Our Presidents

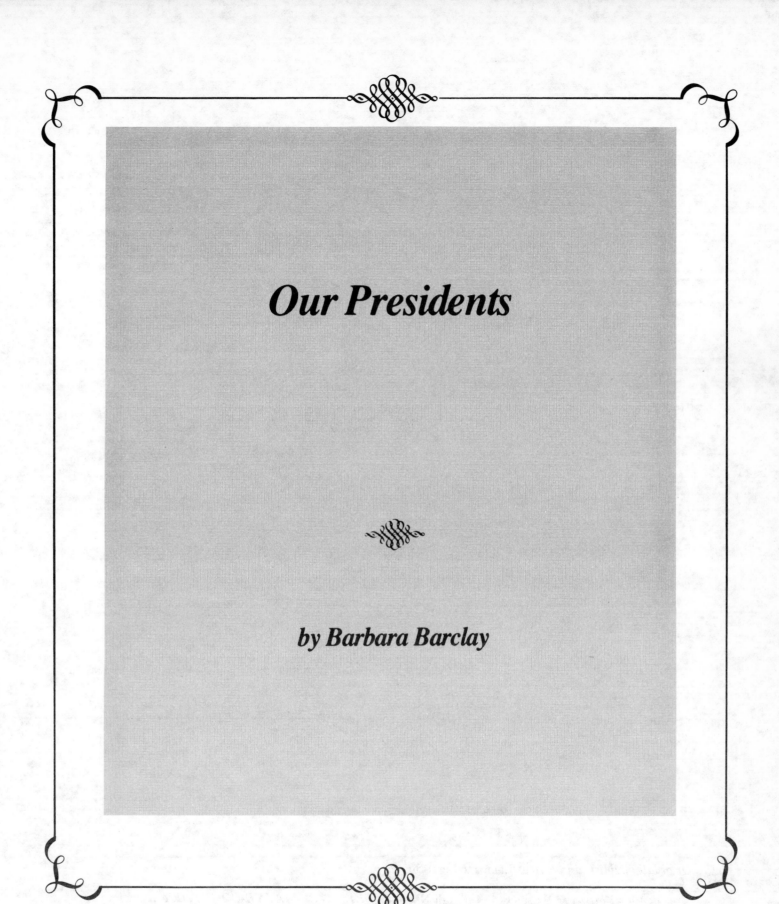

by Barbara Barclay

Originally published in 1970 as Lamps to Light the Way

Presidential Portraits: Washington through Nixon *by CELESTE SWAYNE-COURTNEY*
Ford and Carter *by GRAM D. MAJORDEN*

Book design: RICHARD DENISON

Copyright© 1970, 1977 by Bowmar Publishing Corp.

All rights reserved including the right to reproduce this book or parts thereof in any form.

Printed in the United States of America. International copyright secured.

Library of Congress Catalog Card Number: 75-42589

ISBN 0-88394-039-6

Published by arrangement with Ottenheimer Publishers

This book is respectfully dedicated to the thirty-eight men

whose lives inspired the author to write it.

ACKNOWLEDGEMENTS

The author wishes to thank the following persons and organizations for their assistance in the selection of and the permission to use the illustrations appearing in this book on the following pages.

The Library of Congress:

14	34	53	67	87	105	126	144	161	177	198	221	242	263	279	295	351
15	35	54	69	88	106	128	145	162	180	199	225	243	264	281	304	368
16	38	55	72	89	107	129	146	164	181	200	228	245	265	284	305	369
17	39	56	74	90	110	130	147	165	182	201	229	246	266	285	308	384
18	40	57	76	91	112	131	150	166	186	204	232	252	267	286	309	385
20	42	58	77	94	113	134	152	169	187	209	233	253	268	287	311	408
22	43	59	78	95	114	136	153	171	188	214	234	254	269	289	312	
23	44	62	79	97	115	137	154	172	189	216	235	255	271	290	313	
26	45	63	82	98	118	138	155	173	192	217	236	256	273	291	316	
27	46	64	83	99	120	139	156	174	194	218	237	257	276	292	319	
29	49	65	84	102	122	142	157	175	195	219	238	261	277	293	322	
32	52	66	86	104	123	143	160	176	196	220	239	262	278	294	340	

White House Historical Association, Hillory A. Tolson:
21 33 168 197 207 226 270 288 369
31 68 184 206 210 247 272 292 395

The Franklin D. Roosevelt Library, James E. O'Neill:
328 329 330 332 333 336 337 338 341 342 344

The Lyndon Baines Johnson Library, Frank Wolfe:
388 389 390 391 392 394 396 397 398 399 400 401 402 403

John F. Kennedy Library, Carolyn O'Leary:
374 376 377 378 380 381 382 391

United Press International:
324 351 353 354 356 371 410

Dwight D. Eisenhower Library, W. A. Scott:
360 364 365 370

The Harding Memorial Association, Mrs. Harold Augenstein:
298 299 300 302 303

Harry S. Truman Library, Philip D. Lagerquist:
348 350 353 357

The Richard M. Nixon Foundation, Loie Gaunt:
407 408

The White House:
45 408 416 417 418 419

United States Department of the Interior, National Parks Service, Cecil W. Stoughton:
355 366

Underwood and Underwood:
318 321 323

The Rutherford B. Hayes Library, Watt P. Marchman: 210 211

Herbert Hoover Presidential Library, Thomas T. Thalken: 317 325

U.S. Army Signal Corps: 362 364

Harris and Ewing: 335 353

The Vermont Historical Society, Charles T. Morrissey: 224

The Gray Line, Inc.: 210

The Fogg Museum, Harvard University: 30

The New York Public Library: 73

The Virginia Historical Society: 58

Lyndon Baines Johnson

Mrs. Herbert J. Sanborn

Wide World Photos 422 423 424 425

The author further wishes to thank the following persons for their assistance in the production of this book: June Mengel, Beth Raphael, Doris Read.

LAMPS TO LIGHT THE WAY

To the traveler passing
from dusk to dawn through the night,
lamplight eases and guides
the way.
Without these cheering lamps he could
easily lose his way and stumble . . . perhaps fall.
With them his direction is
well assured.
Lamps can flicker and dim
and the traveler slows his pace.
Too, they can blaze out their illumination
and cut through the
night's darkest shadows.
Now the heartened traveler increases his speed.
No matter how the lamps' power varies,
the traveler is glad for their encouraging glow.
In the following pages
think of the traveler as America.
Our presidents are the lamps
that light the way.

Barbara Barclay

PREFACE

   In the age of computers and consequent
depersonalization, the human touch at times seems close
to extinction. *Our Presidents* develops a
personal approach to United States history for the
reader. This book of presidential biographies
includes the major achievements in the public career of
each president from George Washington through
James Earl Carter, Jr. Of particular importance is the
personal approach taken to each chief executive. In photographs
and text the presidents are shown as real human
beings with families, hobbies, special interests, and,
most importantly, as men with whom the reader
can identify.

   The author wishes to take this opportunity to express
her thanks for the editorial assistance of Norman
Hunter, Karle Lindstrom, and Tom Moon.

TABLE OF CONTENTS

CHAPTERS

Our Presidents

GEORGE WASHINGTON

First President (1789-1797)

Our first president has been painted,
etched, carved in stone and wood, and cast in
bronze through the decades by
adoring American artists.
Poets, biographers, and novelists have
praised him with thousands of flowery phrases
and millions of words.
The simplest deeds of his youth have
become legendary, some blown so out of proportion
that they have become folklore.
People through the span of American
history have idolized him to such
a degree that it might cause
great embarrassment to the man were he alive.
Above all the admiration and praise,
there was truly a humble soul—a sincere
and generous man.
George Washington, the quiet man
from the banks of the Potomac, was throughout
his remarkable life very much
a human being.

Washington is shown here during his first meeting with the Widow Custis.

THE CORNERSTONE OF OUR COUNTRY

George Washington was born February 22, 1732, the son of Augustine Washington, a wealthy Virginia planter and Mary Ball Washington, his second wife. George, the fifth child in a family of ten, spent most of his childhood at Hunting Creek, Virginia.

Young George had little formal education and did not attend college. Orphaned at fifteen with no money to continue his education, he left school with a basic knowledge of mathematics, reading, and spelling. But George rated high marks as a student when following his special interests. These interests were of a practical nature and included surveying and the study of scientific farming. At age fifteen he became a junior member of an expedition sent to measure the lands of the Shenandoah Valley in Virginia.

The orphaned youth went to live with his half brother, Lawrence Washington, whom he admired greatly. Lawrence taught him many of the things which he had himself learned from his schooling in England. Horseback riding was one of these. Under the older brother's instruction, George enthusiastically took up riding and later became known as the foremost horseman of his day. Many years older than his orphaned brother, Lawrence gave George much more than in-

struction. He provided his younger brother with a fine example to follow and with the love and affection he needed in his parentless state. When death came to Lawrence in 1752, he left his estate, Mount Vernon, to his younger brother.

Feeling that he might make his mark in the world as a soldier, twenty year old George joined the Virginia militia as a major. Although strong and vigorous, the young officer suffered from constant exposure to bad weather. Many times during his early military career it seemed as if he might not live long enough to distinguish himself. Before he was thirty Washington had been ill with pleurisy, smallpox, dysentery, and malaria. On one army expedition in 1753 he fell off a raft and nearly lost his life by drowning in the Allegheny River. Another time he was shot at by Indians standing less than fifty feet away. Luckily they were poor marksmen.

Washington grew into manhood shy among strangers, but he was always a person of great charm and courtesy and at his attentive best with the ladies. His was a romantic heart and in his youth he wrote poetry to a number of young women. As an officer on the lonely western frontier during the French and Indian War, he wrote to a friend that he was in love with someone far away. The thought of the pretty Widow Custis haunted him with thoughts of "a thousand tender passages."

He did not pine for long; he married Martha Custis on January 6, 1759. Throughout his life George Washington's physical appearance impressed all who saw him. His wedding was no exception. His servant, recalling the wedding day, said there was nobody in the great party like the young Colonel: "So tall and straight... and with such an air!" This marriage was a comfortable and happy one. By marrying Martha another plantation of 17,000 acres and 300 slaves was added to the Washington holdings. More important, Martha Washington brought a cheery, chatty nature into her husband's life. She was to prove a handy ally through his times of trial and stress. George and Martha had no children of their own. She had two children by her first marriage, a daughter who died in 1773, and a son Jack Custis. George later adopted his wife's two grandchildren George Washington Custis and Eleanor Custis.

The land Martha brought into the marriage made her husband a prominent Virginia landowner. He devoted the majority of his time from 1759 to 1774 to these land holdings. Washington proved to be a very able manager. He was interested in raising livestock and continued the study of modern agricultural methods. He grew wheat and pecans, as well as the staple tobacco crop. His interest in the land and the public welfare led him to plan the drainage of the nearby Dismal Swamp, and as a public service he operated a ferry across the Potomac River. Because of able management and his fairness to those with whom he did business, George Washington became one of the wealthiest and most respected landowners of his time.

Landowners in colonial Virginia had many responsibilities. For sixteen years Washington was a member of the Virginia House of Burgesses at Williamsburg. He was not a good speaker, but was highly thought of because of his honesty and fairness and his great interest in the public welfare. His physical appearance was a further asset. Six feet, two inches tall, and one hundred seventy-five pounds, Washington's powerful, erect physique commanded respect.

When differences with England over taxation and other matters became very serious, delegates from all the American colonies met in Philadel-phia. George Washington was one of Virginia's delegates to the Continental Congress of 1774 and 1775. There he continued to earn high respect and esteem from all the delegates. Patrick Henry said of him, "Colonel Washington... is a man of more solid judgement and information than any man on the floor."

It became clear that war with England was coming soon. John Adams, a Massachusetts delegate, recommended that Washington be Commander-in-Chief of the American Army. His past military experience in the French and

George Washington developed his lifelong interest in surveying at a young age. At seventeen he was licensed by the college of William and Mary and became the official surveyor for Culpeper County, Virginia.

...orge and Martha Custis Washington were married January 6, 1759. ...was twenty-six and she was twenty-seven.

...shington's home, Mount Vernon, has been restored and is maintained ...The Mount Vernon Ladies' Association. The estate is located on the ...nks of the Potomac River a few miles outside the nation's capital. It ...pen to the public every day of the year.

Washington was a busy farmer who carefully supervised every detail of ...lantation production and management. In the time he could manage ...way from the fields or his account books, he read books on scientific ...arming. A favorite book was A New System of Agriculture or a ...Speedy Way to Grow Rich.

...une 15, 1775, was the date Washington was elected Commander-in-...Chief of the forces raised for the defense of the American colonies.

Indian War and his ability as a strong leader convinced the delegates. Washington accepted his commission as the commander of the American Army, June 15, 1775, and served without pay through the war.

For the next eight years he led his country on battlefields throughout the east. General Washington did not have a brilliant military mind, in fact, he won very few battles. His strength lay in his unbreakable spirit. Washington did not give up against the well-trained, larger British army. He was an inspiring leader and would not allow his men to quit. This can be seen in the terrible winter the American forces spent at Valley Forge, Pennsylvania. General Washington's little army was beaten down, threadbare, frost-bitten, and hungry. From his own pocket he often bought food to feed them. The war-weary men longed for their families and their homes. The British had pushed them back on too many occasions. Why go on? Why not surrender? Submit, indeed! As their tall, strong general walked calmly among them, his unwavering vision of what America could be was passed on to them. They would survive. They would win in the end. He would see to it. The men stayed throughout the bitter winter – belief in their commander greater than their hardships and hunger.

The Revolutionary War ended with an American victory. With his work completed, General George Washington resigned his commission at the Fraunces Tavern in New York City in December 1783. Here he was able to overcome his customary shyness and reveal his deep emotions and great heart. The general stood before his men and with tears in his eyes said in a trembling voice: "I cannot come to each of you to take my leave, but shall be obliged if you will each come and shake me by the hand."

Returning to civilian life, Washington worked diligently to restore his neglected Virginia farmlands. He renewed his interest in surveying and engineering and gathered men at Mount Vernon to discuss improvement of navigation on the Potomac. But he was not allowed to continue his good deeds in private life for long.

America needed him. The new nation needed a firm government and a strong leader. George Washington was asked to preside over the Constitutional Convention of 1789. The basic foundations of our American government were set up during this historic convention. It was there the Federalists nominated Washington to be the first President of the United States.

At first, the hero of the Revolutionary War was not sure he was the man for this high office. He felt uncertain and inexperienced in this new world of politics. Gouverneur Morris, a convention delegate, strongly urged him to accept and wisely wrote to Washington: "No constitution is the same on paper and in life. The exercise of authority depends upon personal character. Your cool, steady temper is indispensibly necessary to give a firm and manly tone to the new government." With powerful persuasion such as this, Washington did accept and became the unanimous choice of the convention.

Gouverneur Morris' words suggesting that George Washington's strong personal character was necessary in the presidency proved correct. In July 1794 one of the great tests of the federal government's strength was placed in Washington's hands. It was colorfully known as the Whiskey Rebellion. Many farmers found it difficult and expensive to transport their corn crop to market – it was much easier and much more profitable to distill it into liquor and transport it to town. They hated the tax placed upon them by the central government and rose up in fierce protest. In western Pennsylvania they frightened tax collectors, forced federal troops guarding the chief tax inspector to surrender, and threatened to march on Pittsburgh. Alarmed that the Whiskey Rebellion might spread, President Washington calmly and firmly went into action. Calling out 15,000 state militiamen to stop the violence, he personally rode out to inspect the troops' readiness. This show of strength on Washington's part quickly stopped the rebellion.

The first President of the United States was inaugurated April 30, 1789, in New York City. President George Washington served his country for eight years. He chose wisely the members of his Cabinet: Thomas Jefferson, Secretary of State; Alexander Hamilton, Secretary of the Treasury; and Henry Knox, Secretary of War. John Jay was chosen the first Chief Justice of the Supreme Court. It was felt that Washington's choice of Hamilton was a particularly excellent one. The main problem of his first presidential term was raising money to run the government. Fortunately, Hamilton was clever in financial

The sight of General Washington often heartened his troops and help them through the terrible winter of 1777 at Valley Forge, Pennsylvan Troubled about lack of food for his nine thousand men, General Was ington issued a desperate proclamation on December 20, 1777. required all farmers within seventy miles of Valley Forge to thre one-half of their grain by February 11, 1778, so that there might food for his ragged, hungry soldiers.

General Washington is shown taking leave of his officers at the Fraun Tavern in New York City on December 4, 1783.

Enthusiastic crowds greeted George Washington as he traveled l horseback on the way to his inauguration at Federal Hall, New Yor City, April 30, 1789.

President Washington is shown here delivering his inauguration spee inside Federal Hall in New York City.

17

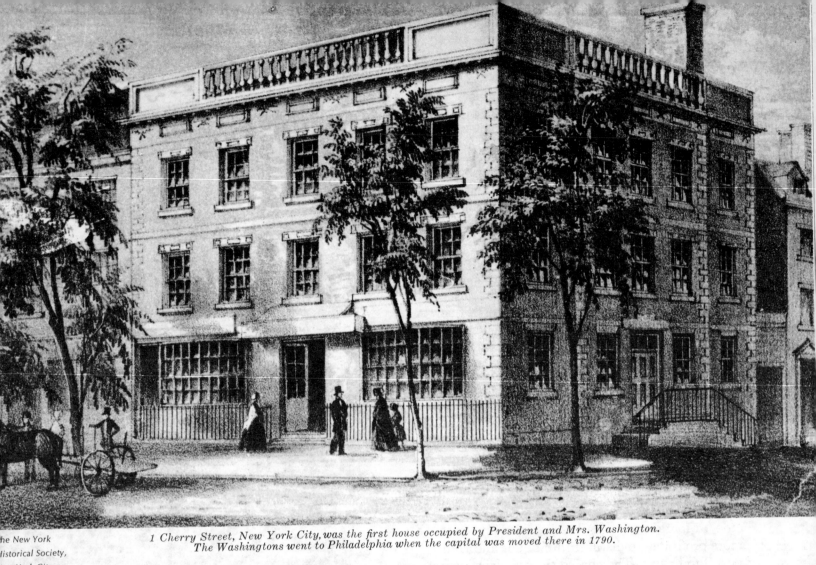

1 Cherry Street, New York City, was the first house occupied by President and Mrs. Washington. The Washingtons went to Philadelphia when the capital was moved there in 1790.

President and Mrs. Washington often entertained elegantly at official receptions.

The Great Seal of the United States was adopted June 20, 1792.

matters. He was an energetic young man who was effective in directing Congress to get the country moving on a sound financial basis.

President Washington in describing himself, said he was a person who had received "inferior endowments from nature." He was too modest. He had the power of inspiring respect in all who met him. As president he knew how to work with men and use them to their best capacity while ignoring any faults they might have. The greatest strength of this quiet man from Mount Vernon was his fine, firm character. This strength allowed him to remain calm, using his powers of common sense and compromise to get the best out of difficult situations and hard-to-handle personalities. It is remarkable that he was able to keep two such spirited colts as Hamilton and Jefferson in his stable for any length of time. These two brilliant statesmen, with such opposing beliefs, were constantly arguing. The president's reassuring hand upon their shoulders did much to ease the way and keep them working to develop their young country.

Washington was not a cold-blooded, mechanical chief executive, perfect in every detail. On rare occasions his outbursts of temper were awe-inspiring. Thomas Jefferson recorded the events of an August 1793 Cabinet meeting after Secretary of War Knox had shown the president a particularly nasty newspaper attack aimed directly at him:

> The President... "got into one of those passions when he cannot command himself, ran on much on the personal abuse which had been bestowed on him (and said)... he had rather be on his farm than to be made emperer of the world and yet they were charging him with wanting to be a king."

President Washington displayed some imperfections outside the Cabinet Room, too. In public he was a plodding, uninteresting speaker. Many people who did not know him mistook his shyness for aloofness and found him stiff and dull. Meeting strangers often embarrassed him and reduced him to an awkward silence. But with his friends he could relax and allow his personal warmth to flow forth. Persons close to Washington knew this side of his nature. With the ladies he continued to be a great success. Always a perfect gentleman, President Washington could often be seen at official receptions and

During her husband's presidency Martha Washington was known as Lady Washington. This formal title was dropped by later presidents' wives.

BUILDING THE FIRST WHITE HOUSE

WASHINGTON D.C. 1798

The District of Columbia was established by Congress in 1791. It was later renamed Washington, D.C., in honor of George Washington. The first president is pictured here in 1798 inspecting the unfinished President's House with James Hoban, the architect and builder.

George Washington enjoyed working close to the earth, but his duties of supervision at Mount Vernon usually kept him away from such activity.

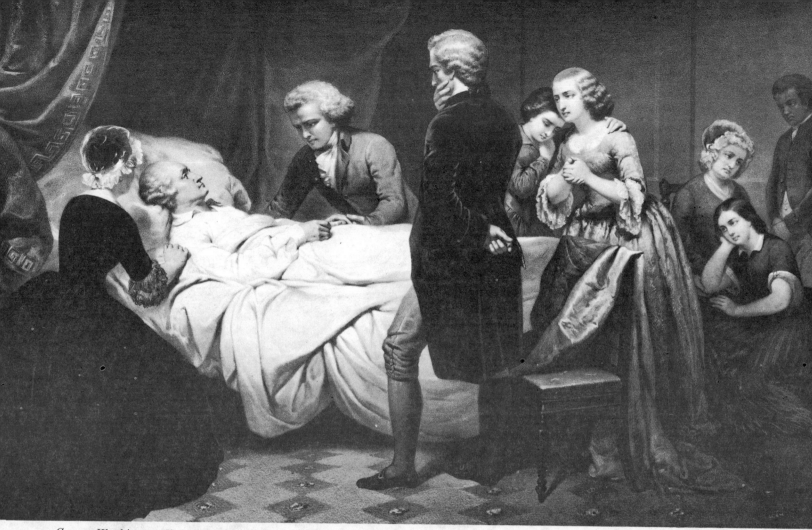

George Washington died December 14, 1799, at his Mount Vernon estate, two-and-a-half years after he retired from the presidency.

balls engaging them in charming conversation and whirling them around the room in a vigorous and graceful dance.

During the Washington administration, Vermont, Kentucky, and Tennessee became states. The State Department, Department of War, Treasury Department, and Office of the Attorney General were established. The first ten amendments to the Constitution, commonly called "The Bill of Rights," became law. In 1790 the first United States census was authorized and the Supreme Court met in its first session. The president's idea for a federal city became a reality as the District of Columbia was established in 1791. And next year the United States Mint began operation in Philadelphia.

No official residence was supplied for George and Martha Washington during the eight years of his presidency. The first president's mansion was located at 1 Cherry Street, New York City. Construction on the Executive Mansion did begin while he was president, but it was not completed in time for the Washingtons' occupancy.

On his next to last day in the presidency, Washington expressed these thoughts: "To the wearied traveler who sees a resting-place, and is

bending his body to lean thereon, I now compare myself . . . The remainder of my life . . . will be occupied in rural amusement."

In March 1797 he returned to private life at Mount Vernon. His last years were well earned, happy ones. He rekindled his interest in farming. There was time for his favorite sports of fox hunting and fishing, and time to participate in a favorite hobby, mule breeding. George and Martha enjoyed giving parties at their plantation home, but guests had to have their good times early because Martha saw to it that our first ex-president was in bed by nine.

If history has done George Washington any disservice, perhaps it is that of stripping him of his status as a man. Honors, historic sites, statues, and words have tried to make him larger than life, almost an American god. This surely would not have pleased him, for Washington undoubtedly would have wished to be remembered as a humble and good man of the earth, with sensitive and deep feelings for family and friends, and a great love for his country. He died December 14, 1799, at Mount Vernon. His last words were, "It is well."

JOHN ADAMS

Second President (1797-1801)

Where America was concerned
he battled for it like a bantam rooster and
hovered over it like a mother hen.
With a range of reactions
like this, he was bound to be misunderstood.
Some people said he wanted to be
King of America.
Yet, as a boy, he happily
hoed corn on his father's Massachusetts farm.
Fellow workers said he was
ambitious, extremely proud, and unusually
quick to anger.
On the other hand, Thomas Jefferson,
who knew Adams throughout his
life, said this man was very
pleasant, possessed a brilliant
mind, and was blessed with great energy.
So many people liked him and so many disliked him
that it is certain John Adams was
a man with many contrasts
in his personality.

This is Harvard University in Massachusetts as it looked when John Adams was a student there. He entered Harvard in 1751, and received a B.A. degree in 1755 and an M.A. degree in 1758. Harvard is the oldest university in the United States. It was founded in 1636.

A MAN OF COURAGE AND CONTRASTS

John Adams was born in Braintree (now Quincy), Massachusetts, the third son of John and Susanna Boylston Adams. His father was of hard-working New England stock, and John spent his boyhood on a farm. Yankee thrift, perseverance, and hard work were well taught on the Adams farm. It required a great deal of sacrifice to give John and his brothers the opportunity for fine educations, but John's parents believed in the power of learning. After graduating from Harvard College, John taught school for a short time to get enough money to study law. And in 1758 he passed the examina-

tions required to become a lawyer in the state of Massachusetts.

Six years later, John married Abigail Smith. The marriage proved to be an ideal match. Their fifty-four years together were happy ones. Both were persons of action and strong ideas. Abigail was a clever and talented woman. Though she never attended school, her published letters reveal her many abilities and are now delightful documents in American history.

Mrs. Adams encouraged and supported her husband every step of the way to the presidency and ran an efficient home at the same time. Discussing the problems of government with her husband, churning butter, and sewing their children's clothing were all one to Abigail Adams. When the well-being of her family or country was at stake, her very best efforts were apparent. She has the unique distinction of being the only woman in our history to be both wife

Paul Revere of Boston sold this engraved picture of the Boston Massacre which took place in King Street on March 5, 1770.

and mother of a president. The eldest Adams' son, John Quincy, followed his father's path to the presidency.

John Adams loved the practice of law and maintained an interest in it throughout his long life. His courtroom eloquence and courage made him a well-known, highly-respected Massachusetts lawyer. One of his most famous cases came after the "Boston Massacre" of 1770. British soldiers were charged with the murder of Massachusetts citizens. There were many reasons for resentment toward the British at that time. One was the English policy of high taxation of the American colonies without allowing them representation in the English Parliament. The English "Redcoats" had been sent to the colonies to enforce this law. Hatred of the English government fell on the accused soldiers. It took a brave man to go against this strong public feeling and defend these English soldiers in court. John Adams was just such a man. During the trial his careful questioning of witnesses and brilliant planning of the defense was admired even by his opponents. The trial ended in the acquittal of the officer in command and most of his soldiers.

The people of Massachusetts admired lawyer Adams' spirited defense and one year later they elected him to the Massachusetts House of Representatives. This began a great career as a public official which took him finally to the office of President of the United States.

As early as 1765, John argued against the Stamp Act, and for American independence, stating that taxation without representation was illegal. Knowing his feelings, Massachusetts sent him as a delegate to the Continental Congress. As a member of the Continental Congress, Adams' powers of debate and persuasion greatly assisted George Washington in becoming Commander-in-Chief of the American Army. He also had the honor to be one of the five men who served on the committee that drew up the Declaration of Independence. This historic document, in which America declared her independence from the mother country, England, is thought to be the birthright of the United States. John Adams was deeply proud of the part he played in the writing of this great document. Thomas Jefferson and Benjamin Franklin were also on this committee of five. As the early pages of American history unfolded, Jefferson, Franklin, and Adams continually crossed paths.

His career in the Continental Congress ended in 1778 when he was sent to Europe to arrange a peace treaty with England. This was a dangerous duty for a signer of the July 4, 1776, Declaration of Independence. Adams was none too safe in France which was only a few miles across the channel from England. He was warned to keep his bag of official documents loaded with rocks so that he might be able to drop them into the Seine River at a moment's notice. Obviously, his American colleagues knew he ran the risk of capture and imprisonment. He worked hard in Paris but even there he revealed his unpredictable personality. Adams' lack of tact and hot temper often flashed in disagreement with Benjamin Franklin, one of the other peace commissioners. Both were patriotic Americans. Unfortunately, both were quick-tempered and at times stubborn. Often they could not get along. Finally, after many months of debate, there was a final agreement and Adams, Franklin, and John Jay were able to bring about a treaty which ended the Revolutionary War. These three American diplomats had done as much in the halls of Paris as George Washington had done on the battlefield to bring the first war in United States history to a successful conclusion.

In 1785 John Adams again returned to Europe, this time with Abigail and his entire family. He was the first American minister to Great Britain. The loneliness of foreign shores was eased for Adams because his family was with him. Abigail was a knowledgeable woman in most things, but she knew next to nothing about the fashions of the English court. Her strange costume, yards and yards of material topped with two enormous white plumes upon her head, caused tongues to wag in the elegant Court of St. James. Ill-mannered court ladies turned their backs on the little country woman from Massachusetts, and England's Queen Charlotte looked upon her with "contempt and scorn." Both Adamses ignored this bad behavior and went about their government's work with courage and dignity.

During this stay in England, Adams wrote a powerful defense of the system of government

During the Revolutionary War this 1776 lithograph of "Yankee Doodle" was published. In it an old man, a young boy, and a battered soldier show the "Spirit of '76", the Americans' determination not to give in to greater British forces.

John Adams worked very hard as a diplomat in Paris to help end the Revolutionary War.

Benjamin Franklin of Philadelphia often worked with John Adams during the years of the American Revolution. The two men were members of the Continental Congress and the committee that wrote the Declaration of Independence. Franklin and Adams helped bring about the signing of the Treaty of Paris which ended the Revolutionary War.

John Adams, Roger Sherman, Robert Livingston, Thomas Jefferson, and Benjamin Franklin, stand with pride before the Continental Congress as the organization officially adopts the Declaration of Independence they drew up. The date was July 4, 1776.

in America. This written work was well accepted in England, but when these ideas appeared in print in America, critics rose up to condemn his writings. Adams' suggestions seemed too aristocratic and seemed to go against the best interests of the common man. This was not John Adams' intention, but was an early example of an unfortunate character trait. He was often unable to get across to the people and the men with whom he worked his great love for the country.

For more than ten years John Adams represented America in many diplomatic posts. He negotiated important treaties, looked after the best interests of the young struggling nation, and sent back good advice for American lawmakers to act upon. With great discomfort and financial cost, he lived in several European capitals during this period. Once he was forced to write Alexander Hamilton asking for money enough to pay his family's living expenses.

Following his return to the United States Adams received the largest number of electoral college votes for vice president in the first presidential election of 1789. As the first vice president in American history, he presided over the

Senate for eight years. In that position he cast more tie-breaking votes than any other vice president. But the active, argumentative Adams did not like being second-in-command. He described the vice president's position as "the most insignificant that ever the invention of man contrived or his imagination conceived."

After 1796 he was no longer second-in-command. John Adams was elected to the presidency as a member of the Federalist Party. This stout, rather unattractive, little man, so different from George Washington in physical appearance and personality, had a fine record as president, but he was never happy holding that office. The lack of tact and self-control he revealed at times, angered his co-workers. One of the most powerful political leaders of that time, Alexander Hamilton, found much fault with Adams and caused him much trouble. Hamilton wanted war with France, President Adams felt it wiser for his new nation to stay out of war. To combat the Hamilton forces he unwisely allowed the passage of the Alien and Sedition Acts which made it unlawful to criticize the government under penalty of deportation, fine, or imprisonment. President

John Adams did not like to sit to have his portrait painted. He wrote in 1809: "I . . . have been too much abused by painters ever to sit (for) any one again."

Abigail Adams was the first president's wife to live in the President's House in Washington, D.C. The Adamses moved into the Executive Mansion in November 1800, just four months before President Adams' term was over.

Here Abigail Adams and her little granddaughter Susanna help a servant hang out the washing in the bare East Room of the President's House.

Adams took further unwise action to keep his country from war by taking part in secret diplomatic actions. When one of these actions, the "XYZ Affair," became known to the public, President Adams' unpopularity increased.

In spite of these difficulties, John Adams achieved a great deal as president. The first American naval vessel, *United States*, was launched in Philadelphia and the Navy Department went into operation. These accomplishments earned him the nickname, "Old Sink or Swim." The United States Marine Corps, the United States Public Health Service, and the Library of Congress were created during his four-year administration. And in 1798, the Mississippi Territory was established.

While Adams was the chief executive, Washington, D.C., became the capital city of the United States. In 1800, John and Abigail Adams became the first tenants of the President's House. In those early days the capital was like a frontier settlement surrounded by thick forests and unhealthy swamps. The Adamses were most uncomfortable in the President's Mansion because construction had not yet been completed. Their nearest neighbor was more than a half-mile away. The First Lady had a difficult time keeping her family warm in the drafty mansion. Letters sent to her Massachusetts friends brought smiles of amusement,

as she told of hanging out washing to dry in the enormous East Room.

John Adams was defeated for reelection in 1801 by Thomas Jefferson. The little man from Massachusetts was not a president who could make the public believe in him. His distinguished career in public life had come to an end.

John Adams was often a difficult man with whom to get along, but he had great strength of character. He was tough-minded and realistic. His high-minded ideas were always for the best interest of the country. Unfortunately, he sometimes made enemies by his discourteous manner when fighting for important goals. For this his reputation suffered. This courageous man of contrasts always fought hard for his country and must be remembered as one of the most distinguished patriots of the American Revolution.

President John Adams was one of the most learned men of his time. A quiet, scholarly study of law, history, and political philosophy occupied his last years. He lived to see his son, John Quincy Adams, inaugurated the sixth President of the United States. He lived to be ninety, longer than any president. The date of his death was, in a way, a tribute to the greatness of his life. He died in Quincy, Massachusetts, July 4, 1826, exactly fifty years after the signing of the Declaration of Independence.

Congress had its first good brawl in 1798 during John Adams' presidency. After insulting each other, House of Representatives members Roger Griswold and Matthew Lyon picked up a cane and fire tongs and battled each other with more than words.

THOMAS JEFFERSON

Third President (1801-1809)

His estate at Monticello, Virginia,
is an American shrine.
When walking through its halls
one can see that its owner was a man of
many interests and talents.
He was regarded as the best thinker of his day,
and Abraham Lincoln said this man's ideas were
the basis of our free society.
He was a writer, a scholar, a planter,
an architect, a scientist,
an inventor, a mathematician, an educator,
a diplomat, even, in emergencies,
a backwoods doctor.
Thomas Jefferson was all of these things,
as well as the third President of
the United States.

Thomas Jefferson served as chairman of the committee of five which drew up and submitted the Declaration of Independence to Congress July 1, 1776.

THE MAN OF A HUNDRED TALENTS

Born to Peter and Jane Randolph Jefferson April 13, 1743, in Albemarle County, Virginia, Thomas was the third child in a family of ten. His father was a planter and a county leader; his mother belonged to one of the most distinguished families in Virginia. Thomas' early years were in some ways like those of many Virginia planters' sons. There was one great exception. Peter Jefferson's plantation, Shadwell, was near the frontier. This area taught young Thomas to use common sense, to do things for himself, and, above all, to respect his fellow man. He learned the arts and crafts of the pioneer from his father, a strapping frontiersman whom even the Indians admired. He learned to ride and shoot, to paddle a canoe, to plant and build, and to size up a man. Through

Colonel Jefferson's example, Thomas gained high respect for truth and knowledge. It was a common sight to see the lad on the hilltop, that would one day become his home, with his head buried in a book.

Like both his presidential predecessors, he lost his father at an early age. When Thomas was fourteen his father died and, as the eldest son, he inherited the Jefferson estate and became the head of a family of nine.

His formal education began at home under tutors who instructed him in the classics, French, dancing, and the violin. At sixteen, Thomas entered the College of William and Mary at Williamsburg. There he developed an interest, which he never lost, in mathematics and the natural

A Declaration by the Representatives of the UNITED STATES OF AMERICA, in General Congress assembled.

When in the course of human events it becomes necessary for one people to dissolve the political bands which have connected them with another, and to ~~advance from that subordination in which they have hitherto remained,~~ & to assume among the powers of the earth the separate and equal station to which the laws of nature & of nature's god entitle them, a decent respect to the opinions of mankind requires that they should declare the causes which impel them to the separation.

We hold these truths to be self-evident; that all men are created equal, that they are endowed by their creator with ~~equal~~ inherent & inalienable rights; that among these are life, & liberty, & the pursuit of happiness; that to secure these rights, governments are instituted among men, deriving their just powers from the consent of the governed; that whenever any form of government becomes destructive of these ends, it is the right of the people to alter or to abolish it, & to institute new government, laying it's foundation on such principles & organising it's powers in such form, as to them shall seem most likely to effect their safety & happiness. prudence indeed will dictate that governments long established should not be changed for light & transient causes: and accordingly all experience hath shewn that mankind are more disposed to suffer while evils are sufferable, than to right themselves by abolishing the forms to which they are accustomed. but when a long train of abuses & usurpations [begun at a distinguished period & pursuing invariably the same object, evinces a design to ~~subject~~ reduce them under absolute Despotism, it is their right, it is their duty, to throw off such ~~government~~ & to provide new guards for their future security. such has been the patient sufferance of these colonies; & such is now the necessity which constrains them to [expunge] their former systems of government. the history of the present king of Great Britain is a history of [unremitting] injuries and usurpations, [among which appears no solitary fact to contradict the uniform tenor of the rest, but all have] in direct object the establishment of an absolute tyranny over these states. to prove this, let facts be submitted to a candid world [for the truth of which we pledge a faith yet unsullied by falsehood]

A copy of the Declaration of Independence in Thomas Jefferson's own handwriting.

In 1769 Thomas Jefferson began designing Monticello which means "little mountain." Although he lived in it through the years, it was not until after he retired from the presidency in 1809 that he completed the building of his thirty-two room home.

sciences. In college he also continued to study foreign and classical languages. Throughout his life the study of language was of great importance to him and before he was through he knew Latin, Greek, Italian, French, and Spanish. At William and Mary he came to feel that the law could be used as a powerful tool to help the common man and to change the form of government. Out of interest and the need to earn money to support his mother and younger brothers on their small estate, he turned to the study of law. After five years of study in George Wyeth's law office, he became a lawyer in 1767.

For seven years he practiced law in Virginia. The money he received from his law practice allowed Jefferson to settle his family comfortably. Thomas doubled the size of their estate. He bought the little mountain where he had read and dreamed as a boy. He proceeded to draw plans and build upon its summit, Monti-

cello, which became the most spectacular country house in all of Virginia.

With his family well taken care of, Thomas Jefferson lost interest in the practice of law. Now he could give his full efforts to political action and philosophy. He entered public service by taking a seat in the Virginia House of Burgesses. He was sent to Philadelphia in 1775 as a Virginia delegate to the Continental Congress. He was a quiet, thoughtful member of this group. Throughout life, the soft-spoken Jefferson firmly believed that men were never convinced by argument, but only by thinking, reading, and calm conversation. When the Continental Congress made its decision for independence from England in June 1776, Jefferson was assigned to the committee to prepare the reasons for this action. John Adams and three other committee members knew of his writing excellence and, after much planning, gave Jefferson the important task of expressing their thoughts. In this way he became the author of the Declaration of Independence.

Returning to the Virginia legislature in October 1776, Thomas Jefferson began work to change that state's laws. He worked to guarantee religious freedom, to end the law stating that the eldest son could be the only heir to his father's property, and for the adoption of a state-supported school system. His first two efforts became law in Virginia within a period of ten years.

In 1779 Thomas Jefferson began a short term as the governor of Virginia. At this time his beloved wife, Martha, died leaving him a widower with two daughters. There was much heartache for the saddened husband. For several months Jefferson did not venture beyond the sound of his wife's voice as she lay dying at Monticello. The devotion between Thomas and Martha was great. Their love was bound close by often sharing the sadness that death brings. Together they buried four of their six children in infancy or early childhood. When he knew that death was near, Jefferson declared to his dying Martha that he would never remarry. He remained true to that promise, carrying this pledge through the remaining forty-four years of his life.

Jefferson's grief was great after Martha's death, but his strong feelings for the public welfare helped him overcome the sadness. In 1783 he was back in Philadelphia, a member of Congress under the Articles of Confederation. There Jefferson's talent for mathematics became apparent when he contributed to a report that brought about the establishment of the decimal money system in the United States. This replaced the more difficult English money system that had formerly been used.

He succeeded Benjamin Franklin as United States minister to France in 1785. Under President Washington he served as Secretary of State. Strong differences between Jefferson and Alexander Hamilton, the Secretary of the Treasury, soon rose. These two, so different in philosophy and life style, sat across from one another in Cabinet meetings and battled "like fighting cocks." Their differences of opinion did much to establish the two-party political system in America. Hamilton became the leader of the Federalist Party which believed in great powers for the central government. In fierce opposition to Hamilton's policies, Jefferson and his friend,

James Madison, founded the Democratic Republican Party. They felt that great powers for the federal government went against the best interests of the majority of the people.

Elected vice president in 1796 under John Adams, Thomas Jefferson served as the presiding officer of the Senate. Here he prepared, from his extensive experience as a lawmaker, his *Manual for Parliamentary Practice*, a work so fine it is still the basis for procedure in the United States Senate.

When Federalist President John Adams ran for reelection his unpopularity was great and Thomas Jefferson, who opposed him as a Democratic Republican candidate, won the election. Jefferson was inaugurated March 4, 1801, in Washington, D.C., and remained in the president's office for the next eight years. Throwing out kingly behavior, the president-elect walked to his inauguration ceremony, and afterward walked back to his boarding house. President Jefferson refused to wear a white, powdered wig, thinking his own red hair was good enough for any occasion. He did away with bowing stiffly at official receptions and to riding around the capital in a horse-drawn coach. Instead he shook the hands of folk he met and rode horseback through the streets of Washington. He ended the custom of nationally celebrating the president's birthday. Some thought he was carrying democracy a bit too far when they found him doing his own shopping at the market. Thomas Jefferson's living style was thought to be a fine example for the American public to follow. To this day many of the simple manners introduced by Jefferson remain the rule of behavior for occupants of the President's House.

The great achievement of his first term was the Louisiana Purchase of 1803. To stimulate trade, President Jefferson felt the United States should acquire ownership of the land at the mouth of the Mississippi River. Inquiries were sent to France, then the owner nation. Napoleon, the French leader, was in need of money and offered to sell the entire Louisiana Territory for fifteen million dollars. Thomas Jefferson jumped at the chance, although to do so he had to go beyond his presidential authority and lay himself open to much criticism. The greatest land bargain in our history was gained because of Jefferson's boldness. The Louisiana Purchase nearly doubled the size of the United States and

The drawing room inside Monticello shows the elegant but simple furnishings selected by Thomas Jefferson.

brought rich new lands and many natural resources to our new nation.

Serving his second term as president, Jefferson ran into problems as do all presidents. He sincerely wanted "peace, commerce, and honest friendships with all nations." To accomplish this he proposed the Embargo Act of 1807 which cut off trade with England and France who were at War. President Jefferson felt, by not taking sides, he could keep his young country out of war. This war in Europe would cut into the economy and manpower of America at a time when neither could stand the strain. The Embargo Act was successful in keeping America from the firing line, but it made enemies for Thomas Jefferson. Yankee traders who received most of their income from trading with England and France were furious with the president.

Thomas Jefferson stepped down from office on March 4, 1809. His good friend James Mad-

ison succeeded him. Then nearly sixty-six, he went home to Monticello. This closed a political career of nearly forty years; a career he could look back upon with great pride. Strangely, Jefferson had become the most successful political leader of his time without making one political speech.

When the ex-president left Washington, D.C., his work was not done. Still remaining was the establishment of a system of public education for which he had been fighting for thirty-three years. "A system of public education ... was the earliest so it will be the latest of all the public concerns in which I shall permit myself to take an interest," he wrote. Through much hard work and planning in many quarters he was able to establish the University of Virginia.

On this project Thomas Jefferson showed his talent for architecture. He designed the uni-

The drawing room and entrance hall of Monticello.

versity's buildings and supervised the construction of the campus down to the smallest detail. Then he found the professors, planned the courses, and selected some of the readings for the classes. For this work he was called "The Father of the University of Virginia," a title which gave him much pride and satisfaction.

Jefferson's great interest in architecture influenced the building style in the United States at that time. He had much to do with the planning of Washington, D.C. Two of his architectural designs, Monticello and Bremo, a mansion he built for a friend in Fluvanna County, Virginia, are still among the most beautiful country houses in America.

At Monticello, his plantation home, Jefferson showed himself to be a happy, humane master. He learned the medical arts well enough to sew up a wound or set the broken bone of an injured slave. He loved his violin and, al-

though he was forced to give up playing the instrument due to a weak wrist, he always delighted in listening to others play. He had a fine singing voice. His manly tones often accompanied him on horseback rides around the plantation.

When time away from public service permitted, Thomas Jefferson practiced scientific farming at Monticello. Once, while visiting Europe in earlier years, he took a terrible chance and smuggled a rare type of rice across the Italian border. This could have led to his arrest, but fortunately he was not caught. In later years he found much satisfaction in improving Monticello farmlands.

Some of Jefferson's inventions can be seen today upon visiting his Virginia plantation home. In our age of advanced technology they remain remarkable. To accommodate his writing, he invented a collapsible writing table which

President Jefferson was a man of simple tastes and actions. When he was president, rather than use a horse-drawn coach, he preferred to ride horseback through the streets of Washington.

could be carried from place to place. A clock of his design, run with cannon balls as weights and balances, is also on view. He also invented a pedometer to measure his walks and a plow that won first place at a French exhibition.

It might be thought that a man of such widespread genius would have little time for people and ordinary things. Thomas Jefferson always had time for people. Sensitive and kind to people he met, he had a charming manner, an even temper, and was the most generous of men. During his later years friends and strangers alike wrote to him for advice or came to visit him at Monticello with or without invitations. Often wearing comfortable clothes and old slippers, he warmly greeted all who came. The tall and lean, carrot-topped Virginian made everyone welcome.

Money problems made Thomas Jefferson's later years difficult. Because he had devoted his life to the public welfare with hardly a thought to his own interests, he was twenty thousand dollars in debt at the end of his presidential term and was forced to borrow money from friends to pay Washington shopkeepers. To keep a home for himself and his large family of grandchildren, grandnieces and grandnephews, the ex-president was forced to sell his cherished ten-thousand volume library to Congress. However, the last months of his life were made happy by a rush of generosity from friends and admirers who learned of his money problems and came to his assistance.

After retiring from politics, Thomas Jefferson again became united in friendship with his old Federalist foe, John Adams. This ended in a remarkable coincidence. Both men gave up life's breath on the same day. As Thomas Jefferson lay weak and dying on the evening of July 3, 1826, he whispered, "Is this the Fourth?" A friend, to quiet him, answered yes. He fell asleep with a smile on his face and he never regained consciousness. Thomas Jefferson's heart continued to beat until the bells and fireworks of the Fourth rang out the next day. Then it stopped. Exactly fifty years after writing the Declaration of Independence, its author ceased to be.

Aaron Burr was Thomas Jefferson's first vice president. When he failed to win Jefferson's support for a second term as vice president and then lost the election for governor of New York, he became a very bitter man. He challenged an old enemy, Alexander Hamilton, to a duel and killed him. He was later charged with treason for trying to raise an army in the western territories to go against the United States. He was acquitted of these charges in 1807, but never held any position of importance in American government again.

Alexander Hamilton was the leader of the Federalist Party in the early years of our country. He believed in a strong central government for America. He wrote many of the Federalist papers which argued for the adoption of the Constitution. As President Washington's Secretary of the Treasury he helped establish a firm banking and currency system in the United States. Although his aristocratic ideas sometimes went against Thomas Jefferson's more democratic ones, Jefferson recognized Hamilton's genius and called him "a colossus."

The Jefferson Memorial in Washington was dedicated April 13, 1943. The architects who designed it were influenced by the classical style of architecture Thomas Jefferson introduced to America. It is maintained by the National Parks Service and is open daily to the public.

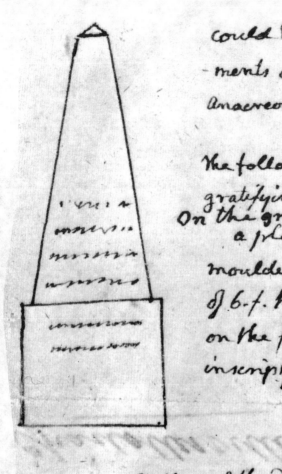

could the dead feel any interest in Monu-
-ments or other remembrances of them, when, as
Anacreon says: Ολιγη δε κεισομεστα
                 κονις, οστεων λυθεντων
the following would be to my Manes the most
gratifying.
On the grave
        a plain die or cube of 3.f without any
mouldings, surmounted by an Obelisk
of 6.f. height, each of a single stone:
on the faces of the Obelisk the following
inscription, & not a word more
        'Here was buried
        Thomas Jefferson
Author of the Declaration of American Independance
        of the Statute of Virginia for religious freedom
& Father of the University of Virginia.'
because by these, as testimonials that I have lived, I wish most to
be remembered. ~~to be~~ to be of the coarse stone of which
my columns are made, that no one might be tempted
hereafter to destroy it for the value of the materials.
my bust by Ciracchi, with the pedestal and truncated
column on which it stands, might be given to the University
if they would place it in the Dome room of the Rotunda.
on the Die of the Obelisk, might be engraved
        Born Apr. 2. 1743. O.S.
        Died ———   ,

Thomas Jefferson left directions for the design of his own gravestone. Included in these
instructions were the words he wanted placed on his grave: "Here was buried Thomas
Jefferson, author of the Declaration of Independence, of the Statute of Virginia for religious freedom, and Father of the University of Virginia."

JAMES MADISON

Fourth President (1809-1817)

He had no children,
yet our fourth president
is one of this country's most
famous fathers.
His great legislative and writing genius
made our federal Constitution the
firm foundation on which our government has
existed for nearly two hundred years.
James Madison is honored
by historians as the
"Father of the Constitution."

Montpelier was James Madison's home in Virginia.

THE FATHER OF OUR CONSTITUTION

Born on March 16, 1751, James was the oldest of ten children born to James and Eleanor Conway Madison. James Madison, Sr., was a Virginia landholder. When he died, young James inherited his estate. It is said that frail James never had much energy for play and spent his childhood years studying at home with private tutors. Boyish games and pranks were unknown to this serious young Virginian. Learning was the important thing in James' young life.

Eighteen year old James enrolled in Princeton University in 1769 and graduated with a Bachelor of Arts degree in 1771. During his first year in college, James organized a debating club called the American Whig Society. This debating experience was going to be a great help to Madison during his future career as a stateman.

He continued in post graduate study at Princeton. This little five-foot, four-inch, hundred-pound man suffered all his life from poor health and after a year he had to return home. Delicate health kept Madison from the outdoor activity enjoyed by most Virginia landowners. Full of melancholy and hating his sickliness, James Madison wasted much of his time brooding. He often stated that he did not "expect a long or healthy life." He first decided not to try to take an active role in any career. Instead, he spent the next three years studying religion and law.

At the age of twenty-four, James Madison was stirred into action by his country's struggle with England. He discovered that his place in life should be that of a public servant and statesman. Madison first came to the attention of the people of Virginia when he was made chairman of the Orange County Revolutionary Committee of Safety. He wrote the committee's anti-British resolutions which were widely read in the Colonies.

When the War for Independence came in 1776, Madison's health was too poor to allow him to enlist in the American Army. But this time he did not allow these problems to idle

A VIEW of the PRESIDENTS HOUSE in the CITY of WASHINGTON

after the Conflagration of the 24th August 1814.

When the British invaded Washington in 1814 they set fire to the President's Mansion. The walls remained standing after the fire, but the inside was completely destroyed. Marks from the smoke can be seen above each window.

him. He knew his country needed him. In the early stages of the war, Madison recruited troops for the American Army and wrote propaganda against the British. He was also elected to the Virginia legislature and it was there that he met Thomas Jefferson. This began an historic friendship that was to last fifty years.

No two men could have been closer, both as friends and as co-workers. They were the leaders in the founding of the Democratic Republican Party. They brought about significant public legislation in Virginia. They acted together to double the size of the United States when Jefferson was president. Privately, Jefferson and Madison always showed great consideration for the other's interests and feelings. James Madison was one of the greatest scholars and most avid readers of his day. At times he lacked the money to buy the books he wanted. Thomas Jefferson knew of this difficulty and, while serving as United States minister to France, took time away from his busy schedule to act

as Madison's bargain book buyer in Paris.

Despite this close friendship, it would be unfair to think of Madison as a carbon copy of Jefferson, whom the younger James called his "Tutelary Genius." The tall, lean Jefferson was a great contrast to tiny James Madison whom Washington Irving called "a withered little apple-john!" Perhaps the most striking difference between the two men was in temperament. Jefferson was very casual about his clothing, Madison always dressed very neatly in black. A servant of Madison's reported the reason for his habit of dressing only in black. Madison was not a wealthy man and could afford to buy only one suit at a time!

Madison was elected to the Continental Congress and remained in that body from 1780 to 1783, during the final years of the Revolutionary War. At times, Congressman Madison angered the people of Virginia by supporting the central government's authority over the states to issue paper money and to establish import duties.

He returned to Virginia in November 1783 and was elected to the state assembly the next year. There he led the successful fight to enact Thomas Jefferson's law providing religious freedom for all the citizens of Virginia. This law was one of the most important in the history of personal freedom in America. Thanks largely to Madison's hard work and powers of debate in the legislature, it was passed in December of 1785.

James Madison attended the Constitutional Convention in Philadelphia in 1787 and became one of its leaders in discussion. His keen writing skill was also exercised. The notes he kept during that time are still history's best source of information about the establishment of the Constitution of the United States. There were objections to the proposed federal constitution of America. James Madison joined John Jay and Alexander Hamilton in writing the *Federalist* papers which supported the new Constitution. Madison wrote twenty-nine of the eighty-five powerful political papers. He did more than any man, with the possible exception of Hamilton, to get the Constitution ac-

cepted by the states. In achieving this goal, he sacrificed himself politically.

While fighting for the federal Constitution, James Madison lost much political support at home. Many Virginians believed strongly that states' rights were superior to the federal government and Madison's actions had not pleased them. He was defeated in the first Virginia election for the United States Senate, but found his way to Washington on another road. Madison's home county believed in him and elected him to the House of Representatives. He was a member of the first Congress to meet in Washington, D.C., taking his seat in 1789. As a Congressman, Madison proposed nine of the first ten amendments to the Constitution, now called the "Bill of Rights." These firm statements for human rights and justice have carried America through extremely trying times. The "Bill of Rights" reveals that the big heart inside little James Madison beat for his fellow Americans.

James Madison retired from Congress in 1797 expecting to spend the rest of his days quietly at his home, Montpelier, in Orange

In this uncomplimentary British cartoon Americans and British both make fun of President Madison's flight from the capital in 1814.

BATTLE OF NEW ORLEANS

And Defeat of the British under the Command of Sir Edward Packenham.

By GEN? ANDREW JACKSON
8th. Jan? 1815.

Published by Wm. H. Morgan No. 114 Chesnut St. Philadelphia.

American force 6100 Militia.
1 Killed 6 Wounded.

British force 14000 Regulars.
Killed and Wounded 2600.

The last great battle of the War of 1812 was the Battle of New Orleans, January 8, 1815.
The British were badly beaten by General Andrew Jackson and his American troops.

County, Virginia. Two years later his life changed greatly when he married Mrs. Dolly Payne Todd, a pretty young widow. She sparked her quiet husband back into the main stream of America. James Madison was a man who could do great things, and Dolly always reminded him of this. Her plump beauty was often contrasted against her husband's small frame and withered face. She was a sparkling hostess, a great wit, and proved to be one of the most memorable and charming First Ladies.

When Thomas Jefferson was elected to the presidency in 1801, Madison again entered public life as Secretary of State. Because President Jefferson was a widower, Dolly Madison often acted as the official hostess at the President's House. The vivacious Mrs. Madison loved the limelight and gladly volunteered to help her husband's friend, the president. As the substitute hostess for Jefferson and then the First Lady for her own husband, Dolly Madison was for sixteen years the Executive Mansion hostess. This was an accomplishment unmatched

by any other woman in American history. During these years she came up with a "first" for which American children through the decades have applauded. At one elegant dinner in the President's House, Dolly introduced ice cream as a dessert in America.

James Madison labored as hard politically, as his wife did socially, for Thomas Jefferson. Madison was a good Secretary of State and worked very closely with his friend President Jefferson. The Madison-Jefferson team was built on such a firm friendship they could be direct with each other and not worry about misunderstanding. This smooth functioning two-man team was directly responsible for the Louisiana Purchase from France in 1803. Secretary of State Madison risked criticism along with Jefferson over this action and was proud to take some of the credit when things worked out nicely. Much to Thomas Jefferson's delight, one-half of this fine team stayed on after his retirement. James Madison was elected to the presidency on March 4, 1809, as our fourth president.

Washington Irving was a popular American author during James Madison's presidency. He is often called the "father of American literature." His greatest success was The Sketch Book published in 1819. This book included the famous stories "The Legend of Sleepy Hollow" and "Rip Van Winkle."

Beginning as Thomas Jefferson's substitute hostess and continuing active in society after her husband's death in 1836, Dolly Madison reigned as a Washington hostess for nearly fifty years. She was a charming woman but was also known for her cool common sense. She took the time to rescue some important government papers and a valuable portrait of George Washington and barely escaped ahead of British troops as they set fire to the President's House in 1814.

Madison remained interested in government activities after he retired from the presidency in 1817. He is shown here debating before the Virginia legislature in 1829.

President Madison had always believed in Thomas Jefferson's ideas and hoped to continue his friend's policies of government. Staying out of war in Europe continued to be of great importance. But, in trying to keep America out of the war between England and France, he was unsuccessful. Events of the time overpowered President Madison and the United States went to war with England in 1812—a war it could not afford.

The War of 1812, or "Madison's War," as it was called at the time, was a disaster to America. As Presidents Jefferson and Madison had feared, the United States was not prepared. American soldiers lost battle after battle. The United States was further distressed when the president and his First Lady barely missed becoming prisoners of the British in August of 1814. At this time British troops captured and burned the President's Mansion and most of Washington, D.C. The War of 1812 took a fortunate turn for America when General Andrew Jackson led the American forces to victory over the English in the Battle of New Orleans in January 1815. Unknown to Jackson and his troops the United States had, a few days earlier, signed a peace treaty with England. Jackson's victory greatly built up Americans' faith in their army and their government. After the war the young American nation settled back to peaceful

expansion and building. The years of Madison's presidency after the war were quiet ones.

After eight years as president, James Madison retired from office in 1817 and returned to Montpelier. During his last years he also took up Thomas Jefferson's great interest in education at the University of Virginia.

Madison also devoted much time to the freeing of slaves. To our fourth ex-president, slavery was ungodly, unjust, and inhumane. It was a black mark on American history. Madison also found time to enjoy Dolly's sparkling parties at Montpelier, and to develop modern agricultural methods at the estate. He died at home on June 28, 1836.

All successful presidents have been good administrators. President Madison was not successful in this area. As the chief executive, James Madison had few close friends and inspired little affection and no enthusiasm in his colleagues and co-workers in Washington, D.C. He was at times stubborn and was not always effective in dealing with Congress. Still he was the greatest scholar among our founding fathers, expert in constitutional history and theory. Our fourth president must be praised as a great statesman. His work as one of the main contributors to our federal Constitution, the rock upon which America rests, has earned him a high place in the history of our country.

President James Madison

JAMES MONROE

Fifth President (1817-1825)

He was called "The Last of
the Cocked Hats."
This nickname, which hinted at
aristocratic dress and manners, was most unfortunate.
As the youngest member of the Virginia
political clan, which included Thomas Jefferson
and James Madison, he did have
well-born friends.
But in many ways, our fifth president was
a very ordinary man.
He was plain, with awkward
manners and modest presence.
He was not a powerful speaker nor a good writer,
and not a man of wealth.
It was his unbreakable spirit that led him
to the president's chair.
Dedication to the country guided James Monroe
through his eight-year presidential
administration which is remembered by historians
as "the era of good feeling."

This plain country home in Westmoreland County, Virginia, was the birthplace of James Monroe.

THE "ERA OF GOOD FEELING" PRESIDENT

James Monroe was born in Westmoreland County, Virginia, April 28, 1758. His parents, Spence and Eliza Jones Monroe, were of the moderately wealthy Virginia planter class. He was the eldest of their five children. From his parents he learned that plain ways were best. As a youth he enjoyed rabbit and squirrel hunting. James could often be seen roaming the woods with gun in hand. His catches often found their way to the Monroe family dinner-table.

Young James's early education took place at a neighborhood school conducted by a clergyman. He entered William and Mary College in 1774 at the age of sixteen. The Revolutionary War interrupted his studies in 1776. Full of patriotic spirit, James Monroe left college and was commissioned a lieutenant in the American Army at the age of eighteen.

During the Battle of Trenton in December 1776, he was wounded in the shoulder. For his valor at Trenton, General Washington promoted young Monroe to captain citing him for "bravery under fire." He continued to do well as an officer, rising to the rank of major, before resigning from the army in 1778.

Two years later he began the study of law under Thomas Jefferson, who was then the governor of Virginia. In 1786 Monroe was admitted to the bar in Virginia. During his years of law study, Jefferson and young James Monroe developed a close friendship which had a powerful influence upon Monroe's future political career. In later years, these three—Jefferson, Madison, and Monroe—united in friendship and political philosophy, were often referred to as the "Virginia dynasty." It was a dynasty of sorts because this brilliant group turned out three presidents.

At twenty-four years of age Monroe was elected to the Virginia House of Delegates. Entering national politics in 1783 he served in Congress under the Articles of Confederation for three years. He returned for one year to the

Virginia Legislature in 1787. After working in national politics, state government seemed almost dull. The next year he decided to try again for the federal government, running for a seat in the House of Representatives against James Madison. This defeat was only the first of many setbacks on James Monroe's hill-and-valley road to the presidency. Through the years he never gave up.

Monroe married Elizabeth Kortright in 1786. Monroe's family became populated with ladies when his wife presented him with two daughters, Eliza and Maria. A son died in infancy.

Monroe's political career soon improved. From 1790-1794 he filled a vacancy in the United States Senate caused by the death of Virginia's Senator Grayson. He immediately joined the Jefferson-Madison Democratic Republicans who vigorously opposed the Federalist tactics of Alexander Hamilton and President Washington. Washington decided to overlook their political differences and made James Monroe minister to France. The president's plan was to send Monroe to improve French-American relations during the troubled times of the French Revolution. Washington, who sympathized with England, knew Monroe favored the new Republic of France. Monroe blundered early by presenting a United States flag to hang on the wall in the rebel headquarters, next to the French Republic's tri-colored flag. Wishing no association with the revolutionaries of France, this "flag friendship" enraged President Washington and many of his followers. From then on they criticized Monroe's every move.

While on duty in Paris, James Monroe discovered his fellow American, Thomas Paine, in a French prison threatened by possible death on the guillotine. Using his high diplomatic position, he rescued Paine and took him into the safety of the American legation. There he nursed this hero of the American Revolution back to health. Again, his actions were attacked. Critics said Monroe was interfering with matters that did not concern him.

After two years in France, President Washington decided that Monroe had not represented his government properly and he curtly recalled him to America. James Monroe returned in a rage and eased his anger with a five-hundred page document written in defense of his actions in France. President Washington took Monroe's

Thomas Paine was one of the most important influences informing public opinion just before and during the Revolutionary War. In January 1776, he published Common Sense, *a pamphlet which powerfully voiced the American people's wish for independence from England.*

This British cartoon is very much against President Monroe. In it he is unfairly portrayed as an American "king" who harshly ruled over the Indians and killed many Englishmen.

pamphlet as a personal attack and never forgave him. At odds with the president and cut off from national politics, Monroe returned home to Virginia. He bounced off the political ropes in 1799 when he was elected governor of Virginia, a position he held until 1802.

In that year James Monroe happily rejoined Thomas Jefferson in national service. It was again a diplomatic post and the area was again France. President Jefferson appointed him a special minister to assist the resident minister, Robert Livingston. The assignment was to arrange the purchase of the Louisiana Territory. This negotiation was one of Monroe's few successes in Europe. For five years as President Jefferson's minister he tried and failed in the difficult tasks of arranging treaties with Spain and England. After five years in European diplomatic posts, President Jefferson also became

displeased with Monroe's work as a diplomat and recalled him to the United Sttaes.

When he returned to Washington, James Monroe did what political experts considered to be a foolish thing. He ran for the presidency. Temporarily in disagreement with Jefferson, James Monroe had little change of winning in 1808 against James Madison. He was badly beaten. Again he returned to Virginia, a failure as a diplomat and out of favor with national leaders. Time heals many wounds. Feeling Monroe's administrative skills could be put to better use on American shores, Thomas Jefferson, in 1811, recommended that the youngest member of the "Virginia dynasty" accept President Madison's offer to become Secretary of State. Delighted with the opportunity to redeem himself, Monroe eagerly accepted this challenging Cabinet position. Unfortunately,

This painting by C. B. King was done in the first year of James Monroe's presidency.

Because she had travelled with her diplomat husband in Europe, Elizabeth Kortright Monroe was familiar with political life when she became First Lady. In the last years of her husband's presidency, due to ill health, she kept away from crowds and did little entertaining.

President Monroe discusses the Monroe Doctrine with his Cabinet.

Secretary Monroe could do nothing to avoid war again with England. During the War of 1812 Monroe took on additional responsibilities when he became Secretary of War. Holding two Cabinet positions and doing each job well, James Monroe displayed great energy and fine administrative ability. At this time James Monroe did as much as any man to keep the seams of government in Washington from splitting apart.

In 1817 the Federalist Party gave up the ghost. With no opposing party and President Madison's retirement, James Monroe swept into the presidency with ease. He is the only president, except for George Washington, ever to run unopposed at the polls. Only one stubborn Federalist from New Hampshire cast his electoral vote against Monroe. President James Monroe was inaugurated March 4, 1817. The plain man from Virginia, overcoming gigantic obstacles, had reached the President's Mansion by his forceful, rugged courage and his hardworking, honest character.

So popular were Monroe's two presidential terms (1817-1825) they were called "the era of good feeling." The United States was weary of war and division within the country. Changes were taking place and Americans were united in national spirit. Congress shared this national spirit and passed the law officially establishing the flag of the United States. Manufacturing replaced shipping as New England's number one industry. Because of Eli Whitney's cotton gin, the cotton industry was spreading across the south to the new gulf states. The American people had jobs, plenty to eat, and a little time

to sit back and enjoy the country's new wealth. James Monroe was fortunate to be president at this time of growth and prosperity. He was also a man who guided the nation with a firm hand.

Monroe had the ability, as did Washington and later Lincoln, to select strong men for his Cabinet. His selection of John Quincy Adams as Secretary of State was particularly wise. This partnership of Monroe and Adams led the country forward. They made great achievements in foreign affairs. In 1819 they signed a treaty with Spain selling Florida to the United States for five million dollars.

In 1823, when trouble began with Russia and other European powers over colonization and land rights in North and South America, President Monroe stepped forward and delivered a strong message to Congress. This message is called the Monroe Doctrine. For many years the Monroe Doctrine has helped to guide United States foreign policy for American presidents. Some consider Secretary of State John Quincy Adams the author of the doctrine. Secretary Adams had no intention of proclaiming his ideas to the world. It was President Monroe who bravely took this responsibility. Historians consider the Monroe Doctrine to be properly named.

"The era of good feeling" unhappily did not work inside the President's House. In the Executive Mansion President Monroe with his quiet, good humor was able to keep warring diplomatic and political factions at peace, but he was not successful with his ladies and their dis-

CAPITOL OF THE U.S. AT WASHINGTON.

From the Original Design of the Architect B.H. Latrobe Esq[r]

The Capitol Building in Washington when James Monroe was president.

The "Virginia dynasty:" (from left to right), James Monroe, James Madison, and Thomas Jefferson.

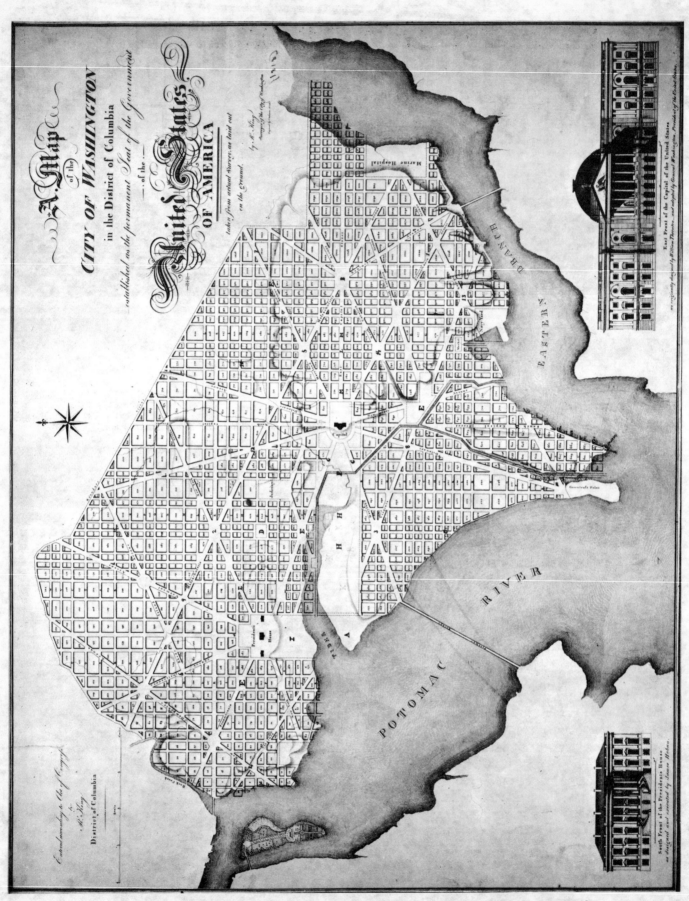

This 1818 street map of Washington shows the location of the President's House and the Capitol Building. Our nation's capital has grown greatly, but both buildings stand in the same place today.

James Monroe moved to New York City to live with his daughter after the death of his wife in 1830. He died in this house, July 4, 1831. This made him the third president to pass away on July 4.

putes. The quiet, modest president was constantly faced with arguments over social rank and behavior brought about by his wife and daughter. Mrs. Monroe and her daughter Eliza were accused by angry Washington wives of putting on royal airs. They would not allow guests to sit in their presence, and thought it beneath them to return social calls.

President Monroe remained a plain and simple man untouched by his ladies' fine airs. It was reported that one day a visiting European diplomat, while walking through the Executive Mansion, found a bald-headed man with an ink-spotted vest and dirty slippers sitting at the president's desk writing. He was shocked to think the president would have such a slovenly clerk in his employ. His astonishment was even greater when he learned that this untidy clerk was President Monroe himself.

Monroe's second term ended in 1825 and he retired once more to his Virginia home, Oak Hill. The next year he became a regent of the University of Virginia. His remaining years were spent in trying to put his business affairs, which he had selflessly ignored for forty-eight years, back into order. To do so Monroe asked Congress to pay him for his expenses while in public service. Congress did pay, but James Monroe still died a poor man on July 4, 1831.

Stoop-shouldered and awkward, Monroe did not possess any commanding physical or personal characteristics. Consequently, he suffered in comparison to other great statesmen of his times. But, in the words of John Quincy Adams, he had "a mind . . . sound in its ultimate judgments, and firm in its final conclusions." President Monroe was a man who lead America firmly along the path of growth and prosperity.

JOHN QUINCY ADAMS

Sixth President (1825-1829)

Fiercely proud of his family's
fine image in the pages of American history,
he battled to make his own place in
history memorable.
The Adamses of Braintree, Massachusetts,
were a political dynasty
for more than one hundred years.
This son did much to
make it so.
He never allowed his physical
appearance—a short, thick-set body,
watery eyes, and a bald head—to keep him back.
He had two famous careers.
He became one of America's greatest
diplomats, a career he began at fourteen.
He was also the outstanding
leader of the anti-slavery movement in the House
of Representatives during the last
eighteen years of his life.
Sandwiched in between these two careers,
John Quincy Adams became our
sixth president.

The birthplace of John Quincy Adams in Braintree, Massachusetts.

A DYNAMIC DIPLOMAT
AND A COURAGEOUS CONGRESSMAN

Born to John and Abigail Adams, July 11, 1767, in Braintree (now Quincy), Massachusetts, young John grew up a child of the American Revolution. When only seven he stood on Penn's Hill holding his mother's hand and watched the Battle of Bunker Hill explode below. Much of his early life was spent with his family in Europe where his father represented the United States on diplomatic missions. John Quincy obtained his education wherever his family happened to be: France, Amsterdam, Leyden, and The Hague. He was extremely bright and his range of interests went far beyond those of the average teenager. Barely fourteen, he went to Russia with Francis Dana, the American minister, as his private secretary and French interpreter. In 1782, he was secretary to his father during the negotiations for the Treaty of Paris which ended the Revolutionary War between the United States and England. The brilliant young man enjoyed conversations with other diplomats. These wise men found the young American to be highly intelligent and a master of several languages.

When John Adams was sent to England in 1785, John Quincy, who disliked the English, decided to leave his family and return to Massachusetts to continue his education at Harvard College. After graduation he studied law and was admitted to the Massachusetts bar in 1790. He had no intention of remaining a lawyer all his life, but law practice was a good way to wait for better opportunities. During his years as a lawyer he was one of the most talented political writers in America. John Quincy Adams enjoyed writing and felt it was a fine way to get other people to understand and accept his ideas. Only twenty-four, he published *Publicola*, a reply to Thomas Paine's *The Rights of Man*. After *Publicola*, he continued his political writing in defense of the Federalist Party's foreign policy and attracted the attention of President Washington. Throughout his life, Adams kept a diary that was to become one of the most famous in American history.

George Washington appointed young Adams as American minister to the Netherlands in 1794. This began a diplomatic career in which

John Quincy Adams at sixteen.

73

John Quincy Adams was an active and effective young diplomat in President Washington's diplomatic corps.

he served as minister to the Netherlands, Sweden, Great Britain, Germany, Portugal, and Russia. George Washington regarded John Quincy as the ablest officer in all of his foreign service. While he was minister to the Netherlands, Adams gathered much vital diplomatic information. With this information President Washington and John Quincy's father were able to keep America out of war.

John Quincy Adams married Louisa Johnson, the daughter of the American consul, in London in 1797. Adams and Louisa soon left for Germany where he was to serve as the American minister. Louisa shared her husband's knowledge of Europe because she had been born and raised there. She first set foot upon American soil four years after her wedding when she returned to the United States with her husband in 1801.

Between diplomatic assignments, John Quincy Adams was elected to the Massachusetts Senate in 1801. Two years later that state's legislature elected him to the United States Senate. He started his political career as a Federalist but Senator Adams was never a man to follow the strict rules of one political party. Adams considered himself to be "a man of my whole country." This ruled out partisanship. He went against the Federalists when he supported the Louisiana Purchase in 1803. Later Senator Adams supported President Jefferson's Embargo Act and the Federalist's anger against him was so great he lost his seat in the Senate in the election of 1808. From 1806 to 1809, Adams divided his time between politics and a professorship of rhetoric and oratory at Harvard College.

Under President Madison in 1809, after a lapse of eight years, John Quincy Adams returned to the diplomatic service as minister to Russia. There in every possible way, he advanced the interests of American trade and became a close friend of Czar Alexander I. Adams ended his diplomatic career as the American minister to Great Britain, a post once held by his father, John Adams. Later John Quincy's son, Charles Francis Adams, was also minister to Great Britain.

Because of John Quincy Adams' great reputation as a diplomat, President James Monroe appointed Adams his Secretary of State in 1817. Secretary Adams played a leading role in the acquisition of the Florida Territory, and in the establishment of the Monroe Doctrine as a part of U.S. foreign policy. He achieved further success in 1819 when he negotiated a treaty with Spain. This treaty established an American boundary stretching from the Atlantic to the Pacific Ocean. To accomplish these things Secretary Adams often labored eighteen to twenty hours a day. The wisdom of President Monroe in picking John Quincy Adams as Secretary of State is a bright page in American history.

John Quincy Adams was elected president in 1825. In the 1825 election no clear majority was won by any of the four candidates. Andrew Jackson won the most votes, but candidate Henry Clay supported Adams when the election was decided by the House of Representatives. Adams promptly made Clay his Secretary of State. Henry Clay was well qualified for the job, but this appointment brought cries of "bargain" and "corruption" from Andrew Jackson supporters.

John Quincy Adams' presidential administration (1825-1829) was the only one in our history with no political party to support it. The sixth president had great legislative vision. Many of his suggestions, such as a department of the interior to regulate natural resources and government aid to education, later became part of the government. Adams simply would not play politics to get a party to back him. With this great handicap, Adams' presidential term was not a shining beacon of success. He would not compromise and, thus remained a man alone, never departing from his fiercely independent path. He had little personal charm nor much sense of humor. It was hard for his associates to feel any great enthusiasm for him.

Eccentric personal characteristics did not help his public relations. They were often the subject of unpleasant public jokes. He was one of the most poorly-dressed men ever to sit in the presidential chair. It is said that he wore the same hat for ten years! A stranger who saw Adams on vacation wearing a beat up old outfit and battered hat, exclaimed, "This is the President of the United States?"

He was criticized for being a gambler because he had installed a billiards table in the President's House and played regularly. Actually, John Quincy Adams' life in the Executive Mansion was a simple one. Long before the rest of

Secretary of State John Quincy Adams gave a ball during
James Monroe's presidency to honor Senator Andrew
Jackson.

THE VELOCIPEDE OF 1827.

An early version of the bicycle, the velocipede, caused a
sensation in 1827 when it first appeared on the streets of
Washington.

Washington was awake, he rose daily at five,
built his own fire, and read the Bible. Then he
took a solitary stroll or swim. One morning
while President Adams was enjoying an early
dip in the Potomac, a thief stole his clothes from
the river bank. A passing boy was greatly surprised to find a short, fat, naked old man shout-
ing to him to run up to the President's House
to fetch a suit of clothes for the president.

Fierce opposition from the followers of Jackson made President Adams' term in office a difficult one. Even so, when the election year of
1828 came up, President Adams decided to run
again. The Adams' personality erased his last
glimmer of hope—Adamses served but Adamses
did not campaign nor defend themselves against
political attack. He was overwhelmingly defeated for reelection by Andrew Jackson. Em-

bittered by what he considered unfair charges of
fraud and extravagance made by the Jackson-
ians, he refused to attend the inauguration. He
left the capital by a backroad on March 4, 1829.

For a brief period of time John Quincy
Adams retired to private life in Massachusetts.
But a great man is never satisfied unless he is
doing worthwhile things. .The people of Massachusetts elected the fiery old Yankee to the
House of Representatives in 1830, and he stayed
there for eighteen years. John Quincy Adams'
long second career as a congressman was as successful and important as his first career in the
diplomatic service. Throughout his nine terms
as a congressman, he fought the expansion of
slavery. Adams proposed many anti-slavery
amendments to the Constitution. Southern congressmen with their famous "gag rule" continu-

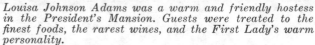

Louisa Johnson Adams was a warm and friendly hostess in the President's Mansion. Guests were treated to the finest foods, the rarest wines, and the First Lady's warm personality.

John Quincy Adams in a portrait by J. P. A. Healy.

ally battled the tough, little New Englander. Adams was often alone in his fight. A visitor to Washington during these times wrote his wife this observation of John Quincy Adams, the "Old Man Eloquent," on the floor of the House of Representatives:

"Old Nestor lifted up his voice like a trumpet; till slave-holding, slave-trading and slave-breeding absolutely quailed and howled under his dissecting knife... Scores ... of slaveholders (members of Congress) ... screaming at the top of their voices: 'That is false!'... Whenever any of them broke out upon him, Mr. Adams would say, ... 'If before I get through every slave-holder, slave-trader and slave-breeder on this floor does not get material for bitter reflection it shall be no fault of mine.' "

In 1844 Congressman Adams' long fight to repeal the "gag rule" was finally won.

Throughout his life the dynamic Adams found time away from public life to devote to the study of science. He was particularly excited about astronomy which he felt was "one of the most important (subjects in which) man could engage." With great satisfaction he helped direct the establishment of the Smithsonian Institute in Washington in 1846.

John Quincy Adams' long and useful life finally came to an end in a most dramatic way. Sitting at his desk while Congress was in session he suffered a cerebral stroke and fell unconscious to the floor of the House of Representatives. Two days later Adams died on February 23, 1848, in the Capitol Building.

THE PRESIDENTS HOUSE

This is the President's House as it appeared during John Quincy Adams presidency. He enjoyed walking down to the Potomac River daily for an early morning swim.

This is the home of John Quincy Adams in Quincy, Massachusetts. He spent a great deal of time there after he retired from the presidency in 1829.

CLIPPER SHIP "GREAT REPUBLIC"
Length on Deck 325 Feet. – Breadth of Beam 53 Feet. – Depth of Hold 38 Feet. – Tonnage per Register 4500.

Yankee clipper ships were in great demand during the first half of the nineteenth century. They were used to carry cargo back and forth between the United States and Europe. Many were used as whaling ships.

Battling Congressman Adams of Massachusetts died in the Capitol Building. He was surrounded by his friends in Congress shortly before he passed away. His last words to them were, "This is the end of earth, I am content."

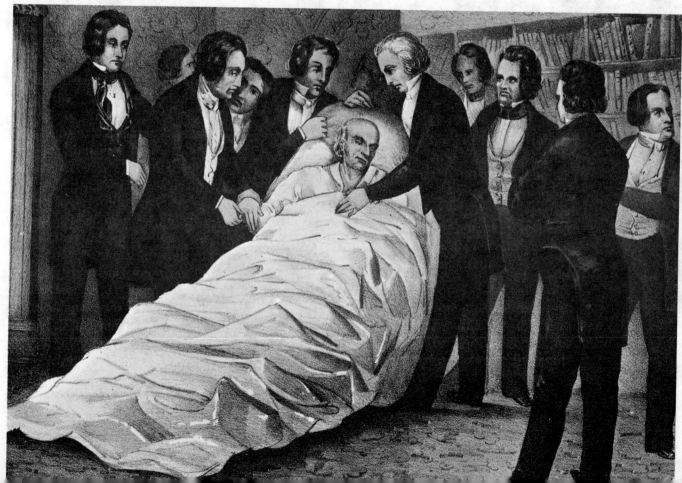

ANDREW JACKSON

Seventh President (1829-1837)

His soldiers called him "Old Hickory"
because that was the toughest wood they knew.
But his other nicknames were not
as tame as this one.
Enemies who hated his domineering ways
in government labeled him
"King Andrew the First."
Throughout his colorful life, he was
an independent spirit who would "battle a bear"
for the best interests of the
American people.
His fiery, dominating personality
won many friends and made
many enemies.
People who knew Andrew Jackson could not
remain in the middle
of the road; they simply had
to take sides.
But in general, the people of America
loved the seventh president.
He was the first president born in a log cabin
and the first born on the new frontier.
This Tennessean was the first
frontiersman to be elected
president—elected directly
by the people.

Andrew Jackson was the first president born in a log cabin. This is his first home in Waxhaw, South Carolina.

A MAN FOR THE PEOPLE

Waxhaw County, South Carolina, was the site of his birth, March 15, 1767. Andrew was the third child in a family of three born to Andrew and Elizabeth Hutchinson Jackson. Battling was in young Andrew's blood from the beginning. His father was an immigrant farmer from Northern Ireland who died the year of Andrew's birth, leaving his widow to struggle on as best she could. Because the Jacksons owned no land, Andrew's mother went to live in the home of her sister. There she acted as housekeeper and brought up her boys. His mother's courageous struggle to keep the family together filled Andrew with admiration and a lifelong reverence for women.

Frontier Waxhaw offered little educational opportunity for young Andrew. As a result, he learned more from men in the woods than he did from books in the schoolhouse. By the time he was eight he had managed, from his spotty schooling, to learn to read and write. The eight year old boy had also developed a fiery temper.

Schoolmates learned that blond, freckle-faced Andy Jackson would fight. Made of little more than skin and bones, he often came out second best in his scuffles, but he never gave up. One combatant recalled that he could throw Andy three out of four times but, "he would never stay throwed."

The Jackson boys' frontier schooling was interrupted by the British invasion of the western Carolinas in 1780. The war brought great misfortune to the Jackson household. The Jackson brothers immediately joined the Revolution although only Hugh was old enough to be a soldier. Hugh was killed in battle. Andrew and Robert volunteered as mounted message-carriers for the American forces. During a skirmish both boys were taken prisoners by the British. Shortly after their capture, Andrew refused the command from an English officer to clean his boots. The cruel officer's response was quick and terrible. The officer drew his saber, cut Andrew's left arm to the bone and gashed his

General Andrew Jackson's fierce fighting spirit and victories during the War of 1812 made him a national hero.

The cruelty to the Jackson brothers by this British officer during the invasion of the Carolinas was never forgotten by young Andrew.

Andrew and Rachel Jackson's home, the Hermitage, was located twelve miles outside Nashville, Tennessee. To the right is the home of their adopted son, Andrew Jackson Donelson.

head. The furious Redcoat then turned his anger upon Robert, cutting him badly with the saber. The wounded brothers, their cuts untended, were then marched forty miles to a British military prison. In this dirty prison the young prisoners fell ill with smallpox. Both boys were released in their mother's custody. These physical misfortunes were too much for sixteen year old Robert. He died at home. Only Andrew's incredible strength, which later became legendary, kept him alive through this terrible time.

For young Andrew Jackson there was still more misfortune. Elizabeth Jackson had left her recuperating son in order to nurse two nephews who lay sick from the plague aboard a British prison ship docked in Charleston. She, too, fell victim to this dreaded disease. Back home, fourteen year old Andrew felt the stinging stab of orphanhood as he learned of his brave mother's death. Now alone in the world, he blamed the death of his mother and brothers on the British. For the rest of his life he never forgot this hatred for the English.

Andrew's grief was great, but his spirit unbroken. The war orphan began to support himself as a chore boy and saddler's apprentice while continuing his education. He gained enough knowledge to develop a strong and effective writing style and enough skill to become a powerful speaker. But he remained an extremely bad speller to his last day. Some Carolina people called the young Jackson "the most roaring, rollicking . . . horseracing . . . mischievous fellow . . . hereabouts." Although young Andrew hid his grief in rowdy activity, he was not lazy or undirected. He had great ambition.

Jackson began to realize his life plan when he began to study law in a lawyer's office in Salisbury, North Carolina. He became a lawyer at the age of twenty. In 1788, he became a prosecuting attorney for the area that was soon to be the state of Tennessee. This rugged Western District was the ideal place for an ambitious young lawyer to cut his teeth. Andrew Jackson was soon a highly successful government attorney. The peak of this career in law was reached when he served as a judge of the Supreme Court of Tennessee from 1798 to 1804.

The events surrounding his marriage to Rachel Donelson, in 1791, illustrate Andrew Jackson's impatient temperament. He fell deeply in love with Rachel, his landlady's daughter, and quickly married her without waiting for her divorce from her first husband to become final. Her first husband had intentionally allowed the false report of his divorce to reach Andrew's and Rachel's ears. After two years of happy marriage, they learned that the divorce had, just then, been granted. This made the first Jackson wedding ceremony illegal and they were required to marry again.

The Jackson marriage was one of great love and devotion, but the confusion surrounding Rachel's divorce put much sadness and strain upon husband and wife. Jackson, always gallant where ladies were concerned, boiled over with rage when he encountered insulting remarks aimed at his beloved Rachel. He fought many duels defending Rachel's honor. One such duel resulted in the death of his opponent, Charles Dickinson, and left Jackson with a bullet (which could not be removed) lodged close to his heart.

Jackson continued to fight against personal criticism he considered unjust. One of the most famous of these brawls occurred in 1813. Angered by Tom Benton's words criticizing his behavior during a friend's duel, Andrew, with horsewhip in hand, followed him into a Nashville hotel. During this fight for his personal honor, Jackson once again received bullet wounds. One shattered his shoulder so badly doctors wanted to amputate the arm that hung lifelessly beneath it. Knowing his vigorous way of life would end with amputation, he refused the operation and risked death instead. Jackson's great strength showed itself once again and he slowly recovered. With three bullets in his body, Andrew Jackson was never again in perfect health or without pain. Feeling that complaints could not ease pain, few people knew of the rugged Jackson's physical discomfort.

With his friends and in his home, no one could be kinder than this rough-hewn, hard-hitting man. Friends knew the warmth which radiated beneath his iron exterior. Andrew Jackson, with his kind and gentle manner, gave his plain little wife the grand attention due a queen. They did not have children of their own so they adopted one of Mrs. Jackson's nephews, Andrew Jackson Donelson.

The study of the Hermitage.

The master bedroom of the Hermitage.

Rachel Donelson Jackson was a quiet, shy woman who loved to spend her time out of the public attention at the Hermitage. She often remained there when her husband's military or political duties took him away. To ease his loneliness when he was away, Jackson carried this miniature picture of Rachel with him.

Andrew Jackson's interest in public affairs and politics was always keen. In politics, he could satisfy his desire to serve his country. He was elected to Congress in 1796, the first representative from the new state of Tennessee.

While in the House of Representatives, his old hatred of the English flared up when he read John Jay's treaty with Great Britain. Jackson felt it was too favorable toward England and hotly returned to Tennessee vowing never again to enter politics. But Andrew Jackson was too great a leader to remain out of things for long. Before the end of the year he returned to Washington as a senator from Tennessee. Unhappy at being away from Rachel and his home near Nashville, he resigned from the Senate after a year. He returned to the Senate twenty-five years later in 1823. This time, he remained for two years before resigning.

One of the more colorful aspects of Andrew Jackson's life began in 1812, when he became a soldier. As the commander of the Tennessee militia he served with valor against the British and their allies, the Creek Indians, in the War of 1812. Angered at first by not being able to fight the British directly, Andrew Jackson

showed he was a brilliant, quick-thinking officer by winning battle after battle against the Indians. His greatest victory over the Creek Indians came at Horseshoe Bend, Alabama, and brought him a promotion to major general. With each victory his men loved him more. General Jackson inspired the war-torn nation and became a national hero after he soundly defeated the British at the Battle of New Orleans, in January 1815. This was a rousing victory for the American people and ended the War of 1812.

General Jackson remained in the army at the close of the war and was sent to a command in the southeastern section of America. There he checked the troublesome Seminole Indians. Jackson was made the territorial governor of Florida in 1821 and remained in that position for six months.

The six-foot, one-inch, lean and wiry, blue-eyed Jackson was now a familiar picture in the minds of the American people. This national hero had distinguished himself in the army and in public service as a governor, congressman, and senator. Of equal importance to his political career was his humble background which made Americans think of him as a man who understood the needs of the frontier folk of the west. These considerations led Jackson to enter the race for the presidency in 1824. Among the four candidates, Jackson won the largest number of electoral college votes — ninety-nine. But this was not a majority. Because no candidate had the majority, the House of Representatives had to decide the election. John Quincy Adams slipped into the president's chair with Henry Clay's support.

During the next four years Andrew and Rachel spent much time at their Tennessee home, the Hermitage. This was a happy time for quiet Mrs. Jackson who hated being separated from her husband. Jackson rode through the Tennessee hills he loved and practiced marksmanship. Rachel occupied herself with the lovely Hermitage gardens. All the while, he was biding his time and preparing to run in the presidential election of 1828.

Jackson defeated John Quincy Adams in 1828 after a long and bitter campaign. The cruel comments, sharply-worded attacks, and personal insults proved too much for Rachel Jackson. She died in December 1828, three months before her husband was inaugurated. The love of his life

This drawing shows the popular "People's President" on his way to Washington to be inaugurated. Jackson was dressed in black because he was mourning his wife Rachel who died a few months earlier.

gone, grief-stricken and drained of his customary vigor, Andrew Jackson was inaugurated March 4, 1829.

His supporters continued to stand in admiration of the new president. Inauguration Day found Washington crowded with people from all walks of life. They overflowed from hotels and boarding houses and gathered on street-corners to praise their man. The saddened president-elect nodded to their cheers and shook their hands on the way to his inauguration. That night, some of President Jackson's supporters ran through the streets of Washington and gleefully rushed into the President's Mansion. America's aristocrats, feeling the country's dignity had suffered with the election of rugged Jackson, renamed the president's house. Formerly called the "President's Mansion" or "President's House," it was renamed the "White House." To these well-born critics it was now

nothing more than an ordinary whitewashed house.

The first frontiersman in the President's House was not a bumpkin from the backwoods. Although he felt free to relax on the White House lawn with a corncob pipe in his mouth, Andrew Jackson was, on state occasions, capable of manners as fine as any of his predecessors.

Jackson's eight years as the "People's President" are regarded as a turning point in American political history. His election came because the people of the west had selected him as their candidate. Jackson had the respect and love of the people because he proved that a man with little formal education, born in a log cabin, could win battles, become a famous general, and become President of the United States. President Andrew Jackson was the ideal picture of the self-made man, an inspiring image for newly-

FIRST RAILWAY TRAIN IN PENNSYLVANIA,

Drawn by "Old Ironsides" on the Phila., Germ. & Norr. R. R.

FIRST TRIP, 23rd NOVEMBER, 1832.

Matthias W. Baldwin was the builder of the first locomotive in Pennsylvania in 1832. It was called "Old Ironsides." As railroad travel became increasingly important in America, the Baldwin Locomotive Works grew. His company built more than 1,500 locomotives. Baldwin is notable for making several improvements in steam locomotives.

BORN TO COMMAND.

KING ANDREW THE FIRST.

This is President Jackson as portrayed by a friendly artist.

This is President Jackson as portrayed by an unkind political cartoonist.

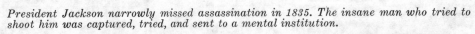

President Jackson narrowly missed assassination in 1835. The insane man who tried to shoot him was captured, tried, and sent to a mental institution.

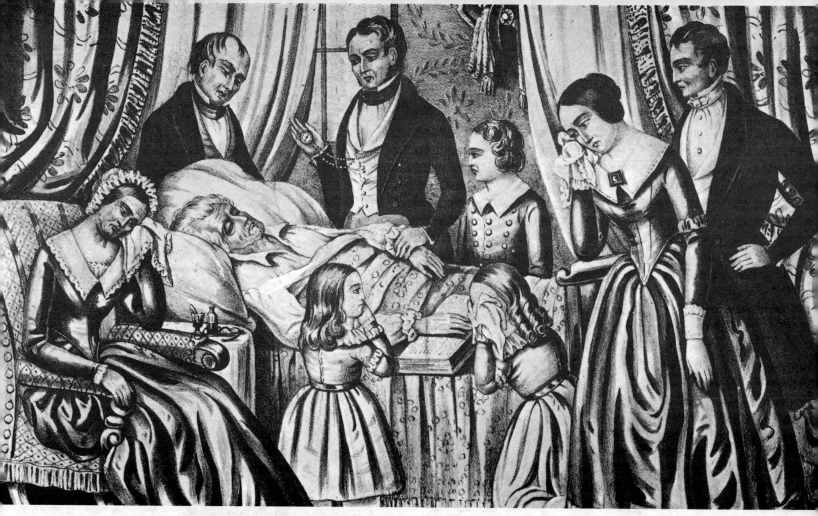

On June 8, 1845, seventy-eight year old Andrew Jackson fainted at his Tennessee home. He died that afternoon with his adopted son, Andrew, Jr., at his side.

emerging middle class America. His fighting ideals, favoring the common man, became the basis of the Democratic Party's political philosophy.

During the Jackson administration America moved westward, expanding and prospering. Arkansas and Michigan became states. The Oregon Trail opened in 1830. The Wisconsin Territory was organized in 1836. That same year Americans, such as James Bowie and Davey Crockett, went to the aid of Texans and bravely fought the battle of the Alamo against superior Mexican forces.

One of the greatest tests yet to be given to a president occurred during President Jackson's administration. In 1832, South Carolina became angered against federal tariff acts and secession rumors brewed. The United States was in danger. Jackson had to act quickly. He agreed the tariff was too high and asked Congress to reduce it. Congress did so and granted President Jackson the authority to send federal troops to South Carolina. The threat of troops quickly stopped secession thoughts. Quick action on the part of the president kept the Union together.

Andrew Jackson retired from office in 1837, even more popular than when he was elected. He was nearly an invalid. In our history few presidents have suffered from so much painful, continuous illness. His pain was increased by his never-ending sorrow for the loss of his wife, Rachel. At the time of his inauguration, the bullets in his body were poisoning his system. He suffered from headaches and at least five other painful diseases. Doctors were in constant attendance while he lived in the White House, but "Old Hickory's" tough body and strong will pulled him through the eight years of his presidency.

Our seventh president was a man who fought vigorously and brilliantly for the causes in which he believed. He was an idealist and a great leader. His decisions were firm and usually correct. On the occasions when Andrew Jackson was wrong, he made bitter enemies. But more often he was loved for his firm belief in the future of his country and the American people. The "People's President" became an inspiring example of vigorous, far-sighted action in the White House.

MARTIN VAN BUREN

Eighth President (1837-1841)

Political allies called him
the "Little Magician." Enemies
named him the "Red Fox of Kinderhook."
Both nicknames credited this active little
man from New York with being a
master politician.
Coming up through the ranks,
he mastered the art of politics as
an artist might master the art
of painting — slowly, carefully, and with love.
Above all, he loved the game of politics
for the good it could do and for the
plain fun of it.
Our eighth president, Martin Van Buren,
was known throughout his life
as a clever, honest, and extremely
likeable man.
He played an important part in
American political history.

THE BIRTH-PLACE OF MARTIN VAN BUREN.

THE POLITICAL WIZARD OF KINDERHOOK

Martin Van Buren was born December 5, 1782, the third of five children of Abraham and Maria Hoes Van Buren. He was raised in the picturesque Dutch town of Kinderhook, New York. His father was the owner of a small farm and tavern, and his interest in local politics was transferred to his son Martin.

While working in his father's tavern serving drinks to the customers young Martin had the opportunity to meet many people. He learned much about human nature and the things that move men or anger them. Martin was educated at the Kinderhook schoolhouse and later at the village academy. The young Dutch-American was only an average student because he preferred action and conversation to book study. Law was quite a different matter for the ambitious Martin; lawyers did things, and more importantly, met influential people. He enthusiastically began the study of law in 1796 and completed his studies in New York City where

he was admitted to the bar in 1803. Lawyer Van Buren then returned to Kinderhook to begin a long and successful career.

In February of 1807 he married Hannah Hoes. His wife died in the twelfth year of their marriage and he was left with the task of bringing up four young sons. He never remarried.

It did not take long for his talents as an industrious and capable attorney to become well-known. About the time he began practicing law, Martin Van Burean became interested in local politics. People just naturally remembered the well-dressed, charming young lawyer. This helped in his 1812 election to the New York State Senate. Senator Van Buren served for eight years in New York's capital, Albany. There he learned the art of politics. Some historians credit Van Burean with being the first real machine politician in America. A good mechanic understands all the parts of the machine with

This photograph of President Van Buren was taken by the famous American photographer Matthew Brady.

Hannah Hoes Van Buren died in 1819, many years before her husband became president.

which he is working. He knows what makes that machine run smoothly and how to fix it when trouble arises. In Van Buren's case, the "machine" was New York politics and the "parts" were the people with whom he dealt. He became a master mechanic.

"Little Van," as his close associates called him, had all the qualities necessary for a successful politician. He was a fine judge of men's actions, always dealing honestly with them. People found him extremely likeable. He had a fine sense of humor and could inspire laughter and good will in others. These personal qualities, combined with his skills as an organizer, soon put Van Buren in command of a strong political faction in New York. This power led to his election to the United States Senate in 1821.

Being elected to the federal government in Washington pleased the little man, but he did not want to give up his political power in Albany. Martin Van Buren's political hold on New York was so firm he was able to establish the "Albany Regency." When he pulled the strings of the powerful political organization from the nation's capital, things jumped back home in New York state. Fellow politicians had to agree, Van Buren was a wonder. Only some sort of wizard could enjoy the best of two political worlds. Martin Van Buren was able to work in Washington and, at the same time, keep his power in New York.

Reelected to the United States Senate in 1827, he resigned the following year to take another step up the political ladder, the governorship of New York. Residence in Washington had brought Martin Van Buren into the world of Andrew Jackson. He could not forget the magnetic Tennessean or his political visions for America. Firmly established in Jackson's camp, Van Buren happily gave up his New York political power when his friend asked for help. He went to work as Andrew Jackson's advisor and his northeastern manager for the 1828 presidential campaign. Van Buren organized Democratic Party workers so well and spent money so wisely that Jackson won the difficult election of 1828 against John Quincy Adams. The tall president-elect was quick to thank those who worked for him. Van Buren, the "Little Wizard" from New York, came in for a large share of Jackson praise.

Knowing Van Buren was a man with whom he could work, President Jackson made him a Cabinet member shortly after his inauguration in March of 1829. Because of his political skill and pleasant personality, Secretary of State Martin Van Buren was soon the strongest member of the Cabinet. Secretary Van Buren was criticized by political foes for extending the spoils system throughout the federal government. The truth was that he did, indeed, hand out federal jobs for loyal party service. On the other hand, Secretary Van Buren was also praised for bringing about cooperation between the president and congressional party leaders. With the government working smoothly, President Jackson accomplished many worthwhile things.

Van Buren's political skills became legendary in the nation's capital. The Peggy Eaton affair well illustrates his political genius. Mrs. John Eaton, the wife of the Secretary of War, was being snubbed by Washington society. Some thought Mrs. Eaton had a questionable past and Washington wives were causing much social embarrassment for the unfortunate woman. Wives of President Jackson's Cabinet members refused to attend social gatherings with Mrs. Eaton. Remembering his own wife's suffering at the hands of wicked gossips, President Jackson stopped all Cabinet meetings until the wives agreed to attend social gatherings with Mrs. Eaton. Van Buren, who was a widower, went out of his way to be kind to Mrs. Eaton. This pleased the president but did not impress the Cabinet wives. Jackson was in a bad position. If he fired the Whigs on the Cabinet, this act would become a serious political issue to be used against him. If he gave in and fired Secretary Eaton, his executive power would be challenged. Martin Van Buren came up with a plan to rescue his president. As a neutral in the affair, he resigned from the Cabinet. This began the action for which he had hoped. All members of the Cabinet followed the example and resigned. Van Buren's selfless actions allowed President Jackson to appoint a new Cabinet and get out of a potentially troublesome situation.

After resigning his post as Secretary of State in 1831, Van Buren was appointed minister to Great Britain. Four months after his arrival in England, he learned the trip had been for nothing. This time he was a victim of the polit-

The White House during Martin Van Buren's presidency.

President Van Buren insisted upon personally greeting the men who came in to the White House to seek office.

President Van Buren is portrayed as being a high-spending man in this 1837 political cartoon. It unfairly suggests that he does not care about the suffering of his people during the financial panic of 1837.

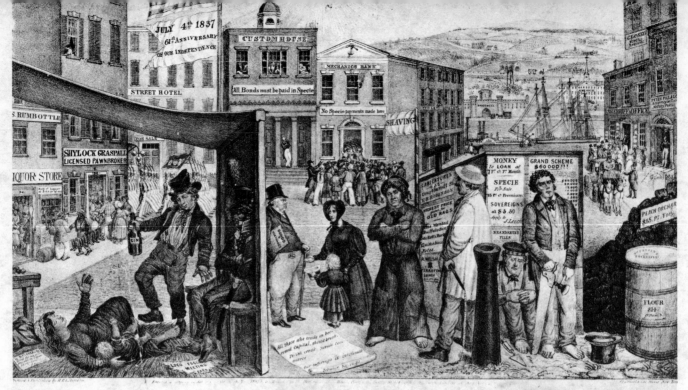

THE TIMES.

This newspaper cartoon shows the hard times many Americans suffered after the financial panic of 1837.

ical game. His nomination as minister to England was defeated in the Senate by the tie-breaking vote of Vice President John C. Calhoun, a long time political rival.

The Eaton affair proved Martin Van Buren was President Jackson's most trusted follower. He wanted the little New Yorker as his second-in-command. In 1832, at the first national convention of the Democratic Party (formerly the Democratic Republicans), he was nominated and elected on the ticket with Jackson. The two popular Democrats proved to be an unbeatable team against their main opponent, Henry Clay. Vice President Van Buren, during his four years in office, was a valued associate and advisor of the president.

Because he was so highly respected by retiring President Jackson, he was nominated unanimously at the Democratic Party convention. Martin Van Buren easily won the presidential election of 1836, coming in on the coattails of Andrew Jackson's great popularity. Shortly after he took office in 1837, things changed greatly. That year a financial panic began to spread throughout America. For the next four years there was much unemployment, many crops failed, and prices were so low that industry was badly hurt. Banks failed and a number of states were not able to meet their financial obligations. Many working men were without jobs. Their families went hungry. These troubles began years earlier. Often when great

trouble arises the president in power is blamed. This happened to President Van Buren. One man alone cannot be the complete cause of trouble, nor can one man alone ease the burden of such troubled times. But the discontented, suffering American public needed a scapegoat and chose to blame the president.

Although greatly hindered by public unpopularity and political maneuvering, President Van Buren did accomplish some good work. He managed to lower the working day for laborers on federal projects to ten hours. In 1840, he managed to get a law passed to establish an independent federal treasury. This was highly important because it took United States government money out of private business hands.

President Van Buren was not unpopular with friendly, bubbling Dolly Madison. During a visit to the White House, this lovely ex-First Lady was shocked to find the total lack of a woman's touch. In Dolly's eyes, the four Van Buren sons and the widower president had turned the Executive Mansion into a barracks. This would never do. Noting Van Buren's eldest son, Abraham, was just of the marrying age, she went to work. Mrs. Madison sent for her pretty cousin, Angelica Singleton (fortunately just Abraham's age), and went about her matchmaking work. Less than a year later, the White House had a woman's touch and a hostess once again – Angelica Van Buren.

A Washington street in 1839.

In the presidential election of 1840, running against the Whig Party candidate William Henry Harrison, Martin Van Buren came up against the greatest challenge of his political career. This election was one of the most colorful in United States history. Martin Van Buren against William Henry Harrison, Democrat against Whig, the "log cabin and hard cider" campaign of 1840 left the starting line at a gallop! The serious issues of the day were pushed aside, the game of politics was on, at its best and worst. Songs, ballyhoo, slogans, and dirty tricks were the weapons of both parties. Van Buren was unkindly labeled "Old Kinderhook" by the Whigs. Midway through the campaign this was shortened to "O.K.". It is said that this American expression started in this way.

During this campaign, "Old Kinderhook" was unjustly attacked by the Whigs for spending much money in the White House while the American people were suffering economic hardship. The Whigs started untrue rumors about an aristocratic chief executive who ate from plates of gold, drank expensive French wines, and paid his chef high wages. Harrison was contrasted as a poor man of the people, a man who enjoyed simple things. Neither picture, of course, was true, but the American voters chose to select the more pleasant image. Harrison beat the little New Yorker badly at the polls. For the first time in twenty-eight years, Martin Van Buren found himself out of a political job.

Martin Van Buren ran twice more for the presidency. In 1844, as a Democratic candidate, his firm stand against slavery kept him from the nomination. He was beaten before he reached the polls. Again in 1848 Van Buren was defeated, this time as a "Barnburner Democrat" and Free Soil candidate. The little ex-president then retired to his estate, Lindenwald, in New York. He enjoyed several years of travel in Europe. He continued active interest in politics until his death in Kinderhook, July 24, 1862.

In firm partnership with Andrew Jackson, Martin Van Buren contributed much to the formation of the principles of the Democratic Party. He played a long and hard political game with many victories and some defeats along the way. He reached the heights in politics because he was able to compromise on some issues, letting people have what they wanted. The "Little Wizard" had great faith in the power of the newly emerging middle class. They had worked hard to get there and deserved to be heard by their leaders. Knowing the rules of the political game so well, he still never quite understood why these people, in whose judgment he placed so much faith, turned against him. In spite of the downward turn at the end, history remembers him for his remarkable political career and as the first "machine-made" president in American politics.

WILLIAM HENRY HARRISON

Ninth President (1841-1841)

*"Granny" was the unfortunate
nickname tacked on to this vigorous
Indian fighter.
He was born into one of the first
families of Virginia.
Yet when he ran for President of the United
States, he was pictured as a
hard cider-drinking frontiersman
who lived in a rugged log cabin.
The campaign of 1840 was filled with ballyhoo,
songs, chants, and slogans.
Candidates took uncomplimentary potshots
at one another daily.
In the end, William Henry Harrison
emerged the victor.
Our ninth president, however, did not live
to show what he could do in office;
he died one month after his inauguration
in Washington, D.C.*

General William Henry Harrison became a national hero after the
Battle of Tippecanoe, November 7, 1811.

TIPPECANOE AND TYLER, TOO!

William Henry Harrison, born February 9, 1773, was the youngest of seven children in Benjamin and Elizabeth Bassett Harrison's family. His birthplace was the Berkeley plantation in Charles County, Virginia. His father was a wealthy planter and an important Virginia politician who served as governor of the state from 1781 to 1784.

Young William Henry grew up in the comfortable plantation atmosphere of aristocratic Virginia. Far from being the rough-hewn pioneer Whig politicians later painted him to be, he grew up trained in good and gracious manners. Throughout his childhood he was educated at home by private tutors. In 1787 he entered Hampden-Sidney College. After graduation in 1790 he began the study of medicine at the College of Physicians and Surgeons in Philadelphia.

To this day Harrison remains the only president to have studied to become a doctor. The young man was greatly intrigued by the science of medicine and the good it could do mankind. But after one year of study, his father died and he left school to enter the army as a junior officer in the first regiment at Fort Washington, Ohio. After six years of army service, he resigned his commission with the rank of captain.

He gained more than military experience in the Ohio wilderness. In November 1795, Harrison married Anna Symmes of North Bend, Ohio. The new Mrs. Harrison was the daughter of a prosperous farmer and judge. Deciding to settle down in Ohio, the young army lieutenant, before his wedding, purchased a parcel of land and there built a five-room log cabin. During the years the Harrisons lived on their North Bend farm, the log cabin was continually improved. By the year 1840, it was only a small annex to a greatly enlarged house.

In May of 1800, President John Adams appointed Harrison governor of the newly created Indiana territory. In many ways William was an average man – ordinary in mental qualities and physical courage – but as a public servant he was exceptionally honest. Harrison attracted attention with his good character. As governor of the Indiana territory, stretching from what is now the state of Ohio to the Rocky Mountains, he had no legislature to watch over him.

He had opportunities for dishonest dealings that would have made him a great deal of money, but he refused them all. Among these was the lucrative offer for about half of the land in and around St. Louis. From this he could have made his fortune, but, of course, Harrison said "no". After twelve years of service, he left the territorial governor's office with a bank account no larger than when he started.

While he was territorial governor, William Henry Harrison was also special commissioner to the Indians. Harrison, pushed by the central government in Washington, brought about a number of treaties which opened new western lands to white settlers. Harrison was in the unpleasant situation of taking away lands from the Indians and trying to make them happy about it.

As may be expected the Indians were greatly dissatisfied with these treaties and with what was happening to their lands. Tecumseh, a chief of the Shawnees, was particularly angry because the Indian nation was losing so much land to the expanding United States. With his brother, Tenskwatawa, known as the Prophet, Tecumseh began to work against the white man's illegal acquisition of Indian lands. Because of these powerful Shawnee brothers, Governor Harrison found it extremely difficult to purchase new lands.

In 1809 Harrison was able to negotiate a treaty to purchase a large piece of land from the Miami Indians. When Tecumseh and the Prophet refused to recognize this treaty, trouble began brewing in the western territory. Two years later President Madison ordered him to lead American troops into the disputed territory while Tecumseh was away. There he fought the famed Battle of Tippecanoe. On the banks of Indiana's Tippecanoe River, on November 7, 1811, Harrison led his troops into action against the Prophet and his Indian forces. The Indians were defeated and Harrison became an American hero. His image as the rugged western man and successful Indian fighter was what the public wanted.

After the victory at Tippecanoe, Harrison was appointed supreme commander of the Army of the Northwest. He went after Tecumseh at the Battle of the Thames in 1813. The great

HARRISONIAN

BALL ROLLING.

KEEP THE

WILLIAM HENRY HARRISON THE FARMER OF NORTH BEND.

RALLY!

A General Meeting

Will be held at the Old COURT ROOM, [Riey's building]

On Saturday Evening,

The 18th instant, at early candle light. A punctual attendance is requested.

MESSRS. DAVIS, BOTKIN, KEATING

And others, will address the Meeting.

R. P. TODD, *Chairman*

July 17, 1840.   *Vigilance Committee.*

The log cabin and barrel of hard cider were the trademarks of the 1840 campaign of Whig candidate William Henry Harrison.

Shawnee chief was killed during the battle and the Indians were beaten. William Henry Harrison's image as a western hero grew. The victorious general was not an Indian-hater as some suggested; he went into these battles only to serve America. Many times, when he was military governor, he had the opportunity to deal justly with Indians in criminal cases and he did so.

During the next seventeen years William Henry Harrison served in a variety of positions in public life with moderate success. He served in Congress from 1816 to 1819. In Ohio, he was a member of the state senate for two years, and from 1825 to 1828 he was a United States senator. John Quincy Adams appointed him the first United States minister to Bolivia in 1828. Dissatisfied with his actions, Adams recalled Harrison from this position after less than a year's service.

Harrison then returned to his farm in North Bend, Ohio, and lived there for the next few

years in semi-retirement, struggling to make his farm profitable. Early in 1835, recalling his heroics at Tippecanoe, the Whigs began mentioning him as their candidate for the presidency. He lost in the election of 1836 to Martin Van Buren, but lost little in the estimation of Whig political leaders. Harrison, with his western heritage, put before the voters' imagination pictures of the adventuresome Davy Crockett type of hero.

The Whigs nominated him again in the election of 1840. Old General Harrison, the hero of Tippecanoe, was a vote-getter, he had political experience with service in both Congress and the Senate. But, even more important, he was not associated with any ideas or legislation that would anger the voters. In the campaign of 1840 the Whig Party won. In William Henry Harrison they had a military hero – a man who could be popularized. The Whigs presented no platform, discussed no real issues, and worked on the emotions rather than the brains of the voters.

"Tippecanoe and Tyler, Too!" became the cry throughout the land. (John Tyler of Virginia was his vice presidential running mate.) President Van Buren was criticized for expensive tastes and luxurious living in the White House. He became known by the uncomplimentary nickname "Old Kinderhook." The Democrats replied by calling Candidate Harrison "Granny," suggesting that, at sixty-seven, he was too old for the job. Campaign songs like this were written and sung:

"Old Tip he wears a homespun coat,
He has no ruffled shirt – wirt – wirt.
But Mat he has the golden plate,
And he's a little squirt – wirt – wirt."

This noisy campaign gave birth to another popular American expression. An enthusiastic team of Whig supporters pushed a gigantic paper ball, as tall as two man and covered with Harrison campaign slogans, from city to city. Newspapers reporting the act said they were "keeping the ball rolling" for Harrison.

What really turned the tide in Harrison's favor was the unlucky comment of a journalist who disliked the plain old man from Ohio. A Baltimore newspaperman suggested that if "Old Tip" were given money and a barrel of hard cider he would prefer a log cabin to the White House. Now it became the "log cabin and hard

PRESIDENTIAL INAUGURATION OF Wᵐ H. HARRISON.
IN WASHINGTON CITY, D.C. ON THE 4ᵀᴴ OF MARCH, 1841.

In this 1840 campaign poster, Candidate Harrison is portrayed at his home in North Bend, Ohio, happily greeting an old soldier who served under him at the Battle of Tippecanoe.

This is William Henry Harrison as he looked at the time of his presidential inauguration.

Anna Symmes Harrison became ill in Ohio one month before her husband's inauguration. She preferred to stay home to recover and planned to join him later in Washington. During President Harrison's brief term of office, his daughter-in-law acted as a temporary hostess of the White House.

cider campaign." Log cabin clubs and log cabin badges sprouted everywhere. There was even a Log Cabin Newspaper. The people gleefully climbed aboard the log cabin bandwagon to support this man whose image appealed to them.

General William Henry Harrison defeated Martin Van Buren by a large electoral college vote. In electing Harrison the voters sent a man to the White House about whom they knew little. To the American public his political thoughts and plans as president were a mystery. This had truly been an election of a personality.

"Old Tip" was exhausted at the end of the campaign. Shortly before taking the oath of office it was announced in the newspapers that President Harrison would shake no hands at the inauguration. His arm was sore and his hand swollen from too many campaign handshakes.

The fourth of March, 1841, was the coldest Inauguration Day in history, but the new president would not wear an overcoat. William Henry Harrison was the oldest man to be elected president, but he didn't want to act it. No one would be able to call him "Granny!" His inauguration speech, the longest in history, kept him in the cold air one hour and forty minutes. President Harrison further weakened himself by riding to and from the ceremony on horseback, and by attending three inauguration balls in his honor that night.

In the damp, unheated White House later in March, he caught a cold. He was further exhausted by a continuous crowd of Whig office seekers who overflowed the White House. The cold turned into pneumonia. He died exactly one month after being sworn in as the chief executive while still trying to carry out his sworn presidential duties. William Henry Harrison's last words were directions addressed to the absent Vice President Tyler.

GEN. WILLIAM HENRY HARRISON

This 1840 campaign poster portrays the major events and achievements
in the lifetime of William Henry Harrison.

President Harrison died April 4, 1841, one month after his inauguration. In attendance at his death were, from left to right, Secretary of the Treasury Thomas Ewing, Secretary of State Daniel Webster, his doctor, his minister, and his niece and nephew.

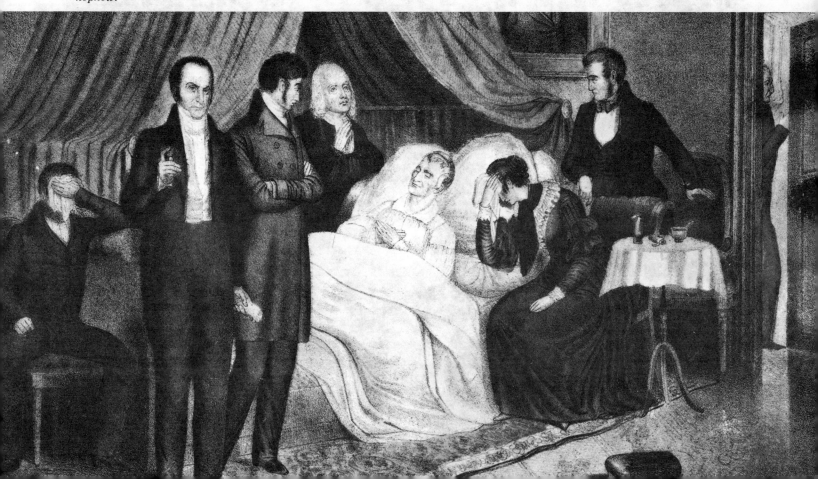

JOHN TYLER

Tenth President (1841-1845)

Like all vice presidents,
he had put ideas of being president
out of his mind.
When a friend brought him word
of William Henry Harrison's death,
he was shocked.
He hadn't even known of the
president's illness!
He raced back to Washington to
begin his new duties.
As he rode, a thousand questions
raced through his head.
What should he do?
How should he act?
No man had ever been placed in
this situation before!
Newspapers called him the "Accidental President,"
after he was sworn in as the tenth
chief executive.
Many persons criticized the
elected vice president for
acting like a president.
Both the Whigs and the Democrats disowned him.
Still he managed to do his job and
keep the country going.
The obstacles were great,
but John Tyler's strong will and love of country
served him throughout the presidential
term which he inherited.

The Peacemaker, a bow gun aboard the U.S.S. Princeton was fired for demonstration on February 28, 1844. Eight men were killed including Secretary of the Navy Thomas Gilmer and David Gardiner, father of President Tyler's fiancee, Julia.

THE ACCIDENTAL PRESIDENT

The tenth President of the United States was born to John and Mary Armistead Tyler in Charles County, Virginia, March 29, 1790. John was the sixth child in a family of eight. His father was a prominent Virginia politician who had been governor of the state for three years and a United States District judge for two more. Little is known of his early years except for the great sadness he suffered, at the age of seven, over his mother's death. Consequently, this motherless boy became very attached to his father and often tried to imitate his forceful ways.

At twelve, John Tyler entered the grammar school of the College of William and Mary. He was graduated from this institution at the age of seventeen and immediately began the study of law in his father's law office. In 1809, he was admitted to the bar of the state of Virginia and began to build a successful practice. For many years he alternated public service with service to the people of Virginia as an attorney. It was a common sight to see Lawyer Tyler astride his horse, "The General," riding around Charles County on his legal duties. When "The General" died, John Tyler had a large grave dug at his Virginia home. Over the grave was this inscription:

"Here lies the body of my good horse, 'The General.' For twenty years he bore me around the circuit of my practice, and in all that time he never made a blunder. Would that his master could say the same!
John Tyler."

Probably Tyler made a few "blunders" in his career in law and public service, but he was successful and diligent in his service to the people of Virginia.

John Tyler began his duties in public office at the age of twenty-one. He was elected to serve five terms in the Virginia state legislature. He served in the United States House of Representatives from 1817 to 1821. As a congressman in 1820, he voted against the Missouri Compromise. Tyler recognized the evils of slavery and hoped it would gradually die out, but he opposed as unconstitutional laws that restricted slaveholders in the territories. As a states' rights man all the way, Tyler felt it was the duty of the states to direct the federal government, not the reverse. He returned to Virginia and was elected governor in 1825, but resigned his position to become a United States senator in 1827.

Tyler's nine-year Senate career was memorable for his courageous beliefs and independence of political parties, his belief in states' rights, and a close interpretation of the Constitution. Fearing that South Carolina would leave the Union, Senator Tyler worked with Henry Clay for the successful passage of the compromise tariff of 1833. Later, Senator Tyler stood bravely by his beliefs when he became the only senator to vote against President Jackson's Force Bill. This bill would allow the president to send federal troops into South Carolina. It was necessary in this emergency. But Senator Tyler felt these actions went against the Constitution. The Force Bill passed in the Senate 32-1; Tyler's was the only "nay" vote. South Carolina did remain in the Union. Some questioned Senator John Tyler's wisdom in taking so strict a stand for states' rights at this time, but none can question his patriotism and hard work when the Union was threatened.

During the Whig convention of 1840, John Tyler was nominated to run as vice president with nominee William Henry Harrison. Being the champion of states' rights, he was placed there chiefly because the Whigs thought he could carry the South. They were correct. After the lively campaign of 1840, the team of "Tippecanoe and Tyler, Too!" won a large electoral college majority over the Democratic opponent, Martin Van Buren.

John Tyler was playing a game of marbles with neighborhood boys in Williamsburg when the news of President Harrison's death reached him. Tyler packed and made haste for the capital. Most of his life he had found himself short of money and even now he had to borrow funds from friends to get to Washington. Few people knew of the dignified Virginian's money problems. The quiet smile on his pleasant face often hid personal worries. Tyler never burdened his friends with his private troubles.

It was suggested by Henry Clay, the Whig leader in Congress, that Tyler was only an acting president and, therefore, could not use the full powers of the presidency. The new president was told that all decisions were made in Cabinet meetings. He was to follow President Harrison's example and cast only one vote. The independent legal mind of President John Tyler took exception to this suggestion. He knew the Constitution; he knew the president was supposed to lead, not be one of a group. With no other example to follow, the first man to be elevated to the presidency through the death of a chief executive bravely showed the way for others. He would lead, and did lead.

His spirit of independence aroused, John Tyler refused to play the lame duck and began exercising the powers of the presidency. This decision led to a feud with the powerful Henry Clay and brought about the resignation of his entire Whig Cabinet, with the exception of his Secretary of State, Daniel Webster. The president was further handicapped by being thrown out of the Whig Party. Tyler was now a man without a party and without support in Congress.

He became known as "Old Veto" because he sent back so much proposed legislation. Congress paid him back by refusing to cooperate on bills the president felt were needed. Now Tyler's independent spirit was truly put to the test. It served him well. His administration was successful in many ways in spite of constant opposition from Congress. The United States Navy was reorganized. A depot for nautical charts and instruments was established that later became the naval observatory. A magnetic telegraph system was tested and developed. The United States Weather Bureau was founded.

Julia Gardiner Tyler became First Lady when she was twenty-four.

His greatest achievement as president was the annexation of Texas which occurred only a few days before he retired from office. President Tyler put in long, hard hours trying to add Texas to the Union. He felt this deed, which had plagued his presidential predecessors, was all important for continued growth and expansion of the United States. The slavery issue held up President Tyler's plans for many, many months but in the end his perseverance won.

John Tyler was the first president to marry while in the White House. His first wife, Letitia, mother of eight of his fifteen children, died in the second year of his term. His second wife, Julia, during their engagement, was literally blasted into his arms! On February 28, 1844, President Tyler, members of his Cabinet, and many important men and their wives were cruising down the Potomac aboard the *U.S.S. Princeton*, the first American propeller-driven warship. On this excursion the *Princeton's* two large guns were to be tested. The United States came close to being without a president that fateful afternoon. About to go on deck to see the guns tested, President Tyler stopped for a moment to listen to a song below deck. Just at that moment one of the *Princeton's* guns exploded killing several people and severely wounding nineteen. Miss Julia Gardner, whose father was one of those killed, fainted in the president's arms. Luckily neither received injury.

They were married in New York City in June of that same year. The slim, handsome president and his lovely, young First Lady cut an elegant path through Washington society. Tyler believed his lovely wife's pleasurable White House entertainments during the last year of his administration helped get votes for the annexation of Texas. To show Julia his thanks, he gave her the gold pen with which he signed the formal annexation papers.

John Tyler was the first man in our history to become president because of the death of the chief executive, thus, serving the American people for nearly four years without being elected by them. In trying to do his duty as he saw fit, he was regarded as a renegade by both political parties. Yet, his administration accomplished much good work. By the end of his term, it was clear that his independence had put him in disfavor with Whigs and Democrats alike. His political career had come to an end. He was not nominated by a major party in the election of 1844. However, he is remembered favorably by historians as a man who successfully carried out the duties of the presidency upon the death of a chief executive. Through the years, Tyler served as an example, a bright light of hope, for other vice presidents who suddenly found themselves serving as the new chief executive.

From original painting by J. R. Lambdin.   Copyrighted by J. C. Tichenot, 1898.

John Tyler

President John Tyler as painted by J. R. Lambdin.

113

President Tyler's granddaughter Mary was a fairy hostess at her third birthday party. Her friends and children of Cabinet members were invited.

Secretary of State Daniel Webster was the only member of the Cabinet who did not resign when John Tyler became president. He began his political career in 1813 as a congressman from New Hampshire. He spent most of the remainder of his life as a legislator and statesman. President Tyler said of him, "You have . . . a true American heart." He died in 1852.

Henry Clay, because of his work on the Compromise of 1820, became known as the "Great Compromiser." This Kentuckian was an active American politician for over four decades. He tried for the Whig presidential nomination in 1840, 1844, and 1848. Winning the Whig nomination in 1844, he lost to Democrat James K. Polk. He sponsored the Compromise of 1850 in the Senate. Clay died two years later thinking his efforts had saved the Union.

Ex-president John Tyler and his wife Julia retired to their Virginia home, Sherwood Forest.

This is another unkind look at a president by a political cartoonist. This cartoon suggested President Tyler used his veto power like a sword to cut down all opposition.

JAMES K. POLK

Eleventh President (1845-1849)

Betting on horseraces
has been a popular sporting activity
in America through the decades.
Discussing the best horses and the reasons
why one is favored over another is as
much fun as watching the fast race.
Racing fans usually hesitate about betting
money on an unknown horse.
The same is true of politicians when they
nominate a candidate at a national convention.
They are unwilling to count on
a man they do not know.
This was the case at the Democratic
National Convention of 1844.
Their candidate came from the hills of Tennessee
and was almost unknown to the nation.
But James K. Polk, the first "dark horse"
candidate to win a presidential election, became
the only president who managed
to fulfill all of his
campaign promises.

GRAND DEMOCRATIC BANNER.

Entered according to Act of Congress in the Year 1844 by J. Baillie in the Clerks Office in the Dt Court of the Sn Dt of N.Y.

Lithd & Pubd by J. Baillie 118 Nassau St N.Y.

James K. Polk and vice presidential candidate George M. Dallas as they appeared on the Grand Democratic Banner during the campaign of 1844.

THE FIRST "DARK HORSE" PRESIDENTIAL CANDIDATE

Our eleventh president was born in Mecklenburg County, North Carolina, November 2, 1795. Born to Samuel and Jane Knox Polk, James K. was the eldest child in a family of ten. At the age of eleven he went with his family to live in Maury County, Tennessee.

His deeply religious mother told him of the strength and power that love of God can give. He needed them at the age of seventeen. Always a sickly child, he was forced to have a painful gallstone operation without anesthesia or antiseptics. Polk survived the operation, his faith in God firmer than ever.

Because of poor health, school attendance was difficult for young James. By the time he was twenty he was strong enough to meet the entrance requirements for the University of North Carolina. He graduated in 1818 as the class scholar in mathematics and classics. James then returned to Nashville to study law. In 1820 he was admitted to the bar of the state of Tennessee and began a career as an attorney.

Politics had long been important in the Polk family. The practice of law brought James K. Polk into contact with the leading political figures of the state. His deep interest in politics was strengthened by meeting dynamic politicians like Andrew Jackson. Soon he began making speeches in support of candidates and legislation. Polk was a strong supporter of Democratic Party policies and a devoted supporter of General Jackson. Throughout Tennessee, James K. Polk's speeches caught the interest of all who heard him. Lawyer Polk had a powerful way with words in spite of his stern and formal manner. The people of the state overlooked these personal drawbacks and listened to his inspiring words. Because Polk's speeches were so effective, he was compared to the powerful French leader Napoleon and labeled "Napoleon of the Stump."

James K. Polk's rise to political power in Tennessee was further helped by his marriage to Sarah Childress in 1824. His bride was a member of one of Tennessee's most socially prominent families. Her quiet charm was a great help to the rising young politician who was then a member of the Tennessee legislature. With no children of her own, Sarah Polk devoted herself to her husband's career.

Later, as the First Lady, she ran the White House with dignity and simplicity. Plain ways prevailed in the White House under Mrs. Polk. Her strict religious beliefs would not permit wine, card playing, or dancing in the Executive Mansion. At public receptions no refreshments were served. In fairness to Mrs. Polk, it must be said that her wishes suited her husband's mood. One of the hardest-working presidents in history, Polk did not like "time unprofitably spent." While the Polk's reigned, fashionable Washington society was kept alive by Dolly Madison's lively parties in her Lafayette Square home. She was still sparkling at the age of eighty.

James K. Polk was a successful public official, but men who worked close to him found his somber ways difficult. His associates accepted, but did not approve of his straight-laced mode of living. Usually wearing clothes two or three sizes too large, his small frame seemed even smaller. This stiff, unhumorous man with sharp gray eyes, a grim mouth, and a sad face, looked like an old man even when very young. It is understandable that he had many acquaintances, but few friends.

Andrew Jackson was one of those friends who was loyal to James K. Polk throughout his lifetime. "Old Hickory's" forceful personality and political power brought James K. from Tennessee into government service in Washington. Polk's enthusiasm for Jackson's policies earned the younger man a "Young Hickory" label. Polk was often criticized for riding on Jackson's coattails. Nevertheless, he entered national politics with vigor and honesty. He firmly and deeply believed in Jackson's politics and never found it difficult to support him. Polk's image lost a great deal of its luster when in the shadow of his political idol.

Beginning in 1825, he served fourteen years as a member of the United States House of Representatives. He became Speaker of the House in 1835, remaining there until 1839. Then

A drawing of James K. Polk's, March 4, 1845, inauguration as it appeared in the
Illustrated London News.

James Marshall discovered gold in California January 24, 1848. This cartoon shows
people heading west in search of gold and riches.

Tennessee politics called Polk home. He returned to be elected governor.

James K. Polk's nomination as the Democratic "dark horse" candidate came as a complete shock to political experts and the nation. Although Polk had served as a congressman for fourteen years, he was not nationally known. In Washington he had simply been thought of as "Jackson's man." At the May 1844 Democratic National Convention in Baltimore, Polk was not originally considered as presidential material. His name did not appear once on the first seven ballots cast at the convention. By then it was clear that a stalemate had been reached by the two most popular candidates; the convention delegates simply could not agree. On the eighth ballot Polk's name came up. He was nominated as a compromise candidate. On the ninth ballot the convention stampeded to support Polk.

Twenty-four hours before the "dark horse" appeared in the winner's circle in Baltimore, no one had mentioned his name for the high office of president. Public surprise at James K. Polk's nomination can be seen in the following event. The first year of the telegraph was 1844 and many people doubted this "new-fangled contraption." The inventor, Samuel Morse, waited in Washington for news of the Democrats' choice. He spelled out in dots and dashes the name of the candidate chosen by the convention . . . P-O-L-K. It was then that the doubters in Washington were sure the telegraph must be a fraud.

Campaigner Polk surprised the nation by standing firm for the acquisition of the Southwest Territory and the re-occupation of the Oregon Territory. His Whig opponent, Henry Clay, did not. At this time, there was growing support for American expansion west to the Pacific Ocean and southwest to the Rio Grande River. The little-known Polk promised the public both and was elected over his well-known opponent.

For years America had been expanding westward. Explorers, trail blazers, traders, trappers, and whalers opened up the rich western regions. Then ranchers and farmers began to settle the land. By 1844 Americans were spreading through these valuable western lands, but they were frustrated. The Oregon Territory was shared with England, and the Southwest Territory belonged to Mexico. Western Americans wanted to own these lands and candidate Polk listened to them.

President Polk was completely successful in living up to his campaign promises. His administration made large territorial gains. Except for President Jefferson's Louisiana Purchase, his administration placed more square miles within United States boundaries than any other. A treaty with England was signed establishing a permanent boundary between the United States and Canada at the forty-ninth parallel. Opponents of President Polk's action, desiring more land to the north, shouted the slogan, "Fifty-four, Forty or Fight!" But Polk knew how to get things done. When he knew he was right, he could not be bluffed or threatened. He held his ground against the "Fifty-forties" and the treaty was ratified.

War with Mexico did come, however, over the acquisition of Texas and the Southwest Territory (now California, Arizona, Nevada, New Mexico, Utah, and sections of Colorado). When diplomatic negotiations with Mexican leaders broke down, President Polk sent the American Army into action. After many battles, the Mexican Army was defeated by American soldiers under the Command of Generals Zachary Taylor and Winfield Scott. After nearly two years of warfare, the Mexican government signed the Treaty of Guadalupe Hidalgo, ceding the Southwest Territory to the United States for fifteen million dollars.

Other accomplishments of James K. Polk's term include the establishment of the Department of the Interior, the United States Naval Academy at Annapolis, and the Smithsonian Institute in Washington. Largely through his untiring efforts and effective communication with both houses of Congress, President Polk managed to push through the legislation for which his administration is known.

President Polk, operating under a serious physical handicap, accomplished all this in a single term. The bad health which plagued him in childhood held him back during his presidential term. The location of the White House on the "foggy bottom" didn't help the president's condition. Swamps along the Potomac acted as breeding grounds for disease-carrying flies and mosquitos. Nor was the president's health helped by the total absence of plumbing in the Executive Mansion.

Sarah Childress Polk ran the White House in a quiet, efficient way when she was First Lady.

James K. Polk was forty-nine when he became president. Up to that time in history, he was the youngest man to serve in the office.

As his term as president wore on, President Polk became more and more burdened with the tremendous duties of his office. In his diary there is much evidence of his great despair over the many office and favor seekers with whom he was forced to deal. These spoils system seekers took much of his time away from more important matters. He felt he must deal with these people. However, he refused to see them in the afternoons because this was the time he dedicated to the more important affairs of state.

As his presidential term approached its end, the burdens of the presidency began to wear away James K. Polk's frail shield of health.

Satisfied with his many accomplishments, he did not seek reelection in 1848. On his last day in office, March 3, 1849, President Polk wrote in his diary:

"I feel exceedingly relieved that I am now free from all public cares. I am sure I shall be a happier man in my retirement than I have been during the four years I have filled the highest office . . ."

He did not have much time left to learn if private life would make him a "happier man." One hundred three days after this hopeful passage was written, James K. Polk died in Nashville, Tennessee.

This cartoon portrays Texas as the pretty lady in the center. It shows Vice President Dallas, President Polk and Henry Clay all trying to "court" her and win her over.

James K. Polk's home in Tennessee.

ZACHARY TAYLOR

Twelfth President (1849-1850)

Affectionately called
"Old Rough and Ready" by his men,
the fourth general to become
president was anything but ready to become
the chief executive.
His military career, which spanned forty years,
never allowed him to stay in one place
long enough to vote.
Politics interested him, but
he never thought of it as a career.
But history sometimes takes strange turns.
General Zachary Taylor found himself in
the midst of one when he moved into
the White House as our
twelfth president.

Captain Zachary Taylor during the 1812 defense of Fort Harrison from Indian attack.

OLD ROUGH AND UNREADY

Born to Richard and Sarah Dabney Taylor in Orange County, Virginia, November 24, 1784, Zachary was the third child in a family of nine. He was still an infant when his father made a new home for the Taylor family in Louisville, Kentucky. There the elder Taylor was appointed collector of the port of Louisville. The port area bordered Spanish and Indian territory, and young Zach grew up in dangerous frontier country. The howling of wolfpacks was common at night, and danger from unfriendly Indians was everywhere. Throughout his frontier youth he had very little formal schooling, but he did receive some tutoring from a man employed by his father.

Zachary's love for adventure was influenced by pioneer life and its constant dangers. As a young man he tried farming, but this did not satisfy his adventuresome nature. At twenty-four he became a lieutenant in the United States Army. He married shortly after this.

Moving from army post to army post around the country with his wife Margaret and their six children, the Taylors rarely knew the ease of a "settled in" existence. Two of their children died as a result of this rough life.

Taylor kept up a second career as a professional farmer. He owned plantations in Louisiana and Mississippi, and loved to talk about crops and new farming methods with his army friends. Much of the directing of his plantation managers was done by mail because army duties usually kept him far away from home.

Zachary Taylor's forty years of soldiering were spent mostly in the cavalry. He was an oddity as an officer. He disliked uniforms and was usually seen with a colorful scarf around his neck flapping in the breeze. It was reported that he only wore his regulation uniform when he had his picture taken! Taylor was of medium height, but his legs were exceptionally short. Because of this he had to be helped into the saddle. He made anything but a dashing picture when on a horse. With his short legs sticking out and his bright scarf and suspenders catching the sunlight, Taylor made an amusing picture. But these things endeared him to his troops.

If he was an affectionately funny sight to his men, he wasn't to his enemies. He never lost a battle. Taylor had the loyalty of the men he led. For them it was a pleasure to serve under such a skillful and exciting officer. The soldiers nicknamed him well, because Zachary Taylor was always ready for anything. Three wars and many uprisings left "Old Rough and Ready" still unafraid. After the Battle of Lake Okeechobee, during the Seminole Indian uprising, he was made a brigadier general.

Taylor's administrative skills were almost as well-known as his military skills. He had a fine reputation for his fairness in dealing with the Indians. He built many roads, bridges, and forts for the army in the western territories. He was known as a commander who could keep his soldiers, stationed at lonely army outposts, happy.

When Texas was annexed in 1845, the United States government feared that Mexico would make war. General Taylor was ordered by the War Department to place his troops in southern Texas. Taylor's forces occupied territory claimed by Mexico. In the spring of 1846, General Taylor had three thousand men encamped in Fort Brown at the mouth of the Rio Grande River. The Mexican Army was stationed across the river at Matamoros. In April, Taylor blockaded the river and cut off Mexican supplies. In response to these actions, the Mexicans sent a force of cavalry across the Rio Grande and engaged in a skirmish with a troop of American soldiers. Several Americans were killed and General Taylor notified President Polk. These actions by Taylor started one of the major wars in our history. The president acted quickly and sent a war message to Congress.

Victorious against the Mexicans in the Battles of Palo Alto and Resaca de la Palma, General Taylor became a hero to the American public. Politicians back in Washington, knowing the American public's fondness for military men, did not like this. They worked to keep the hero of the Mexican war under wraps. General Taylor suspected political tricks when President Polk refused to send him reinforcements and supplies. The president expected Taylor and his men to live off the land, but his army was encamped in a dry desert area. He began to complain and soon a few more men were sent.

Taylor and his troops then advanced and captured the town of Monterey. Politics flared up again, because President Polk did not approve of some of General Taylor's actions at Monterey and said so publicly. Believing the president was playing politics, Zachary Taylor began sending letters in his own defense to newspapers back home.

"Old Rough and Ready," the outspoken soldier, was becoming dangerously popular. Victories in Mexico and letters to American newspapers were making him a light in the public eye. Washington politicians began to worry. A popular general who wrote "letters to the editor" must certainly want to become president. Taylor had no such idea; he was merely defending himself against attack.

President Polk decided to remove General Taylor from the limelight and ordered him to take up a defensive position at Monterey. The greater glories of the Mexican War were turned over to General Winfield Scott. Angered by this, General Taylor disobeyed these orders and crossed the mountains to meet the army of Santa Anna at the Battle of Buena Vista. Buena Vista was a great victory for the Americans. General Taylor is remembered standing calmly giving orders during the battle with a hail of bullets whizzing by. Some bullets came so close they ripped his clothing. Outnumbered four to one, the Americans were inspired by this picture of their general's bravery and gained one of the greatest victories of the war.

At home, wise Whig politicians had closely followed the career of the brave old general and made their decision. They wanted Zachary Taylor as their next presidential candidate. As a hero he would win the North, and as a planta-

A lieutenant of artillery drew this sketch of "Old Rough and Ready" and "Whitey" during the Battle of Palo Alto.

tion owner and slaveholder he would carry the South.

While waiting in Louisiana for news of the Whig convention's decision, General Taylor became impatient at the silence from back east. Without knowing it, he refused to accept his own nomination for president. In those days, the post office sent letters collect, and the thrifty old soldier sent back the Whig's nomination unopened because of unpaid postage. He finally received news of his nomination and entered into politics in the election of 1848. Zachary Taylor won a close victory and became the twelfth president on March 4, 1849.

Taylor's inauguration was a happy event for the public, much like the spirited Andrew Jackson ceremonies. The crowds that greeted the popular general were said to be larger than those that welcomed Jackson. People cheered him and cannons boomed welcoming salutes. On his inauguration night, the new president was greeted with welcoming bonfires and fireworks displays.

Zachary Taylor, the "Brave Old Feller," was the fourth distinguished general to become president and, certainly, the least prepared man to that time in American history to reach this high office. President Taylor was a simple, straightforward man who hated playing the political game. He wished to leave politics to politicians in Congress. He wanted only to carry out the laws of the land. Perhaps he was a man who saw things too simply to be a successful presi-

dent. A lifetime spent in the army made him see things in an oversimplified manner. As a soldier he had learned to locate the objective, attack, and conquer it. Unfortunately, a president can seldom run his job in such a cut-and-dry fashion. Compromises are necessary, but this type of action did not sit too well with the rugged old army man from Louisiana.

Unhappy with presidential problems, Zachary Taylor would get away from it all on many occasions. He was often seen saddling up "Whitey," his faithful cavalry horse, whom he kept pastured on the White House lawn. A White House doorman replaced his military aide and hoisted the vigorous old president into the saddle. These quick gallops around Washington cooled off the red-faced anger of the fiery chief executive. Congressmen and government officials never knew how often they were saved from President Taylor's angry words because of the swift Whitey.

Slavery was the greatest problem facing President Taylor. The president saw no reason why the South should be bribed to allow admission of California and New Mexico as states. He saw the necessity for stable governments in the newly-acquired southwestern territories. Statehood was necessary and these states should be free of slavery. To protesting senators from the South, he declared his determination to crush secession threats wherever and whenever they appeared, even if he had to lead the army personally.

The slavery question was much too complicated for such a simple solution. Over the president's protests, the Compromise of 1850 was proposed in Congress. The Compromise upset him greatly. Then a scheme to cheat the government, involving G. W. Crawford, Taylor's Secretary of War, added to the president's troubles. During these times "Whitey" was saddled up more than ever!

President Taylor, depressed by these problems, attended official ceremonies in Washington on the Fourth of July, 1850. The sun was boiling and the humidity unbearable. To make matters worse, the president was forced to listen to a two-hour speech. To cool off, he ate a large number of sliced cucumbers and drank great quantities of iced milk. Washington, with its open sewers and flies, was always unhealthy in the summer. Eating outdoors could be a risky

General Zachary Taylor at the Battle of Buena Vista.

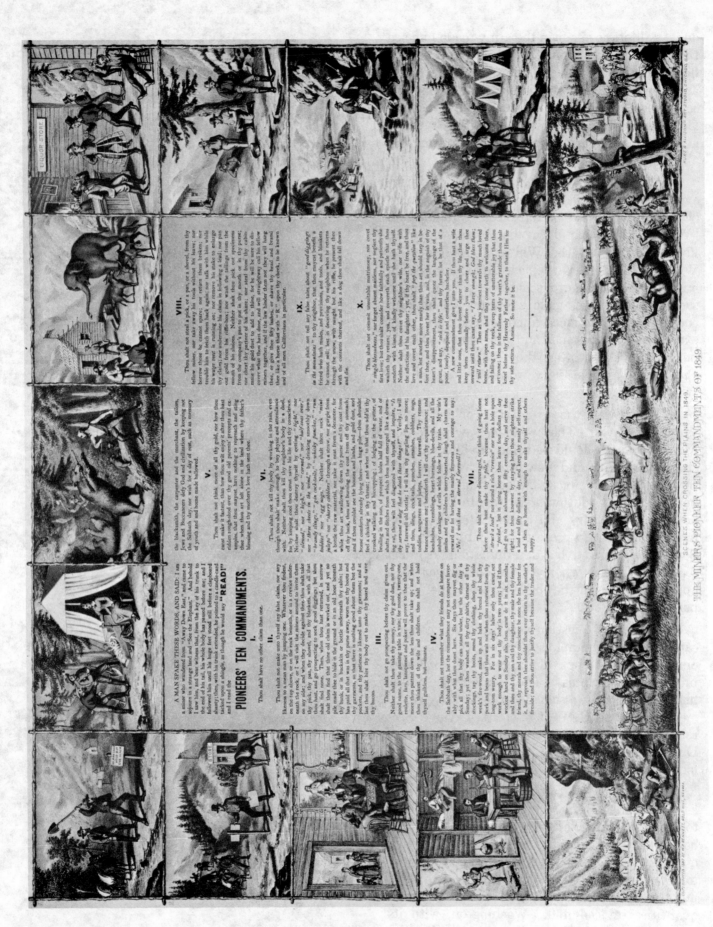

Pictured here are scenes showing the dangers and hardships faced by the "forty-niners" gold mining in California.

business. Shortly after the Independence Day ceremony, the president came down with a serious stomach illness. Some think that perhaps a diseased fly landed on one of the cucumbers the president ate.

He was a strong old man and if left alone, probably would have recovered. Because Zachary Taylor was the President of the United States, doctors flocked to him. The physicians of the capital drugged him, dosed him, even blistered him. Another medical treatment of the day did the final damage. At that time doctors thought bleeding a patient helped to cure him. The president was drained of much of his blood by attending physicians. In his weakened condition, this was too much. Surrounded by doctors, Zachary Taylor died in the White House, July 9, 1850, only sixteen months after taking office.

At his state funeral, a procession nearly two miles long followed the popular president to his grave. Thousands lined the funeral route to pay their last respects to the brave old soldier. Across the land, millions wondered, would his successor take up Zachary Taylor's firm stand against the expansion of slavery?

This is one of many lively 1848 campaign songs written about Candidate Taylor.

President Taylor and his Cabinet. From left to right: Attorney General Reverdy Johnson, Secretary of the Treasury William M. Meredith, Secretary of the Navy William B. Preston, Secretary of War George W. Crawford, Postmaster General Jacob Collamer, Secretary of the Interior Thomas Ewing, and Secretary of State John M. Clayton.

MILLARD FILLMORE

Thirteenth President (1850-1853)

As a nearly-illiterate
clothmaker's apprentice, the future
did not look bright for the
teenager who was to be our thirteenth president.
He was a clever lad, but the long, hard
hours on his father's New York farm
allowed him little time for an education
in his early years.
He was seventeen before he saw
his first dictionary.
From then on, his interest in books grew rapidly.
In fact, the first library in the White House
was established while he lived there.
Historians call him one of our
least effective chief executives, but it was
one of Millard Fillmore's presidential decisions
that kept this nation from
civil war for ten years.

GRAND, NATIONAL, WHIG BANNER.
PRESS ONWARD.

Vice Presidential Candidate Fillmore and Presidential Candidate Taylor as they appeared on the Grand National Whig Banner during the election of 1848.

FROM CLOTHMAKER TO CHIEF EXECUTIVE

Millard was born January 7, 1800. Early life was a struggle for him, his father, mother, and eight brothers and sisters. The Fillmores' New York farm was an extremely poor one. The land was rocky and the soil thin. There was a constant struggle to keep food on the table in their log cabin. This left young Millard with little time for schooling. In his teens he was apprenticed to a wool carder and all thoughts of learning faded away. He hated the clothmaker's trade and worked to buy his way out of his apprenticeship. To do this, he had to borrow thirty dollars. Having bought his freedom, he walked one hundred miles back to his home.

In his teenage years he met Miss Abigail Powers, a schoolteacher. She became a friend and counselor to young Millard. With her love for learning, she suggested he further his education. At nineteen, he fell in love with her, although she was two years older. Admiration of this intelligent young lady made him desirous of more education. It caused Fillmore to spend many hours poring over books. Abigail Powers encouraged and applauded him all along the way.

Fillmore decided to study law after becoming acquainted with the village lawyer. Young Millard worked at his law studies with such gusto that Miss Powers was impressed. He succeeded in his studies and, at the same time, won the schoolteacher's heart. After admission to the bar in 1823, he began practicing as an attorney in East Aurora, New York. Three years later he married Abigail Powers. Their marriage was one of mutual support, respect, and affection. The Fillmores had two children.

Energetic Millard Fillmore soon found time for politics as well as law. In 1830 he moved his law practice to Buffalo, New York, because it was the center of political activity. This hearty New Yorker certainly had an appealing political appearance. Tall and strong, ruddy-faced and handsome, the log cabin boy grown to manhood, had the appeal of a vigorous backwoodsman. This sort of appeal was important in the days of Andrew Jackson. Along with this fine appearance, he had a good mind, a deep speaking voice, and an easy manner of addressing the public. In short, he looked like a winner to New York political bosses. He was.

Millard Fillmore was elected to three terms in the New York legislature at Albany, and was able to work for the passage of much good legislation. There was one law in particular for which he was most proud. At that time, in New York State, a person who had come upon bad luck and was not able to pay his debts could be, and often was, thrown into prison. Recalling his penniless youth, he knew what hard times were. He strongly felt the injustice of this law. How could a man who wanted to pay his debts do so while locked up in prison? Fillmore used his political skill. He succeeded in getting passed a law which ended imprisonment for unpaid debts in New York.

He left the state assembly when the people of New York elected him to the House of Representatives in Washington. Hardworking Millard Fillmore quickly became one of the outstanding leaders of the northern wing of the Whig Party. He left Congress after six years of service to run for governor of New York.

Congressman Fillmore's capacity for organized good work in the national legislature was deeply appreciated by fellow congressman John Quincy Adams. Saddened at Fillmore's retirement from the House of Representatives, "Old Man Eloquent" said: "I hope and trust he will soon return, for whether to the nation or to the state no service can be or ever will be (given) by a more able or a more faithful public servant."

Narrowly defeated in the New York gubernatorial election, Fillmore made a political comeback in 1847 by winning the election for the Comptrollership of New York. By this time he was well-known as a politician in the northeastern section of the country. This led the Whig Party to nominate him as their vice presidential candidate in 1848. Fillmore, running with Louisianan Zachary Taylor, made a sectionally balanced ticket that could win votes in the North and in the South. This Whig strategy was effective, for Millard Fillmore became the vice president under Taylor in 1849. He was

DANIEL WEBSTER ADDRESSING THE UNITED STATES SENATE

IN THE GREAT DEBATE ON THE CONSTITUTION AND THE UNION 1850.

Northern newspapers, with drawings such as this one, continually attacked the effects of the Fugitive Slave Law. This cruel law required the return of escaped black men to their southern owners. Many northerners refused to obey this law.

Stephen Foster (1826-1864), an American composer of popular ballads and minstrel songs, began composing music as a young boy. One of his most famous songs, "Oh! Susanna," was published in 1848. It was a popular song of the gold rush of 1849. Although many of his songs were inspired by the south, he traveled there only once. Among the most famous of his 180 songs are "Old Folks at Home," "Camptown Races," and "Beautiful Dreamer."

elevated to the presidency, July 9, 1850, after the untimely death of President Taylor.

When Fillmore was told of the death of Zachary Taylor he experienced a great shock. Like John Tyler, he had not thought of being president. When the news reached him, he shut himself up in his room and spent a restless, sleepless night thinking of the great challenge that lay before him. Sleeplessness was practically unknown to the healthy new president. A non-drinker and non-smoker, he had taken good care of himself all his life. But the strains of the presidency take their toll on even the most robust of men. In those days, living in the White House was not as pleasant as we may think. Mosquitoes from nearby swamps made malaria a constant danger at the Executive Mansion. It was damp and cold in winter and hot and sticky in summer. President Fillmore found brief trips away from Washington a fine tonic for his health.

The slavery question which had plagued Taylor now haunted President Fillmore. The president wrote to his friend Daniel Webster that deep in his heart he hated slavery as an institution. But he felt it should be protected by the Constitution until the time when it could be ended without splitting the nation in two. With these last thoughts, Fillmore was to prove a political prophet.

Slavery was such an explosive issue at that time, President Fillmore felt only a great compromise would keep the Union together. Some people already knew that this inhumane institution, hated in the North and favored for economic reasons by some in the South, was beyond compromise. President Fillmore was not one of them. He joined with Daniel Webster and Henry Clay in urging the Compromise

The pick, shovel, and rocker were popular tools of the "forty-niners."

Commodore Perry's men delivered American gifts of goodwill to the Japanese Emperor's men at the port of Yokohama.

Abigail Powers Fillmore was ill much of the time she served as First Lady. Many of her responsibilities were passed on to her daughter Mary.

President Millard Fillmore.

of 1850. With the passage of this Compromise, the situation calmed down in the South, where secession had been threatened, but tempers still raged in the North. However, it successfulv kept the nation out of war for ten years.

The most unpopular law to come from the Compromise of 1850 was the Fugitive Slave Act. This law stated that runaway slaves, if caught, must be returned to their legal owners in the South. Many northerners refused to do this. They felt that escaped black men had the right to freedom and dignity. Northerners blamed President Fillmore for putting them in the position of breaking the law. The Fugitive

Slave Act proved to be his political death warrant.

The Whig Party was also in trouble. The great fury over the Fugitive Slave Act split the party so far apart it never recovered. While abolitionist northern Whigs raged red hot, southern Whigs sat back and calmly chuckled as some runaway slaves were returned to them.

Inside the walls of the White House, life was smoother for the embattled president. When he came home to his kind and efficient Abigail, things ran smoothly. She was shocked when she discovered the Executive Mansion had no library. Taking matters into her own hands, Mrs. Fillmore succeeded in talking Congress into a $250.00 grant for books. She established the first library in the White House in a small room on the second floor. She also had water pipes and a cookstove installed, which must have been a relief to her health-conscious husband and to later First Ladies.

The president enjoyed things which took him briefly away from the troubles of America. He made improvements in the gardens and grounds of the capital. He hired Andrew Jackson Downing, a Massachusetts landscape architect, to beautify the grounds of the White House, the Capitol Building, and the Smithsonian Institute.

President Fillmore had a great interest in expanding the development of America. He wanted to help all sections of the country work together in harmony. He worked to bring the west, with its new state of California, in closer cooperation with the older parts of the nation. Of equal importance was his desire to open up the Pacific to America. He was one of the first presidents to recognize the importance of extending the United States' influence in the Pacific. To do this, he sent Commodore Matthew Perry with a fleet to Japan in 1853. Japan at that time was a country closed to all foreigners. Commodore Perry, on the president's orders, so impressed the Emperor of Japan with intelligent words and interesting gifts (a toy train and a toy telegraph) that the Japanese government softened its attitudes toward foreigners. Because of President Fillmore's farsightedness, Japan and the United States entered into trade and diplomatic relations.

Fillmore further distinguished himself in foreign affairs by beginning to patch up differences between the United States and Mexico. He authorized an American-built railroad across the Isthmus of Tehuantepec. Pacific trade was growing and Hawaii became an important port. The American president, with firm action, stopped the French from taking over the little island nation in 1851. But all his good work in foreign affairs was largely overlooked. The black clouds of slavery and sectional splits hung over America. The slavery issue would not go away and President Fillmore was not able to find a solution. Because of this, the American people turned against him.

Millard Fillmore was an unsuccessful candidate for the Whig presidential nomination in the election of 1852. He retired from office in March 1853. A double tragedy then entered Fillmore's life. He lost his beloved Abigail a month after he retired from the presidency. A short time later his daughter Mary died, a victim of the dreaded disease cholera.

The grieving ex-president moved back to Buffalo where he continued to work for the public welfare of his home city. He helped to found the University of Buffalo and served as its chancellor. He helped establish the General Hospital, the Society of Natural Sciences, the Fine Arts Academy, the Historical Society, and many other cultural institutions.

Millard Fillmore's life ended March 8, 1874, after serving his city, state, and country in an earnest and dignified manner for most of his seventy-four years. His presidential record probably would have been treated more kindly by history if he not had the misfortune of serving when the evils of slavery were about to split the nation in two.

RESIDENCE OF MILLARD FILLMORE.

In 1888, The American Nation *published this picture of Ex-president Fillmore's home in Buffalo.*

FRANKLIN PIERCE

Fourteenth President (1853-1857)

His private and public lives
were like a roller coaster ride.
Early life was like a beautiful carnival
balloon for this man.
Then the balloon popped.
He was the youngest man in his time to serve
in the Senate, and the youngest yet
elected President of the United States.
Franklin Pierce, the handsome,
friendly "dark horse" from New Hampshire, became
our fourteenth president at a time when
America was deeply troubled and hopelessly
divided over the issue of slavery.
His presidential term, 1853-1857, was a time
that would have taxed the
greatest of men.

WEST VIEW OF BOWDOIN COLLEGE, BRUNSWICK, MAINE.

Franklin Pierce graduated September 1, 1824, from Bowdoin College in Brunswick, Maine. He was nineteen.

NEW HAMPSHIRE'S HANDSOME FRANK

Young Frank was born into a politically prominent New Hampshire family on November 23, 1804. He was one of eight children born to Benjamin and Anna Kendrick Pierce. His father was a Democratic member of the New Hampshire legislature and later served as governor of that state. The Pierces' children were free from worry or hardship. There was always time for fun and always opportunity for an education. As a youth, Franklin attended the academies at Hancock and Francestown in New Hampshire, and later enrolled in Exeter.

In 1824 he graduated from Maine's Bowdoin College, but it was not easy. Popular, handsome, and full of good-natured charm, Franklin thought college was for friends and fun. At the beginning of his college career, he was a very poor student who spent hours in the carefree pursuit of pleasant pastimes. He was particularly admired by Jane Appleton, the daughter

of the college president. Ten years after his graduation he married this young lady.

During his third year, he was told that he had the poorest marks in his class. Frank's friends challenged him to stay in school and to seriously try for good grades. Showing the strong character that had been buried for so long, he began studying twenty hours a day and sleeping only four. Three months later his marks were respectable. By graduation he stood third from the top in his class. His self discipline had paid off. Franklin's formal education ended when he completed his study of law and was admitted to the New Hampshire bar.

At Bowdoin College he met and began a lifelong friendship with Nathaniel Hawthorne. Hawthorne, with his polished writing style, later presented Pierce with a fine campaign biography. When he reached the presidency, Franklin rewarded his writer friend with an appointment

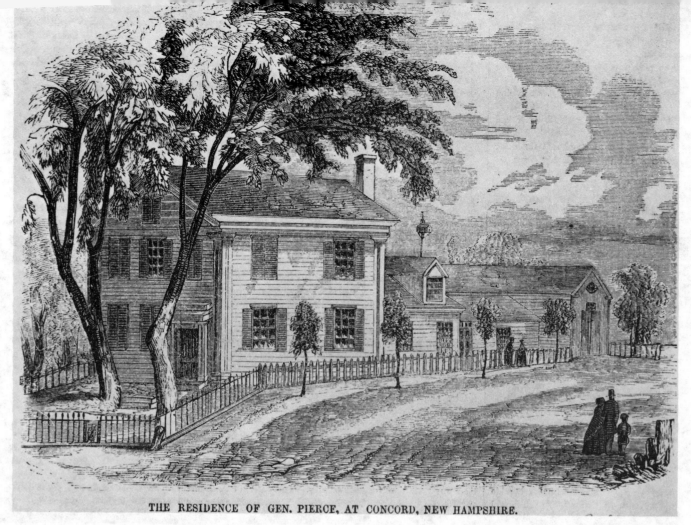

THE RESIDENCE OF GEN. PIERCE, AT CONCORD, NEW HAMPSHIRE.

as consul at Liverpool. This employment provided Hawthorne with the money he desperately needed to support himself while writing some of his greatest works. The friendship of these old college chums ended only in death. Hawthorne died in the company of Franklin Pierce while the two were on vacation in the White Mountains of New Hampshire in 1864.

His early political career quickly rose like a gas-inflated balloon. Only twenty-five, Franklin Pierce entered politics as a member of the New Hampshire House of Representatives. Four years later he was elected to the United States House of Representatives. After two terms in Congress, the people of New Hampshire elected him to the United States Senate. But Pierce did not have a happy time as the nation's youngest senator. His youth and inexperience could not compete with brilliant lawmakers, such as Senators Henry Clay and Daniel Webster. Disappointed in his lack of success, he resigned his seat in 1842 and returned to his law practice in New Hampshire, determined never again to enter public life.

After his disappointment in Washington, Pierce's zest for public service was somewhat dampened, but not his love of country. The drums of patriotism beat for Franklin Pierce at

the outbreak of the Mexican War. At the age of forty-two he entered the army as a private. He was a born leader and within a year's time he attained the rank of brigadier general. He served with distinction as an officer under General Winfield Scott on the march toward Mexico City. During the Battle of Contreras he was suddenly thrown forward on his horse and received painful injuries. Pierce tried to remain in the saddle but soon fainted from the pain. Later, during his presidential campaign, his political enemies suggested he had fainted out of fear. Candidates for the presidency have learned to expect such unkind barbs, but these are always bitter pills to swallow. Franklin Pierce continued soldiering until the end of the Mexican War and then returned to his New Hampshire law practice.

At the Democratic Convention in 1852, Lewis Cass, Stephen Douglas, and James Buchanan were the three strongest candidates in the running. These men split the convention delegates so that no one could get the two-thirds majority needed for the presidential nomination. A few wise politicians, remembering James K. Polk in 1844, put their own "dark horse" on the thirty-fifth ballot. He was Franklin Pierce of New Hampshire. On the forty-ninth ballot, he won

Enthusiastic crowds attended Franklin Pierce's March 4, 1853, inauguration.

the Democratic nomination. Pierce went on to win the presidency over General Winfield Scott, his former commander, who was the candidate of the badly-split Whig Party. Pierce won the greatest electoral victory since that of James Monroe.

The happy winner began vigorously planning for his administration after the November 1852 election. President-elect Pierce had high hopes for his country. He would stick to the Compromise of 1850 and this would calm the country down. He would ease sectional splits by having men from all parts of the country in his Cabinet. He would have a strong foreign policy. Above all, he would be a careful, honest leader. With such soaring hopes for America, things never seemed better for the handsome man from New Hampshire.

His fortunes quickly changed in January 1853. That month tragedy entered the Pierce household. Their two eldest sons had died at early ages, and Jane and Franklin had turned all their hopes and love upon their youngest son Benjamin. The Pierce family was traveling from Boston to New Hampshire by train just two

months before Franklin's inauguration. The railroad car in which they were riding rolled off the track and killed Benjamin. Neither parent was physically hurt, but emotionally they were shattered.

Mrs. Pierce never recovered from the shock of losing her last son. From then on, she showed no interest in acting as First Lady. She wore black throughout her husband's presidential term and refused to attend any official events. The White House became as somber as a funeral parlor. The religious First Lady asked only one thing of her servants, that they attend Sunday church services for her sake. President Pierce's aunt, Mrs. Abby Means, had to act as the White House hostess during his administration.

When his saddened wife told him that Benjamin's death was a sign from God that he should turn away from his family and devote all his energies to the presidency, Franklin Pierce was torn with grief and guilt feelings. His pre-inauguration vigor was replaced by shyness and uncertainty. President Pierce rarely showed the sparks of the earlier "Handsome Frank."

144

However, as president he never forgot his fine manners. Pierce's kindness and courtesy went out to everyone. A White House doorman noted that the president treated him as grandly as he did heads of state. But the fact remained that his son's death took from him some inner spirit that was never replaced. In those dark and troubled times, a president needed all the strength he could get.

President Pierce was inaugurated March 4, 1853. He entered office with a handsome face and a good record as a general in the Mexican War. His political thoughts were unknown, but not for long. He was a member of the eastern Democratic group that wanted peace, harmony, and economic prosperity. To achieve these things, Pierce and his followers felt they must ease southern feelings and avoid trouble over the slavery issue. Some of his pre-inauguration ideas became reality. He made the South happy by placing southern planters as well as northern businessmen in his Cabinet. But the slavery issue was not to be put aside for long, certainly not by such obvious measures.

As president, Pierce had some success in foreign affairs. He established the first American consulate in Japan, carrying on the good work begun by President Fillmore and Commodore Perry. But these good marks were erased when he brought his country to the brink of war with England because of mistaken actions in Nicaragua. Pierce sent the *U.S.S. Cyane* to bombard Greytown, Nicaragua, in hopes of gaining an unnecessary apology for the injury done to an American minister. Fortunately, things calmed down. In July of 1853, he brought prestige to this country by opening the Crystal Palace Exposition in New York City. This was the first world's fair in the United States and it displayed many American inventions.

One of the chief domestic plans of President Pierce's administration was the building of a transcontinental railroad. Pierce and his Secretary of War, Jefferson Davis, wanted a southern route to California. It soon became clear the railroad would have to pass through Mexican territory. Davis persuaded the president to buy the needed land in the Gila River Valley of southern Arizona. The Mexican government needed money and sold the Gadsden Purchase land to the United States for ten million dollars. The southern railway was not built, but this valuable land remained a United States possession.

Guests meet President Pierce during a White House reception.

Nathaniel Hawthorne was one of the greatest fiction writers in American literature. He was born July 4, 1804, in Salem, Massachusetts. Among the most famous of his works are The Scarlet Letter, The House of the Seven Gables, *and* Twice-Told Tales.

General John Charles Fremont was a popular national figure during Franklin Pierce's presidency. His victories in California during the Mexican War and his expeditions into Utah in 1853-1854 led to his presidential nomination by the new Republican Party in 1856. In the election he was defeated by James Buchanan.

Mourning the death of her third son, Benjamin, Jane Appleton Pierce lost all interest in her duties as First Lady.

Fireworks started over the slavery issue when the 1820 Missouri Compromise was repealed by the passage of the Kansas-Nebraska Act. Both northern and southern tempers raged at the idea that Kansas should be allowed to decide whether to be a free or a slave state. Northerners were afraid of the possible extension of slavery and angered that the thirty year old compromise was destroyed. The proud southerners demanded that slavery be allowed to follow United States expansion. "Bleeding Kansas" was the result. Abolitionists and pro-slavery forces met head on in gun battles. Each tried to turn Kansas their way. Unfortunately, President Pierce was not effective in dealing with this bloody prelude to the Civil War.

Opposition to the passage of the Kansas-Nebraska Act and to President Pierce's weak actions brought about the formation of the Republican Party. Near the end of his presidential term, the Republicans and a great many of his own Democratic Party were against him. Pierce was found unacceptable to the majority of the Democrats as their presidential candidate in the election of 1856. He retired from office and public life on March 3, 1857. The rest of his life was spent quietly in New Hampshire.

During his presidency, anti- and pro-slavery feelings were ready to explode like a keg of dynamite. Franklin Pierce did not want to strike the match that would send the nation into violent action. Many cautious and thoughtful men would have felt the same in his position. It is best to remember him as a man so devoted to his country that, at forty-two, he gave up wealth and comfort to enter the army as a private. Pierce was a patriot through and through.

President Franklin Pierce.

JAMES BUCHANAN

Fifteenth President (1857-1861)

Three times he entered the race
for the presidency and three times he
finished out of the money.
But this unsuccessful presidential
candidate of 1844, 1848, and
1852 refused to give up.
James Buchanan finally arrived in the White House
in 1857 with over forty years experience
as a diplomat, Cabinet member, and legislator.
No one could have been better trained
for the presidency than the fifteenth president.
As he took the presidential oath, a
troubled and hopeful nation stood behind him.
Surely with his experience he could bring the
divided country together.
James Buchanan soon discovered
that qualifications alone
do not make a president.
His experience and desire to
do well were crushed by avalanches of change.
Sadly, he left behind him one of the most
unsuccessful administrations
in our history.

Wheatland, the Pennsylvania home of James Buchanan.

A FORTY YEAR CLIMB TO THE PRESIDENCY

James was the second child in a family of eleven born to James and Elizabeth Speer Buchanan. He was born on April 23, 1791, in a Pennsylvania log cabin. But young James' early life was not filled with the usual hardships of log-cabin living. His father became a prosperous storekeeper and was able to send James to college. Upon first entering Pennsylvania's Dickinson College, Buchanan showed that the frontier living of his early days had not entirely rubbed off. He had such an untamed spirit that the faculty had him dismissed from the school. Then the Buchanan family minister took up the young man's cause. He pleaded for James' readmission, promising that he would greatly change his ways. He did. In an amazing turnabout, James Buchanan graduated from Dickinson College first in his class.

His interests then turned to law and he was admitted to the Pennsylvania bar in 1812. Law practice was soon interrupted by army service

in the War of 1812. Buchanan left the army filled with a desire to serve his country. Politics, he felt, was the answer. He was elected to the lower house of the Pennsylvania legislature in 1814.

James fell in love and became engaged to Ann Coleman. However, when he was away on political duties, unkind neighborhood gossips linked him with other women and caused Ann to become jealous. She did not wait to ask him the truth. Ann wrote a letter dismissing him from her life. Both were proud, angry young people. James felt the broken engagement was unjust. Ann believed the stories were true. Heartsick, Ann died in December 1819 of an overdose of laudanum when on a trip to Philadelphia. Some say it was suicide. The Coleman family would not forgive James for his supposed contribution to their daughter's death, and did not allow him to attend the funeral. Buchanan remained a bachelor throughout his life.

He always held his head tilted slightly to one side because one eye was near-sighted, the other was far-sighted. Recalling the tragic end of his engagement to Ann Coleman, one malicious political enemy invented the terrible lie that this "tilt" was caused by a neck injury suffered when he tried to hang himself after her death. Unfortunately, all our presidents have been attacked by evil, sharp-tongued foes.

Although he remained a bachelor, he was by no means a woman hater. Tall and strong, Buchanan was always courteous and attentive to the ladies. Women considered him charming and good-looking. His strong fatherly spirit was shown when he raised the orphaned son of one of his sisters and the orphaned daughter of another sister. He did this with pleasure. Both were brought up as his own children, with kindness and care. His adopted daughter, Harriet Lane Johnston, later showed her deep devotion to Buchanan by acting as a charming and efficient White House hostess for her uncle.

When Buchanan had recovered from the shock of Ann Coleman's death he reentered politics as a United States Congressman in 1821. He became a friend and strong ally of Andrew Jackson during his ten years in Congress. In 1832 he was sent to Russia as a United States minister. He returned to Washington two years later and was elected a United States senator. Later, in 1845, President James K. Polk made Buchanan his Secretary of State. The president and Secretary Buchanan were a good team and among their accomplishments was the acquisition of the Southwest Territory from Mexico.

During the 1830's, and probably because of close association with Andrew Jackson, James Buchanan was filled with a great ambition to be president of the United States. This Jackson clan, inspired by its dynamic leader, had several of its members aspire to the political heights in America. Three made it: Martin Van Buren, James K. Polk, and James Buchanan. Feeling he must gain southern votes in order to succeed in his plan to become president, Buchanan knew his stand on the slavery issue was important. Although he felt slavery was morally wrong, he believed that Congress must not act against it in states where slavery was permanently established. Nor should Congress react out of fear by creating anti-slavery laws in the western territories. This satisfied the southerners but not the northerners. With this philosophy, Buchanan ran for the presidency three times and three times he lost.

On his fourth attempt, at the Democratic National Convention of 1856, he finally succeeded. Before the convention, he had been out of the country for three years as the United States minister to Great Britain and no one was really sure of where he stood on the slavery issue. Buchanan was nominated over his Democratic rivals, Stephen Douglas and Franklin Pierce, because the delegates did not approve of their stand on slavery. In the election campaign that followed, Buchanan beat his Republican rival, John C. Fremont, by a half million votes.

President James Buchanan had slowly climbed the ladder of national acclaim through forty years of public service. When he reached the top, he was too old and too tired to be a successful president. He was inaugurated, March 4, 1857. The terrible weight of his office came down upon President Buchanan two days later when the Supreme Court announced its decision against Dred Scott. Scott was a slave, owned by an army doctor, who had moved from slave territory into free territory. Scott petitioned the court stating he was a free man because he had set foot on free land. The Supreme Court said no.

Dred Scott's bravery in this instance was remarkable. He spoke out for his own freedom and also for the rights of his people. Southerners rejoiced at the decision against him while northerners raged. The gap between North and South widened. Northern writers shouted their indignation. One of the loudest cries came from Harriet Beecher Stowe in her book *Uncle Tom's Cabin.* She wrote in the preface:

"The object of these sketches is to awaken sympathy and feeling for the African race, as they exist among us; to show their wrongs and sorrows, under a system so necessarily cruel and unjust as to defeat and do away the good effects of all that can be attempted for them, by their best friends, under it."

Influenced by religion and inflamed by words like these, northern abolitionist and anti-slavery advocate, John Brown, with a few Negro and white followers, led a raid on the federal arsenal

An enormous building was erected in Washington for the March 4, 1857, inauguration ball of President James Buchanan.

at Harper's Ferry, Virginia in 1858. Brown hoped to start an uprising by giving the captured guns to Negro slaves. The Harper's Ferry raid failed. Federal troops soon captured the raiders. For his leading role in the uprising, John Brown was tried, found guilty, and hanged. Although the North tried and convicted Brown, the South still feared the Yankee's were plotting to destroy their society. Brown became the image of no compromise to both North and South.

In quieter times, President Buchanan's legislative programs might have made him an empire-builder in the pages of history. He worked to enlarge American influence in Mexico and Central and South America, always with United States expansion in mind. He also wished to ease political problems in the western hemisphere that might bring European intervention. Buying Cuba was another of his expansion ideas. All these proposals, and even bills needed to keep the government running, were stopped in Congress. Sectional splits between the North, the South, and the West, weakened Congressional cooperation. Congressmen and senators thought only of their part of the country. The welfare of the federal government became buried in the dust of their bickering. With it was buried the efforts and spirit of President James Buchanan.

President Buchanan's experience as congressman, Cabinet member, and diplomat, would have made him an excellent president in ordinary times. But these days were the most

NOTICE TO OUR READERS.

WE commence in the present number to publish a new story of thrilling interest, by one of the first writers of the age, called

"The Chronicles of the Bastile."

It is especially interesting to Americans, as exhibiting the terrible effects of despotism. This story will be finely illustrated.

THE ATLANTIC TELEGRAPH COMPLETED.
Transmission of the Messages of
QUEEN VICTORIA AND PRESIDENT BUCHANAN
Great Rejoicings throughout the United States.

WE were enabled in our last to bring down the account of the successful laying of the Atlantic telegraph cable to the arrival of the Niagara and Gorgon in Newfoundland, and the transmission of the great intelligence to every accessible part of the United States. Since then the crowning success has been attained by the transmission of Queen Victoria's message to the President of the United States, and the frigate Niagara has arrived at New York, amid the acclamations of an entire people, and glorious in the termination of her peaceful task. We are now able to present illustrations, from the pencil of our own correspondent, of the arrival of the Niagara and Gorgon in Trinity Bay, and of the

THE QUEEN'S MESSAGE.

TO THE PRESIDENT OF THE UNITED STATES, WASHINGTON :—

The Queen desires to congratulate the President upon the successful completion of this great international work, in which the Queen has taken the deepest interest.

The Queen is convinced that the President will join with her in fervently hoping that the electric cable which now connects Great Britain with the United States will prove an additional link between the nations, whose friendship is founded upon their common interest and reciprocal esteem.

The Queen has much pleasure in thus communicating with the President, and renewing to him her wishes for the prosperity of the United States.

THE PRESIDENT'S REPLY.

WASHINGTON CITY, August 16, 1858.

TO HER MAJESTY VICTORIA, THE QUEEN OF GREAT BRITAIN :—

The President cordially reciprocates the congratulations of her Majesty the Queen, on the success of the great international enterprise accomplished by the science, skill and indomitable energy of the two countries.

It is a triumph more glorious, because far more useful to mankind, than was ever won by conqueror on the field of battle.

May the Atlantic telegraph, under the blessing of Heaven, prove to be a bond of perpetual peace and friendship between the kindred nations, and an instrument destined by Divine Providence to diffuse religion, civilization, liberty and law throughout the world.

In this view, will not all nations of Christendom spontaneously unite in the declaration that it shall be for ever neutral, and that its communications shall be held sacred in passing to their places of destination, even in the midst of hostilities ?

JAMES BUCHANAN.

16th August 1858.

THE TELEGRAPHIC MESSAGES OF QUEEN VICTORIA AND PRESIDENT BUCHANAN.

*Queen Victoria of England and President Buchanan of the United States
exchanged telegraphic messages, August 16, 1858.*

JOHN BROWN

Meeting the Slave-mother and her Child on the steps of Charlestown jail on his way to execution!

The Artist has represented Capt Brown regarding with a look of compassion a Slave-mother and Child who obstructed
the passage on his way to the Scaffold. — Capt Brown stooped and kissed the Child — then met his fate.

FROM THE ORIGINAL PAINTING BY LOUIS RANSOM.

For leading the raid on Harper's Ferry, abolitionist John
Brown was tried and sentenced to death. On the way to his
execution Brown stopped to comfort a slave mother and
child.

The Pony Express mail service between St. Joseph, Missouri, and Sacramento, California,
began April 3, 1860. This was the fastest mail service to that time in U.S. history. For
$5.10 a letter was delivered over the eighteen-hundred mile route in ten days.

James Buchanan

attorney, Edwin Stanton, warned the president, "You are sleeping on a volcano!" The unhappy Buchanan replied, "Mr. Stanton, for God's sake, come and help me." Stanton entered Buchanan's Cabinet but it was too late. The war clouds were about to burst.

Buchanan decided not to run in 1860. He left the Democratic Party without one candidate to unite behind. Republican Abraham Lincoln, who was firmly against slavery, won the presidency.

The South looked upon Lincoln's election as their political and economic death warrant. South Carolina seceded from the Union in December 1860, and was followed soon after by Mississippi, Florida, Alabama, Georgia, Louisiana, and Texas. The Confederate States were organized in February 1861. The scene was ominously set when Abraham Lincoln took office in March of 1861. When Buchanan handed over his office to the tall man from Illinois, both sides stood quietly alert at Fort Sumter.

For years before James Buchanan's presidency, politicians and the courts tried to compromise on the evils of slavery. All presidents immediately preceding the Civil War were elected to leave things alone. Millard Fillmore, Franklin Pierce, James Buchanan, and the voters who sent them to the White House hoped that the great moral evil would somehow go away. It did not. The problem was too great and the gap between North and South too wide to be settled peaceably. It remained for the cannon and the rifle to settle the slavery question.

OLD MOTHER BUCHANAN AT WHEATLAND.

This political cartoon criticizes President Buchanan and suggests he was like an "old woman" refusing to act to solve the problems of his administration.

turbulent our country had known. They were times that required a man with a mountain of iron will. James Buchanan was always a political compromiser. Knowledge that his compromise tactics were not working weighed heavily on him. There were too many things against him. He seemed helpless. One day famous Ohio

Jefferson Davis was inaugurated president of the newly-formed Confederate States of America in front of the state capital at Montgomery, Alabama, February 18, 1861.

President Buchanan's face shows the terrible weight of the office of the presidency in the pre-Civil War years. He is discussing the problems of the presidency with president-elect Abraham Lincoln shortly before Lincoln was inaugurated.

The funeral of Ex-President James Buchanan, June 4, 1868.

ABRAHAM LINCOLN

Sixteenth President (1861-1865)

In the yard bordering a humble
farm home in Kentucky there stands today
an oak tree, tens of feet tall and
three hundred years strong.
It reigns over its surroundings, a towering and
lasting reminder of the great man who
sat beneath its soothing shade in summer,
and watched it win an annual battle
with the elements in winter.
The oak will not bend to stress and gives life
and heart to the things around it.
It remains nature's fitting model for the
child grown to greatness who
once leaned against its solid base.
Abraham Lincoln grew to be the American oak.
His strength and memory will stand
through the ages.

Abraham Lincoln's log cabin home in Illinois.

THE AMERICAN OAK

Abraham was born to Thomas and Nancy Hanks Lincoln on February 12, 1809, in a backwoods cabin in Hodgenville, Kentucky. The Lincolns were a poor, hard-working, farm family. When Abe was two the family moved to the neighboring valley of Knob Creek. Among his earliest memories of this home was a flash flood that swept away all the corn and pumpkin seeds he had just helped his father plant.

In 1816 Thomas Lincoln was faced with a lawsuit challenging his title to his land. He then decided to move his family to Indiana. The Lincolns' first winter there was a terrible one. The journey from Kentucky had taken so long there was barely time for them to put up a rough, three-sided structure of logs before the bitter winter began. They tried to keep warm by huddling together by a blazing fire in the cabin entrance.

One of the unhappiest periods of Abraham's life followed the death of his mother in the autumn of 1818. Death was no stranger to Abraham; his baby brother had died a few years before in Kentucky. But death was terribly hard to accept, especially that of his mother. Lonely Abe grew even closer to his sister, Sarah, who was his good friend and advisor in his early years. Death came into his family a third time when Sarah died shortly after her marriage. Before he reached manhood Abraham had seen death three times. Although it saddened him, it did not defeat him. Losing his loved ones gave him a deep respect and love for life.

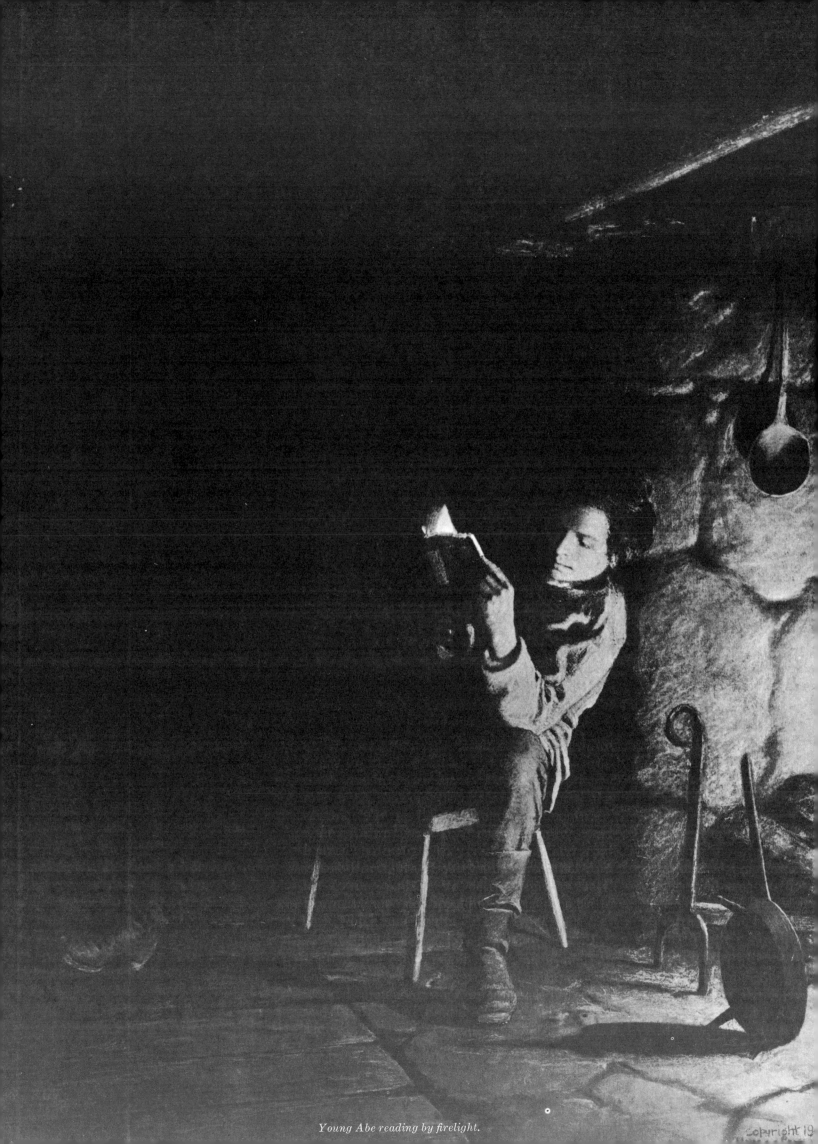

Young Abe reading by firelight.

LINCOLN AS A FLATBOATMAN ON THE MISSISSIPPI RIVER.

Lincoln's home in Springfield, Illinois in 1860.

Fortunately for young Abe, only a year went by before he had a new mother. On a trip back to Kentucky, in 1819, Thomas Lincoln married Sarah Johnston, a widow with three children of her own. Abe's stepmother had energy and affection to spare. She ran the Lincoln household in a warm, efficient manner and treated all the children equally well. She was especially fond of her stepson, and he of her. Sarah Lincoln encouraged him to speak freely of his dreams and encouraged him to continue learning. Later in life he often referred to her as his "angel mother."

Abraham Lincoln wrote in his 1859 autobiography describing the conditions of his schooling in Indiana:

"It was a wild region, with many bears and other wild animals still in the woods. There I grew up. There were some schools, so called; but no qualification was ever required of a teacher beyond readin', writin', and chipperin'... There was absolutely nothing to excite ambition for education... I have not been to school since. The little advance I now have upon this store of education, I have picked up from time to time under the pressure of necessity."

"From time to time" may have been an example of Lincoln's modesty. His cousin, Dennis Hanks, once said, "I (have) never seen Abe after he was twelve that he didn't have a book somewheres around." With his stepmother's encouragement, Abe would read whatever he could lay his hands upon, reading and rereading the books until he understood them. By sunlight, candlelight, and firelight he read whenever he had a spare moment. The book he knew best was the Bible because it was the only book the Lincolns owned. He would walk miles when he learned that there was a book to borrow. His favorites were *Aesop's Fables*, *The Arabian Nights*, *Pilgrims Progress*, and *The Life of George Washington*.

As an adult, Lincoln read to learn; he rarely read only for entertainment. His law partner and close friend, William Herndon, said, "Mr. Lincoln read less and thought more than any man in his sphere in America."

The Lincoln family moved again to Illinois when Abraham was twenty-one. By this time he was six-feet, four-inches tall, lanky and strong. He was well-known for his skill and strength with an ax. In manhood his physical appearance alone made him memorable. Writer Sherwood Anderson described him this way: "He was like a tree, having its roots in black mire, its upper branches reaching toward the sky." He stood tall over the tallest of men. His dark hair was coarse, his skin sallow, his neck scrawny, his arms exceptionally long, his feet big, and his movements awkward. Ill-fitting clothes exaggerated his thin, wiry appearance.

He had a face that most people liked, but some felt it seemed hollow and unhealthy. During the presidential campaign of 1860, Lincoln's face moved eleven year old Grace Bedell of Westfield, New York, to write: "Dear Sir, I am a little girl ... but want you should be President of the United States very much ... If you will let your whiskers grow ... you would look a great deal better for your face is so thin." When a train taking him to Washington stopped in Westfield, Lincoln called out into the crowd for his little correspondent. When Grace came forward he hugged and kissed her and told the crowd, "She wrote me that she thought I'd look better in whiskers." He took Grace's advice and become the first president to wear a beard.

The Lincoln family started farming again in Illinois. Abe the railsplitter helped to clear and fence his father's new farm. But farming did not appeal to him. After his family was settled, he hired out as a flatboatman and made a voyage down the Mississippi River to New Orleans. When he returned to New Salem, Illinois, he worked there as a storekeeper, postmaster, and surveyor. In 1832 he enlisted as a volunteer in the Black Hawk War and became a captain of his company. Recalling this experience, Lincoln later joked that the only battles he had as a soldier were "a good many bloody struggles with the mosquitoes."

Retiring from the army in June 1832, Lincoln returned to New Salem, Illinois. He had decided upon law as a profession. At that time, law students prepared for the bar examination by studying with an attorney. But Abraham had already taught himself grammar and mathematics and now wanted to teach himself law. He was successful and passed the bar examination four years later.

The young lawyer moved to Springfield, Illinois, a year later. There he met Mary Todd and fell in love. It was a stormy courtship because Miss Todd's aristocratic friends frowned upon the unpolished Lincoln as her suitor. In spite of this, Mary and Abraham became engaged. Then Lincoln, doubting he could make her happy, broke the engagement. He was moody and saddened by her loss and returned to ask her to be his wife. The two were reunited and on November 4, 1842, were married.

In 1844, Lincoln entered into a prosperous law practice with William Herndon. Lawyer Lincoln represented prosperous businesses, such as the Illinois Central Railroad, and humble folk alike. Each spring and fall he would set out on horseback or buggy to travel hundreds of miles over the thinly-settled prairie, from one county seat to another. For very small fees, he often helped those who needed him. His fame as an attorney of great skill and integrity spread throughout Illinois. His most famous case involved a murder. A witness claimed that, by

moonlight, he had seen Lincoln's client take part in a killing. With the aid of an almanac, Lincoln showed that it had been too dark on that night for the witness to have seen anything. His client was acquitted.

His prominence as an attorney started him on a career in politics, and, in 1834, this political newcomer was elected to the Illinois state legislature. His four-term career was outstanding. Lincoln quickly learned the political ropes. His keen mind easily grasped the methods of bargaining and vote-swapping so necessary for political success. Following these political rules, Lincoln carefully guided the 1837 movement to transfer the state capital from Vandalia to his own hometown, Springfield. Lincoln's reputation as a legislator increased as his bills passed. He was still a rough-hewn frontier man at times. He once tried to avoid a quorum and a vote showdown on one of his pet projects by leaping out of the window of the state capital building. However, each year spent in the legislature smoothed off a few more of his rough edges.

THE REPUBLICAN WIGWAM AT CHICAGO, ILLINOIS, IN WHICH THE REPUBLICAN CONVENTION WILL BE HELD, MAY 16, 1860.

Democrat Stephen A. Douglas of Illinois was Abraham Lincoln's chief political opponent during the 1850's. The "Little Giant" began his national political career when he was elected to Congress in 1843. During the Illinois senatorial election of 1858 his Republican opponent was Abraham Lincoln. Douglas felt slavery in the territories should be left up to the settlers. Lincoln was a firm anti-slavery man. The Lincoln-Douglas debates that took place during that campaign are considered to be the most eloquent in U.S. political history. Douglas narrowly won the Senate election but was defeated two years later when he ran against Lincoln for president. He died of typhoid fever in June 1861.

By the mid-1840's, Abraham Lincoln decided to try for higher political office. He won his campaign and served for a single term in the House of Representatives in Washington (1847-1849) as a member of the Whig Party. Congressman Lincoln then became a great admirer of Henry Clay and Daniel Webster. Because of his opposition to the Mexican War, he was not returned to Congress by the Illinois voters. However, Lincoln did stay in Washington long enough to help another Whig, Zachary Taylor, become president.

Then for nearly five years he concentrated on his Illinois law practice and took little part in politics. When Stephen A. Douglas helped maneuver the Kansas-Nebraska Act through Congress, Lincoln was roused into action. He hated slavery and insisted that Congress must keep it out of the territories. The Whig Party was no longer a political power so Lincoln formed a firm alliance with the new Republican Party. He was an unsuccessful candidate for the vice-presidency at the Republican Convention in 1856.

He was again an unsuccessful candidate in 1858. This time he tried for a United States Senate seat from Illinois. Stephen A. Douglas was his Democratic opponent. The Lincoln-Douglas debates of that year are considered to be among the most eloquent and powerful in American history. Lincoln's speaking powers, his ability to turn simple words into poetry, had a great effect on listeners. The issue was slavery. He declared: " 'A house divided against itself cannot stand.' I believe this government cannot endure permanently half slave and half free." Lincoln won a narrow victory in the debates; Douglas won a narrow victory at the polls. But Lincoln's strength as an orator paved his way to the presidency.

Though he failed to obtain a Senate seat, Lincoln's name was known nationally because of the debates. In May 1860, in Chicago's "Wigwam," the first building especially built and telegraphically equipped for a political convention, Abraham Lincoln received the Republican presidential nomination. The Democratic Party was split among four candidates, the Republicans were united behind Lincoln. He carried the election of 1860 over Stephen A. Douglas and

This photograph from the New York Times *shows Abraham Lincoln taking the oath of office, March 4, 1861.*

John C. Breckenridge, the two main candidates running for the split Democratic Party.

When Lincoln's election was certain, the South went into an uproar. An Atlanta newspaper wailed "...the South will never submit to...the inauguration of Abraham Lincoln." Secession began immediately. Southerners looked upon the president-elect as a northern politician who would surely ruin them. Guns were drawn and waiting on both sides at Fort Sumter, South Carolina, when Abraham Lincoln took the oath of office March 4, 1861. Ex-president Buchanan greeted the incoming president on the White House steps saying, "If you are as happy, my dear sir, on entering this house as I am on leaving it and returning home, you are the happiest man on earth." War clouds hung heavily over Washington on Inauguration Day. Lincoln was the first president whose military escort was really a guard instead of an honorary escort.

Fort Sumter in Charleston Harbor, during the months before the inauguration, was an example of the North's determination not to recognize the Confederacy. If Major Anderson and his small troop of soldiers surrendered to the Confederacy this would be an act of recognition of the new Confederate States of America. The Confederates were equally determined that Fort Sumter was in their territory and must be turned over to them. Meanwhile, inside the fort, there was a growing shortage of food for the Union soldiers.

For several weeks the Fort Sumter problem troubled the new president. Then he decided to act. The government would send an expedition with food to Major Anderson and his men at the fort. President Lincoln informed South Carolina's governor of the peaceful nature of the mission. The Confederate authorities did not wait for Lincoln's expedition; they bombarded Fort Sumter at dawn on April 12, 1861. The War Between the States, that was to go on for four terrible years, had begun. The country was ripped apart, brother against brother, and son against father. American democracy was torn to shreds by bullets and bombs. The rest of the world watched and waited.

Only a man with a will of granite and the strength of an oak, a man of heroic proportions, could take command in times like these. Pres-

ident Abraham Lincoln—born American, trained American, steeped in Americana—was this dream of American greatness come to life. As president he was Commander-in-Chief of the Army and the Navy. Patiently, he controlled temperamental generals, often changing them and countermanding their orders. President Lincoln's great aim was to help the Union win the war and to preserve the nation.

At the beginning, the actual military conduct of the war was directed by President Lincoln. Because he had no general in whom he had complete faith, the president was the Commander-in-Chief. Day after tiring day, the weary president went to the War Department reading telegraph messages from the front. He answered them with tactical instructions. Sometimes he was forced to gently chastise a Union general who hadn't followed orders. He felt great anguish over each death report. Every day Americans were killing Americans by the hundreds. It was almost more than Abraham Lincoln could bear. Finally some of the weight of the war was lifted from his shoulders. Lincoln found an able general, Ulysses S. Grant. In Grant, the president had a general he could trust to handle the fighting.

President Lincoln was now free to fight to preserve the Union with legislative acts. Some of his wartime measures were extreme but Abraham Lincoln thought them necessary. To restore a whole America, Lincoln considered no act too harsh. He said, "These rebels are violating the Constitution to destroy the Union." He increased the size of the Army and the Navy, placed a naval blockade on the South, and put those suspected of treason in military prisons.

Other men of political importance had shared President Lincoln's hatred of slavery, but none had met the problem head on. Abraham Lincoln did just this. In January 1861, his Emancipation Proclamation declared all slaves under Confederate control to be free at once. Black men were soon in blue Union Army uniforms fighting for their freedom and for the country. Northerners slowly began to realize this terrible war was a fight against slavery, a fight for human dignity, as well as an effort to save the Union.

The president knew he needed more than a proclamation to rid the nation of slavery. A law was necessary. Lincoln's presidential cam-

The Civil War began when Confederate troops bombarded Union troops at Fort Sumter on April 12, 1861.

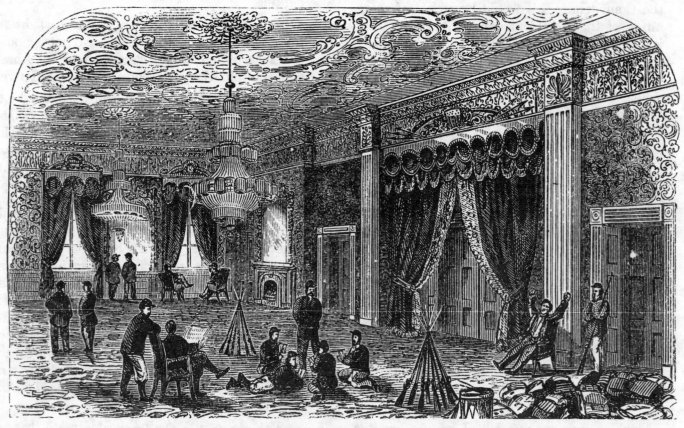

The East Room of the White House has known many uses. During Lincoln's presidency, Union soldiers were quartered there.

Confederate Generals Robert E. Lee (left) and "Stonewall" Jackson (right) led their troops to many victories during the first part of the Civil War.

Lincoln's Address at the Dedication of the Gettysburg National Cemetery, November 19, 1863.

Fourscore and seven years ago our Fathers brought forth on this continent a new nation conceived in liberty, and dedicated to the proposition that all men are created equal. Now we are engaged in a great civil war, testing whether that nation, or any nation so conceived and dedicated, can long endure. We are met on a great battlefield of that war. We have come to dedicate a portion of that field as a final resting-place for those who here gave their lives that that nation might live. It is altogether fitting and proper that we should do this. But in a larger sense, we cannot dedicate—we cannot consecrate—we cannot hallow—this ground. The brave men, living and dead, who struggled here, have consecrated it far above our poor powers to add or detract. The world will little note nor long remember what we say here. It is for us, the living, rather, to be dedicated here to the unfinished work which they who fought here have thus far so nobly advanced. It is rather for us to be here dedicated to the great task remaining before us—that from these honored dead we take increased devotion to that cause for which they gave the last full measure of devotion; that we here highly resolve that these dead shall not have died in vain; that this nation, under GOD, shall have a new birth of freedom; and that government of the people, by the people, for the people, shall not perish from the earth.

CONGRESS ADDRESS RE-ELECTED FOUR YEARS

This 1864 political cartoon from Harper's Weekly affectionately pokes fun at President Lincoln's great height.

Mary Todd Lincoln served as First Lady in a very simple and quiet way. The war years dampened Washington's enthusiasm for social functions.

President Lincoln and his son Tad, February 9, 1864.

paign of 1864 was based upon his firm idea that the country had to pass laws making slavery illegal. He won a narrow victory over his Democratic opponent General George McClellan.

With a Republican majority in Congress and Abraham Lincoln in the president's chair, the Thirteenth Amendment to the Constitution, outlawing slavery forever, became law.

President Lincoln was a leader who truly lived by the laws in which he believed. During his last two years in the White House, Negroes were welcomed as visitors and friends by the president. One of these friends was Frederick Douglass, a former slave who had become a distinguished writer, lecturer, and freedom fighter. Douglass wrote this of the president, "In all my interviews with Mr. Lincoln I was impressed with his entire freedom from prejudice against the colored race."

Unhappily, there was some turmoil for "The Great Emancipator" inside the White House. Mrs. Lincoln had always been a high-strung woman, and the death of her young son, Willie, from typhoid fever added to her troubles. There

Ford's Theater in Washington, 1865.

John Wilkes Booth.   President Lincoln   Mrs. Lincoln   Major Rathbone   Miss Harris

ASSASSINATION OF PRESIDENT LINCOLN FORD'S THEATRE WASHINGTON APRIL 14 1865.

were also rumors that she was a spy because she had relatives in the Confederate Army. At one time, Lincoln feared that her outbursts of temper, severe headaches, and strange acts might best be cured in a mental institution. Grieving over Willie's death, she held spiritual seances in the Executive Mansion's Red Room, trying to communicate with her dead son. These actions embarrassed her worried husband. Mrs. Lincoln's reckless spending was another source of trouble. Her debts for clothing alone ran over $25,000.00. One item on her list was for three hundred pairs of gloves.

Lincoln's ability to tell a good story and his tremendous sense of humor were fine assets to him throughout his career in law and in public life. As president, he would tell jokes at the most critical times. He had a habit of starting every conference or meeting with a "that reminds me" story. He loved to tell stories just for the fun of it, but there was often more to his humor than mere personal pleasure. He found that his jokes had a way of leading into plain talk. This is the way he spoke to poorly-educated country audiences. Those jokes also helped him cover up his deeply sensitive heart. A congressman, reporting a particularly disastrous event during the Civil War, flew into a rage when President Lincoln began his reply with "That reminds me." Lincoln gently replied, "Now you sit down! If I couldn't tell these stories I would die."

To take his mind off his home and presidential problems, Lincoln often attended the theater or the opera. He also enjoyed reading in bed, especially the plays of William Shakespeare. A great comfort to the troubled chief executive was his youngest son, Tad. The boy had a lively personality and his father loved talking with him. Tad sometimes sat on Lincoln's lap during meetings in the White House, and occasionally slept in his father's bed.

While Abraham Lincoln's family problems ebbed and flowed, the war took a turn in the Union's favor. The North won battle after battle and the South began to see the approaching doom. President Lincoln, a man not capable of hatred or revenge, looked forward to the day when America would again be a united nation. His wish was granted. General Robert E. Lee of the Confederacy surrendered to General Ulysses S. Grant at Appomatox Courthouse, Virginia,

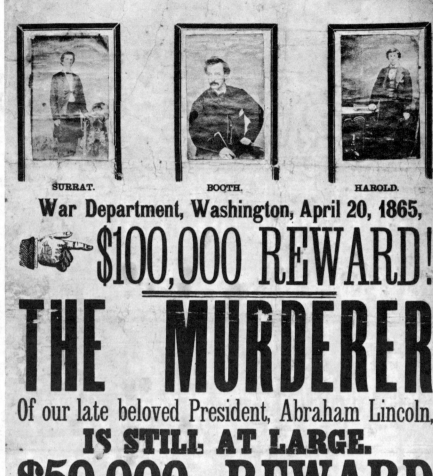

SURRAT.   BOOTH.   HAROLD.

War Department, Washington, April 20, 1865,

$100,000 REWARD!

THE MURDERER

Of our late beloved President, Abraham Lincoln,

IS STILL AT LARGE.

$50,000 REWARD

Will be paid by this Department for his apprehension, in addition to any reward offered by Municipal Authorities or State Executives.

$25,000 REWARD

Will be paid for the apprehension of JOHN H. SURRATT, one of Booth's Accomplices.

$25,000 REWARD

Will be paid for the apprehension of David C. Harold, another of Booth's accomplices.

LIBERAL REWARDS will be paid for any information that shall conduce to the arrest of either of the above-named criminals, or their accomplices.

All persons harboring or secreting the said persons, or either of them, or aiding or assisting their concealment or escape, will be treated as accomplices in the murder of the President and the attempted assassination of the Secretary of State, and shall be subject to trial before a Military Commission and the punishment of DEATH.

Let the stain of innocent blood be removed from the land by the arrest and punishment of the murderers.

All good citizens are exhorted to aid public justice on this occasion. Every man should consider his own conscience charged with this solemn duty, and rest neither night nor day until it be accomplished.

EDWIN M. STANTON, Secretary of War.

DESCRIPTIONS.—BOOTH is Five Feet 7 or 8 inches high, slender build, high forehead, black hair, black eyes, and wears a heavy black moustache.

JOHN H. SURRAT is about 5 feet, 9 inches. Hair rather thin and dark; eyes rather light; no beard. Would weigh 145 or 150 pounds. Complexion rather pale and clear, with color in his cheeks. Wore light clothes of fine quality. Shoulders square; cheek bones rather prominent; chin narrow; ears projecting at the top; forehead rather low and square, but broad. Parts his hair on the right side; neck rather long. His lips are firmly set. A slim man.

DAVID C. HAROLD is five feet six inches high, hair dark, eyes dark, eyebrows rather heavy, full face, nose short, hand short and fleshy, feet small, instep high, round bodied, naturally quick and active, slightly closes his eyes when looking at a person.

NOTICE.—In addition to the above, State and other authorities have offered rewards amounting to almost one hundred thousand dollars, making an aggregate of about TWO HUNDRED THOUSAND DOLLARS.

FRANK LESLIE'S
ILLUSTRATED
NEWSPAPER

Entered according to the Act of Congress in the year 1864, by FRANK LESLIE, in the Clerk's Office of the District Court for the Southern District of New York.

No. 503. Vol. XX.]   NEW YORK, MAY 20, 1865.   [PRICE 10 CENTS. $4 00 YEARLY. 12 WEEKS $1 00.

The sketch below was furnished by one of the two officers employed in the duty of sinking the body of Booth in the middle of the Potomac. Although not authorised to divulge his name, I am able to vouch for the truth of the representation.

New York, May 10th, 1865.   F. LESLIE.

The assassin's body was quietly disposed of in the waters of the Potomac River.

on April 9, 1865. Returning from a visit with General and Mrs. Grant at his rear guard headquarters in Virginia, Mrs. Lincoln remarked on the drive from the Potomac wharf to the White House, "The city is full of enemies." The president retorted, "Enemies—never again must we repeat that word."

Mrs. Lincoln's words soon became terrible truth. On the evening of April 14, 1865, Lincoln took his wife and two friends to Ford's Theater to see a play called "Our American Cousin." An actor, with southern sympathies and a deep hatred of the president, was also there. He was the leader of a plot to assassinate the president and other important government officials. The theater was as well-known to the vengeful assassin as his face was to the theater employees. He moved easily through the theater lobby and up the stairs to the president's box. At 10:13 a pistol shot rang out and the president slumped in his seat. The actor leaped from the box to the stage screaming threats. He rushed through the rear exit and was off on horseback. Three days later he was found and shot to death.

The wounded Lincoln was carried across the street to a lodging house. The bullet had torn through his brain and rested behind one of his eyes. There was no hope for him. Secretary of the Navy Gideon Welles described the grim scene: "The giant sufferer lay extended diagonally across the bed, which was not long enough for him." Through the gloom of night the deathwatch was kept. Mrs. Lincoln was in near-shock over the shooting. Lincoln's oldest son, Robert, sobbed on the shoulder of a friend as he watched his father's life flicker away. Shortly before dawn it began to rain. At 7:22 the next morning Abraham Lincoln died.

It was one of the most tragic days in the history of the nation. Crowds of newly-freed slaves stood around on Washington streets, helpless and speechless. Men wept openly. A death hush fell across the land. The sadness caused physical pain to many. Secretary of War, Edwin Stanton, sadly summarized the scene when he said, "Now he belongs to the ages."

After more than one hundred years Stanton's words still ring true. Abraham Lincoln is the timeless strength of nature. He was truly the American oak, with roots buried so firm and so deep the ages cannot forget him.

Lincoln National Life Foundation

This is an interior view of the Abraham Lincoln Memorial in Washington. It was dedicated May 30, 1922. The Memorial is maintained by the National Parks Service and is open daily to the public.

ANDREW JOHNSON

Seventeenth President (1865-1869)

The sign over the door
read "A. Johnson, Tailor."
The tailoring trade was the only
private occupation the seventeenth
president ever knew.
Even after he entered public
life, Andrew Johnson was rarely away from
the needle and thread, the
tools he knew so well.
He continued to make his own clothes
throughout his life.
Once, while he was governor of Tennessee,
he thanked the governor of Kentucky
for a favor by making him
a suit of clothes.

The birthplace of Andrew Johnson in Raleigh, North Carolina.

ANDREW JOHNSON'S TAILOR SHOP, AT EAST GREENVILLE, EAST TENN.

Shortly after Abraham Lincoln's death, Andrew Johnson took the presidential oath in the small parlor of Kirkwood House in Washington.

THE TOUGH TENNESSEE TAILOR

None of our presidents came from more humble beginnings than Andrew Johnson. He was born December 29, 1808, in Raleigh, North Carolina, the third child of Jacob and Mary McDonough Johnson. The family was extremely poor and matters were made worse when Andrew's father died while the boy was very young.

At the age of ten young Andrew and his brother were "bound out" to a Raleigh tailor. This meant they were "owned" by their employer until they reached a certain age. In exchange for room and board and learning the tailor's trade, the young apprentices had to work without salary. Six years of this hard life was enough for the brothers and they ran away. After the Johnson brothers' escape in 1824, this advertisement appeared in the *Raleigh Gazette:*

"Ran away from the Subscriber two apprentice boys, legally bound, named William and Andrew Johnson . . . I will pay . . . (ten dollars) to any person who will deliver the said apprentices to me in Raleigh . . . James J. Selby, Tailor."

The reward was never collected. After a year, the conscience-stricken brothers returned to Raleigh on their own to serve out the time of their apprenticeship. Mr. Selby had retired, but threatened legal action against the Johnson brothers.

Seventeen year old Andrew then moved with his family to the hills of eastern Tennessee. After a year of aimless odd jobs, young Johnson learned that the tailor of Greenville, Tennessee had retired. He traveled to that town and set up his own tailoring shop in a simple, two-room house.

Andrew's poverty during his early years did not allow him time for an education. At nineteen he met and married seventeen year old Eliza McCardle. The young Mrs. Johnson was fairly well-educated and saw that her husband

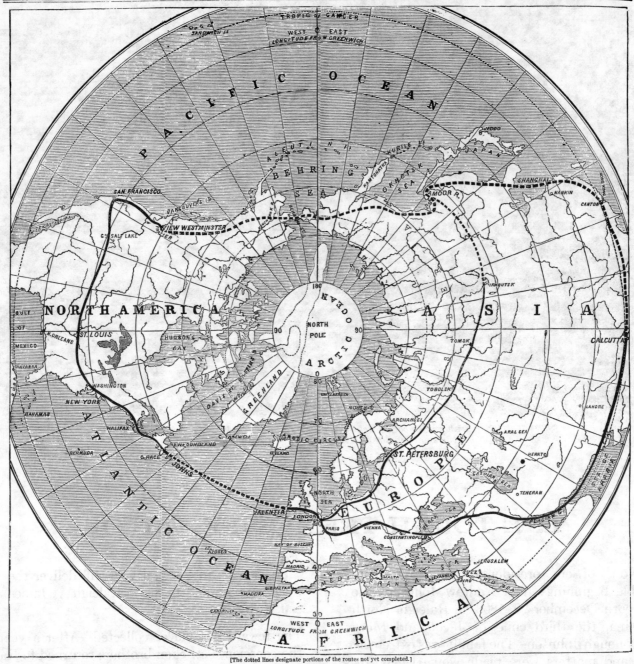

[The dotted lines designate portions of the routes not yet completed.]

MAP OF THE WORLD, SHOWING THE TELEGRAPHIC SYSTEMS FOR ENCIRCLING THE ENTIRE GLOBE.

*The Atlantic cable was completed in August of 1858. Telegraphic communications
systems were world wide in 1865.*

needed more learning. The Tennessee tailor shop became his classroom and his bride became his first and only schoolteacher. She read to him while he worked his needle through the cloth, and guided his unsure hand while he practiced writing. Eliza was a good teacher. In a short time, Andrew had improved his reading skill and had learned writing and arithmetic.

Soon the tailor shop was a meeting place for the young workingmen of Greenville. It was a

place to learn more about words and ideas and a fine place to debate. It was also the spot where Andrew Johnson's political ambitions were kindled. Education gave him confidence. with his wife's love and his friend's encouragement, he became a fine speaker who could express his ideas clearly and powerfully. Tailor Johnson became the leader of the young workingmen who gathered in his shop. Before he was twenty-one he had organized a workingman's party which first elected him alderman and then mayor of Greenville.

Andrew Johnson had begun his long career in public service. This vigorous public life included eight years in the Tennessee legislature, ten years as a congressman in the House of Representatives, two terms as the governor of Tennessee, and finally, election to the United States Senate. From time to time, some people would unkindly criticize Johnson because he was a workingman and had little education. The plain-living, neatly-dressed Tennessean answered the critics with actions, not words. He worked harder and longer than most politicians and usually knew the facts and issues better than they did. Rather than feeling ashamed, he was proud of his background and worked constantly for the best interests of the humble people he represented. With Andrew Johnson, the needs of the people came first. The people loved him and many politicians hated him.

When Tennessee Whigs gerrymandered him out of his congressional seat, the Tennessee people elected him governor. As governor he established the first public school system in the state. In 1857 the Tennessee legislature elected him to the United States Senate. When notified of this honor, the proud Johnson said, "I have reached the summit of my ambition." As a senator from Tennessee, he managed to pass the Homestead Act of 1862. He considered this act to be his best work as a law maker. Johnson was always a champion of the poor farmer. The passage of this act opened up huge amounts of rich western land to any poor man who was willing to work it.

When Abraham Lincoln was elected to the presidency, Senator Johnson argued that the South had no reason for secession. One by one, the southern states left the Union. Andrew Johnson remained the only one of twenty-two southern senators who stood firm for the Union.

After Lincoln became president, Andrew Johnson rushed back to Tennessee in spite of threats against his life. Although threatened by a lynch mob, Senator Johnson worked to keep his state in the Union. The little people to whom Johnson was an idol voted to stay in the Union, but the richer more populated western districts were too strong. The final vote took Tennessee into the Confederacy. Branded a traitor, Johnson had to quickly flee for his life

to Kentucky. The two oldest Johnson boys entered the Union Army. His wife and small son, labeled traitors and Unionists, were turned out of their eastern Tennessee home. Back in Washington, Senator Johnson worked to gain assistance for the hill people of eastern Tennessee who were suffering at the hands of the Confederates because of their Unionist views.

Because of Johnson's courageous, unwavering support of the Union, President Lincoln appointed him military governor of war-torn Tennessee early in 1862. Throughout a battle-scarred two-year term, Johnson served in this position. Continually denounced and threatened by many Tennesseans, Andrew Johnson was loyal to the Union's stars and stripes through the thick of battle. For his vigorous support, he was called by Abraham Lincoln to be his vice presidential running mate in the election of 1864. They won the election easily. The inauguration took place March 4, 1865. One month later the presidency was thrust upon Andrew Johnson by an assassin's well-placed bullet.

Both North and South felt great anxiety after Lincoln's assassination. What would the new president do? Radical Republicans were pleased by the thought that now they had a president who would help them get even with the South. Here was a man who would help them control the southern vote by giving the newly freed black men the right to vote and take it away from those men who had been loyal to the Confederacy. Southerners worried at the thought that one of their own poor whites, a traitor to them during the war, was now in the president's chair. President Johnson only wanted to cool passions on both sides and attempted to carry out President Lincoln's peace program as best he could.

Radical Republicans in and out of the government began to hate him because Johnson checked them time and time again with the power of the presidential veto. He would not allow them to shower their vengeance upon the South or upon specific individuals as revenge for the Civil War and President Lincoln's assassination. The Radicals began plotting against the president. Foremost among them was a member of his own Cabinet, Secretary of War, Edwin Stanton.

To gain public support President Johnson spoke often in public. Here he addresses citizens of Washington on February 22, 1866.

The Oval Room in the White House was a library when Andrew Johnson lived there.

The Reconstruction period following the war would have proven a heavy load even for the Illinois ironman; it certainly was too much for his successor. Andrew Johnson had few of Lincoln's warm personality traits and he did not have the confidence of the American public. He wanted desperately to carry out Lincoln's fair rebuilding policies in the South, but he could not bring them about.

In hopes of regaining the public support and placing more legislative allies in Congress, he made a "swing 'round the circle" in 1866. On this tour of major eastern and midwestern cities he hoped to help elect congressmen who would support him in Washington. But the president succeeded only in kindling more public flames of fury against himself. Time and time again, when faced with angry, jeering audiences, he would lose control of himself and let loose his fiery temper. At one stop, his companion on the "swing 'round the circle," Ulysses S. Grant, feared for Johnson's life as a hail of bullets greeted his arrival upon the stage.

These times were as terrible for the South as they were for the president. Northern "carpetbaggers" and Southern "scalawags" gained control of southern governments. Corruption and injustice became common in the South. A southern group, the fear-inspiring and illegal Ku Klux Klan, rose up to frighten these outsiders and the newly freed black man.

In the North, the Radicals plotted to rid themselves of their uncooperative president. Congress passed the Tenure of Office Act, which was later proven illegal by the Supreme Court. President Johnson felt this act unlawfully cut into his presidential powers. He went ahead and fired the disloyal, scheming Secretary Stanton.

The scene was now set for one of the blackest moments in the history of the United States government. The Radical Republicans felt they had a case because the president had willingly broken the law by firing Secretary Stanton. Impeachment proceedings began. President Andrew Johnson became a victim of the tyrannous times he was trying to control. The case against the president was, at best, extremely weak. At worst, it was non-existent. But Johnson's enemies filled the Capitol to see "Andy walk the plank."

Under the Constitution the power of impeachment belongs to the House of Representatives. The Senate conducts the trial in its chambers, listening to the evidence and voting for or against impeachment. There were fifty-four senators at the time; a two-thirds majority of thirty-six was needed for conviction. At the beginning of the trial, which lasted nearly three months, the Radicals had thirty certain votes and Johnson had twelve. There were twelve undecided.

As the lengthy trial went on, President Johnson went about the country's business in the White House. He longed to walk across to the Capitol Building and do some "plain talking" to the group that was trying him. He knew this action was unfair, with politics, not justice, as its basis. He was not allowed to defend himself and his ideas. Each day as the trial progressed he waited nervously for news of its developments. As the days passed the news was not good, five of the undecided senators were now going to vote him guilty.

All the Radicals had to do was get one more vote from the seven undecided Republican senators. The pressure and the threats upon these seven men were tremendous. Their political careers were at stake. But more important to these brave men was the threat against the office of the presidency. When the final vote came, all seven ended their political careers by voting for the president's acquittal. Andrew Johnson was saved by one vote.

Andrew Johnson's administration, through agony, disruption, and trouble, illustrated one great truth to Americans. The government goes on no matter how great the obstacle. Of particularly great assistance to the president during these trying times was his loyal Secretary of State, William H. Seward. Seward constantly supported Johnson and wrote many of his veto messages. The Secretary of State's most famous achievement was his 1867 purchase of Alaska from Russia for seven million dollars. Known as "Seward's folly" or "Johnson's polar bear garden," the Alaska purchase was at first unpopular. But as the months and years went by the nation came to see Seward's wisdom in making this great land purchase.

Andrew Johnson

Eliza McCardle Johnson was an invalid when her husband became president. The Johnson's daughter, Martha Johnson Patterson, acted as White House hostess for her father.

Westward expansion of the U.S. population increased after the Civil War. Americans found the rich lands of the west ideal for farming, sheep-raising and cattle-ranching. Here Texas cowboys are driving cattle to the nearest railroad depot. Beef prices were high on the eastern market.

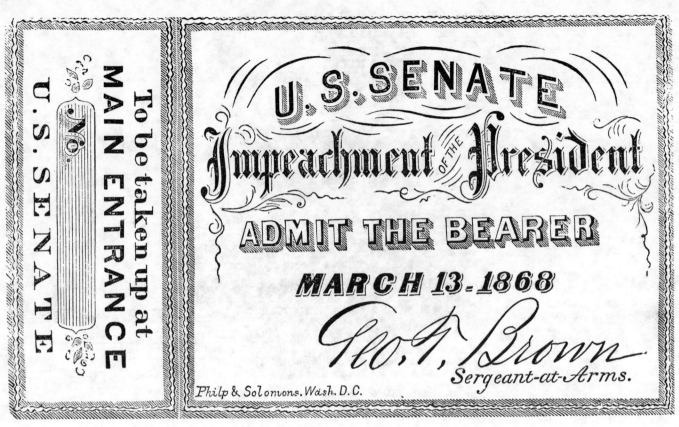

Thousands of people flocked to Washington to see the presidential impeachment trial.
Tickets were difficult to obtain.

Harper's Weekly *showed this drawing of the impeachment proceedings.*

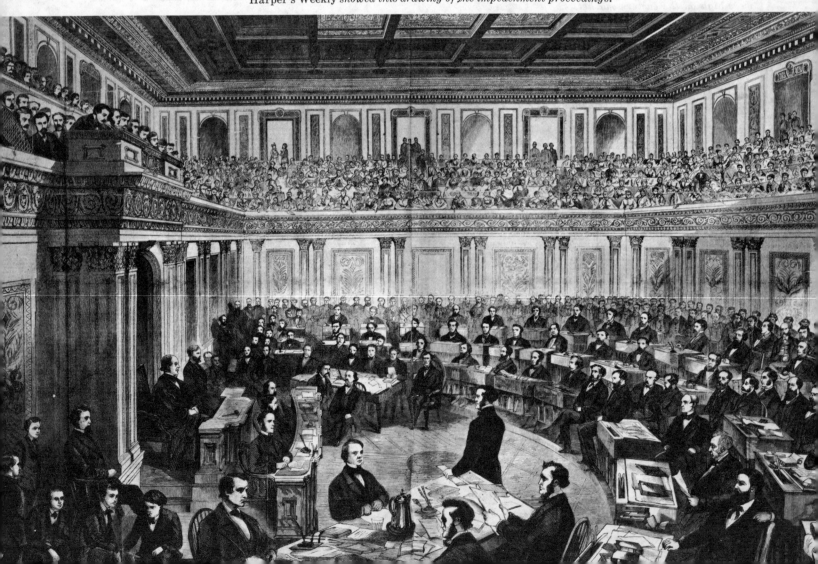

Andrew Johnson's home in Greenville, Tennessee.

Andrew Johnson retired from office in March 1869. After the terrible effects of his near impeachment, it would have been understandable if he had slipped away and hidden himself in the Tennessee hills. But he was not a coward. He was back in Washington less than seven years after his impeachment trial, again as a United States Senator from Tennessee. He carried his triumph with dignity. As he greeted old senate colleagues, Johnson said sadly, "I miss my old friends Fessenden, Fowler, Trumbull, Grimes, Henderson, Ross, all are gone..." Indeed they were gone. He had named six of the seven courageous Republican senators who had ended their legislative careers by voting for his acquittal.

Andrew Johnson's triumphant return to the Senate was a short-lived one. In less than four months he died of a stroke. The tough Tennessee tailor was buried on a hillside overlooking Greenville with a copy of the Constitution of the United States resting under his head.

ULYSSES S. GRANT

Eighteenth President (1869-1877)

Hiram Ulysses Grant,
Ulysses Hiram Grant, Ulysses S. Grant —
which name was correct?
The answer is all of them.
His correct name has been a problem
to historians recording his life.
Defending his good name was
one of Grant's greatest concerns.
In his lifetime he was given such names
as "The Butcher from Galena,"
"The Hero of Appomatox,"
"Uncle Sam," "Useless Grant," and
"Old Three Stars."
Which of these fit him?
It all depends on who
tells his story.

The birthplace of Ulysses S. Grant, Point Pleasant, Ohio.

A MAN OF FICKLE FORTUNE

Ulysses, born April 27, 1822, in the Ohio River town of Point Pleasant, was the eldest of six children born to Jesse and Hannah Simpson Grant. He was christened Hiram Ulysses Grant, but later changed the name to Ulysses Hiram Grant to avoid being teased with initials that spelled "HUG." When Ulysses was a tot, Jesse Grant moved his family to Georgetown, Ohio. There his father set up a tanning business and worked a small farm. Ulysses had a pleasant childhood. He attended school regularly, helped his father at the tannery and on the farm, and followed his own special interests. Ambitious young Ulysses had his own business at ten, running a wagon-taxi to Cincinnati. As a teenager, he developed a reputation for being able to gentle hard-to-handle horses.

When Ulysses was seventeen, Jesse Grant received word that the appointment he sought for his son at the United States Military Academy at West Point had been approved. The appointment read "Ulysses S. Grant." The congressman who recommended the appointment had misunderstood young Grant's given names and, to avoid confusion, had made his middle name "Simpson," his mother's maiden name. Ulysses Simpson Grant was the name that remained for the rest of his life.

For some reason Ulysses did not want to attend West Point. "I won't go!" he stormed at his father. Jesse could not understand his son's reluctance to take advantage of this fine opportunity. Perhaps it was embarrassment over his size that held the boy back. At seventeen, Ulysses was a strong, muscular youth, but stood a bare five-feet, one-inch tall. He later grew seven inches at West Point. Father and son disagreed hotly for days. In the end, when Jesse said he must go, Ulysses agreed. Traveling by steamboat and train to West Point, the sad, soon-to-be soldier wished for a train wreck, boat explosion, or anything, to keep him away from the Academy.

Grant was not a model cadet; he disliked the hardship and rules of military life. He received many demerits for slovenly dress and tardiness. Only an average soldier, he loved reading books, particularly adventure novels such as Sir Walter Scott's *Ivanhoe*. There were also happy times at West Point for "Uncle Sam" Grant, as he was called by his classmates. He was popular with the other cadets and was elected president of the Academy's literary society. He became the best horseman at West Point and established a record high jump on horseback that stood for twenty-five years. Cadet Grant also developed an interest in and ability for mathematics. In spite of his early reluctance to attend West Point, he learned to admire the United States Military Academy, calling its Hudson River campus, ". . . the most beautiful place I have ever seen." He graduated in 1843.

The Academy's best horseman asked to be assigned to the cavalry, but the army put the young second lieutenant in the infantry. During his first two army years, Grant was stationed in Missouri, Mississippi, and Louisiana. At the outbreak of the Mexican War he was ordered to join General Zachary Taylor's army. Like Abraham Lincoln, Lieutenant Grant did not agree with the war's purpose, but he served with distinction, taking part in all but one of the major battles.

Service in the Mexican War allowed this man of action much opportunity to show his worth. As gunfire and cannon fire burst all around the American soldiers during the Battle of Monterey, Grant noticed that some soldiers were out of ammunition. Without a thought for his own personal safety, he leaped upon his horse, clung to one side of the saddle, and galloped through a hail of bullets to get help for these men.

At the close of the war, he was ordered to Jefferson Barracks, near St. Louis, where he had been stationed before the war. There he had the opportunity to court pretty Miss Julia Dent, the sister of one of his West Point classmates. Julia shared Lieutenant Grant's love of horses. She was an excellent horsewoman and put love-light in his eyes at first sight. The two were married in August of 1848. They shared a happy thirty-seven year marriage filled with horses, travels, and the raising of four children.

In 1852 Grant entered his worst years—a period that shadowed and stained him for the remainder of his life. He was assigned to a bleak frontier post on the Pacific Coast and was forced to leave Julia and his small son behind. His army troop made a dangerous crossing at the Isthmus of Panama. During the trek through the thick jungle, cholera killed one third of the men. Grant survived and, upon reaching the Pacific Coast, was stationed at Fort Vancouver. There he was overcome with loneliness for his wife and little son. He brooded over the fact that he had never seen his newly-born second son, and he could not afford to bring his family west. He began to drink whiskey to forget his sorrow and to ease his mind of the lonely life about him. In April 1854, a superior officer discovered Captain Grant drinking heavily in public. He threatened a court martial. Grant did not want to embarrass his wife and her high-ranking army officer father; he quietly resigned without defending himself.

Grant's next eight years were filled with poverty and failure. He tried unsuccessfully to farm outside St. Louis. He failed in his efforts to be a bill collector and a real estate agent. Then Julia's father, Colonel Dent, offered him a low-paying job as a clerk in his Galena, Illinois, leather shop. Grant was spiritually at the bottom of the well. For eight-hundred dollars a

Frank Leslie's Illustrated Newspaper *published this sketch in 1869. It shows Captain Grant leaving his home in Galena, Illinois, to join the Union Army.*

In this May 1864 letter to Secretary of War Stanton, Grant reveals the fighting spirit that helped make him Commander-in-Chief of the Union Army. A sentence from this letter captured the public's and the president's attention. It said, "I propose to fight it out on this line if it takes all summer."

MEETING OF GENERALS GRANT AND LEE PREPARATORY TO

THE SURRENDER OF GENERAL LEE

AND HIS ENTIRE ARMY TO LIEUT GENERAL U S GRANT APRIL 9th 1865

The Civil War officially ended when Confederate General Robert E. Lee (third from right) surrendered to Union General Ulysses S. Grant (far right), April 9, 1865.

year he unloaded wagons, kept books, and sometimes took the unkind barbs of Julia's two
younger brothers. Through it all the Grant family kept together, its strong devotion intact.

He was beaten down by these years but not
defeated. Even in those times Grant had the
sly sense of humor that endeared him to friends
throughout his life. Standing around with Galena friends, he loved to swap stories. Grant
particularly enjoyed telling stories on himself.
Recalling early school years and his lack of interest in studies, he stated that he had been
told "the noun is the name of a thing" so often
that he had to believe it. He joked about his

lack of musical ability claiming he knew only
two tunes; one was "Yankee Doodle" and one
wasn't.

At the outbreak of the War Between the
States, Ulysses S. Grant's life again took on
meaning. When President Lincoln asked for
seventy-five thousand Union volunteers, Captain Sam Grant answered the president's call.
This was a war in which he believed. This was
a chance to erase the black mark upon his army
record. During this terrible time in American
history, Grant went far beyond his dreams of
service to the Union. He began the war by drill-
ing a company of Galena volunteers and ended

it by handing Confederate Commanding General Robert E. Lee a pen for signing the statement of surrender.

Between the start and finish of the war Grant's military star rose high on the horizon. He was the victorious general at the Battles of Shiloh, Memphis, Vicksburg, Port Hudson, and Chattanooga. President Lincoln had much trouble dealing with his generals. Some were reckless, some ambitious, and a few made terrible blunders. He watched Grant's pursuit of victory with interest. When Lincoln made him a three-star general and Commander of all Union forces in March 1864, he said, "I want that man; he fights."

General Grant fought hard to destroy the institution of slavery he had hated since youth. Standing in his war-torn victory trail, beaten southerners called him the "Butcher from Galena." War is never pretty and General Ulysses S. Grant hated it. To be a general was not a glorious thing to him, but winning the war was something that had to be done. It was the aftermath of battle, the torn and mangled bodies of the wounded, that hurt him most. The Union commander would sometimes stand outside a warm tent, soaked to the skin by heavy rains, rather than remain inside where he might see the blood of his soldiers in surgery.

Laughter in times of great trouble sometimes helps to keep men sane. The general was no exception. The humor that carried him through his eight years of failure in civilian life, now helped him through the horror of war. With a sly look upon his face, he explained why he always had a big, black cigar in his mouth:

"I had been a light smoker ... In accounts published in the papers, I was represented as smoking a cigar in the midst of . . . conflict; and many persons, thinking, no doubt, that tobacco was my chief solace, sent me boxes of the choicest brands . . . As many as ten thousand were soon received. I gave away all I could get rid of, but having such a quantity on hand I naturally smoked more than I would have done under ordinary circumstances, and I have continued the habit ever since."

The convention chairman announced the Republican presidential nomination of Ulysses S. Grant at the Academy of Music in Philadelphia in June 1872.

And he did, smoking an average of twenty cigars a day for the rest of his life.

As the war went on, victories for the North continued at Petersburg, at Atlanta, and finally at Richmond on April 3, 1865. On Palm Sunday, April 9, General Lee surrendered to General Grant at the Appomatox Courthouse in Virginia. Although Grant felt the southerners' cause to be "one of the worst for which people ever fought," he could feel nothing but compassion for the gallant Lee and his soldiers. Grant was told that Lee's men were hungry and immediately ordered that his troops' rations be shared with the Confederates. He also would not allow his men to shoot off cannon bursts celebrating the surrender. "We did not want to exalt in their downfall," he later said.

The bloodiest war in our history was over and General Ulysses S. Grant was the victor — the man who had saved the Union on the battlefield. He was mobbed by crowds wherever he went. In Washington, President Lincoln greeted him warmly and invited the general and his wife to attend a play at Ford's Theater. Because Julia Grant wanted to get back to her children, an even greater tragedy was avoided April 14, 1865. The assassins had wanted Grant, too.

He left the army with high ambitions for service as a civilian. The General sat out Andrew Johnson's stormy Reconstruction years, quietly waiting for a chance in politics. For Grant knew that "nothing so popularizes a candidate for high civil positions as military victories." And Grant wanted the highest of them all, the presidency. His desires overcame his judgment at times, and the political newcomer placed himself in the hands of people who used him. Ulysses S. Grant was nominated by the Republicans on the first ballot of the 1868 Chicago convention. Four words stood out in his acceptance speech, "Let us have peace."

President Grant was exceptionally honest, but some men in his administration were not. As a political newcomer his "on the job training" sometimes proved disastrous. With the exception of his Secretary of State, Hamilton Fish, most of his Cabinet appointments were unfortunate ones made out of friendship, not good judgment. His administration was riddled with great scandals: The "Black Friday" financial panic of 1869, the "Whiskey Ring" uncovered in 1875, and the discovery of dishonest

President Grant's two young sons, Jesse and Ulysses, Jr., were driven to school daily in this cart. The horses were named "Reb" and "Billy Button."

President Grant and his family relaxed in 1869 on this presidential vacation by the sea.

197

The "golden spike", driven at Promontory, Utah, May 10, 1869, began transcontinental railroad service. Trade and travel between the eastern and western United States increased greatly after this date.

activities by Secretary of War William Belknap, were among the most sensational. President Grant was innocent of illegal activity in these notorious affairs, but guilty of extremely bad judgment in dealing with the scandals. Newspapers openly questioned some of his actions. Again his reputation had become somewhat stained.

Grant's eight years in the White House were not all bad. There was high achievement on some domestic issues. It was an era called "The Gilded Age." It was the time of Mark Twain, Boss Tweed, Susan B. Anthony, and J. P. Morgan. Business prospered and the arts flourished. Social reform was helped by a growing public conscience. People and products got places faster. In 1869 the Union Pacific and Central Pacific Railroads were linked at Promontory,

Utah, and this established the first transcontinental train service. The Homestead Act of 1862 had sent settlers by the thousands west to farm. These rich western lands helped America grow and expand. Industry increased with the inventions of Westinghouse's air brake, Bell's telephone, and the refrigerated railroad car.

Grant carried his love of horses with him into the presidency. For relaxation he enjoyed driving a horse and carriage around Washington. One afternoon he was driving his carriage west on M Street at a fast pace when a police officer stopped him for speeding. When the embarrassed policeman learned he was dealing with the president, he hesitated before issuing the ticket. President Grant insisted he do his duty and paid a twenty-dollar fine. The president later wrote a letter to the Washington

Police Department complimenting the policeman on his fine sense of duty.

The House of Representatives considered legislation allowing him to run for a third term. But after the ups and downs of Grant's eight years in office, they decided not to act. The General showed he was not disappointed by saying, "I never wanted to get out of a place as much as I did the Presidency." He left office in 1877 and, with Julia, soon began to realize a lifelong dream—a trip around the world. The trip began in the Court of Queen Victoria of England, and ended two years later in the Court of the Emperor of Japan. Everywhere the Grants were received like royalty. The ruler of Egypt gave them a palace in which to stay and a boat to tour the Nile. At India's Taj Mahal, the gardener showered Julia with roses. This was all very different from their pork and bean days in Galena. Grant's popularity was on the rise at home, too. Friends who hoped to return him to the White House advised him to stay away until the 1880 Republican Convention. He did, but wrote in 1879, "I dread going home."

There was an ominous ring of truth in these words. Ulysses S. Grant's last years were filled with poverty and pain. The Republicans did not nominate him at their 1880 convention. Grant moved to New York and invested heavily with Grant and Ward, a banking house. When this business failed in 1884, it wiped out his fortune. This misfortune was made worse by tragic personal news. Only a few months before Grant and Ward failed, he felt the first stabbing pains of cancer in his throat. Grant knew he was dying when a publishing house made him a generous offer to write his *Memoirs*.

General George Armstrong Custer was a hero of the Union Army during the Civil War. He continued his military career in the west, winning many battles against the Indians after the war. One June 25, 1876, Custer lost his life and his troops were routed by Chief Sitting Bull and his Sioux Indians at the Little Big Horn in Montana.

*On his world tour Ex-president Grant in 1879 visited
Li Heing Chang, the Viceroy of China.*

This began his final battle with time and onrushing death. The money for the book was necessary to see his family provided for after he was gone. But the dreadful pain of his illness fought his efforts to write every hour of the way. Gradually the cancer ate away his voice so that he could no longer even whisper dictation. He had to use pen and ink. When the pain made this writing difficult, he switched to rough student scratch pads. Julia and the children must not be left penniless! Propped up in an armchair to keep from choking to death, he wrote on.

The rugged old hero of the Civil War won his greatest struggle, the battle of his strong body against pain and death. In his middle years he joked about finally learning what a noun was. Close to death, the ex-president was not joking when he scribbled, "A verb is anything that signifies to be, to do, or to suffer. I signify all three." Seven days before his death, he finished his 200,000 word *Memoirs*, which was to earn nearly a half a million dollars for his family. Fickle fortune finished with Ulysses S. Grant, July 23, 1885.

Grant battled against cancer to stay alive and complete his Memoirs.
He is shown here at work writing a few weeks before his death.

RUTHERFORD B. HAYES

Nineteenth President (1877-1881)

Imagine a basketball game
forced into overtime; a football
game where the winning points are scored
in the final seconds; and a baseball
game that goes into extra innings—thirteen,
fourteen, fifteen—before a victor emerges.
These nip and tuck sporting contests
can be called "cliff-hangers" because their
closeness leaves the audience feeling breathless
and weak, as if they had been hanging
on the edge of a cliff.
Imagine a political contest where
the two opponents did not learn who
the winner was for months.
This surely is the
"cliff-hanger" of all times!
It happened during the
presidential election of 1876.
The opponents were Samuel J. Tilden
and Rutherford B. Hayes.
The prize to be won was the presidency.
Hayes finally won after four months
of suspense and became the
nineteenth president.

The birthplace of Rutherford B. Hayes in Delaware, Ohio.

OHIO'S "CLIFF-HANGER" CANDIDATE

Rutherford B. Hayes was born October 4, 1822, in Delaware, Ohio. He was named for his father who had died of a fever two-and-a-half months before his birth. Young Rutherford was a sickly child. His youth was a very quiet one. He experienced few of the interesting things that happen to boys growing up in small towns. He seemed to act more like a serious little man with no time for frolicking and outdoor activities.

In spite of his father's death, his childhood was free from hardship. He was given the things that interested him. His mother, Sophia Hayes, saw to her son's every wish. She had lost her husband and three of her children to sickness. She was not going to lose Rutherford and his older sister Fanny. She was determined that what was left of her family would survive.

With only women at home, young Rutherford longed for male friends. Sardis Birchard, his understanding uncle, helped as much as he could. Uncle Sardis spent much time with Rutherford and also helped to pay for his education.

The boy attended private schools in Connecticut and Ohio before enrolling at Kenyon College in Gambier, Ohio. He had little interest in sports or other activities outside school. Young Mr. Hayes was always a serious, straight-laced student. According to Stanley Matthews, one of his college classmates, Hayes "never got caught in any scrapes; he never had any boyish foolishness" about him. Nineteen year old Hayes wrote in his diary that he was "determined . . . to use what means I have to acquire a character distinguished for energy, firmness, and perseverance." Hayes stuck firmly to these principles throughout his college career and throughout his life. He was graduated from Kenyon College as the class valedictorian.

After thinking about several careers he decided upon law and began his studies at Harvard Law School in 1842. Three years later he graduated and passed the Ohio bar examination. He began his first law practice in Fremont, Ohio, the hometown of his friend and relative Sardis

Birchard. Having Uncle Sardis nearby was pleasant for Rutherford. But making enough money to live on and building a strong reputation for himself was difficult in Fremont. There was not much opportunity for an ambitious young man in such a small town. Hayes decided to move to Cincinnati in 1849 and try again. He soon had considerable success there by acting as defense attorney in a number of sensational criminal cases.

Hayes had long hated slavery, thinking it a stain on the pages of American history. Because of his humane feelings, he defended several fugitive slaves who awaited trials in Cincinnati and probable return to the South. Although Hayes was not a wealthy man, he never took payment for these cases.

In another way, this was a good time for the quiet, unassuming lawyer. Soon after arriving in Cincinnati, he met Lucy Webb who was a student at Wesleyan Female College. She was like Rutherford, quiet and hard-working. Their common interests, her pleasant voice and beautiful eyes, soon captured the young lawyer's heart. After a long engagement the pair was married in December of 1852. It was a successful marriage. Rutherford and Lucy Hayes shared the same humane and strong religious views. Both were prepared to work in an effort to make these views a reality. They had a family of seven sons and one daughter. Chuckling over all the males in his house, Hayes often remarked that he and Lucy were in "the boy business."

Since childhood, Rutherford B. Hayes had closely followed politics. Political action seemed to him to be a firm and lasting way to accomplish much good work for the country. The newly-formed Republican Party was firmly against slavery. So was he. Shortly after his arrival in Cincinnati he helped organize the Ohio Republican Party. Hayes enjoyed political activity and was a strong party man. But he did not act the role of a partisan politician when elected to office. This sometimes made Republican Party bosses extremely unhappy. Hayes' first elected office was as Cincinnati's solicitor, and he worked to serve the best interests of all the city, not just the interests of his party. Hayes' long success in public service was due to this honest, above board behavior. The voters trusted him.

After the attack on Fort Sumter in April 1861, Hayes felt the strong pull of a new duty—military service. As a soldier he could fight to end the wicked institution of slavery and to hold the Union together. He entered the army as a major in the 23rd Ohio Volunteers and prepared for soldiering as diligently as he did everything else in life. He pored over training and tactical manuals until he could properly lead his men into battle. These efforts soon brought him promotion to the rank of brigadier general.

As a general, Hayes was a strong and courageous officer who was admired and respected by his men and fellow officers. During the war he was wounded four times. Each time he recovered and returned to the battlefield. His bravery made General Hayes memorable to all who learned of it. News of his heroic actions carried all the way back to Ohio. Still in the thick of battle in the summer of 1864, he became an absentee nominee for a seat in the United States House of Representatives. The General scoffed at this, stating, "An officer fit for duty who at this crisis would abandon his post to electioneer for a seat in Congress ought to be scalped!" This quotation caught the fancy of Ohio voters. Hayes was elected without leaving his post. "Scalping" was not necessary. The war ended just as his term in Congress started.

The tired soldier headed straight from the battlefield to the Capitol Building in Washington to serve as a member of the Thirty-Ninth Congress. As an active, honest congressman, his political career was soon firmly reestablished. In 1867 the Ohio Republicans nominated him for governor. Delighted with the opportunity to return home, Hayes won the governorship after a vigorous campaign. As Ohio's top elected officer, he pressed for reform in several areas. Governor Hayes wanted a system of voter registration to help stop election frauds. He wanted a safety code to make mines safer for the men who worked in them. He wished to improve conditions for inmates in prison and mental hospitals. He also worked to establish the college that later became Ohio State University.

Briefly retiring from public life in 1872, he spent three years with his family at his Fremont home, Spiegel Grove. There he attended to private business matters. But his beliefs were too strong to let him remain away from public service very long. The Republican trumpet blew again in 1875. He returned to politics, again as

*President Rutherford B. Hayes taking the oath of office,
March 4, 1877.*

*President Hayes samples the seafood at a Rhode Island
clambake, June 28, 1877.*

*Office-seekers await an interview with President Hayes. These interviews with spoilsmen
took much time away from his other presidential duties.*

President Hayes greeted the first Chinese minister to the United States, September 28, 1878.

Ohio's governor. At this time, Republican colleagues made it clear to Rutherford B. Hayes that his political image was now well-known across America. The presidency became a strong possibility. Just like so many fine men before him, Hayes was caught up by the desire to hold the nation's highest office. This is shown in a March 1876 extract from his diary: "It seems to me that good purposes and the judgment, experience, and firmness I possess, would enable me to execute the duties of the office well."

Three months later the Republican National Convention met in Cincinnati and took up Hayes' banner. His candidacy was helped by much hometown support. But it was Hayes' sincerity and honesty that most impressed the delegates. The Hayes forces defeated James G. Blaine of Maine and captured the presidential nomination. Samuel J. Tilden was his Democratic opponent.

During the campaign of 1876, Candidate Hayes remained quite a mystery to the voters outside Ohio. He rarely appeared in public, feeling his words and deeds should stand by themselves. However, he did attend Philadelphia's Centennial Exhibition in September, one month before election day. This was unwise. Hayes was short, average-looking, had a rat's nest beard, and dressed in rumpled clothing. The *New York Times*, commenting on his appearance at the Exhibition, damaged his political image by saying he wore a "dreadfully shabby coat and a shockingly bad hat."

The election of November 1876 is unique in American political history. The experts who watched the back-and-forth campaign predicted it would be close. Few dreamed how close. Democrat Tilden went to bed election night believing he had won the presidency. Republican Hayes woke up the morning after the election hoping that he had won. The country was completely confused. The Democratic *Chicago Times* mirrored the frustration of America over the indecisive election returns. Thinking the Democrats had won, the *Times* headline writer wrote on Wednesday, the day after the election, "Glory to God in the Highest." On Thursday, he was less certain as the headline read "Lord, We Believe." On Friday, he had thrown up his hands in despair as the headline read "Let Us Pray."

This election dispute led to Democratic shouts of fraud. Nasty names for Hayes, such as "Rutherfraud" and "The Fraud President," were heard around the country. The trouble was in the states of Louisiana, Florida, and South Carolina. In November Tilden had 184 electoral votes, just one short of the majority needed to win. Hayes had 166. The Republicans reasoned if Hayes could capture the twenty electoral votes from the three states in question he would win with 186 electoral votes, one more than majority.

Then the fun began. Each of the three southern states sent in two sets of voter returns, one for Tilden and one for Hayes. Both political camps claimed victory as the weeks wore on, and neither party would give an inch. Angry Democratic and Republican partisans considered taking up the rifle and rapier to settle the matter. Cooler heads prevailed and a special commission of fifteen men was set up to rule over the dispute. This commission, with members from Congress, the Senate, and the Supreme Court, was composed of seven Democrats, seven Republicans, and one Independent. Then Justice David Davis, the Independent, resigned to take a seat in the Senate and the Republicans replaced him with one of their own. The Commission now stood with eight Republicans and seven Democrats.

The days were dragging on and still there was no president. Unhappy Democrats reluctantly agreed to start to work. The special commission sat as joint chairmen over Congress as that body counted and recounted the votes. Each time there was a dispute, the Commission ruled 8 to 7 for Hayes and the Republicans. The Democrats watching this, turned red with anger and screamed corruption each time they heard the dreaded "Hayes, 8 aye, 7 nay" decision.

Almost four months after the election and only fifty-six hours before Inauguration Day 1877, the issue was settled. Rutherford B. Hayes was to be the next president. He had captured all twenty disputed electoral college votes. The final tabulation of the electoral college was Hayes 186, Tilden 185. The nation was relieved, but many Democratic voters still cried "fraud."

Hayes came through this four months of rough and tumble politics with dignified self-restraint. He took no part in the tricky political manipulations that put him into the White House. People had to admire that. With the same strong purpose that had guided him throughout his political life, the president set out to serve the entire country. He appointed a strong Cabinet he believed would work for the best interests of everyone in the country: William Evarts, a noted lawyer, as Secretary of State; John Sherman, a fine financial expert, as Secretary of the Treasury; Carl Schurz, an uncompromising reformer, as Secretary of the Interior; Senator David M. Kay of Tennessee, as Postmaster General.

These Cabinet appointments and President Hayes' efforts to make civil service appointments for merit and not for party benefit, enraged the "Stalwart" faction of the Republican Party. Stalwart boss, Senator Roscoe Conkling of New York, was furious when the president announced that all men then holding federal jobs must give up all political activity. President Hayes fired Conkling's friend, Chester A. Arthur, from his post at the New York Custom House because he continued to be active in Republican politics. This dismissal held up over Conkling's outcries. Hayes had won a satisfying battle against the spoils system, but the war lay ahead

President Hayes believed that it was unjust to have federal troops stationed in the South to support northern "carpetbag" governments. Southern political leaders promised that they would protect the constitutional rights of all men. President Hayes accepted their word and ordered federal troops withdrawn from South Carolina and Louisiana. The Stalwarts howled their dissatisfaction. The president was taking away their power in the South and turning it over to Democrats. They longed to turn back the clock and put Tilden in the president's chair. Hayes just wasn't cooperating! By this brave deed, which practically ended his political career, Rutherford B. Hayes brought the terrible Reconstruction period to an end in the South. Once more all American states governed themselves. The northern president's unusual sense of justice started the slow process of making his country whole once again.

President Hayes handled himself well in the dispute that arose over the great eastern railroad strikes of 1877. He had great sympathy for the strikers' demands but did not approve of their methods. The president sent in federal troops to stop the disorder. He felt that violence would not help the workers' cause. It would only widen the gap between themselves and their employers.

Mrs. Rutherford B. Hayes.

President Rutherford B. Hayes.

209

President Hayes and his family gathered each evening in the Oval Room of the White House. Secretary of the Interior Carl Schurz entertained them this evening on the piano.

The White House egg-roll became an annual Easter event during Rutherford B. Hayes' presidency.

"The White House carriage of President Rutherford B. Hayes"

The Gray Line, Inc., Washington, D.C.

As chief executive, Rutherford B. Hayes did more traveling than any of his predecessors. In 1880 he made a goodwill tour through the South. Later he became the first president to visit the West Coast while in office.

The Hayes' were both colorful and controversial residents of the White House. President and Mrs. Hayes did not drink alcoholic beverages. The First Lady was nicknamed "Lemonade Lucy" because she served lemonade and soft drinks instead of liquor at the White House receptions. Religion was an important part of the Hayes' life and this did not stop when they moved into the Executive Mansion. Each day began with morning prayers for the entire household. And in the evening the Hayes and their guests could often be found gathering around the piano singing church hymns.

Some Washingtonians found the Hayes way of life too dull for their liking. Rutherford and Lucy Hayes were warm-hearted, outgoing people, and their years in the White House were far from solemn ones. They loved receiving people, the more the merrier. Downstairs, the reception rooms at the White House were often filled with cots and couches for overnight visitors. Occasionally one of their sons had to give his bed to a guest and sleep on the unused billiard table in the attic. Sometimes the White House was so overrun with people that President Hayes had to lock himself up in the bathroom to get his work done.

The orderly Hayes way of life was continued in the presidency. His presidential days were highly organized. The president rose each day at 7:00 a.m., ate breakfast promptly at 8:30, and then began meetings and conferences. He carried on the work of the nation until 2:00 p.m. when he stopped for lunch. In the afternoon he wrote letters, took a long carriage ride through the streets of Washington, and then settled down for a nap. The carriage ride and sleep refreshed the president for dinner, official evening receptions, and appointments.

"Lemonade Lucy" was not the sort of person her nickname suggested. Mrs. Hayes was the first college graduate to be mistress of the White House. She had a good mind, a sweet disposition, and a generous nature. The Easter egg-rolling contest that takes place today on the White House lawn began at her request. She loved the elegant, Victorian style of the White House rooms, and sometimes added her own hand-painted china plates to the scheme of decoration.

Rutherford B. Hayes left the presidency March 3, 1881, quite happy. He lived on for twelve more years and continued to work for educational and prison reform. He was president of the National Prison Association for ten years; worked to establish better school facilities for southern Negroes; and became a trustee for three universities—Western Reserve, Ohio Wesleyan, and Ohio State.

Life was not the same for him after Lucy's death in 1889. Hayes missed her loving attention and common sense. Four years later, on one of his regular visits to her grave, he wrote in his diary: "My feeling was one of longing to be quietly resting by her side." This wish was soon granted to the steadfast husband and servant of America. Nine days later he died of heart disease.

"Spiegel Grove", Rutherford B. Hayes home, Fremont, Ohio.

JAMES A. GARFIELD

Twentieth President (1881-1881)

Taught the love of God
by his mother in their log cabin home,
his religious faith and love for his country
supported him all through his life.
It was his faith and patriotism
that carried him into the
Civil War to battle against slavery.
Shortly after the war ended,
he calmed a crazed mob in New York City with
his courageous and hopeful words.
When our twentieth president lay in bed with two
assassin's bullets eroding his body,
his only comment about the man who shot him was,
"he must be insane. Why should
he want to kill me?"
And history still asks this question.
Why should anyone wish to murder
kind and gentle,
James A. Garfield?

Republican National Convention at Chicago, June 2, 1880,

Garfield was walking this convention floor working for his candidate when he heard his name announced as the Republican presidential candidate.

THE PREACHER PRESIDENT

Few people found fault with this sunny, warm-hearted man from Ohio. Early in life, tragedy taught James A. Garfield to face life with courage and with faith in God. Young James lost his father Abram when he was only two. But he was left with a remarkable mother.

Eliza Ballou Garfield became a widow with "four young saplings" when her husband was killed fighting a forest fire in the woods near their log cabin home. Eliza's spirit sparked her family to carve out good lives for themselves on the frontier. The oldest daughter helped in the cabin, the eldest son helped in the fields. With

their help, she grew their food, wove the material and made their clothes, and taught them. She gave the young Garfields the love and guidance that shaped their strong characters. Many years later, Eliza Garfield reaped the rewards of her sacrifice when she watched her youngest son James sworn in as President of the United States.

Young James held great love and respect for his mother throughout his life. In the typical Garfield manner, he helped the family as soon as he was able. At the age of twelve, he chopped wood for seventy-five cents a cord, plus meals. Later he worked as a canal boatman for ten dollars a month and his keep. Encouraged by his mother's example and affection, he found time to study while working to help support the family. He worked as a janitor and attended Hiram College. There his talent for teaching was discovered and he left his job for a teaching position. From his teacher's salary, he was able to save enough money by July of 1854 to enroll at Williams College in Massachusetts.

Garfield's degree from Williams College made him a person of high scholastic standing in Ohio. The first of his many successes was in 1857 when he became president of little Hiram College where he once worked as a janitor. During his years at Hiram, he directed a faculty of five, and also acted as an instructor. As Hiram's professor of classical languages, his powers of scholarship became well-known. His sly sense of humor also flourished. Professor Garfield enjoyed little jokes and loved to amaze onlookers by writing Greek with one hand and Latin with the other—at the same time! While at Hiram, he found time to study law and was admitted to the Ohio bar in 1860.

During these happy years, James A. Garfield's faith in God became known to others. He became a fine preacher. In his sermons he encouraged his listeners to love God. The audience felt the warmth of his religious message, rather than the fear of God put forth by so many preachers of that time. Garfield's voice was clear and pleasant, his words soft yet powerful. Because of his good looks, broad shoulders, and six-foot frame, he was impressive as he preached under the blue skies of Ohio. A friend said that he made his audience feel "as if they had been transplanted away from earth to . . . heaven." His preaching put more than love of God into the heart of Lucretia Rudolph when she listened to his sermons. Garfield had been courting her since childhood. Lucretia agreed at last to be his wife and the two were married November 11, 1858.

When the Englishman, John Denton, came to the United States to lecture on the laws of scientific evolution over the laws of God, James A. Garfield rose up in indignation. The Ohio preacher would not let God take a back seat to anyone. Denton planned to come to Ohio and Garfield began to prepare for the debate. News reached Garfield that the scholarly English-man had easily won all his debates. Unlike Denton's other debating foes, Garfield did not study just to strengthen his own ideas; he prepared carefully by reading Denton's writings. He studied geology and anthropology in order to better understand the ideas of evolution. The coming debate created great interest in Ohio. How would the preacher do against the brilliant Englishman? Their debate took place in a large hall in Chagrin Falls, Ohio. One thousand people watched and listened for five days as the two men presented their arguments. When the debate ended, John Denton stated James Garfield was the strongest opponent he had met. The preacher immediately began a lecture tour through Ohio speaking on "Geology and Religion." He appeared before huge audiences and made them believe.

Garfield joined the army when the Civil War began. This gentle man of God felt a strong need to fight against slavery. He entered as a colonel of an Ohio regiment and his patriotic zeal impressed the men he commanded. Knowing little about soldiering, he began studying army training manuals. He read descriptions of the famous battles of Napoleon of France and England's Duke of Wellington. Colonel Garfield made a model battlefield and used wooden soldiers to teach his men tactics. This hard work led to victories against the Confederates and soon brought him a promotion to major general. In January of 1862, at the age of thirty-one, James A. Garfield became one of the youngest generals in the Union Army.

Military success, coupled with a fine reputation for debate, brought him to the attention of the Ohio Republican Party. The Republicans made General Garfield their candidate for the United States House of Representatives. Still an active officer on the battlefields of the Civil War, General Garfield beat all opponents and won the seat in Congress. He believed he could better serve his country in government and resigned from the army in December of 1863.

Garfield then began a memorable eighteen-year career as a congressman. His powerful speeches in the House soon elevated him in the eyes of his colleagues. He became a member of the Military Affairs, Appropriations, and Ways and Means Committees. Garfield was personally honest, but some of his congressional activities

THE EXPOSITION BUILDING, WHERE THE CONVENTION WAS HELD.

THE CROWDED HOTELS.
The gentleman from Michigan has the floor.

AN ALTERNATE'S ALTERNATIVE.
Brown pays for forty shaves, and gets luxuriant quarters in a barber's shop.

*This political cartoon shows the crowded conditions in Chicago
during the Republican National Convention of 1880.*

FARMER GARFIELD
Cutting a Swath to the White House.

could be questioned. He joined the Radical Republicans in opposing Abraham Lincoln's Reconstruction policies. Later he voted for Andrew Johnson's impeachment. He was one of the Republican politicians who worked in New Orleans to deliver Louisiana's electoral votes to Rutherford B. Hayes.

Congressman Garfield was visiting Wall Street in New York City when news of President Lincoln's assassination came by telegraph. Garfield's grief was great. Outside angry crowds assembled. Two men who spoke against Lincoln were attacked. One man was killed, the other beaten savagely. The crowd wanted to take revenge on a Democratic newspaper, *The New York World*, for its editorials against the

This is the famous "front porch" of Garfield's home in Mentor, Ohio. From it he gave many speeches during the presidential campaign of 1880.

President Garfield takes the oath of office from Chief Justice Waite, March 4, 1881.
His mother (at the far left) proudly looks on.

murdered president. Garfield could not bear this useless violence. He stepped out into the midst of the ugly mob. His words rang out over the noise: "Fellow citizens, God reigns, and the Government at Washington still lives!" he cried. His words quieted the mob and it quietly dissolved.

By 1880 Garfield was being mentioned as a presidential candidate. But the Ohio Republican did not think his nomination was possible. He went to the Republican national convention that year to work for John Sherman, a compromise candidate whom he hoped would bring the "Stalwarts" and "Half-Breeds" together. The Stalwarts wanted Ulysses S. Grant; the Half-Breeds wanted James G. Blaine. On the second day of the convention, the delegates startled everybody by coming out for the surprised James A. Garfield. This happened as he walked the convention floors working for John Sherman. Garfield was the only man in history to be present at his own presidential nomination. To quiet the Stalwarts, the Republicans made Chester A. Arthur of New York the vice presidential candidate.

The Republicans in 1880 invented a new way of campaigning called the "front porch" method. Great crowds were shipped by train from all parts of the country to Candidate Garfield's home in Mentor, Ohio. Every day he held discussions and made speeches to the crowds from the front porch of his house. These talks were filled with smooth words, practical ideas, and good sense. They won him many admirers. On

The Inauguration Ball honoring President Garfield.

one occasion, Garfield surprised a large crowd of German-Americans by welcoming them in German. Garfield's efforts to make the new Americans feel at home impressed voters all over the country.

During the course of the presidential campaign, Garfield's political enemies made a serious mistake. Some unscrupulous Democrats forged a letter in Garfield's handwriting which said he favored the unlimited importation of Chinese workers. This letter was made public in the hope that it would turn workingmen against the Republican presidential candidate. Instead, it won him sympathy when the truth was discovered. The letter had two spelling errors and Garfield's spelling was known to be perfect.

James A. Garfield won the election of 1880 and became the twentieth president on March 4, 1881. This man who loved poetry, literature, and all beautiful things soon learned the hard realities of the presidency. The president found it difficult to say "no" to the flood of office-seekers who descended on the White House. As the avalanche of job seekers increased, the president, at times, handed out jobs to the wrong people because he could not stand to see them disappointed.

But there came a time when he had to say "no." President Garfield began to stand his ground by refusing to go along with the request of New York Stalwarts for federal job appointments. During the political in-fighting that followed, Stalwart bosses Conkling and Platt

President James A. Garfield as photographed by Matthew Brady.

Lucretia Rudolph Garfield.

resigned their Senate seats. The country was pleased that another president stood against the spoils system.

One Stalwart, who had unsuccessfully tried for a diplomatic appointment, had the mad idea of revenging all the Stalwarts by shooting President Garfield. He waited with a gun in the Washington railway station. President Garfield was taking a trip to Massachusetts to a Williams College class reunion. As the genial Garfield walked through the station waiting room greeting people, the madman stepped up and fired two bullets into the president saying, "I am a Stalwart and now Arthur is president." He was immediately arrested and later hanged.

For seventy-nine days James A. Garfield clung to life. "The people must be tired of hearing my symptoms," the president said as he lay in bed. This was not so because Americans read every medical bulletin and every scrap of information they could get about the president. The Baltimore and Ohio Railroad issued daily bulletins on the president's progress.

While treating President Garfield, his doctors made a serious error. The bullet wound in the president's arm had healed, but they could not locate the other bullet which was somewhere in his back. Without the x-ray machine that assists doctors today, the medical men did not know the bullet was close to the surface and fairly harmless because a protective cyst was growing around it. The doctors wanted the bullet out. They poked and probed the president with unclean instruments increasing the infection in his system. Puzzled by the president's lack of progress, the doctors invited Alexander Graham Bell to try to find the illusive bullet with his new electronic listening device. Nothing worked. If President Garfield had been made to get up and walk around taking in sunshine and fresh air, his strong body might have recovered. Instead, the doctors' treatment only increased his infection and weakened his body. On September 19, 1881, the exhausted president died.

Saddened Americans mourned for the sunny preacher from Ohio. James A. Garfield was the second president in twenty years to be murdered while serving his country. Was there an ominous cloud of doom over the presidency? Why had such a terrible thing happened to this gentle man of God?

The assassination of President Garfield.

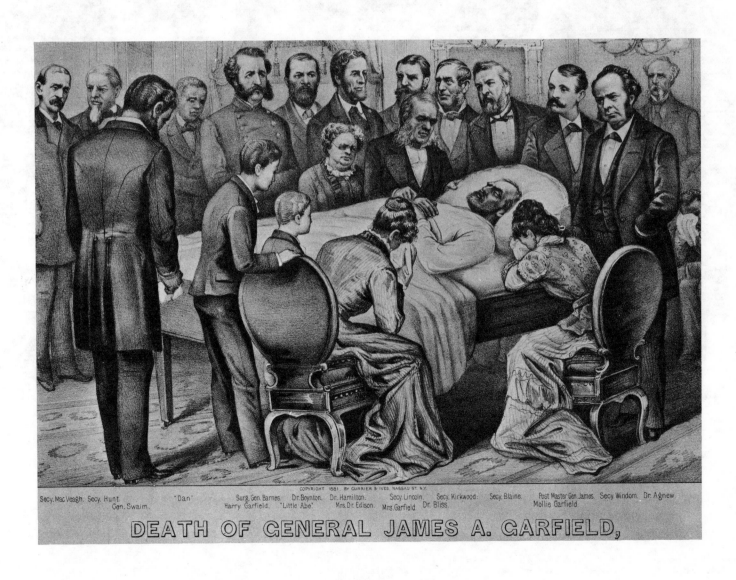

Secy. Mac Veagh. Secy. Hunt.   "Dan"   Surg. Gen. Barnes. Dr. Boynton. Dr. Hamilton.   Secy. Lincoln. Secy. Kirkwood.   Secy. Blaine.   Post Master Gen. James. Secy. Windom. Dr. Agnew.
          Gen. Swaim.   Harry Garfield. "Little Abe".   Mrs. Dr. Edison.   Mrs. Garfield.   Dr. Bliss.   Mollie Garfield

DEATH OF GENERAL JAMES A. GARFIELD,

CHESTER A. ARTHUR

Twenty-First President (1881-1885)

No man ever looked
more like a president.
During his years in the White House,
newspapermen and friends gave
him the nicknames "Prince Arthur,"
"The First Gentleman of the Land," and
"America's First Gentleman."
He rose from childhood in a simple Vermont
parsonage to membership in New York's
highest society where he knew such prominent
families as the Vanderbilts and the Astors.
But looking like a president was
not enough for America.
When he became president after James A. Garfield's
death, the people worried about his actions.
No one knew much about this man,
except for his close association with
the well-known "Stalwart," Roscoe Conkling.
Would he be a political president
or would he be president to all the people?
America anxiously waited and watched
as Chester A. Arthur was sworn in as
the twenty-first president.

HOUSE IN WHICH CHESTER A. ARTHUR WAS BORN, AT FAIRFIELD, IN 1830.

From a Photograph taken in 1880.

PRINCE ARTHUR, THE SPOILS SYSTEM FOIL

Chester was born the eldest son of William and Malvina Stone Arthur on October 5, 1830, in Fairfield, Vermont. Chester's family lived an unsettled existence because his father was a Baptist minister who moved from church to church. The Arthurs lived a quiet and religious life. Reverend Arthur insisted upon personally teaching Chester his lessons during the early years. At nine he allowed the boy to attend public school for the first time. He was a very bright student and at fifteen entered Union College in Schenectady, New York. While a student there, young Arthur helped pay his way by teaching school. Instruction in penmanship was his specialty.

After graduation from college, at the age of eighteen, with high academic honors, he moved back to Vermont to become the principal of an academy in North Pownal. He combined the study of law with his principal's duties. In 1853, he moved to New York City for a year of hard study in the law office of a family friend. The next year, Chester A. Arthur was admitted to the bar and immediately set up practice in the New York metropolis.

Although Arthur was handsome, well-mannered, and intelligent, he was for a time just another struggling young lawyer. Arthur's strong religious beliefs made him a firm anti-

President Arthur took the oath of office in his private residence September 20, 1881.

slavery man. His name first came to public attention with the famous "Lemmon slave case." During this trial Arthur acted as a special counsel for New York state. He won a decision from the courts which declared that slaves traveling in New York were to be treated as free men.

The public noticed him again when he represented a Negro woman who had been removed from a streetcar in Brooklyn because of her race. Attorney Arthur won five hundred dollars damages for his client, and the decision made it clear that all Negroes using public transportation in New York City must be treated fairly.

Outside the courtroom, Manhattan society took to Arthur and he to it. He was a fine-looking man, tall, with dark hair and brown eyes.

Ellen Herndon Arthur died twenty months before her husband ascended to the presidency. President Arthur's two children, Chester, Jr. and Ellen, lived with him in the Executive Mansion.

225

President Arthur at his desk in the White House.

Spoilsmen waiting to see President Arthur were often angered when he refused them jobs.

The Victorian decor of a White House dining room after the redecoration authorized by President Arthur.

With his distinguished-looking side whiskers and full mustache he was handsome enough to be taken for an actor on the New York stage. In 1859 he married Ellen Lewis Herndon of Virginia. This marriage made Arthur's social position even stronger because Miss Herndon was the daughter of Navy Captain William Herndon, the well-known explorer of South America's Amazon Basin.

Arthur married Ellen for love, not social position. In their happy twenty-one years together, they brought up two sons and a daughter. However, their marriage was cut short by the early death of Mrs. Arthur. Arthur grieved so deeply over the loss of his Ellen that after the funeral he would not allow anyone to touch the things in her room. Even the needle she had placed in her unfinished sewing remained unmoved.

While occupied with his law career, he became a member of the peacetime New York militia. This was supposed to be an honorary position, but when the Civil War started, he spent all his time as assistant quartermaster general of New York. This position put Arthur in charge of feeding, housing, and equipping the thousands of New York soldiers headed for the battlefields. The businessman-soldier worked at his duties far away from gunfire. General Arthur was known for his honesty and efficiency in handling a most difficult and trying task.

When the war ended, Chester A. Arthur turned his attention to politics. He knew that his reputation as an anti-slavery lawyer, an efficient army general, and as a member of New York society would help establish him in the Republican Party. His better instincts flinched at some of the methods used by machine politicians of the time, but he felt he must try his hand at this highly important and exciting activity. The up-and-coming Manhattan attorney did not take much time to become well-known in the fast-rising Republican Party. He was a delegate to the New York Republican's first convention and became an important person backstage in political activity there.

New York political boss, Senator Roscoe Conkling, soon became interested in the handsome, young lawyer. This association with "Stalwart" Conkling both advanced and darkened Arthur's public life. Conkling believed in the spoils system of politics. This meant that men who worked for the party and paid their party dues should get the government jobs handed out by elected party officials. These handouts reached their peak in 1869 when Ulysses S. Grant, who was a close associate of Senator Conkling, became president. Grant paid off the Stalwart's support by giving out a great number of government jobs.

Chester A. Arthur knew about the evils of the spoils system, yet he remained with the New York Republicans. He loved the political game too much to quit. He concentrated on doing his work honestly and enjoyed his role as a quiet, behind-the-scenes organizer of party affairs. By 1871 there were so many "spoilsmen" in federal jobs that public outcries against corruption and scandal in the Grant administration became strong. Grant needed a man with a good reputation to take over one of the worst dens of corruption, the New York Custom House. Chester A. Arthur was his man. Reluctantly, he took his first public office as collector of customs for the Port of New York.

Chester A. Arthur was now in charge of over one thousand men. His supervision of this small army was better than most of his predecessors. He tried to carry out reform measures suggested by lawmakers and certainly took no part in corrupt activities. Nevertheless, the Custom House was so overstaffed with spoilsmen who did little to earn their wages, and much to illegally increase the size of their wallets, that President Rutherford B. Hayes had to take action. Arthur was caught in the middle of the battle between Hayes and the Stalwarts. Although he had no part in the spoils system graft, he had become a victim of guilt by association. His public image was badly damaged when President Hayes forced him to resign from his post at the Custom House.

This unpleasant episode was the total of Arthur's public political career until political plotting at the 1880 Republican national convention placed him in public view again. Conkling and the Stalwarts fought hard against the compromise candidate, James A. Garfield, but he won the presidential nomination. To smooth ruffled Stalwart feathers and to keep the party together, Chester A. Arthur was suggested as Garfield's vice presidential running mate. Roscoe Conkling did not want this "deal." He raged against it and ordered Arthur to refuse. Arthur

then showed great strength of character. He said "no" to Conkling and the other Stalwarts. A simple, patriotic New England heart had always beat deep within this sophisticated man. Arthur was deeply moved by the vice-presidential nomination. He told Conkling, "The offer of Vice President is the greatest honor that I ever dreamed of attaining." This Republican backstage worker made his political debut at a very high level. This first time his name appeared for public office was as a candidate for the nation's second highest office.

Seven months after his inauguration, James A. Garfield breathed his last as the result of wounds received from the hand of an assassin. The little bit that Americans knew of the vice president was cloudy and unclear. Arthur, so far as the country knew, was a machine politician. The country was filled with anxiety over its new president.

President Arthur's appearance reassured the public slightly. He looked like a president. No chief executive since George Washington had dressed in such elegant clothing. A Washington observer described President Arthur's dress this way: "The Gentleman Boss usually (wore) a Prince Albert coat... with a flower in one upper button hole and the corner of a silk handkerchief visible from a side pocket." His manners added to his personal appeal. To everyone, President Arthur was as charming and courteous as a European prince.

This sophisticated man from Manhattan liked rich living. Upon first examining the White House, the new president was shocked at the state of its furnishings. He hired twenty-four wagons to cart away the dilapidated furniture. He refurnished the Executive Mansion in an elegant Victorian style. He refused to move into the White House until the redecoration was completed. Then he brought with him a French chef and a valet. His sister, Mrs. John McElroy, was the White House hostess for her widower brother.

The great responsibility of the president's position brings out the best in a man. Chester A. Arthur, inspired by the challenge of his office, soon began to act like a president. The spoils system caused him trouble as it had many former chief executives. One day, early in his presidential term, an observer noting President Arthur's troubled expression asked if he had been given the news of some great disaster. "No," the president sighed, "It is not (a) war that is bothering me, it is the appointment of a postmaster for Brownstown, Indiana."

Something had to be done about the spoils system which had been blocking the national government's path of progress for years. It had been the death of one president, James K. Polk, and harmed the health of many others. It left a trail of corruption and fraud that greatly troubled most of the voting public. The situation was described in a book by a young Princeton professor, Woodrow Wilson, in 1885. Just before an assassin's bullet struck him down, President Garfield had said, "I'm going to find out whether I am merely a recording clerk for the Senate or chief executive of the United States." He never found out, but Chester A. Arthur took up the fight against the spoils system.

To weaken the spoils system and create a more sound federal government, he had to put his neck into a political noose. There were many spoilsmen in government offices and all of them would fight to destroy any man who threatened them. But President Arthur could no longer put up with the evils he saw in this system of politics. He joined congressional leaders in supporting the Pendleton Bill of 1883. The bill passed and led to the establishment of a Civil Service Commission. A new policy for placing people in federal jobs was now the law. Now competitive examinations were given and those who passed qualified for government employment. The public and legislators who fought for the establishment of the Civil Service Commission praised President Arthur for his strong support. His political party did not. To make matters worse between himself and the Stalwarts, he vetoed a graft-ridden river and harbor bill. Then he prosecuted spoilsmen who were cheating the United States Post Office.

Chester A. Arthur joined many presidents in finding the duties of his office exhausting. When his presidential schedule allowed, he took time off for outdoor vacations. He was an expert fisherman and enjoyed quiet, out-of-the-way spots where he could cast his line into a bubbling brook. The most famous of his vacations was in the summer of 1883. With personal friends, high-ranking army officers, seventy-five cavalry troopers, Indian guides, and one hundred seventy-

A U.S. Cavalryman painted by the famous American painter Frederic Remington (1861-1909). Remington specialized in scenes of the American west. His popularity began after his return from the west to New York in 1884. He once said, "I paint for boys... boys from 10 to 70."

five pack horses, President Arthur toured Yellowstone National Park. He fished, watched Indian ceremonies, and was given a pinto pony by a Shoshoni chief for his daughter. He was delighted when a Wyoming mountain peak was named in his honor.

When the Civil Service Commission was established, President Arthur knew his political life was over. The voters never had a chance to show their appreciation for his good work. The Stalwarts had only hard thoughts for the man who had worked against them. They used their influence in the 1884 Republican convention to nominate James G. Blaine. But President Arthur was not forgotten by the American public. Mark Twain nicely summed up his presidency with the statement, "I am but one... still in the opinion of this one... it would be hard to better President Arthur's Administration."

*Handsome President Arthur tips his hat to lady vacationers
on a trip to Newport, Rhode Island, in 1884.*

President Arthur's love for the outdoors was always great.

GROVER CLEVELAND

Twenty-Second President (1885-1889)
Twenty-Fourth President (1893-1897)

In his lifetime he was
called "The Buffalo Hangman"
and "Grover the Good."
Strangely enough, both titles
pay tribute to the hard work and honesty
of this man while he was in public office.
He was a Democrat surrounded by a
sea of Republican presidents,
and an untarnished office holder
embedded in a swamp of spoils system politicians.
To the public, Grover Cleveland proved that
honesty certainly is the best policy.
The greatest tribute to his straightforward
approach to public office was
his election as our twenty-second
and twenty-fourth president.
He was the only man in our history
to run for reelection
as president, to be defeated, and then to
run again successfully.

A Democratic campaign banner for the election of 1884.

THE RETURN OF GROVER THE GOOD

He was born Stephen Grover Cleveland on March 18, 1837, in Caldwell, New Jersey, the fifth child of Richard and Ann Neal Cleveland. Young Grover chose to drop his first name. His father was a Presbyterian minister and from him the Cleveland children gained their firmness and integrity. The children were active in the family worship held each evening. When quite young, Grover greatly pleased his father by memorizing *The Pilgrims Progress*, a book of religious teachings and good advice.

When Reverend Cleveland received a position with the American Home Mission Society, the family moved to New York. In Clinton, New York, Grover and his brothers and sisters attended the town academy. He was a fine stu-dent and hoped to enter Hamilton College, but his father's death in 1853 made this impossible. Grover's plans for a higher education had to be abandoned so he could help support his mother and his younger brothers and sisters.

Cleveland's father taught him that life can sometimes be hard, but a man must hold his head up and carry out God's will. Grover prac-ticed this lesson by never complaining about the sacrifice he had to make for his struggling fam-ily. He worked first as a clerk in a village store for wages of fifty dollars a year. Then he was a teacher in a school for the blind in New York City. At the end of that year, seventeen year old Grover returned briefly to his home in Hol-land Patent. Restless, he borrowed twenty-five

The wedding of Grover Cleveland and Frances Folsom, June 2, 1886, in the Blue Room of the White House.

dollars from an elder of the Presbyterian Church and with a friend started west.

Grover got as far as Buffalo where an uncle helped him land a job as a law clerk. He first worked for no salary, then was paid four dollars a week. The slim salary was unimportant to the energetic young man. Now he had the opportunity he had always wanted. He could send money home to his family and, at the same time, study law. Grover continued to work at his clerking duties during the day and studied law at night. Sometimes he stayed up through the night poring over his law books. This hard work paid off. He was admitted to the New York bar in 1859 at the age of twenty-two.

Cleveland's habit of working hard continued when he started his law practice in Buffalo. He became known as a lawyer who could always be

The youngest First Lady in history, twenty-one year old Frances Folsom Cleveland.

233

John Philip Sousa (1854-1932) was America's most famous bandmaster and composer of march music. Sousa's marches are believed to be among the best of their kind.

trusted to do a good job for his clients. Slowly he managed to earn a comfortable income. As a young bachelor he found time for fun as well as for work. During these years another aspect of his personality appeared. The public knew Grover Cleveland as a strong and dignified citizen, a lawyer who got things done honestly and well. Privately, with his bachelor friends, he had to unwind from all the work and sacrifices of his early years. Like many young bachelors, Cleveland could often be found with cronies out at night drinking beer, smoking cigars, and singing happily. Schenkelburger's German Restaurant in Buffalo was a place he often visited. He especially liked sausage and other rich German foods, and loved to drink down the thick-foamed German beer. This rich food put a great deal of weight upon his powerful frame. A favorite evening pastime was playing cards with friends after dinner.

Cleveland's friends had no idea that this fun-loving man had serious political ambitions. Grover seldom became angry, but when he had a fist fight with Mike Falvey over Democratic politics in Buffalo, then those who knew him decided he was serious. Cleveland had long held a desire for public service. But his way of getting into politics was strange for the times.

The 1860's were years so full of corrupt political activity that the people's only defense became bitter jokes and indifference. Many politicians sold their votes to the highest bidder. Private individuals and large companies bought these votes to help themselves. To these politicians the country came second. One joke of the time said that the Standard Oil Company had done everything with the government except refine it.

Cleveland was determined to never owe favors to any man, to any political machine, or to any company when he took office. He would be an independent, honest public servant whom people could look up to. Some politicians at that time thought only men who had never held public office could be idealists. Grover Cleveland proved them wrong. He held fast to his beliefs all through his long career in public service.

His first public office was in 1863 when he became an assistant district attorney for Erie County, New York. At the age of thirty-four he was elected sheriff of that county. Some people laughed at the thought of a minister's son taking on the tough duties of a sheriff. They didn't laugh for long because Cleveland proved to be an excellent lawman. He showed his integrity in this office by refusing to pass disagreeable jobs on to the men who worked under him. His heart was torn when he had to attend hangings of convicted murderers, but he would not order any of his men to take this dreadful aspect of a policeman's job. These years as assistant district attorney and county sheriff were valuable ones for Cleveland. They taught him much about crime and corruption. They strengthened his ideas on the way a government should be run.

In the search for an honest mayoral candidate in 1881, a reform group in Buffalo thought Sheriff Cleveland might be their man. They asked him to try for city hall. He agreed and campaigned true to his ideals, without making deals, without spending a penny for votes, and without owing favors. He easily won and within a year had become famous throughout New York state as Buffalo's "veto mayor," a man who stood firm against corruption. Mayor Cleveland saved his city a million dollars by vetoing a dishonest sewage and street cleaning contract. Before long, the Buffalo newspapers began talking of their fighting mayor as a candidate for governor.

This idea interested Cleveland, but again he would make no deals. His fine record in office brought him Democratic support. Without making a speech, he allowed his honest record in office to campaign for him. He won the Democratic nomination and then the election. Grover Cleveland became New York's governor by the greatest number of votes in the state's political history. He wrote to his brother after the election: "I am honest and sincere in my desire to do well but the question is whether I know enough to accomplish what I desire."

Governor Cleveland's firmness and common sense helped him do his job well. His fame began to spread throughout the land. Two successful years in the governor's chair made him a delightful dish to ravenous Democrats who had been out of the White House since James Buchanan was president. At the Chicago Democratic convention in 1884, Cleveland was supported by delegates in large blocs. They were inspired by the stand he took against Tammany Hall, New York City's all powerful political machine. One supporter of Grover Cleveland at this convention shouted, "We love him for the enemies he has made!"

He won the Democratic nomination and started campaigning. There was some dreadful mudslinging between the Democrats and Republicans that election year. The Republican presidential candidate, James G. Blaine, was accused of illegal dealings in railroad stocks. The Democrats serenaded him savagely with this song:

"Blaine, Blaine, James G. Blaine,
the continental liar
from the state of Maine."

The Republicans returned the favor with songs and mudslinging of their own, crying out against Grover Cleveland for an unsavory incident in his early private life.

The American public watched the black words fly, then voted narrowly in favor of Grover

In May of 1885 Geronimo and his Apache Indians went on the warpath in Arizona and New Mexico.

Children of the 1880's singing "The Star Spangled Banner."

Cleveland. The election was close, but Cleveland emerged the victor because his past record showed he was independent of political pressure and political machines.

No man ever skyrocketed into the public attention more quickly than Grover Cleveland. At forty-five, he was the mayor of a middle-sized American city. At forty-eight, he held the highest office in the land as the twenty-second president.

The Democrats went out of power with bachelor Buchanan and came back to power with bachelor Cleveland. The new president was fairly young, not elderly like James Buchanan, and matchmakers in Washington began at once to select a First Lady for him. Tongues wagged in high gear about Mrs. Emma Folsom, the pretty widowed mother of his former law partner in Buffalo. Mrs. Folsom and her daughter Frances were White House guests of President Cleveland and his sister Rose during the early months of his administration. Washington gossips never guessed it was the daughter who interested the president, not the mother.

Twenty-one year old Frances Folsom had graduated from Wells College and was traveling in Europe when she announced her engagement to President Cleveland. When she returned home her picture appeared in all the newspapers. Her name was on every tongue. When she appeared in public, crowds gathered and bands serenaded her with love songs. The marriage of a bachelor president to a lovely, young woman was a national event.

The wedding, held in the Blue Room of the White House, was celebrated in the public imagination, but not in the public presence. It was a simple ceremony with only President Cleveland's Cabinet and a few close friends and relatives in attendance. Society reporters were excited by the fifteen foot train on the bride's wedding gown. The Wedding March was played by John Philip Sousa. After the ceremony the bride and groom left by a back door of the White House for their honeymoon retreat in the mountains of Maryland. But it is difficult to have privacy when one is President of the United States. Industrious members of the press soon located them.

Unfriendly reporters continued to hound Cleveland throughout his presidential terms by writing about private matters not connected with his duties as president. He longed to keep his family life private, but could not. The president was unjustly accused of being an unkind husband and father. He never replied to these false charges, but he did show his displeasure by continuing battles with the press.

The twenty-seven year difference in their ages did not matter to the Clevelands. Theirs was a marriage of love and devotion. Our history's youngest First Lady brightened capital society and her husband's life. During difficult times for the president, she was able to put a smile upon his face, make him relax, and calm his worries. At official functions, Frances Cleveland was a beautiful and sunny hostess. In a warm and friendly manner, she would greet hundreds of guests while her proud husband stood by quietly.

President Cleveland knew the mudslinging campaign he had been through had nothing to do with the issues at hand. He knew exactly what he wanted to do the day he stepped into office. Honesty and honor were his key words. From the nation's railroads, he recovered thousands of acres of land that had been taken illegally, and he opened it for homesteading. He changed a government ruling and gave reservation land back to peaceful Indian tribes. Not all Indian tribes, however, had smoked the peace pipe. President Cleveland was forced to send federal troops to fight Chief Geronimo's Apaches in Arizona, and the Utes in Colorado.

He would not allow the Democratic political bosses to dictate orders to him. President Cleveland refused to hand out government jobs to gain votes or to get laws passed by Congress. He would not make appointments to undeserving Democratic supporters. This firmness cost him the presidential election of 1888. Republican Benjamin Harrison won because of the support he received from Democratic Tammany Hall bosses who were angered because they could not control Grover Cleveland. Democratic disloyalty troubled him deeply, but Mrs. Cleveland did not seem too worried by her husband's defeat. The young First Lady had such faith in her husband's future that she told the White House staff shortly before their departure, "I want to see everything just as it is now when we come back."

After four years of private life, the Clevelands did come back to Washington as residents of the Executive Mansion. Grover Cleveland ran against Benjamin Harrison again in 1892. This time he won. In this manner he became the twenty-second and the twenty-fourth President of the United States. The returning president began his second administration under a gloomy cloud, the financial panic of 1893. That year the Philadelphia and Reading Railroad went bankrupt and five hundred banks failed. Over two million workers lost their jobs. Many could not pay their bills. Many lost their homes. Some went hungry.

President Cleveland knew firm action must be taken at once to help the country recover from these troubles. He felt the Sherman Silver Purchase Act must be repealed. Confidence in the American dollar had to be restored and the economy stabilized. The nation had to remain on the gold standard. With this proposal, shouts went up from silver speculators throughout the country. But he went ahead and called a special session of Congress to repeal the Sherman Act.

During these troubled times, the president revealed his strong character to close associates. While preparing his case for the repeal of the Sherman Act, he noticed a sore spot on the roof of his mouth and asked his doctors to look at it.

This political cartoon shows President Cleveland faced with the gold and silver standard problem during his second administration.

The doctors took one look and told him it was cancer. The president was worried about the effect news of his illness might have upon the troubled country. He wanted absolute secrecy.

The public never knew of Grover Cleveland's battle for life against cancer. Surgeons removed the growth from his mouth in complete secrecy aboard a private yacht in the middle of Long Island Sound. To cut out the cancer, the surgeons had to remove Grover Cleveland's upper left jaw. For the rest of his life he wore an artificial jaw made of vulcanized rubber. The cancer was cured but took its toll upon the hardworking president. After the operation he never regained his full strength or his ability to work the long hours he had previously worked.

When he stepped off the yacht after surgery, he was healthy enough to vigorously renew his battle against silver. After two months of debate and filibustering, Congress suggested a compromise to the president. President Cleveland became furious, banged his fist on the desk, and refused to give in. This strong refusal gave new

Ex-president Cleveland in 1900 on the porch of his home in Princeton, New Jersey.

ident seemed to be an enemy of labor when he sent federal troops to Washington to stop the unemployed marchers in "Coxey's Army." He also sent troops against the striking Pullman Car workers in Chicago. Cleveland made enemies outside the labor movement, too. He was rude to newspapermen because they intruded on his private life. He deeply offended Union Army veterans by placing two former "Rebels" on his Cabinet. Because of these errors and his firm refusal to deal out federal jobs, the Democrats turned away from him in 1896. They gave their nomination to William Jennings Bryan.

Grover Cleveland retired from office in 1897 and took his wife and children to a quiet life in Princeton, New Jersey. The Clevelands were immediately welcomed by a community delighted to have the honest, ex-president living there. In 1901 he was elected to the board of trustees of Princeton University. He became a very close friend of the University's president, Woodrow Wilson, and was in great demand there as a lecturer. He died June 24, 1908, a respected member of the college community and the nation as a whole.

Grover Cleveland once said of the presidential office he held, "What is there in this office that any man should ever want to get into it!" These words were probably spoken after a bad day in the executive office. These days are encountered by all presidents. The words he spoke which came closest to his true feelings were the last he uttered on earth, "I have tried so hard to do right."

vigor to his followers in Congress and, with a new wave of activity in October 1893, they were able to repeal the Sherman Silver Act. This stand taken by Grover Cleveland reestablished faith in the American dollar and the gold reserve that backed it.

President Cleveland's firm stands were not always on the winning side of the coin. He made mistakes in handling labor problems. Sympathetic to the working man, he did not really understand their problems and needs. The pres-

President Cleveland and friends relax in camp on the Santee River in South Carolina.   They were on a duck hunting trip.

"Thrift and carefulness of expenditure among the people tend to secure a thrifty government."

GROVER CLEVELAND

Grover Cleveland. Born 1837. Died 1908. Twice elected President of the United States, and the only one to serve two terms not in succession. Went to school until sixteen, when it became necessary for him to support his mother and sisters. Studied law in Buffalo; admitted to the bar and soon entered political life. Was assistant district attorney; sheriff; mayor of Buffalo; governor of New York; elected President first in 1884; again in 1892. He was calm and deliberate, independent and thorough, unswayed by public clamor. Careful and painstaking, his administrations were characterized by efficiency and economy; he extended the Civil Service merit system and used his veto power without fear or favor. He at no time sought public office, but in his life filled many great positions with credit to himself and benefit to his country.

A printed tribute to Grover Cleveland, our twenty-second and twenty-fourth president.

BENJAMIN HARRISON

Twenty-Third President (1889-1893)

Considering length of service
to the country, his family
is the most distinguished in
American history.
He was named for his great-grandfather,
one of the signers of the
Declaration of Independence.
His father was a two-term member
of the United States House
of Representatives from Ohio.
His grandson has served in the same position
several times since 1951, as a
congressman from the state of Wyoming.
The "hat" his grandfather passed
on to him was the presidency.
Benjamin Harrison proudly wore the "hat"
of his grandfather, William Henry Harrison,
when he became the twenty-third
president in 1889.

INAUGURATION OF PRESIDENT HARRISON,
MARCH 4th, 1889.

Benjamin Harrison posed for this photograph in college.

HE WORE "HIS GRANDFATHER'S HAT"

Benjamin was born August 20, 1833, into the family of John and Elizabeth Irwin Harrison. The Harrison household was a plain one with no frills. The children grew up on their grandfather's farm at North Bend, Ohio. Benjamin began to help his father around the farm at an early age. When he was eight, he had extra duty helping his father with farmyard chores because his grandfather, William Henry Harrison, was away campaigning to become our ninth president. When Benjamin was older, he helped with the more strenuous tasks of plowing and wood-chopping. He was a fine athlete and particularly enjoyed swimming in the Ohio River, which ran by the Harrison farm.

Education was important in the Harrison household. John Harrison made sure his children attended the local schools, even when money was scarce. When he could, he hired private tutors for his children. Benjamin was always a good student and, at sixteen, entered Farmers' College in Cincinnati, Ohio. Three years later he transferred to Miami University of Ohio. He particularly enjoyed classes in political science and history, and developed a talent for public speaking. He graduated with a fine record in 1852. While in college, he met Caroline Scott. She admired his beard, a rare thing for a young man to have in those times, and he

admired her intelligence and attractive appearance. One year after Benjamin's graduation, they were married in Oxford, Ohio. When he married Caroline, he was studying law with a Cincinnati firm. He was admitted to the Ohio bar in 1853, at the age of twenty.

Harrison moved his wife and infant son, Russell, to Indianapolis, Indiana, in 1854. It was a growing city and a good place to settle down and establish a law practice. The first two years were difficult for the young lawyer and his family. There were not many clients. Money was very scarce. Harrison said of his early days in Indianapolis, "A five-dollar bill was an event." Just as he had with his studies, Harrison kept at his law practice and slowly began to build a name for himself in the community. In 1855 he formed a law partnership with William Wallace.

Wallace devoted most of his time to politics, Harrison concentrated on the clients. He had a fine memory and the ability to quickly analyze many facts and figures. These were excellent tools for a lawyer. In court he could sway the judge and the jury with his powerful speeches. He became known to the people of Indianapolis as an able and honest lawyer.

Harrison had a cool and controlled personality. Because of this he did not make many close friends. An Indianapolis neighbor, Dr.

John Kitchen, said of Benjamin Harrison, "He made a success of everything he undertook . . . I do not think he ever had an acquaintance with anyone that ripened into the hottest kind of friendship." Harrison was respected by most people he met. But they could not warm up to him. Small and stocky, Harrison made a poor impression when he appeared in public wearing gloves to protect himself from other people's germs. This seemed downright unfriendly. When he ran for governor of Indiana, political enemies criticized him for this cold behavior by calling him "Kid Glove Harrison."

The private personality of Benjamin Harrison was quite different. At home he was an affectionate husband and kind father to his son and daughter. All of the Harrisons were religious and attended the Presbyterian Church regularly.

President Benjamin Harrison presided over the banquet in honor of our nation's one hundredth anniversary, April 29, 1889. The banquet was an elegant affair and went on for hours. This menu from the banquet is printed in French.

CENTENNIAL CELEBRATION
OF THE INAUGURATION OF
GEORGE WASHINGTON.
BALL
HELD AT THE METROPOLITAN OPERA HOUSE, APRIL 29TH
1889.

BUFFET

Chaud
Consommé en tasse   Huîtres à la poulette
Bouchées à la reine   Timbales vénitiennes   Croquettes de volaille
Terrapin, Maryland   Filets de boeuf aux champignons
Chapons rôtis aux marrons

Froid
Saumon du Canada au beurre Montpelier
Bass rayée à la Borgia   Truites saumonées à la Bayadère
Filets de boeuf à la russe   Aspics de foie-gras en Belle-vue
Pâtés à la Washington   Jambons historiques
Tartines de foie-gras
Buissons de truffes du Périgord   Langues de boeuf à l'ecarlate
Noix de veau à la ravigote   Galantines de chapon aux truffes
Chaud-froid d'ortolans   Bécassines et pluviers à la gelée
Agneaux du printemps rôtis entiers
Sandwiches de foie-gras   Salade de volaille   Salade d'homard

Sucres
Pièces montées en patisserie
Gelée aux fruits   Gelée Orientale   Charlotte russe   Charlotte Doria
Gaufres à la Chantilly   Biscuits des Princes
Diplomates à la crème, Chantilly
Brioches en moules   Savarins en moules
Quartiers d'oranges glacés au caramel
Nougat parisien   Napolitaines   Châteaubriands   Meringues suisses
Fantaisies   Sultanes   Cornes d'abondance   Petits gâteaux
Petits fours   Mottoes   Bonbons

Glaces
Vanille   Pistache   Framboise   Ananas

Café
Corbeilles de fruits   Pièces montées

MOËT & CHANDON WHITE SEAL   MOËT & CHANDON BRUT
MUMM'S EXTRA   GIESLER GREEN SEAL
JULES MUMM'S GRAND SEC   APOLLINARIS
HOFFMAN HOUSE.

He was an elder in the church and once taught a men's Bible class.

Back in Ohio his father was elected to Congress in 1852. Although he worked hard to be a successful congressman, John Harrison did not like professional politicians and the games they played. After two terms in Congress, he returned to farming life at North Bend. He warned his son Benjamin to stay away from politics and its many chances to do wrong. Benjamin was strongly attracted to the Harrison family tradition of public service. He respected his father's advice but had to try his hand at politics. It worried his father when he joined the Republican Party in Indiana and, in 1857, successfully ran for public office in Indianapolis.

The Civil War changed Benjamin Harrison's political plans. In July of 1862, he was made a colonel of the 70th Indiana Volunteers, an infantry regiment. Colonel Harrison and his men were sent to Kentucky to guard the Louisville and Nashville Railroad. Like his grandfather, the "Hero of Tippecanoe," the new colonel became a successful soldier. He soon learned that his troops were raw and inexperienced. To save their lives and help them do their duty Colonel Harrison drilled and disciplined his men until they were ready for war. As an officer, he was responsible and efficient, but also cold and short-tempered. His men obeyed his orders but did not like him. After taking part in minor battles in Kentucky and Tennessee, the 70th Volunteers were attached to General William T. Sherman's army. The Indiana regiment did a lot of hard fighting in Georgia, and Harrison was promoted to the rank of brigadier general. Senior officers liked his "ability . . . energy and gallantry in command of a brigade."

He served in the army until the Civil War ended and then returned home to continue his law practice and his career in politics. By working diligently for the Indiana Republican Party, he began to make a name for himself with the party leaders. In 1876 Harrison's reputation as a successful lawyer and loyal party worker helped him win the Republican nomination for governor of Indiana. He lost a hard-fought campaign to his Democratic opponent. However, the loss of this election did not stop him. In 1880 he was chairman of the Indiana delegation to the Republican National Convention. There he helped nominate James A. Garfield as the presidential candidate.

That same year, Indiana voters elected the vigorous little politician to a six-year term in the United States Senate. Senator Harrison continued his work as a loyal Republican during his time in Washington. But occasionally he detoured from party policy to serve the interest of the people. He had great sympathy for the problems of Indians and poor homesteaders in their land disputes with the railroads. Harrison wanted laws to protect them from unscrupulous railroads.

When Grover Cleveland became president in 1884 the Democrats came into power in Indiana. After they gained control of the state legislature, they changed legislative districts to favor their candidates. When Republican Senator Harrison came up for reelection in 1886, this gerrymandering cost him his seat in the Senate. He left active political work, but not for long.

Early in 1888, James G. Blaine announced he would not seek the Republican nomination for president. Many party members decided to support "Hoosier" Harrison. He did not seem interested in promoting his own candidacy and supporters began to worry. Somehow they succeeded in convincing the hard-headed little man to promote himself at a Washington's Birthday celebration in Detroit. This proved a wise move. Harrison's powers of oratory were well displayed and a phrase from his Detroit speech, "rejuvenated Republicanism" was taken up by the nation's newspapers. At the 1888 Chicago convention, Benjamin Harrison became the Republican torchbearer. His cause was aided when James G. Blaine, on vacation in Scotland, wired his support for "Old Tip's" grandson.

The Republicans tried to turn grandson Harrison into a "Young Tippecanoe." Campaign offices were built to resemble log cabins in hopes of reminding voters of the zesty "log cabin and hard cider" campaign of 1840. This was not successful. Harrison could not capture the voters' fancy as his grandfather had. His cold public personality simply was not one for songs, cider, and ballyhoo. He did not gain the majority of the popular vote either, coming in 100,000 votes behind Grover Cleveland. But Benjamin slipped into the president's chair with a narrow win in the electoral college.

President Harrison told Republican boss, Senator Matt Quay of Pennsylvania, that his election was "providence." This was not so.

Hard work and sharp dealing by the Republicans won him the election. During the campaign large groups of voters were shipped to Harrison's home state by Pennsylvania Railroad freight trains. Government jobs were promised to Tammany Hall bosses in New York. Some manufacturers went so far as to threaten workers with the loss of their jobs if Harrison was not elected!

Although Benjamin Harrison did not know about this kind of campaigning, his presidency was held back by the "deals" made by his supporters. He hoped to make federal job appointments on the basis of ability, not politics. "When I came into power, I found that the party managers . . . had sold out every place to pay the election expenses," he later lamented. The efforts he made to improve the Civil Service were only successful in making Matt Quay and other Republican bosses angry.

Harrison's colorless personality haunted his campaign managers and held him back while he was the chief executive. Newspaper cartoons portrayed him as a colorless little man whose head was completely buried in an enormous hat. The words underneath usually suggested that he was too small a man to fill his grandfather's hat. All through life, Benjamin Harrison found it easy to convince large audiences with his gift for public speaking. Alone he found it difficult to sway one man in his favor.

President Harrison did not try very hard to influence the men under the Capitol dome. He preferred to let Congress run itself while he sat in the White House going about his presidential business in an aloof and cold manner. Working in the president's executive office, he at times showed a lack of consideration for others. He rarely offered a chair to his visitors and often sat tapping his fingers on his desk, waiting impatiently for them to go. Those close to the president warned guests not to be hurt by his manner, explaining, "It is only his way." This warning did not help. President Harrison often offended his guests with his impolite actions. Some fellow Republicans found it hard to like President Harrison and said so openly. Theodore Roosevelt referred to him as "the little gray man."

Harrison was fortunate to be president at a time when United States expansion and the economy were booming. Population had been on the increase in the northwestern territories

Benjamin Harrison as photographed by Joseph Kitchell in 1897.

for some time. In 1889 and 1890, North Dakota, South Dakota, Montana, Washington, Idaho, and Wyoming were added to the Union. Big business, was growing by leaps and bounds and government business grew along with it. Congress passed its first billion-dollar budget in 1891.

As America was growing and prospering, the president sat on the sidelines applauding, not leading. President Harrison seemed willing to let Republican politicians run his Cabinet and the Congress. This lack of leadership frustrated lawmakers who knew the need for great changes, especially in settling the problems of the workingman and the farmer. America was rapidly changing from a small-town farming country to a big-city manufacturing society.

Points were scored in President Harrison's favor in the field of foreign affairs. With the help of his Secretary of State, James G. Blaine, he improved relations with South American countries. The president felt relations with our Western Hemisphere neighbors had been neglected too long. Largely due to his efforts, a

Caroline Scott Harrison was an active First Lady. She was the first President General of the National Society of the Daughters of the American Revolution. She died during the third year of her husband's presidency.

245

In this uncomplimentary political cartoon President Benjamin Harrison is shown wearing "his grandfather's hat" and having a tantrum over problems of taxation and the tariff. Uncle Sam doesn't know what to do with him.

Pan American Conference was held in October of 1889. Later it became the Pan American Union. Its purpose was to develop understanding and economic growth between the United States and the countries of South America. In 1891, Harrison showed surprising spunk in dealing quickly with Chile in a dispute over the death of two American sailors.

Inside the White House during the twenty-third presidential administration there were many changes. Electricity was installed throughout, but the Harrison family was a bit cautious about using it. Afraid of getting a shock from the light switches, they would often leave lights in the White House burning late into the night. Members of the staff usually came along to turn them off.

The president insisted upon an orderly schedule in the Executive Mansion. His enemies said it was a boring schedule that matched the man who established it. Breakfast was always

at eight, followed by family prayers. Lunch was served promptly at one. In the evening, dinner and bedtime came early. These activities rarely changed. Occasionally the schedule would vary when the president was away. For relaxation the stout little man enjoyed short hunting trips. He liked duck hunting and made an amusing sight wading through the water carrying a gun that seemed almost as long as he was tall.

Caroline Harrison died in the third year of her husband's presidency. Saddened by her death, Benjamin Harrison became more withdrawn than ever. His wife's niece, Mary Dimmick, acted as a substitute hostess at official receptions until he retired from office in March 1893. Harrison later married her and they had one daughter.

Ex-president Harrison left Washington in 1893 for Indianapolis and there resumed his lucrative law practice. He distinguished himself in international legal circles by representing Venezuela in a border dispute with England in 1899. Harrison, with his usual thoroughness, took two years preparing his case. So powerful were his arguments for Venezuela before the tribunal in Paris that England's attorney sent a message of defeat to his government before the decision was announced. Republican bosses back home sighed. Why hadn't Harrison revealed his strong courtroom personality when he was president?

Away from his law practice, writing took much of Benjamin Harrison's time during his last years. He wrote magazine articles and was the author of two books, *This Country of Ours* and *Views of the Ex-President*. He died of pneumonia in 1901.

Benjamin Harrison was not an inspiring leader while in the White House. Some would argue that he did not wear his grandfather's "hat" very well, but none would question his honesty and dignity while serving in that office. It is interesting that a member of such a distinguished American political family was president in 1889, the one hundredth anniversary of the nation.

The grandchildren of President Harrison sometimes went for a goatcart ride on the White House lawn. In this photograph their Uncle Russell Harrison supervises. Mary Mc Kee is holding her uncle's hand while her younger brother drives. Marthena Harrison hangs on behind him. The goat's name was His Whiskers.

PRESIDENT BEN? HARRISON.

HON. JAMES G. BLAINE,
Secy. of State.

HON. W™ WINDOM
Secy. of the Treasury.

HON. BEN? F. TRACEY,
Secy. of the Navy.

HON. J. M. RUSK,
Secy. of Agriculture.

HON. W. H. H. MILLER,
Attorney General.

HON. JOHN WANAMAKER,
Postmaster General.

HON. JNO. W. NOBLE
Secy. of the Interior.

HON. REDFIELD PROCTOR,
Secy. of War.

PRESIDENT HARRISON AND HIS CABINET.

COPYRIGHT 1889 BY CURRIER & IVES N.Y.

WILLIAM McKINLEY

Twenty-Fifth President (1897-1901)

Towering above the
North American continent,
there is a snow-capped mountain
named for the twenty-fifth president.
This powerful peak,
the tallest on the continent,
stands proudly against time and
nature's most terrible attacks.
The mountain humbles those who seek to climb it,
and thrills those who look upon it.
Alaska's foremost sentinel, Mount McKinley,
towers majestically over the land.
Its namesake, William McKinley, the gentle
and humane president from Ohio,
would have stood in awe of
this great tribute.

LAUNCHED 1890. BLOWN UP IN HAVANA HARBOR AT 9:40 P.M.
DIMENSIONS:- LENGTH OVERALL 324 FT 4½ INCHES, BREADTH EXTREME 57 FT;
MEAN DRAUGHT 21 FEET 6 INCHES: DISPLACEMENT 6682 TONS, SPEED 17 KNOTS
AN HOUR. 9293 HORSE POWER: TURRET ARMOUR 8½ INCHES THICK; COST $3,000,000.

DESTRUCTION OF THE U.S. BATTLESHIP MAINE
IN HAVANA HARBOR FEBY 15TH 1898.

COPYRIGHTED 1898 BY KURZ & ALLISON, 267-269 WABASH AVE., CHICAGO,
ARMAMENT:- 4-10 INCH BREECH-LOAD; 6 RIFLES: 14 RAPID FIRE GUNS;
4 REVOLVING CANNONS: 4 GATLINGS: 7 TORPEDO TUBES. THE SIDE BELT WAS
12 INCHES THICK & 180 FEET LONG. OFFICERS & CREW 453, KILLED & DROWNED 258.

This violent action in Cuba started the Spanish-American War.

*President McKinley and his Cabinet met often to determine U.S. policy
and military actions during the Spanish-American War.*

THE GENTLE CAMPAIGNER FROM CANTON

William McKinley was born on January 29, 1843, in Niles, Ohio, the seventh child in a family of nine. As a child his health was poor so he spent much time studying. He was an excellent student and developed great powers of observation. He received a secondary school education at an academy in Poland, Ohio, excelling in public speaking and debate. Young William was so deeply religious his mother hoped he would one day become a Methodist minister. This was not his desire, although strong religious principles guided him all his life. He was always kind and considerate when he met people from each level of society.

At seventeen he entered Allegheny College at Meadville, Pennsylvania. He had always been an excellent student and his family held high hopes for their kindly William. But illness forced him to withdraw after one term, and lack of money kept him from returning. Throughout his childhood, the McKinley family suffered from lack of money. His father was a foundryman. As the owner of two small iron furnaces, he provided only a meager living for his family. At an early age, William knew the ways of industry and the hard life of workingmen. He often carried his father's dinner pail to him at the foundry. The flaming furnaces fascinated the boy. Observing his father hard at work, William developed a sympathy for men who used their hands. This feeling stayed with him all his life.

To help his family, William took a job as a teacher in 1859. Stirred by his love of God's ways and his family's strong anti-slavery feelings, he enlisted as a private in the 23rd Ohio Volunteers at the beginning of the Civil War. Young McKinley became a fine soldier and was popular with all who were around him. A little more than a year after his enlistment, his regiment fought in the bloody battle of Antietam. Now a sergeant, McKinley was in charge of feeding the men of the 23rd. A few hours after the worst of the fighting, the regiment was amazed and delighted to see a wagon bumping along the front lines with Sergeant McKinley at the reins. Delicious smells emerged and heartened the weary men. Hot food on the battlefields was unknown. Every man in the regiment was served hot coffee and warm food.

The "chow" sergeant's bravery was noticed by his commanding officer, Rutherford B. Hayes. Colonel Hayes promoted his kind and brave sergeant to lieutenant. As an officer, McKinley repeatedly proved his courage. He was involved in some of the most terrible battles of the war. This brave, inspiring young officer was loved by his men and his fellow officers. Talking with him took away some of their fears of battle, some of their sadness over dead comrades, and much of their hardships in the field. All through his life, the people who knew McKinley best liked him most. When the Civil War ended, General Hayes called his friend and junior officer, Major William McKinley, "one of the bravest and finest officers in the army."

McKinley retired from the army and returned to Ohio to study law. He was admitted to the bar in 1867 and set up a practice in Canton, Ohio. The young lawyer's friendly ways quickly impressed the people of the town. McKinley entered Republican politics to support Rutherford B. Hayes, when his old commander ran for governor of Ohio. Using his fine speaking skills, McKinley became known as a vigorous campaigner.

William McKinley was definitely an up and coming young man. The handsome young bachelor attorney was also the object of much female attention. The banker's daughter, Ida Saxton, was no exception. McKinley became very attentive to the attractive Miss Saxton and one sunny afternoon while they were taking a buggy ride, he asked her to be his wife.

William McKinley's marriage was filled with sorrow. Ida gave birth to a daughter, Katherine, on Christmas Day, 1871. For two years they were a happy and handsome family. Just before their second child was born, Mrs. McKinley's mother died. Then her newborn baby girl died. Ida McKinley was never a strong woman and this double tragedy was more than she could bear. She sank into a great mental depression. Her physical condition became worse and for the rest of her life she suffered from epilepsy. During attacks from this illness, she fainted without warning and her face twisted in ter-

Ida Saxton McKinley lived the life of a semi-invalid in the White House during her years as First Lady.

rible ways. William constantly feared for his wife at these times.

Ida's illness did not dim his love. Throughout their lifetime, McKinley remained as devoted and attentive as he was when Ida was his bride. He suffered the sadness of her disability in silence. She was always his companion. She stood by his side as he rose in state and national politics.

Following his election as governor of Ohio, McKinley moved into a hotel across from his offices in the capitol building in Columbus. Each morning before entering his offices, passers-by could see the governor raising his hat to his wife who was sitting in the window across the street. Every day exactly at three, no matter what he was doing, he stepped to his window and waved a handkerchief to Ida, who watched for him from her room.

She became bored with sitting at home so much of the time and insisted upon attending social affairs with her husband. This caused him great worry but he remained kind and considerate. Her attacks came often. When one did

occur he reacted swiftly. He would immediately place a handkerchief over her face and carry her into another room. These painful scenes happened dozens of times during his political career. They always upset the people who were present, and emotionally drained McKinley. Only a man of great goodness and courage could withstand this pressure without complaint. William McKinley was such a man.

Politics was a relief from these personal problems, an outlet for his energies and emotions. Political activity provided him with the companionship of vigorous men like himself. His honest, pleasant manner impressed his co-workers and won him votes. He was elected to Congress in 1876. In Washington he settled Ida comfortably in a hotel and then went to work. McKinley's old friend, Rutherford B. Hayes, was president and this helped the friendly congressman become known in national politics. But his honesty and kindness helped him as much as his friendship with President Hayes. It was not long before William McKinley was well known to all congressmen.

His great interest was the tariff. He was a champion of the tariff's protection. McKinley believed that its barriers against importation of foreign goods would protect the wages of American workers and increase the growth of American industry. He became known nationally when he managed to get the McKinley Tariff of 1890 passed.

The Tariff Act was a great achievement and brought Congressman McKinley to the attention of Marcus A. Hanna, a millionaire businessman and a tough Ohio Republican political boss. Hanna was a hardheaded politician who knew success in politics meant winning. McKinley impressed him with his honesty, goodness, and political idealism. "I love McKinley! He is the best man I ever knew," declared the powerful Ohio boss. The two men became close friends and a fine team. McKinley's honesty checked Hanna's "win at any cost" policies, and Hanna's great fortune helped McKinley every step of the way to the White House.

McKinley returned to Ohio to be elected governor in 1892. After two terms as governor, William McKinley was a popular, well-known national figure. Mark Hanna said it was time to make a serious try for the presidency. The Republican presidential nomination was decided

President William McKinley in 1900.

The caption underneath this political cartoon read: "A new bird for Thanksgiving. Spain's goose is cooked, and William McKinley is the man who cooked it!" Americans were proud of President McKinley's leadership role in guiding the United States to a rapid conclusion to the Spanish-American War.

does not talk wildly, and his appearance is that of a president."

In 1896, the Republicans were the first political party to use telephones during a presidential campaign. William McKinley remained in Canton directing his campaign managers in each of the thirty-eight states by telephone.

Without making one deal or buying one vote, William McKinley won the presidency. In March 1897 he became president. There were problems in America, but they were small in comparison to the prosperity that bloomed throughout the land. Industry was booming. There was enough to eat. The times were good for all levels of American society.

Not even a war could stop American growth during McKinley's administration. The Cubans had been fighting against Spanish control since 1895. There was great loss of American property in Cuba during these times. President McKinley did not want a war with Spain, but he believed he had to protect American interests in Cuba. He tried to do this with diplomacy. He failed and in February 1898, the United States battleship *Maine* was blown up in Havana Harbor killing two hundred sixty American sailors. There was great anger in the country. Cries of "Remember the Maine" echoed throughout the land. The president sent a war message to Congress in April.

Acting as Commander-in-Chief during the Spanish-American War, President McKinley showed the tough, fighting part of his personality. He sent Commodore Dewey from Hong Kong to the Philippines. Dewey's ships quickly sent the Spanish fleet to the bottom of Manila Bay. Americans went wild with the news of this great naval victory. In June, United States troops landed in Cuba. By late July another American force had landed in Puerto Rico. Spain had enough and surrendered to the United States. With President McKinley's firm guidance, the terms of the peace treaty were good for the United States: independence for Cuba and the acquisition of Puerto Rico as a United States territory.

For the first time the United States was a world power. Before the Spanish-American War, the Philippines was an unknown place to most Americans. The Treaty of Paris, an aftermath of the war, gave the Pacific islands of the Philippines and Guam to the United States in return

even before the delegates arrived. Hanna did not have to buy their votes because McKinley's warm personality touched everyone. McKinley became the Republican candidate when the convention started.

Passing out gold pins representing their gold standard platform, the Republicans went after their Democratic opponent, William Jennings Bryan, with the vigorous slogan "Good work, good wages, and good money." Hanna, the campaign manager, flooded the country with colorful McKinley posters and badges. There were even cut-out McKinley paper dolls for the children. While Democrat Bryan toured the country making political speeches, Hanna brought the voters by the trainload to meet McKinley in his hometown of Canton. Front porch campaigning was working to perfection. McKinley's personal warmth won as many votes as his words. A New England lady remarked upon hearing him, "He

for a twenty million dollar payment to Spain. That same year the Hawaiian Islands were annexed by the United States. In 1899 American Samoa was acquired by treaty. Now the American flag waved half way around the world.

Through all this prosperity and expansion President William McKinley remained one of the kindest and most soft-spoken men ever to occupy the White House. He quarreled with no one. Opponents could feel no anger toward his quietly dynamic ways. One day the president asked a senator, who favored the other side of an issue, if the senator would be angry if he opposed him. The senator replied, "Mr. President, I could not get angry at you if I tried!"

McKinley was renominated in the 1900 election and easily defeated Democrat William Jennings Bryan. McKinley's vice president was Theodore Roosevelt. The nation's prosperity continued in his second term, and the McKinley popularity continued to grow. Shortly after his second inaugural ceremony, President McKinley began a goodwill journey around the country with members of his Cabinet and his good friend, Mark Hanna. Cheering crowds greeted the presidential party at every stop.

Tragedy silenced the cheering and ended the trip. The president arrived in Buffalo to open the Pan American Exposition. His secret service advisors were warned of a plot by anarchists to kill the heads of several world governments. McKinley was one of them. Italy's leader had already been murdered. Secret service men asked the president to stay away from the Exposition crowds. But the kindly chief executive refused.

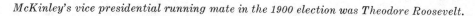

McKinley's vice presidential running mate in the 1900 election was Theodore Roosevelt.

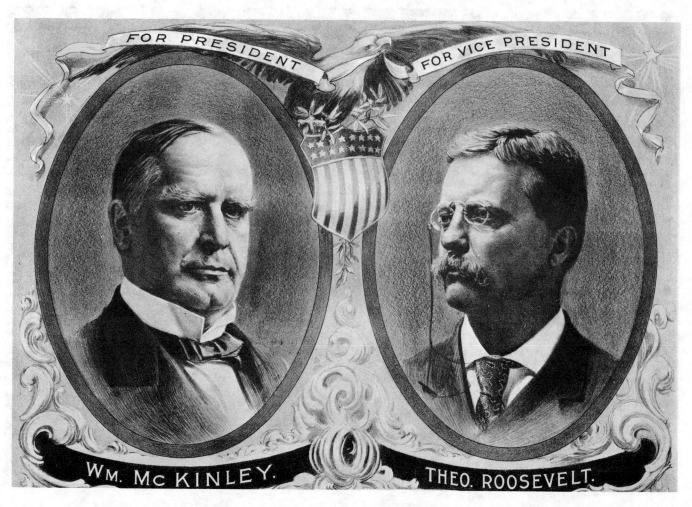

FOR PRESIDENT   FOR VICE PRESIDENT

WM. McKINLEY.   THEO. ROOSEVELT.

President McKinley was warmly welcomed by school teachers and children on a visit to El Paso, Texas in 1901.

This last photograph of President McKinley was taken as he left the International Hotel in Niagara Falls, New York, September 6, 1901.

The assassination of President William McKinley.

He was president and he would meet the public.

On September 6, 1901, President McKinley held a public reception in the Temple of Music on the Exposition grounds. The reception was crowded. The kindly president smiled and shook hands with all who passed. As he reached out to a man with a bandaged hand, two bullets ripped into his body from a gun hidden inside the bandage. The anarchists had succeeded. The assassin was seized immediately and later tried and executed in New York state's electric chair.

Nine days after the shooting William McKinley was dead. He had fought a brave but useless battle against the bullets.

At the news of William McKinley's death the nation went into a state of shock. Another president had been cut down by the bullets of an assassin. Americans wore black and wept openly as the body of their murdered chief lay in state in Washington. As William McKinley's body moved slowly in the funeral procession to its final resting place, Canton, Ohio, Americans watched in silent respect and were troubled. For the third time in less than forty years a president had been murdered in office. How strange that these three presidents were the gentlest of men to serve in that high office. First Abraham Lincoln, the emancipator from Illinois. Then Garfield, the peace-loving preacher from Ohio. And now, the gentle man from Canton.

As the murdered President McKinley's funeral train passed somberly through town after town on its way to Canton, Americans who loved him waited silently to pay their last respects.

THEODORE ROOSEVELT

Twenty-Sixth President (1901-1909)

"Now look," wailed Mark Hanna,
as the twenty-sixth chief executive
took office,"A cowboy is
President of the United States!"
Among the many interests this vigorous man
pursued during his colorful life, cow-punching
was high on the list.
He was the exact opposite of his
silkpurse, high-society New York background.
An asthmatic weakling during his
childhood, little "Teedie" began to build up his
body in his father's gym.
This body-building program worked.
He became very muscular and, as a college
student, he tried for the lightweight boxing
championship of Harvard University.
Nothing could hold Theodore Roosevelt down
when his mind was set, not even
the wound from an assassin's bullet
buried four inches deep
in his chest.

"T.R.," THE TOUGH REBEL
FROM SILKPURSE SOCIETY

Theodore Roosevelt was born in New York City, October 27, 1858, the son of Theodore and Martha Bullock Roosevelt. Little Teedie's family was one of great wealth. His grandfather, Cornelius Roosevelt, was an investment banker and his father a prosperous glass importer. The four Roosevelt children grew up in a happy, active household. Constructive and interesting family projects were the custom and this habit remained with Teddy all his life.

Teddy said his father was, "the best man I ever knew." The boy had good reason to love his father. He remembered his father carrying him around his bedroom all night, holding his frail body upright so he could breath. These continued asthma attacks left his body thin and weak. Teddy was such a sickly child he could not attend regular school. His eyesight was so poor he often bumped into things. Confined to the life of a semi-invalid, he had to study at home with private tutors.

This was a strange start for a man who grew to be our most vigorous and athletic president. Teddy's invalid life changed at thirteen. While visiting Moosehead Lake in Maine to recover from an asthma attack, he was bullied by two local boys who did not like his city manners. The Roosevelt fighting spirit was there, but his body was not strong enough. In the skirmish, the city boy was given a bad beating.

From then on he called himself "T.R." and he was set on strengthening his frail body. He vowed that he would never again be humiliated in such a way. His father built a gymnasium for him inside their New York home. T.R. gradually built up his body by working with bar bells, a punching bag, Indian clubs, and the horizontal bars. By the time he entered Harvard University at eighteen, he was muscular and strong. He took up boxing and became known as a fine boxer. His motto from that time forward was, "Don't hit at all if it is honorably possible to avoid hitting, but never hit soft."

In addition to boxing, T.R. proved to be a fine student. As a Harvard freshman, his great interest was in the natural sciences. He wanted to become a naturalist like John Audubon. However, he was a good scholar in all subjects and in his senior year became interested in American naval history. Roosevelt also wrote well and began work on his book, *The Naval War of 1812*, shortly before graduation. This was the first of more than two thousand works he authored during his lifetime. In 1880 he graduated from Harvard near the top of his class. That same year he married Alice Lee, a member of Boston society.

The newlyweds moved into the Roosevelt family house in New York City. T.R. began the study of law at Columbia University but soon grew to dislike it. Grinning, he would say that he thought lawyers were too interested in freeing crooks. His manner of speech was quick, witty, often cutting. All his life, people either loved the way he spoke or were enraged by it.

Law was out. The vigorous bridegroom quickly turned his interests to other things. It was time to have fun in the social world, time to show off his lovely bride. At home he took up horseback riding and mountain climbing. Theodore climbed Switzerland's rugged Matterhorn while on vacation in Europe. He attended the balls and parties of New York society.

But Theodore Roosevelt became tired of playing. He chose politics as a way to do worthwhile things. His elegant society friends turned up their noses at his thought of politics. They warned Roosevelt that he would be spoiled by associating with the lower elements of society. "Ridiculous" was Teddy's quick response. He turned his back on these friends and joined the local Republican Club. Then he ran for the New York State Assembly and won the election at the age of twenty-three. With the volcanic vigor that typified his activities throughout life, Assemblyman Roosevelt jumped into legislative affairs in Albany and made a name for himself.

Double tragedy interrupted his budding political career in 1884. On the same day, Theodore Roosevelt lost two of the people he loved most—his wife and his mother. His wife, Alice, died of Bright's disease two days after giving

The birthplace of Theodore Roosevelt, 28 East 20th Street, New York City.

Teddy went west to his North Dakota ranch to work off his sorrow over the death of his wife and mother. He is shown here without the glasses he usually wore.

birth to their daughter. The daughter lived. Roosevelt, who had received many blows in his life, could not bounce back after this double dose of death. Filled with grief, he left his infant daughter, Alice, in New York and went west to his Elkhorn Ranch in the Badlands of the wild Dakota territory. He remained there for two years working the sadness out of his heart.

At first the hearty Elkhorn cowboys made fun of the "four-eyed tenderfoot" from eastern society, but not for long. The Elkhorn hands took Teddy to a saloon one evening and watched a gun-carrying bully walk up to their group and poke fun at Roosevelt because of his pince-nez glasses. "Four-eyes" calmly got up, knocked the bully to the floor, and took away his gun. From that time on, the cowboys of the Elkhorn had nothing but the greatest respect for their tough eastern co-worker. As a rancher Roosevelt worked as hard as any of the men. He would sit in the saddle for forty hours at a stretch during roundup time. He rounded up stray calves for branding. He delivered feed to hungry cattle during blizzards. He mended fences. At the end of his stay, his heart had also mended.

Teddy returned to the east in 1886 and married Edith Carow. This polished, gentle lady was a great contrast to her active, excitable husband. Teddy's second wife was a fine match for him. She helped him in political life with her quiet words and common sense. The Roosevelts had five children, and Edith was a kind parent to her step-daughter Alice.

T.R.'s reputation as a strong, reform politician was developed soon after his 1889 appointment by President Benjamin Harrison to the U.S. Civil Service Commission. During his six years as a commissioner, he enraged political bosses by moving thousands of federal jobs out of the spoils system. His reputation for toughness grew when Mayor William Strong appointed him one of New York City's four police commissioners. As a director of the police department, Commissioner Roosevelt would walk beats with his patrolmen through the night. He wanted to see, first hand, that the law was properly enforced. Again he angered the spoilsmen when he established a merit system for police promotion.

Alice Lee Roosevelt died three-and-a-half years after her marriage to Theodore.

President William McKinley appointed "Terrible Teddy" to be Assistant Secretary of the Navy in 1897. He did not remain in that position for long. Angered by the sinking of the *Maine* in Havana Harbor, Roosevelt resigned his position to join the army. With his usual drive, he gathered a group of Texas Rangers and personal friends and worked them into fighting shape, forming the first U.S. Volunteer Regiment. During the Spanish American War, they became known as "The Rough Riders." Patriotic Americans were thrilled when news of their courageous charge up San Juan Hill in Cuba appeared in the American newspapers. Riding into heavy Spanish gunfire, they captured the hill and defeated the enemy. Leading them on the charge was colorful Colonel Roosevelt, who came home a hero to his fellow Americans.

Leaving the army in 1898, Colonel Teddy Roosevelt was ready again for political life. In

Colonel Roosevelt at the head of the Rough Riders leading a battle charge
in Cuba during the Spanish-American War.

spite of his great wealth and high social position, this vigorous, thick-necked, mustachioed New Yorker was the image of the self-made man to New York voters. Republican political bosses shuddered at his stubborn, unbending ways but could not afford to turn down a sure winner. They ran Roosevelt as their 1899 gubernatorial candidate and he won the governor's chair with ease. Soon, because of his honesty and personality, he was one of the most famous politicians in America.

When Governor Teddy said, with a wide grin, "Speak softly and carry a big stick," the political bosses knew he meant it. The people thought of him as a fearless hunter on a trek through a jungle of enemies. They laughed with him and loved him for his tough policies against corruption. Governor Roosevelt enforced the law without fear. He began important reforms in the handling of food and drugs in New York

state. He promoted laws to shorten the workday for women and children. Proudly, he pushed a bill through his legislature in Albany to stop racial discrimination in New York schools.

Roosevelt's path of reform ruffled many political feathers. Very annoyed by what he considered Teddy's "theatrics," New York's Boss Platt decided to stop the Roosevelt show. He had a tiger by the tail and this worried Platt. Teddy Roosevelt was much too popular to eliminate from the political roll call altogether. Finally Platt came up with an answer. He would put this wild mustang into a side corral away from the main herd. Platt and his colleagues decided, in the 1900 presidential election, to give Teddy the vice presidential nomination on the ticket with William McKinley. The mustang from Manhattan would not be able to do much damage from that position. So they

264

thought, until an assassin's bullet changed their scheme.

Teddy Roosevelt was on a hunting trip in the Adirondack Mountains when he received word that President McKinley was close to death. He leaped into a carriage and began a dangerous journey over fifty-five miles of twisting, rainwashed mountain roads. "Push on," Roosevelt urged his terrified driver, "Push on! If you are not afraid, I'm not." And indeed, as president he was not afraid of anyone or anything he felt would keep him from bettering his country. President Theodore Roosevelt's eight-year administration was the most productive one since Abraham Lincoln's.

"President Teddy" would challenge any foe if he felt it was best for the United States. This notice went out to all in 1903 when he began his "Square Deal" program. The president told the nation it was his business to see to it that every man had a square deal. He would play favorites with no one. Some kinds of big business stood in the way of the Square Deal and he went after them. Roosevelt became known as "The Trust Buster." Trusts were enormous companies within industries like coal, steel, and railroads. The president worried that trusts might become so powerful they would control the federal government. "The Trust Buster" went after the powerful Northern Securities Company first. Men of great wealth, like J. P. Morgan, were very angry. But the president went on with his fight.

Theodore Roosevelt considered conservation of national resources just as important as trust busting. He pushed through the Reclamation Act of 1902 and made the Bureau of Forestry larger. In 1903 he named a special commission to study national resources. He set aside thousands of acres of western land for public use. Conservationist Roosevelt, in eight years, doubled the number of national parks, and established sixteen national monuments, and fifty game reserves.

Once, on a western hunting trip, an act of kindness by the president warmed the hearts of all Americans. Coming upon a small brown bear

cub, he refused to shoot it. Newspaper cartoonists drew many pictures of the event. In children's stores across the country, fat, stuffed "Teddy-bears" were soon top sellers.

Roosevelt's greatest success in foreign policy was the acquisition of the Panama Canal Zone. From the beginning of Roosevelt's administration, he was determined to build a canal across a narrow stretch of Central American land. The United States was a world power with territories in the Caribbean and in the Pacific. Roosevelt believed the American Navy had to have a shortcut route across the Isthmus of Panama. To do this, he had to have the land. He began to negotiate with the Republic of Colombia, which then owned Panama. These negotiations failed. A revolution broke out in Panama City. Two weeks later the new Republic of Panama had signed a treaty with the United States leas-

Colonel Roosevelt during the Spanish-American War as portrayed by an unkind political cartoonist. He is shown here sending off his own press notices for personal publicity instead of leading his men in battle.

The Wright brothers, Wilbur and Orville, made the first airplane flight at Kitty Hawk, North Carolina, on December 17, 1903.

President Roosevelt addressing a crowd in Evanston, Illinois in 1903.

President Roosevelt giving his inaugural address March 4, 1905.

This political cartoon was titled "The president's dream of a successful hunt." The prey was large American trusts, and President Roosevelt is congratulated by the artist for going after them.

ing a ten-mile strip running from the Atlantic to the Pacific. Because of President Roosevelt's actions, the Panama Canal soon made America a great sea power.

The six vigorous Roosevelt offspring were as popular as their father. Newspapers delighted in reporting their daily actions. The younger Roosevelts walked on stilts inside the White House and slid down bannisters. One day they took their pony upstairs, using the White House elevator, to visit a brother in bed with the measles. Theodore, Jr., Kermit, Ethel, Archie, and Quentin, amused the nation by romping about on the White House lawn with a bear named Jonathan and a guinea pig named Father Grady.

Even her father admitted that Alice, the oldest, was a bit hard to handle. He often said he could run the country, but not the country and Alice! She was seen running about Washington smoking cigarettes in public. She loved

When President Roosevelt planted this tree in Fort Worth, Texas, he uttered a quote which captured America's fancy: "May American manhood be sturdy as the oak."

President Roosevelt was proud of the role he played in acquiring the Panama Canal Zone for the United States in 1904. Here he is shown running a steam shovel at Culera Cut during the building of the Panama Canal.

to startle acquaintances by pulling a pet garter snake out of her handbag saying, "Isn't he bully." Mrs. Roosevelt remained a calm mother through it all and is remembered as one of our most dignified First Ladies.

"I enjoy being President!" roared the enthusiastic Teddy. And America loved to watch him in action. The public was fascinated with the report that he wore a ring containing a lock of Abraham Lincoln's hair. They were excited with reports of his cougar hunts in Colorado, boxing matches with heavyweight champion John L. Sullivan, and tennis and football games on the White House lawn. The president took fifty-mile hikes and said that everyone should do the same. He had pillow fights with his children in their bedrooms. He took time away from his presidential duties to be head of a Boy Scout troop at his family home in Oyster Bay, New York. In his spare time he wrote a book, *Winning the West*, which delighted the reading public.

He had more visitors at the White House than any president in our history. Theodore Roosevelt enjoyed meeting people and loved his friends about him. His friendships were as varied as his interests. Author Rudyard Kipling, western lawman Bat Masterson, educator and black leader Booker T. Washington, and naturalist John Burroughs were visitors at the White House during Roosevelt's residence there.

Theodore Roosevelt was a president with many "firsts" to his credit. He was the first president, while in office, to visit every state. He was the first to travel to a foreign country. He was the first president to ride in an automobile and, after his retirement, one of the first to fly in an airplane. In 1906 Theodore Roosevelt became the first American president to win the Nobel Peace Prize for arranging the treaty between Russia and Japan that ended the Russo-Japanese War.

Retiring from office in March 1909, Teddy was just fifty and as energetic as ever. Now he had time to follow his special interests. Nineteen days after he moved out of the White House he began a hunting trip to Africa.

T.R.'s strong sense of public responsibility did not allow him to follow only pleasure for the rest of his life. Roosevelt decided to run again

Edith Carow Roosevelt was a dignified and efficient First Lady during her seven years in the White House. She managed her family of six and her husband's official receptions "without making a mistake."

Theodore Roosevelt, Jr., bore a remarkable resemblance to his father. He is shown here, at the age of fifteen, with his pet parrot Eli.

for the presidency in 1912. He announced his intention with another famous phrase, "My hat is in the ring." However, the regular Republican politicians wanted to reelect President Taft. Many of them must have remembered that Theodore Roosevelt could not be managed by anyone. Taft was renominated.

Roosevelt immediately organized his progressive Republican followers into a third party nicknamed "The Bull Moose" Party after its vigorous leader. Candidate Roosevelt stumped the country and delighted his audiences with zesty, humorous speeches.

The campaign came to a sudden but brief halt in Wisconsin. Preparing to step onto the stage of a Milwaukee auditorium to speak, Theodore Roosevelt was shot in the chest by an insane saloon keeper. He was saved from certain death by the things in his breast pocket—his metal glasses case and the manuscript of his speech. Feeling great pain, T.R. coughed, saw there was no blood in his lungs, and went on to amaze his audience by delivering a fifty-minute speech with a bullet lodged four inches deep in his muscular chest. Afterwards he was taken to a local hospital where he quickly recovered from the wound.

After losing the 1912 election, Roosevelt never again ran for public office. But his love for America remained strong. He stayed in the public eye by working vigorously to raise money for the American war effort in 1917. His spirit was greatly weakened when his son Quentin died in France in 1918. As a friend said, "this was the blow that finally ended the boyhood of Theodore Roosevelt."

Archie Roosevelt (saluting) and Quentin Roosevelt (on the end) often joined the White House policemen for their daily inspection.

Sagamore Hill was the cozy and hospitable summer home of President Roosevelt located at Oyster Bay, New York.

Theodore Roosevelt's last adventure was typical of his fine, productive life. He was told of an unexplored river in the jungles of the Amazon Basin in Brazil. Called the River of Doubt, it ran through terrifying and primitive lands. Although the danger from swirling rapids and fierce water animals was great, T.R. decided to explore it. "You'll be lucky to come back alive," friends warned. For two months, while he battled jungle sickness and rode out the rapids, nothing was heard of him. He returned home with an injured leg and a body weakened by jungle fever. At the age of fifty-six, Roosevelt knew he could never again play the part of the vigorous explorer of faraway places.

Theodore Roosevelt died January 6, 1919, at his family home in Oyster Bay, New York. Five thousand miles south, in the wild Brazilian jungle he had once roamed, the "Rio Theodoro" flowed on in silent tribute to the great man for whom it was named.

Roosevelt arriving at the Alamo Plaza, San Antonio, Tex

Teddy Roosevelt and guides take a moment out for relaxation on a hunting safari in Brazil.

"Algonquin," the pony, was the Roosevelt children's favorite pet. One day Quentin and Kermit Roosevelt sneaked him upstairs in the White House elevator to visit their brother, Archie, who was sick in bed with the measles.

WILLIAM HOWARD TAFT

Twenty-Seventh President (1909-1913)

He was always called
"Big Bill."
Even in infancy, his mother
said he had such a large waist
it was hard to fit him into baby clothes.
The name stayed with him all his life.
When he graduated from Yale University weighing
two hundred twenty five pounds,
he was seventy-five pounds heavier than
the average classmate.
He was also big in brain power, serving
with great distinction as a lawyer, professor,
college dean, public official, and judge.
History records William Howard Taft's
bigness in another way.
He was the only American to hold
our nation's two highest offices. He was the
twenty-seventh President of the United States
and the tenth Chief Justice of
the Supreme Court.

The birthplace of William Howard Taft in Cincinnati, Ohio.

"BIG BILL" TAFT, THE JUDICIAL GIANT

The future president and Chief Justice was born into the large family of Alphonso and Louise Torrey Taft, September 15, 1857, in Cincinnati, Ohio. Alphonso Taft had served two presidents. He was President Grant's Attorney General and Secretary of War, and President Arthur's Minister to Austria-Hungary and then, Russia. He was determined his sons would rise to heights greater than he had reached. The senior Taft was a remarkable man and parent. If any fault can be found in his fatherly actions, it is that he drove his children a bit too hard.

One day teenage William, affectionately called "Big Lub" by his Woodward High classmates, proudly brought home grades that showed he was fifth from the top in his class. Alphonso Taft took one look and exclaimed, "Mediocrity will not do, Will." Will dug deeper into his studies hoping to please his father. But Woodward High wasn't all work for the young man. "Big Lub" found time to play on the baseball team. He wasn't much of a hitter, but he prided himself on his fine throwing arm. He graduated in June 1874, standing second from the top in his class.

Will Taft continued his education at Yale University in September of that year. At Yale he grew in knowledge, size, and personal popularity. A college friend said he was "the most admired and respected man . . . in all Yale." Will graduated from the university in June 1878. Again standing second in his class, he slightly disappointed his ambitious father.

Alphonso Taft was happy when William decided to follow him into the legal profession. Soon after graduation from Yale, he began studying law in his father's Cincinnati law office. During the months he studied law, he also became active in Republican politics, participating in his father's campaign for governor of Ohio. When Alphonso Taft lost this election he became determined that Will would reach the political heights that had escaped him.

The genial William listened to his father and smiled. By this time he knew his real interest was not politics, but the less spectacular career of law. William enjoyed studying the carefully organized legal processes. He believed a strong society could be created by law. He became a lawyer in 1880 and spent the next seven years in private practice in Cincinnati. In 1886 he married Helen Herron. William's wife delighted his father because she was also extremely ambitious for her young husband. Alphonso Taft smiled with satisfaction at the story of seventeen year old "Nellie" Herron telling her friends she would one day marry a man who would be president. Maybe she had something there. Nellie and Alphonso Taft became allies and enjoyed planning William's steps to the presidency.

Only his quiet, understanding mother knew of William's real desires. She smiled with quiet satisfaction when her son became judge of the Ohio Superior Court. To his wife and father it was only a stepping stone to bigger and better places in politics. To the young judge and his mother, it was the start of a meaningful judicial career. William Howard Taft's law career took a giant step forward in 1890 when he was appointed U.S. Solicitor General. With their small son Robert, Nellie and William went to live in Washington. One year later, Taft was offered a job that filled his legal heart with joy, a federal judgeship on the Sixth Circuit. Nellie disliked the idea because it took her husband out of the capital limelight, away from important people. As he accepted the judgeship, William Howard Taft smiled and expressed his feelings about the order and tradition of American law this way: "I love judges and I love courts. They are my ideals that typify on earth what we shall meet hereafter in heaven under a just God."

He traveled the Sixth Circuit, which included Ohio, Michigan, Kentucky, and Tennessee, and did much good work. Taft was the first American judge with the courage to say that workers had the legal right to strike. He ruled in favor of workers who had been injured while at work, and made their employers responsible for payment of medical and injury claims. It wasn't long before he was known as an outstanding judge by his hardest jury, his judicial colleagues.

In 1899, Judge Taft's life took a new turn. On a train ride through Ohio, he became friendly with a fellow passenger, General Corbin. The General, impressed with Taft's learning and good sense, returned to Washington and rec-

Taft returned to the Philippines in 1905 on official duties as Secretary of War under President Roosevelt. He is shown here on an official tour with the president's daughter, Alice Roosevelt.

ommended him for the position of Governor-General of the Philippine Territory. President McKinley was impressed by Corbin's recommendation and sent for Taft. McKinley offered him the appointment. Taft hesitated. He did not want to leave the judicial world, but his sense of duty to America was greater. Accepting the appointment, the ex-judge packed up Nellie and their three children and sailed for the Philippines in 1900.

Four years later, his work unfinished, William Howard Taft again had to make a hard decision. The position most lawyer's desire from the time they hang out their shingle was offered to him by President Roosevelt. It was a place upon the Supreme Court of the United States. Governor-General Taft, torn with inner turmoil, finally turned him down. His lawyer's sense of thoroughness would not let him leave incomplete his work with the Philippine people.

William Howard Taft believed the people of the Philippines must be taught self-government before they could be granted independence from America. He had a genuine liking for the people and, as their Governor-General, set out to show them the way to independence. He put Filipino citizens in responsible government positions, made their courts follow more honest procedures, and built up their school systems. Through these months of guidance and decision-making, the kind Taft was often ill with tropical diseases and fevers. He suffered greatly from the sticky heat because of his great size.

When he believed the Filipinos were well on their way toward self-government, Taft returned to Washington. In 1904 he joined Theodore Roosevelt's Cabinet. Roosevelt reasoned that

The Republican Party is often called the "Grand Old Party" (GOP). Here is the GOP's 1908 campaign poster featuring their presidential and vice presidential candidates, William Howard Taft and James S. Sherman. Clockwise from the bottom left are other GOP presidential candidates: William McKinley, James G. Blaine, James A. Garfield, Ulysses S. Grant, John C. Fremont (the first Republican presidential candidate in 1856), Abraham Lincoln, Rutherford B. Hayes, Chester A. Arthur, Benjamin Harrison, and Theodore Roosevelt.

any man who worked so well on foreign shores would do better by his side. The position Taft accepted, Secretary of War, was appealing to the man from Ohio because it allowed him to help guide the interests of his Filipino friends far away in the Pacific.

His friendship with Theodore Roosevelt blossomed into a remarkable relationship. The public chuckled at the roly-poly Secretary Taft as he walked down capital streets at the side of the strong, muscular Roosevelt. But the president did not laugh. He knew a good man when he saw one. These two men, so unlike in body build, strengthened each other. The calm and thoughtful Taft often kept the excitable president from making mistakes. The fiery Roosevelt

sometimes pushed his thoughtful friend into quicker action. Secretary of War Taft was more than a Cabinet member. He was an advisor, close friend, and sometimes a stand-in president when Roosevelt went off on one of his hunting trips. The Roosevelts and the Tafts had many pleasant evenings in the White House library. Wanting the best for him, Roosevelt would offer Taft a remarkable choice—the president's chair or the Chief Justice's bench. "Make it the presidency," Nellie Taft quickly retorted. "Make it the chief justiceship," her husband would calmly reply. The matter was settled by a man in another part of Washington. Chief Justice Fuller was not ready to retire. Nellie Taft now began thinking in earnest about life as the First Lady.

President and Mrs. Taft leave the U.S. Capitol to head the inaugural parade, March 4, 1909.

TAKING NO SIDES.

This political cartoon shows President Taft trying to do his duty as he best saw fit. But President Roosevelt (portrayed by the Teddy bear) is not far away.

A 1909 photograph of President Taft and his sons Charles (left) and Robert (right). Robert Taft grew up to become a nationally famous Republican senator from Ohio.

This photograph was taken of Helen Herron Taft in 1908, shortly before she became First Lady. When she became ill during her husband's administration her sister, Mrs. Louis More, often acted as White House hostess.

The political campaign of 1912. President Taft rides the Republican elephant, Candidate Woodrow Wilson rides the Democratic donkey, and Ex-president Roosevelt takes up the rear on a Bull Moose.

279

These fireside plans between the two friends became known to the public near the end of Roosevelt's second term. Taft was Teddy's choice and the Republicans would have to play ball. Encouraged by his family and with Roosevelt's strong backing, William Howard Taft threw his "hat into the ring" and became the 1908 Republican presidential nominee. The lively campaign song "Keep on the Raft with Taft" serenaded the country, and Taft rode the fair winds of Roosevelt's tremendous popularity. He defeated Democrat William Jennings Bryan by more than a million votes. In "Big Bill" Taft the American public expected a carbon copy of their Teddy. They were in for a surprise.

Our twenty-seventh president was one of the best-liked and best-natured men ever to become president, and one of the most unhappy while in office. His personality was that of a judge, not a politician. Most of his life had been in the courtroom, and he was uncertain of his political and administrative abilities as president. After an eight year roller-coaster ride with Roosevelt, Taft knew the public would be disappointed with his personality. Writing to his dear friend Roosevelt shortly before he left on his African safari, the new chief executive confessed that whenever he was addressed as "Mr. President," out of habit, he turned around to look for President Roosevelt.

In spite of these private doubts, William Howard Taft did an effective job as president. During his four-year administration the postal savings bank and parcel post services were established. New Mexico and Arizona became our forty-seventh and forty-eighth states, and the Alaskan Territory was organized. The Sixteenth Amendment to the Constitution, creating the federal income tax, was passed by Congress.

With his judicial thoroughness, President Taft stabilized many of the policies begun by Roosevelt. Continuing his friend's "trust busting" policies, the Taft administration prosecuted nearly twice as many anti-trust cases in four years as Roosevelt had in eight. Conservation worried President Taft because of the way Roosevelt took over millions of acres of land for public use. Taft had a law passed that made this kind of presidential action legal.

The president also worried about government spending. He saved the country millions of dollars by keeping a careful watch on his administration's finances. He established a Commission on Economy and Efficiency to report on federal government spending and to suggest ways to save money in the future. Because President Taft's constructive work was done in a quiet, legal manner, without the trumpeting that accompanied much of Teddy Roosevelt's actions, it often went largely unnoticed by the public. This would have bothered a true politician, but Taft was happy to know that he was strengthening the country.

Although William Howard Taft could not match Roosevelt's colorful personality, he was by no means a colorless man. He was the first president to play golf and the first to have an official presidential automobile. In 1910, he started the presidential custom of throwing out the first ball to open the baseball season in Washington. His great girth did not keep him from playing a fast set of tennis with friends, or maneuvering Washington ladies lightly around a dance floor.

President Taft's size was the source of much joking. The president was always good-natured about his weight and enjoyed telling stories on himself. He laughed about the time he tried to impress President Roosevelt with his athletic abilities in the White House gymnasium. He dressed his enormous frame in the traditional white judo costume and confidently approached his tiny Japanese opponent. One quick motion by his opponent and his three hundred pounds were thrown to the mat while Roosevelt laughed. Another favorite story was about the twenty-five mile horseback ride he took into the Philippine hills when he was Governor-General. When a Washington friend heard he had survived the ride, he wired Taft to ask, "How is the horse?" The American public laughed over a popular newspaper photograph which appeared at the beginning of Taft's presidency. The photograph showed four average-sized workmen comfortably sitting in the enormous bathtub they had just installed in a White House bathroom for the new president.

Mrs. Taft was an able First Lady. She loved the oriental style and brought many Philippine-style furnishings and jungle plants into the Executive Mansion. The White House took on such an Oriental flair, it became known during the Taft's stay as "The Malacanan Palace." This was the name of the governor's house in the Philippines. Sadly, the wife who so long wanted to be First Lady, had a stroke shortly after her husband was inaugurated. The president took time away from his busy schedule each day to work patiently with Nellie to teach her how to speak again. Mrs. Taft recovered from her illness well enough to give Washington one of its most cherished gifts. She supervised the planting of the famous Washington cherry trees. Since 1912 this project has been appreciated by Washington citizens. Each spring the city becomes beautifully alive in a blaze of pink cherry blossoms.

In spite of his many administrative successes, William Howard Taft was not popular with some Republican politicians. His ways were much too slow and his personality too colorless for their liking. These "Progressives" believed the jolly president was not moving their policies forward fast enough. They wanted Teddy back in the saddle. They began talking against Taft to Roosevelt. Roosevelt began to believe them, and, bored by his inactivity, began making public speeches criticizing his friend. With each speech the Roosevelt-Taft friendship was pulled farther apart. The president was hurt and puzzled by Roosevelt's actions, but he refused to reply. The criticism continued and Taft's political popularity went downhill fast. His political advisors urged him to defend himself. The genial giant held back as long as he could, but was finally forced to reply to Roosevelt and the Progressives in a speech on April 25, 1912. The strain of making the reply was too much for the kindly president. A reporter, looking for an interview after the speech, found the president backstage weeping. "Roosevelt was my closest friend," was his only comment.

The Republicans again nominated William Howard Taft in 1912. He was reluctant to accept but felt he must stay on and fight the unfair charges of the Progressives. Roosevelt pulled the Progressives out of the Republican Party into his "Bull Moose" Party. Republican in-fighting was on. Democratic candidate, Woodrow Wilson, carried on an efficient campaign and let the Republicans hack away at each other. He easily won the election.

Non-political William Howard Taft sighed with relief as Wilson's March 4, 1913, inauguration approached. Now he could rejoin the calm world of law. He was happy to be appointed as Professor of Law at Yale University. In 1921, President Warren Harding appointed him to the position he had sought for many years. That year William Howard Taft became Chief Justice of the Supreme Court. Taft's Supreme Court years have often been compared to his presidential administration. During his nine years as Chief Justice, he ran an efficient, thoughtful court, noted for its unspectacular but orderly achievements.

The nine years he wore the Chief Justice's robes were the most satisfying of William Howard Taft's remarkable and productive life. The presidency and the political plotting that surrounded him became only a blur. Chief Justice Taft died on March 8, 1930, in the sunshine period of his life.

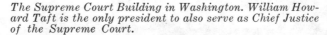

The Supreme Court Building in Washington. William Howard Taft is the only president to also serve as Chief Justice of the Supreme Court.

WOODROW WILSON

Twenty-Eighth President (1913-1921)

Our twenty-eighth president
had more formal education than
any other chief executive.
He is the only president
who earned a Ph.D. degree.
During his years as a graduate student
and a college professor,
he wrote textbooks discussing
the proper way to run a government.
Unsuspecting political bosses in New Jersey
thought this "Professor," with his reputation
as a fine scholar and honest university
administrator, would be a perfect pawn in
their hands if they ran him for governor.
After all, they reasoned, he only
wrote about politicians; he didn't
know how to be one.
They were greatly surprised when
Governor Woodrow Wilson began to act,
not like a puppet they could manipulate,
but like the producer of a show, pulling
the strings and giving
the orders himself.

In August 1920, during Woodrow Wilson's administration, the Nineteenth Amendment to the Constitution was ratified allowing American women to vote. Here "suffragettes" (women who sought the right to vote) march to the Capitol Building, April 7, 1913.

Silent motion pictures became a popular form of entertainment while President Wilson was in office. This is a scene from a 1915 motion picture starring Mary Pickford.

HIS TEXTBOOK CAME TO LIFE

Thomas Woodrow Wilson (he later dropped his first name) was born, December 28, 1856, in Staunton, Virginia. He was the third of four children born to Joseph and Jessie Woodrow Wilson. His father was a Presbyterian minister. One year after Woodrow's birth, Reverend Wilson was called to a church in Augusta, Georgia. Young Woodrow's earliest memories were of Augusta. At the age of four he recalled family friends saying there would be a war because Abraham Lincoln had been elected president. The Civil War brought hardships to the Wilsons, as it did to most families in the South. News of the death of friends and homes destroyed in battle, a scarcity of food and other necessary life-giving materials was common. After the war the Wilsons were typical of southerners who lived through the terrible years of Reconstruction. The Wilsons felt that with prayer and patience better times would come.

Young Woodrow was frail and in bad health for most of his childhood. His father taught him at home. He was a good student and entered North Carolina's Davidson College at the age of sixteen. Bad health forced him to withdraw after only a year's study. After fourteen months of rest, Woodrow was strong enough to reenter college. This time he became a student at Princeton University in New Jersey. This university was the most important place in his life

for the next thirty-five years. At Princeton Wilson was a fine student and debater. Politics also interest him. Once, daydreaming of political possibilities in the future, he wrote on cards ... "Woodrow Wilson, Senator from Virginia."

He graduated from Princeton in 1879 and entered the University of Virginia law school. Again poor health changed his plans and he had to return home to rest. Continuing his law studies at home, Wilson became a member of the Georgia bar in 1882. Soon his love for the university atmosphere and the scholarly life returned. He saw that a career as a lawyer would not fulfill these wishes.

Woodrow Wilson left his law practice after one year and went back to the academic world as a graduate student at John Hopkins University in Baltimore. Two years later he published his first book on political philosophy, *Congressional Government*. The book was highly praised. In his book, the young author argued that American government would be greatly improved if governors and presidents had more power to lead and to make decisions. Little did he dream that years later he would prove his ideas could work. He received a Ph.D. degree in political science in June 1886.

To Woodrow Wilson, 1885 was a rewarding year. In addition to publishing his first book, he married. Three years earlier, Woodrow had seen

Two of President Wilson's daughters married while he was in the White House. The photograph is of the wedding party of his daughter, Jessie, who married Francis Sayre, November 25, 1913.

pretty Miss Ellen Axson during church services in Rome, Georgia. He decided that this was the woman for him. They were engaged six months later. During their engagement, he revealed his warm, fun-loving nature to Ellen. "Can you love me in every humor?" he wrote to her, "Or would you prefer to think of me as always dignified? I am afraid it would kill me to be always thoughtful and sensible." But Wilson could not unbend and relax with many people other than his wife. The world saw him as a stiff, efficient leader who got the job done.

Woodrow and Ellen spent the early years of their marriage in the Midwest where he taught at two universities. His academic career took a turn upward in 1890 when he was offered a full professorship of political science at Princeton. The New Jersey campus was a place Wilson had always loved and he accepted with enthusiasm. Life in the East was happy for Woodrow, his wife, and three small daughters. The young professor loved the challenge of his job. Lecturing, counselling eager students, and writing occupied much of his time. While on the staff at Princeton, he wrote textbooks and articles which expressed his ideas about government. Professor Wilson also enjoyed the fun of campus life, and often attended Princeton sporting events, rooting loudly from the stands for his beloved "Tigers."

In 1902 Princeton's Board of Trustees was looking for a university president. They discussed Wilson. He was a fine teacher. His writ-

ten works were famous in the political science field. He was respected by his students and faculty colleagues, and he loved the university. The board unanimously elected him president. Wilson's years as Princeton's chief administrator began on a winning note. He reorganized the departments within the university. He had trouble later when he took an unbending stand against the location of the new graduate school. Wilson wanted the graduate school on campus. Other people wanted the graduate school off the campus. Wilson refused to compromise and a bitter battle went on for two years. After the smoke had cleared, Woodrow Wilson had lost. The site of the graduate school would be off campus.

After a time, the professor-turned-college-president tired of his job. For a long time he had wanted to put his textbook theories into practice. The scholarly teacher had caught the political fever. He resigned his post at Princeton in October of 1910. For years he had been spoken of as a possible political candidate, and Democratic political bosses of New Jersey were desperate. Voters were fed up with grafters and corrupt politicians. The Democratic bosses needed someone well-known, with a reputation for intelligence and honesty, to run as their candidate for governor. Woodrow Wilson filled this order nicely. The bosses believed his lack of experience would make him an easy mark for their "suggestions" once he was in office.

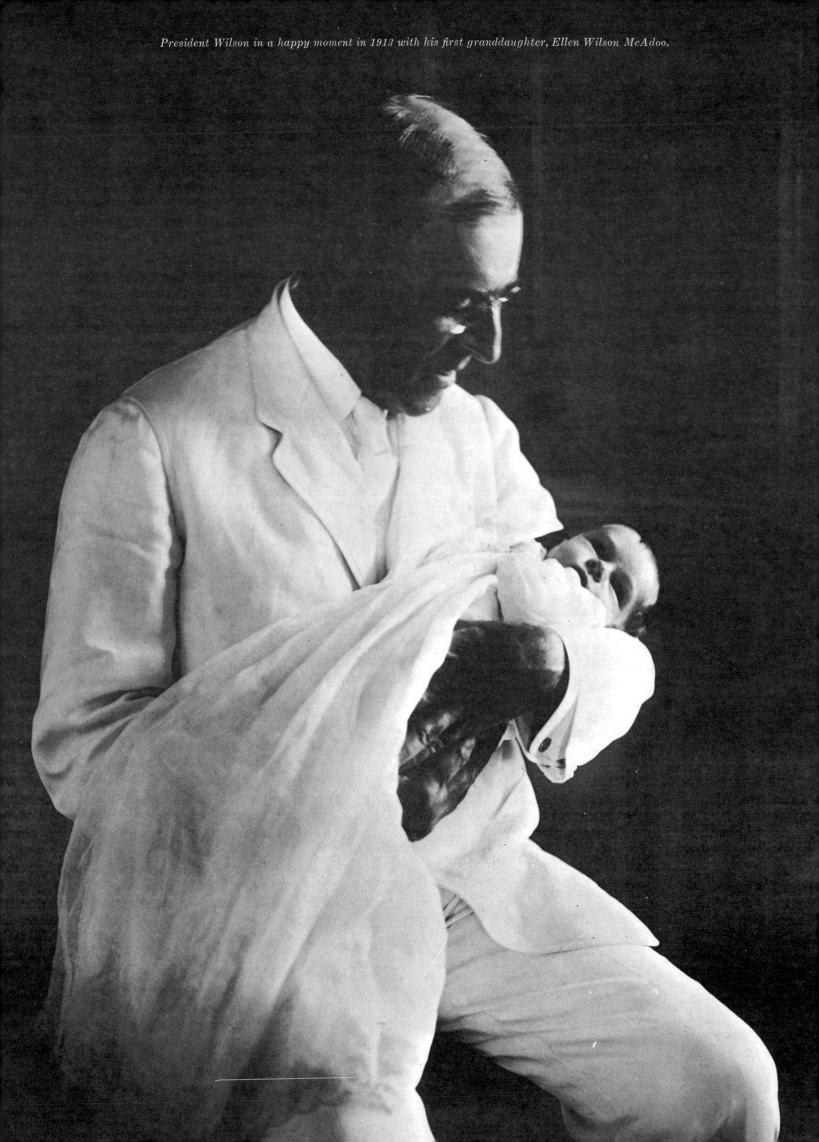

President Wilson in a happy moment in 1913 with his first granddaughter, Ellen Wilson McAdoo.

Ellen Axson Wilson's death in 1914 broke her husband's heart.

Wilson was easily elected governor and took office in January 1911. At first the political science professor amused the Democratic politicians of New Jersey. He began his governorship by following the directions from his own books. Their laughter soon changed to frowns when "The Professor" let them know that he was the boss and would act like one. Wilson was a very successful governor. He had laws passed to rid the state of crooks in government jobs. He had a law passed forcing employers to pay workers injured on the job. He forced honest regulation of public utilities such as the gas and electric companies.

Democratic leaders across the nation began to watch as the New Jersey bosses retreated before the spunky scholar. Some began to think that Wilson might be the man to dump the Republicans out of the presidential chair they had occupied for fifteen years. In a tightly contested race at the June 1912 Democratic National Convention in Baltimore, Woodrow Wilson won the presidential nomination. The voters had three choices that year—Democratic Woodrow Wilson, Republican William Howard Taft, and "Bull Moose" Theodore Roosevelt.

The three-way race soon became a contest between the fiery Roosevelt and the dignified Wilson. The Democratic candidate was a bit slow getting started but, once he did, he enjoyed

the campaign. Wilson met voters all over the country from the rear platform of his campaign train. His managers passed out "Win With Wilson" badges while the candidate spoke to his audiences. The voters were impressed with his "New Freedom" platform to reform the federal government. The November 5, 1912, election results showed Republican Taft and Bull Moose Roosevelt had cancelled each other out. Their scholarly opponent walked off with a whopping electoral college victory: Wilson 435, Roosevelt 88, and Taft 8.

Shortly after his March 4, 1913, inauguration, President Wilson began work on his New Freedom platform promises. To accomplish these goals he used methods new to the presidency. He started presidential press conferences to let the nation know his ideas. By using the President's Room in the Capitol Building, he became well acquainted with congressmen and senators who made the laws of the land. Many of the presidents before Wilson had thought of the Legislative Branch almost as a foreign country. President Wilson did not agree. He often appeared in the House or the Senate unannounced to talk things over with the men whose votes he needed to get his programs made into law. Congressmen and senators were at first startled and then pleased by the president's common sense approach. Woodrow Wilson also showed the American public that harmonious teamwork between the Executive and Legislative Branches could be managed.

With this spirit of cooperation the New Freedom literally galloped along! The high tariff was investigated. It protected our manufactured goods by keeping out cheaper foreign goods, but tended to make the cost of these things higher to the American buyer. American industry was strong enough now to compete with foreign goods, and President Wilson persuaded Congress to lower the tariff. During his administration, the Federal Reserve Board was established to strengthen the system of national banking.

Woodrow Wilson enjoyed being president and watching the theories of his textbooks work effectively in real life. During the Wilson years the Seventeenth, Eighteenth, and Nineteenth Amendments to the Constitution were passed. These amendments provided for the direct election of United States senators by the voters, prohibited the manufacture and sale of

This caricature done in 1915 was one of President Wilson's favorites.

alcoholic beverages, and gave American women the right to vote. Laws were also passed which helped needy farmers borrow money more easily, and shortened the hours of work for railroad men. New Freedom legislation also improved working conditions for children and placed some controls on big business.

The nation enjoyed news about the president and his family inside the White House. Reporters joked that the White House seemed like a happy finishing school with the four Wilson women running about. The inauguration ceremonies were only just over when newsmen started writing with delight about Woodrow Wilson's ladies as they ran through the Executive Mansion exclaiming happily every time they made some new discovery. Ellen Wilson supervised her daughters Margaret, Eleanor, and Jessie. All four Wilson ladies greatly enjoyed being members of the nation's first family. The White House was a happy place for the public to read about. The First Lady changed the upstairs

Oval Room into a family room filled with books and fine paintings. She was a talented painter in her own right. Her daughters were sparkling socialites in Washington. The Wilson girls loved music, dancing, and the theater. They often appeared in amateur theatrical productions to raise money for charity. Jessie and Eleanor were both married during their father's first term. Two White House weddings within six months of each other delighted the entire country. News of bridesmaids dresses, flower arrangements, and guests lists sped all over the nation.

This happy life was shattered shortly after Eleanor was married. In August 1914, the nation was shocked with the news of Ellen Wilson's death. The president was a broken man. How could he live without the advice and gentle humor of his wife? She was the one person who shared his innermost thoughts and knew his complicated personal nature. Sitting by her bedside minutes after her death, he gently laid down her hand and cried out to his family, "Oh my God, what am I to do?" After her funeral, he told friends that loneliness had only been a word to him, but now it was a way of life.

Dr. Cary T. Grayson, his friend and personal physician, worried about the president's state of mind and health, and urged Wilson to take up golf for relaxation. The doctor became President Wilson's partner on the golf course. Dr. Grayson knew Woodrow Wilson was not a man who could live alone. He approved of the president's interest in Mrs. Edith Galt, an attractive widow he met several months after Ellen Wilson's death. The president began taking drives with her and invited her to dinner at the White House. Washington gossips had a field day commenting on the presidential courtship, but Wilson paid no attention to them. He spoke the truth at this time when he wrote about Mrs. Galt to a close friend: "She seemed to come into our life here like a special gift from Heaven." Mrs. Galt was just the woman to ease the terrible strain of his presidential duties and his loneliness. Wilson proposed marriage and Mrs. Galt accepted. Their marriage took place quietly in the widow's Washington home on December 18, 1915.

During the campaign months of 1912, Woodrow Wilson's speeches were almost entirely based upon problems inside the United States. He worked diligently to make his New Freedom plans a reality. But world problems dominated the later years of his administration. In August 1914, World War I broke out in Europe, and President Wilson was faced with an international issue more awesome and far-reaching than any other president had faced. The president had no historic guidelines to follow. He was on his own. World War I caused Woodrow Wilson many great problems and led to his greatest triumphs as President of the United States.

At first Wilson insisted upon American neutrality. The Allies were England, France and Russia. On the other side was Germany and Austria-Hungary. Wilson's neutral policies worked until submarine warfare on the high seas began to alarm the American public against Germany. On May 7, 1915, a German submarine sank the British passenger ship, *Lusitania*, killing 1,198 people, among them 128 United States citizens. Americans were angry, but President Wilson continued with his neutral policies. He just barely won the presidential election of 1916 with the slogan "He Kept Us Out of War."

War fever rose early in 1917 when Germany announced that her submarines would attack any ship at sea, neutral or not. This time the tide was too strong against the president. The United States entered World War I on the side of the Allies in April 1917. In his war message to Congress, President Wilson stated, "The world must be safe for democracy."

World War I was well described by its name. Before it was over, sixteen nations were fighting on one side or the other. President Wilson had asked for a declaration of war with a heavy heart. He did not want war and he was determined to finish it as quickly as possible. Wisely, he chose General John J. Pershing of the regular army to lead the American forces. The American First Army joined the tired French and British armies.

At home, American civilians rose to the task. A War Industries Board was created and had great authority over American life. Patriotic citizens willingly accepted "Wheatless Mondays" and "Meatless Tuesdays." Americans made these small sacrifices so desperately needed food and supplies could be sent to Europe. Woodrow Wilson soon became the outstanding leader of the Allied nations. He began writing powerful messages of propaganda and, when they were dropped from airplanes all over Europe, he became an international hero. Victory was only a matter of time when President Wilson appeared before Congress with his famous "Fourteen Points" for peace on January 8, 1918. The shooting stopped with the signing of an armistice, November 11, 1918.

President Wilson's marriage to Edith Galt in December of 1915 revitalized his spirit. The nation rejoiced for the president, too.

President Wilson threw out the first ball to open the baseball season in 1916.

Headquarters for Democratic candidates in the 1916 presidential election, Woodrow Wilson and Thomas Marshall.

Recruiting posters like this appeared around the country after the United States entered World War I in April 1917. Many American young men believed Uncle Sam and joined the army to fight the war in Europe.

While American soldiers battled the enemy in Europe during World War I, Americans at home practiced economies to help the war effort. The White House was no exception. Sheep were grazed on the White House lawn to raise wool for the Red Cross.

World War I was over, but for Woodrow Wilson the fight was not over. He dreamed of a world government. He believed an international government, to be called the League of Nations, would prevent all future wars. Wilson hoped when the peace treaty was signed the League of Nations would be born. In December 1918 and again in March 1919, he sailed to Europe to work toward this goal. Each time, cheering crowds of Europeans greeted Wilson. The people of Europe believed in his vision of peace. At the Paris peace conferences, European leaders listened to Wilson and accepted the American president's ideas. The League of Nations went into operation in January 1920.

Unfortunately, many political leaders at home did not share President Wilson's hopes

for the League of Nations. Conservative members of Congress opposed President Wilson's efforts for American membership in the League. Where the League of Nations was concerned, Wilson refused to compromise upon any point with those members of Congress who opposed him.

Realizing the Senate might not agree to United States membership in the world organization, Wilson decided to appeal directly to the American people. To do this he traveled nearly 10,000 miles and, in three weeks, spoke forty times for the League. The president completely exhausted himself. On the evening of September 25, 1919, the long months as a wartime president, the tiring weeks spent negotiating the peace treaty in Paris, and the time spent arguing with Congress over the League of Nations issue, all took their toll upon Woodrow Wilson's health. From his railroad compartment the president called his wife, "Can you come to me, Edith, I'm terribly sick." Indeed he was. The stroke he suffered that night was followed by a more severe stroke a week later. These strokes paralyzed his left side and Dr. Grayson feared they had also caused severe damage to the president's brain. Wilson's health was not improved when he learned that Congress had voted against United States membership in the League of Nations.

For more than six months the nation ran without an active president at the helm. Little was known of the president's condition because Dr. Grayson and Edith Wilson kept him sheltered from the world. Because Edith Wilson protected her husband, she was accused of being America's first Lady President. She allowed only one visitor a day. She looked at the messages that were sent to him. Official documents would be returned with a scrawly signature that government officials were not sure was the president's. No one was exactly sure of President Wilson's disability, although Secretary of Agriculture David Houston, who had seen him, said the president "looked old, worn, and haggard . . . enough to make one weep."

Six months passed without a presidential Cabinet meeting, and high government officials worried that the president could no longer lead the nation. Congress sent a committee to investigate Wilson's health. The committee came back uncertain. Then the president slowly began to improve. Letters and other correspondence began to come out of the White House. The president still hoped for American membership in the League of Nations, but this wish did not come true. He was too weak and the nation would not listen.

Woodrow Wilson retired from office, March 4, 1921, and became the only ex-president to take up residence in Washington. With his faithful friend, Dr. Grayson, and his loving wife,

President and Mrs. Wilson attended the ceremonies to open air mail service between Washington, D.C., and New York City, May 15, 1918.

Edith, he lived out the last three years of his life as an invalid. In February 1924 word leaked out that Woodrow Wilson was dying. Crowds gathered outside his house on Washington's S Street to wait in silent tribute. On February 3rd they learned Woodrow Wilson was dead.

Although the United States never joined the League of Nations, Woodrow Wilson's work to establish this world organization won him the Nobel Peace Prize in 1919. The League of Nations was the forerunner of today's United Nations. Edith Galt Wilson lived to see her husband's dream come true when the United States became a charter member of the United Nations in 1945. She must then have remembered her husband's words, "Ideas live; men die."

After his return from Europe where he addressed the opening of the Paris Peace Conference, President Wilson (center) returned to march in this "welcome home" parade, February 27, 1919.

President Wilson sat for this portrait by the famous British artist, Sir William Orpen, in 1919. The painting now hangs in the Red Room of the White House.

WARREN HARDING

Twenty-Ninth President (1921-1923)

There was an easy,
folksy quality about this man,
from a small town in Ohio,
that intrigued the people of the country.
By a seven million majority, they
voted him into the presidency.
Prior to becoming our chief executive,
life had been good to this genial, handsome man.
He was a successful businessman, the
publisher of a prosperous Ohio newspaper,
and a well-known Republican politician.
He had many friends and was
intensely loyal to them.
It was this sometimes ill-placed
loyalty that shattered the
image of the twenty-ninth president,
Warren Harding, and his
presidential administration.
Some historians now consider him
to be one of our weakest
chief executives.

The birthplace of Warren Harding in Blooming Grove, Ohio.

Editor Harding at work in the office of his newspaper, The Marion Star.

Seven year old Warren ("X" above his head)
at a school gathering in Blooming Grove.

High school student Warren Harding in his band uniform.

Presidential candidate Harding's home in Marion, Ohio showing the
famous front porch where he made so many of his campaign speeches
in 1920.

During his 1920 front porch campaign, people traveled from all over the country to meet Candidate Harding. Here he greets entertainers Blanche Ring and Al Jolson.

This 1920 political cartoon kids the two presidential candidates for their methods of campaigning. Harding fishes (campaigns) in one place hoping to "catch" voters, while his Democratic opponent, James M. Cox, keeps moving around to do his "fishing."

THE "TEAPOT DOME" BOILS OVER

Warren Harding was born November 2, 1865, the oldest of eight children in the family of George and Phoebe Dickerson Harding. The Harding family lived on a small farm just outside Blooming Grove, Ohio. His father was a doctor and made enough money to speculate in several small businesses. It was one of these business investments that took young Warren away from the farm chores he disliked so much. The boy was delighted to have a part-time job as a printer's errand boy on the newspaper his father owned. This started him in newspaper work. Life in town proved exciting and the lad persuaded his father to let him work at other jobs away from the farm.

Warren's mother knew her son was not much of a scholar. Hoping he would change his study habits and work hard to become a minister, she sent him to Ohio Central College in 1879. The ministry did not interest him but he made the best of these years in college. Warren was a popular student on the campus. He played the althorn in the college band and did some debating. His old interest in journalism came back to life when he served as editor of the college yearbook.

He graduated from college in 1882 and went to work as a schoolteacher, but quit after one term, saying this was the hardest job he ever held. The young man was not easily kept down because he failed at one occupation. Returning

to his family, now living in Marion, Ohio, he decided to try law. But law required serious study and Harding had never found reading and note-taking easy, so he also abandoned these plans. Being a lawyer was not for this carefree young man, but the town of Marion suited him. Warren loved the pretty little town and its people, and they soon learned to like the friendly, handsome, doctor's son. Warren found his career there, working with people. He was pleasant and easy-going and was thought to be a good businessman. He was given the jobs of handling the finances of Marion's baseball team and cornet band. To Warren both jobs were more pleasure than business.

He was only nineteen when his big opportunity came. Marion's newspaper, *The Star*, was up for sale for three hundred dollars. Hearing this, young Harding's newspaperman's instincts came to life. He knew Marion was a growing town and talked two friends into believing *The Star* would be a sound investment. It was, but not immediately. The first few years were a struggle just to keep the paper from going out of business. Harding's two friends finally gave up, but he would not. Marion did grow and *The Star* grew along with it.

Things changed greatly for Warren Harding and his newspaper in 1891. This was the year of his marriage to Florence Kling, the daughter of a wealthy Marion businessman. The marriage puzzled everyone who knew them. Harding was twenty-six, handsome, pleasant, and easy-going. The bride was five years older, plain, independent, and aggressive. But their marriage was a fine partnership in business and politics. Shortly after their wedding, Florence Harding stopped by *The Star* office to see her husband and was horrified with the disorganization there. As she put it, she "stayed for fourteen years." Her husband handled the writing and editorializing; Florence Harding handled the money and did the hiring and firing of employees. Her energy and cool business head soon had the newspaper showing a fine profiit.

Mrs. Harding did not like to give many raises to *Star* employees. Mr. Harding did not mind sharing the profits with his workers and sometimes he secretly raised their pay. He often got his money back by playing poker in a back room of the newspaper building. Harding chuckled about his secret. At least his employees were

having a little fun with their money before it came back to *The Star* treasury. The money would never have left if his efficient wife had known.

As the newspaper prospered, Warren Harding turned some of his energies to other businesses. By the mid-1890's he was a board member of several Marion corporations, and had become influential in town and church affairs. The minister probably would not have approved of Harding's poker playing, but his friends enjoyed these evenings, with cards, cigars, and friendly talk. It was always fun to spend an evening with Harding, even when losing, which his friends usually did.

Political activity seemed a natural occupation for this pleasant, outgoing man. Florence Harding recognized this and urged him to try another game—politics. Warren Harding didn't need much of a push. Games were always fun for him and politics was the biggest game of

The election of 1920 was the first opportunity women had to vote for a president. Here Mrs. Harding stands in line in front of her husband waiting to cast her vote for him.

all. He joined the Republican Party and found he enjoyed political work which took him among people, talking, debating, and socializing. By 1898 politics was no longer a game; it had become serious work. That year he was elected an Ohio state senator.

It wasn't long before the new senator was the most popular man in the legislature at Columbus. Senator Harding was an average lawmaker, but he was a great peacemaker. His charm and friendliness made him a leader in the state Republican Party. He had a pleasant way of working with others. He settled many disagreements, smoothed over arguments, and helped keep the party machine running smoothly in the state capital.

Warren Harding's activities in Ohio's senate attracted the attention of Harry Daugherty, a clever and powerful Republican machine politician. In 1902, with encouragement from his wife and his new advisor, Harding won the lieutenant governorship of Ohio. After two years in that office, over the protests of Florence Harding and Daugherty, the pleasant peacemaker threw in the towel. He was through with the political game. The splits in the Ohio Republican Party, and the arguments and the plots that surrounded him in the state capital made political office too heavy a load.

Returning home to Marion, he devoted his time to *The Star* and other business opportunities. Most important, he had plenty of time for his friends. The Harding's bankbook prospered. Warren's honesty and personal appeal, combined with Florence's energy and good sense, soon added up to wealth for the couple.

Mrs. Harding and Harry Daugherty never stopped encouraging Harding to go back into politics. They very nearly crushed his political ambition by talking him into running for governor of Ohio in 1910 and 1912. Harding lost both elections. But Daugherty knew a winner when he saw one. He explained to Harding that the governorship was not the right office for him. Daugherty would not allow him to give up. He persuaded Harding to enter the 1914 race in Ohio for United States senator. Daugherty managed a smooth campaign and this time guided the personable publisher to victory.

Always comfortable with the title "Senator," it did not take long for Harding to become a prominent politician in Washington. Senator Harding was not known for his work in the Sen-

ate, but was known for his many friendships with fellow senators. He enjoyed playing golf and attending baseball games with his colleagues; they in turn were refreshed by being with him. When they learned the Ohio senator was coming, Washington wives put out the poker table. Even in the nation's capital, Warren Harding had time for his favorite game. He was still winning, and his opponents still didn't seem to mind losing.

Florence Harding also took to the Washington social whirl. She became a fine party-giver and enjoyed being a senator's wife, especially on official trips with her husband. At the same time she was making even bigger plans for Warren.

His six-year career in the Senate can be summed up in two ways. He was a lawmaker of average distinction who voted with the conservative Republicans most of the time. But he was a gentleman of great distinction, generous in nature and popular with his Washington coworkers. He enjoyed being a senator and the senators enjoyed having him in the Senate.

There were also some serious bones in Harding's body. The years immediately after World War I were frustrating ones for the American people. Inflation caused prices to rise while Congress spent much of its time debating over the League of Nations. Realizing these things, the senator from Ohio became very serious. He spoke out for America saying it was Congress' duty to think of America first, to protect America first, and to make America prosper. Foreign matters should come second. Harding coined a new word in one of his speeches when he said the country needed to return to "normalcy." Americans also wanted "normalcy" and they began to hope Warren Harding could bring it to them.

Harding's vigorous speeches showed his genuine love for his country. They also revealed his desire to return to the Senate in the 1920 election. When Harry Daugherty suggested he might try for the White House instead, Harding was not very interested. He felt he might not be able to handle the job. Daugherty scoffed at his friend's humility and went to work on Florence Harding. With his wife on Daugherty's side, Harding gave in and agreed to make a run for the presidency in 1920. Still not certain they were right, he allowed them to push him into the race.

Daugherty's work at the 1920 Republican

THE MARION DAILY STAR.

VOL XLIV, NO. 289. ENTERED AS SECOND-CLASS MATTER AT POSTOFFICE AT MARION, OHIO. MARION, OHIO, WEDNESDAY, NOVEMBER 3, 1920. SIXTEEN PAGES PRICE TWO CENTS, EXCEPTING SATURDAY, THREE CENTS.

Harding Wins

HARDING BREAKS SOUTH IN A STUPENDOUS VICTORY SCORED BY REPUBLICANS

SENATOR WILL HAVE AT LEAST 391 ELECTORAL VOTES AND MAY HAVE OVER 400, SAY RETURNS

Republicans Will Have Big Working Majorities in Both Houses of Congress—Gain Twenty More Seats in House—Majority of Twelve to Sixteen in the Senate—All Records Are Broken.

New York, Nov. 3.—As late returns came in, today, from all parts of the United States, piling up the Republican lead, the victory over the Democrats was increased to stupendous proportions.

Senator Harding and Governor Coolidge swept Tennessee, returns now indicate, breaking the "Solid South."

This was the first time the Republicans had carried Tennessee since General Grant won the state in 1868.

Under the lead of Senator Harding and Governor Coolidge, the Republicans carried at least thirty-two states; probably more. The New York World, Democratic and the chief press supporter of Governor Cox, estimated there were thirty-seven states in the Republican column.

Senator Harding will have at least 391 electoral votes, whereas only 266 were necessary to elect. The total may go above 400.

The Republicans will have big working majorities in both houses of congress. They gained twenty more seats in the house of representatives and will have a majority of from twelve to sixteen in the senate.

A record vote was polled by Socialists, especially in the cities. There were indications that complete tabulation will show about 2,000,000 votes for Eugene V. Debs, but the Socialist leaders claim even more. The extent of their representation in the next national congress is still problematical.

Still in Doubt.

Arizona and New Mexico were still in doubt at last reports, but the Republicans were making strong claims for the former.

Senator Harding carried Ohio by more than 400,000.

Incomplete returns from Missouri indicated that former Speaker Champ Clark, one of the "wheel horses" of the Democratic party, had been defeated.

Senator Harding and Governor Coolidge carried New York City with a plurality of over 440,000, the biggest plurality ever given a presidential nominee in this city.

The Harding plurality in New York state is unofficially estimated at 1,100,000.

The outcome of the struggle for the governship was still in doubt this afternoon. The complete New York City vote gave Governor Smith, Democrat, a majority, but upstate districts where Judge Miller, the Republican candidate, was strong, were still missing. New York City's complete returns gave Harding 785,576; Cox, 345,635 and Debs 131,856.

An Avalanche.

New York, Nov. 3.—The Republican avalanche which struck the country, yesterday, burying Democratic national and state administrations under a staggering total of votes, was still too big, today, to be estimated in other than general terms.

Early figures available, however made certain that Senator Warren G. Harding and Governor Calvin Coolidge swept at least thirty-one states, with unprecedented pluralities and carried to victory with them twenty-three Republican governors; a majority of at least twelve in the United States senate and a preponderantly Republican house of representatives.

The electoral votes of only two states appeared to be in doubt today—those of Arizona and New Mexico, each with three. Returns in these were so slow and the contests so close that it may take several days to determine the results.

The Cox-Roosevelt ticket carried the Solid South, comprising thirteen states and nothing else, barring possibly victories in Arizona and New Mexico.

The Harding-Coolidge ticket carried every state north of the Mason-Dixon line and every state west of the Mississippi river, with the exception of Arkansas, Louisiana, Oklahoma and Texas and possibly the two doubtful states of the Mexican border.

On the face of today's returns, Harding's popular plurality is estimated anywhere from 4,000,000 to 7,000,000 votes, possibly more, and the Ohio senator seemed assured of having around 389 votes in the electoral college.

Greatest Victory.

It is the greatest victory ever scored by a Republican candidate for the presidency, for exceeding that of Theodore Roosevelt in 1904.

Staggering pluralities were run up in many states, due to the addition of millions of woman votes. The Republican national ticket appears to have captured most of the new vote.

New York gave Harding a plurality estimated roundly at 1,000,000; Pennsylvania, a Republican stronghold, three-quarters of a million; Illinois, 800,000; Michigan, 400,000; California, 500,000; Massachusetts, 300,000, and Ohio, the home state of both candidates, gave Harding a victory roundly estimated at 350,000.

The Republicans succeeded in turning back into the Republican column every northern and western state which Woodrow Wilson carried over Charles Evans Hughes in 1916. Four years ago, the Central and Far West elected Wilson. Yesterday, those same states rolled up impressive majorities for Harding.

Fourteen states which, in 1916, were carried by Wilson and which Harding carried yesterday, were California, Colorado, Idaho, Kansas, Missouri, Montana, Nebraska, Maryland, Nevada, New Hampshire, North Dakota, Utah, Washington and Wyoming.

Southern States.

Even in the southern states, the Democratic majority showed in many cases heavy declines from 1916. Where Texas, four years ago, gave Wilson a handsome majority of 221,515, it was generally estimated, today, that Cox's majority will be many thousands less. Republicans even had strong hopes, today, of electing their men in several congressional fights.

Other southern states showed like decreases.

The thirteen states which Governor Cox appeared, today, to have certainly carried are: Alabama, Arkansas, Florida, Georgia, Louisiana, Mississippi, North Carolina, Oklahoma, Kentucky, South Carolina, Tennessee, Texas and Virginia.

Republican national headquarters here were literally flooded with telegrams today and some of these would not concede the Democrats the so-called border states of Kentucky and Oklahoma, until the last vote was counted. On the face of returns, however, they appeared to be safely in the Democratic column.

Unusual Features.

One of the unusual features of the election, was that of Judge Nathan L. Miller, Republican candidate for governor of New York, ran nearly 1,000,000 votes behind the national ticket and yet was elected by a substantial plurality.

Al. Smith, Tammany hall's favorite son, polled nearly a million more votes in New York than Cox and yet was defeated. Miller's plurality was estimated, today, between 60,000 and 80,000.

While definite figures were not available today, it appeared that the Socialist popular vote is going to be considerable as compared with former years.

In New York City alone, Eugene V. Debs, the prisoner-candidate, rolled up nearly 150,000 votes.

Figures on the Farmer-Labor ticket, headed by Parley P. Christensen, of Utah, were not available this forenoon. The figures on other minor parties are not believed to be impressive.

Breaks "Solid South."

Nashville, Tennessee, Nov. 3.—Tennessee, for the first time since 1868, when Grant received its electoral vote over Seymour, has gone Republican in a national election. The "Solid South" at last has been broken by the cohorts of Republicanism, for Senator Warren G. Harding, according to incomplete, but fairly accurate, returns, has received the state over Governor James M. Cox, between 5,000 and 10,000 votes.

New York City.

New York, Nov. 3.—New York City, complete, gave Harding, 785,776; Cox, 345,535; Debs, 131,856.

In the gubernatorial race New York City, complete, gave Smith, 709,746; Miller, 390,135.

Governor Smith led Miller by 319,611 votes in the completed returns from New York City.

West Virginia.

Huntington, W. Virginia—Republican state headquarters claim Harding carried the state by not less than 40,000. They also claim the election of Morgan, Republican, by 20,000, with the entire state ticket. Cabell county went Republican with a small majority, electing practically the entire ticket.

Democratic state headquarters practically admit the defeat of Arthur S. Koonts, Democrat.

Non-Partisan headquarters still claim Montgomery, Non-Partisan, is elected. Montgomery made a poor showing in Cabell county.

THE STAR OFFICE CREED

Remember there are two sides to every question. Get Both.

Be truthful.

Get the facts. Mistakes are inevitable, but strive for accuracy. I would rather have one story exactly right than a hundred half wrong.

Be decent. Be fair. Be generous.

Boost — don't knock. There's good in everybody. Bring out the good in everybody, and never needlessly hurt the feelings of anybody.

In reporting a political gathering, get the facts; tell the story as it is, not as you would like to have it.

Treat all parties alike. If there's any politics to be played, we will play it in our editorial columns.

Treat all religious matters reverently.

If it can possibly be avoided, never bring ignominy to an innocent woman or child in telling of the misdeeds or misfortune of a relative. Don't wait to be asked, but do it without asking.

And, above all, be clean. Never let a dirty word or suggestive story get into type.

I want this paper so conducted that it can go into any home without destroying the innocence of any child.

WARREN G. HARDING
EDITOR & PUBLISHER OF THE MARION STAR

A MIGHTY LANDSLIDE SWEEPS REPUBLICANS TO UNPRECEDENTED VICTORY

HARDING CARRIES OHIO BY AT LEAST 400,000; WILLIS CARRIES BUCKEYE STATE BY 300,000

Davis Wins in Race for Governor by 125,000 to 140,000—Rest of Repblican State Ticket is Elected by Majorities Ranging Upwards from 25,000 to 140,000. Late Retrns This Afternoon.

Columbus, Nov. 3.—"Harding has carried Ohio by 400,000, Willis by 300,000, Davis by from 125,000 to 140,000 and the rest of the Republican state ticket has been elected by majorities over their Democratic opponents ranging upwards from 125,000 to 140,000," says a statement issued at Republican state headquarters here this afternoon by George H. Clark, chairman of the Republican state executive committee.

At the same time, W. W. Durbin, chairman of the Democratic state executive committee, announced at Democratic state headquarters that he was unable to make any definite statement relative to the gubernatorial race.

Although Chairman Durbin was without figures upon which to base such a statement, he said he was unwilling to concede the defeat of State Auditor Donahey, Democratic candidate for governor, pending receipt of returns which he had asked the various Democratic county chairmen to wire him as soon as possible.

Chairman Durbin, however, conceded Republican victory outside the gubernatorial contest.

Tabulated returns or other figures than those quoted above by Chairman Clark, were not available this afternoon, at either Republican or Democratic state headquarters.

A Big Lead.

Returns from 2,950 of 7,209 precincts gave Davis a lead over Donahey of 60,650, the vote being, Davis, 386,436; Donahey, 325,836.

Returns from 4,460 precincts give Senator Harding a lead over Governor James M. Cox of 218,880. The vote was: Harding, 692,005; Cox, 473,125.

Frank B. Willis is continuing to pile up a staggering lead over W. A. Julian Democratic nominee for United States senator. His plurality may exceed 250,000, according to indications when 2,668 precincts in the state were compiled, the vote being: Willis, 386,324; Julian, 277,579 a plurality for Willis of 108,745.

Returns received on other state officers were scattering and incomplete but there is no doubt that Brown, for lieutenant governor; Smith, for secretary of state; Price, for attorney general; Tracy for auditor, and Archer, for treasurer, had won by handsome pluralities.

The only race now remaining in doubt is that for chief justice of the supreme court where Nichols, Democrat, and Marshall, Republican, are running neck and neck.

Early Returns.

Columbus, Nov. 3.—That Senator Harding has carried Ohio by over 400,000; that the entire Republican state ticket has won in this state; Davis' majority over Donahey exceeds 100,000; that the Crabbe prohibition enforcement act has been severely beaten; that not one Democratic candidate for congress has been elected in Ohio; that former Governor Willis, Republican, has defeated W. A. Julian, Democrat, for United States senator, by a substantial plurality and that the next state legislature will be strongly Republican, are indications, this morning, based upon unofficial returns received outside the secretary of state's office, from more than fifty per cent. of the state's total precincts.

Returns from 3,512 precincts give: Harding, 643,085; Cox, 371,822. Harding's majority over Cox, 172,263.

Returns from 1,727 precincts give: Davis, 200,131; Donahey, 160,189. Davis' majority over Donahey, 39,942.

Returns from 1,605 precincts give: Willis, 185,668; Julian, 134,345. Willis' majority over Julian, 51,323.

A majority of 116,965 for Secretary of State Smith, Republican, over former Secretary of State Fulton, Democrat, is shown by returns from 556 precincts which give Smith 166,836; Fulton, 49,871.

Returns from 435 precincts give Chief Justice Nichols, of the state supreme court, Democratic candidate for reelection, 31,840; Attorney C. T. Marshall, Republican candidate for chief justice, 31,990. Marshall's lead over Nichols, 150 votes.

That the next state legislature, convening here next January, will be "drier than any Ohio legislature in years," was the claim made at the Ohio Anti-Saloon league headquarters.

Male opponents won out over at least two women candidates. Mrs. Dora Sandoe Bachman, Independent, Columbus, was defeated as a candidate for common pleas judge.

Mrs. Etta Freeman Lane, London, Madison county, lost out as Democratic candidate for member of the state legislature.

Ohio congressmen just elected, it appears, include: Former United States Theodore E. Burton, Cleveland, Twenty-Second district; Congressman Nick Longworth, reelected, First district; Stephens, Second; Thompson, Fifth; Kearns, Sixth; Fess Seventh; Cole Eighth; Chalmers, Ninth; Foster, Tenth; Ricketts, Eleventh; Speaks, Twelfth; Murphy, Eighteenth; Hoover, Nineteenth.

In Queen City.

Cincinnati, Nov. 3.—494 precincts out of 559 in Hamilton county, unofficial, give Harding, 92,240; Cox, 66,467.

For governor: Davis, 92,479; Donahey, 71,458.

For United States senator: Willis, Republican, 90,271; Julian, Democrat, 73,233.

For congress, First district: Longworth, Republican, 60,958; Allen, Democrat, 53,037.

Second district: Stephens, Republican, 39,941; Morrow, Democrat, 35,891.

Hamilton county defeated the

Continued on Page Three.

MOTORCYCLE RIDER KILLED IN DAYTON

Police Are Searching for an Automobile Driver.

Dayton, Nov. 3.—In a head-on collision, last night, between his motorcycle and an unknown man's automobile, Clyde Nicholas, twenty-nine, suffered a fractured skull which caused his death in an hour. Police are looking for the automobile driver who they say did not stop.

Watching an election bulletin board, Mrs. Nellie Streill and Ollie Waitley, her niece, each suffered broken legs when they were struck by an automobile. The driver, police say, drove away without being detected.

President Harding enjoyed moments on the golf course away from his official duties.

National Convention in Chicago was a masterful example of the "favorite son" political tactic. The delegates sweltered in the Chicago summer heat in the muggy convention center and argued over three candidates. Daugherty kept his Ohio "favorite son" waiting calmly in the background. At just the right moment, when the wilted delegates faced a second week of squabbling and sweating (at $25.00 a day in Chicago hotels), he acted. Daugherty told the Harding supporters to shout, "Let's nominate Harding and go home!" The delegates had little fight left in them and Warren Harding was handsome and amiable. Why not? Just in time to avoid beginning a second expensive week in Chicago, the tired Republicans compromised and made the Ohio senator their presidential candidate.

The Republicans ran another front porch campaign for Warren Harding, shipping thousands of voters to meet the friendly senator in his own front yard. Candidate Harding was a first-rate handshaker and charmed the people who came by train to Marion to meet him. It was a happy time for Harding. He told jokes and played his althorn. In return, bands played for him, glee clubs sang for him, and Al Jolson

wrote a song for him. Women, who were voting for the first time, were thrilled with his pleasant smile and handsome face. But above all the songs and hubbub, the people knew Warren Harding genuinely loved them and America. They elected him by a seven million vote majority over his Democratic opponent, James M. Cox.

Always a kind and considerate person, Warren Harding had a great moment on Inauguration Day. It was the custom for the president-elect and the outgoing president to ride through Washington streets together to the inauguration ceremonies. Both men raise their hats and wave to the cheering crowds who stand at curbside waiting to greet them. On this greatest day of his life, Harding felt like waving to every soul on earth. However, he noticed that waving caused great pain to stroke-injured President Wilson. The healthy and kind Harding stopped waving so the ill president could also stop.

President Harding began his term by making some very fine appointments. His selection of William Howard Taft as Chief Justice of the Supreme Court was popular with politicians and the people. Harding's Cabinet had three outstanding men: Charles Evans Hughes, Secretary of State; Andrew Mellon, Secretary of the Treasury; and Herbert Hoover, Secretary of Commerce. Secretary Mellon brought praise to Harding's administration when his budget reform program was adopted in 1921. This reform established the Budget Bureau which brought about more efficient government spending. Secretary of State Hughes' work on the Conference for the Limitation of Armament was highly successful. This conference limited the building of warships by America and other leading naval powers.

On Armistice Day, November 11, 1921, President Harding made a moving dedication speech at the Tomb of the Unknown Soldier in Arlington National Cemetery. His words brought tears to the eyes of listeners when they thought

"Laddie Boy" was an airedale given to President Harding as a gift while he was in the White House.

President Harding with the territorial governor (in parka) and Mrs. Harding, aboard ship on his way to Alaska in 1923.

of the thousands who had given their lives during World War I and now rested in graves in Europe.

At times the great demands of the presidency puzzled and frightened Warren Harding. A particularly heavy decision was resting upon his shoulders one day when he said to a White House visitor, "I knew this job would be too much for me." One night several months after his inauguration, a friend went with the president to the back lawn of the White House. There in the privacy of the quiet Washington night, Harding broke into sobs from the strain of his job.

Although the careworn chief executive found little fun in the White House, he remained constant in one way. Warren Harding was a man with many friends, and he took care of his friends. Even when they had poor qualifications, he placed some of them in his Cabinet and many in other high government offices. For a time everything seemed to work well. The Executive Branch functioned smoothly, it seemed almost like a friendly club of political friends. It was a pleasure for their friend the president to see them work so well together. Warren Harding trusted these men completely and he thought all was well.

Early in 1922, the rumors started. These tales of corruption, graft, and dishonest dealing would not go away. The next year two government officials who had been appointed by President Harding committed suicide. Secretary of the Interior Albert B. Fall, another associate of the president, resigned in the furor that accompanied these deaths.

Black clouds of doubt began to fill Warren Harding's mind. He would not believe his friends had betrayed him and the country. The pressure of these doubts became so great he decided to take a trip with Mrs. Harding across the country and then north to Alaska. But the tour

of the northern territory and western Canada did not ease the chief executive's troubled mind. Speech-making and official receptions wore down the president who was already weakened by doubt.

In San Francisco, President Harding became ill with pneumonia. The First Lady sat by his bedside and the nation sat by their radios, waiting for news of the dangerously ill chief executive. Harding improved a little and his wife and the country regained hope. On the afternoon of August 2, 1923, Mrs. Harding sat by her husband's bedside reading aloud a favorable news report. He seemed to be falling asleep when he said in drowsy tones, "That's good, go on." Before she could continue, he was dead, swiftly and silently, of a blood clot on the brain.

Death for the first time had been merciful to a president in office. In the months that followed, scandal after scandal was reported in the nation's newspapers. The Marion *Star* sadly had to report that Warren Harding's friends had betrayed him and their country for profit. Some of Harding's friends were tried, convicted, and sent to jail. Harding's old friend Harry Daugherty, whom he had made Attorney General, was caught taking bribes from prohibition violators. As each scandal broke, Harding's name was further blackened by his lack of leadership and the greed of his friends.

Most spectacular among the numerous scandals was the "Teapot Dome" affair. Secretary of the Interior Fall had made a crooked business deal with two oil companies. In return for an illegal payment of $400,000.00, Fall turned over two valuable government petroleum deposits to private companies. They were the Teapot Dome oil reserve in Wyoming and the Elk Hill oil reserve in California. For cheating the government Secretary Fall and one oil company executive were tried and sent to prison.

Warren Harding never knew how much his good name was blackened by the corrupt activity of his friends. Although he was never personally involved, the American people were terribly angry at the president lying in his grave. They knew that every team must have someone in control, and saw that the Harding team had gone wild without its driver. Warren Harding was not a leader. But the American people can look back upon him now as a man overcome by the terrible responsibilities of the presidency, and as a man betrayed by his friends.

304

This 1923 poster shows newspaper headlines that pay tribute to the
four Republican presidents who had died in office.

CALVIN COOLIDGE

Thirtieth President (1923-1929)

His swearing-in as president
was the plainest in all
American history.
This silent, shy man took the oath
of office as the thirtieth president from
his father, a justice of the peace,
in their kerosene-lit farmhouse
in the Green Mountains of Vermont.
Born and raised in New England, he
possessed the "Yankee" virtues
of honesty, hard work, and quiet
perseverance. He was precisely the man
America needed in the turbulent mid-1920's.
Sandwiched between the notorious
"Teapot Dome" activities and the terrible
economic depression of the early 1930's,
Calvin Coolidge provided our country with the
breath of calm it needed to survive
these ordeals of scandal,
poverty, and change.

President Coolidge had his picture taken more than any other president to that time in American history. Here he poses with visiting Indian chiefs on the White House lawn.

"KEEP COOL WITH COOLIDGE"

This political cartoon deals with the presidential campaign of 1924. It shows other presidential candidates throwing bricks trying to knock the Coolidge hat "out of the ring." Silent Cal stands quietly by looking out from a window in the White House. He knows he has the election won.

John Calvin Coolidge (he later dropped the first name) was born July 4, 1872, in Plymouth Notch, Vermont, the oldest child of John and Victoria Moor Coolidge. The Coolidges had worked on this Green Mountain farm, earning a meager living from the poor soil for four generations. Calvin lived the life of a New England farm boy, and learned the Yankee ways from his parents. On his father's small farm he chopped firewood, planted corn, milked cows, and collected maple syrup. He particularly enjoyed pitching hay, which he thought of more as a sporting contest than work.

His father worked him hard, but was always patient with Calvin. He took time to explain the things the boy questioned. Calvin both loved and respected his father's hard-driving fairness. From him he learned the virtues of thrift, love of his fellow man, and how to work hard. In 1885, twelve year old Calvin lost his mother. It was difficult for his father to explain the will of God to his grief-stricken son.

Calvin's father was a highly respected man in the community. His reputation for good sense and trustworthiness elected him to several local offices, and helped to make the small store he ran earn enough money to provide for his son's education. Calvin first went to local schools. At thirteen he proved himself a good enough student to pass the examination qualifying him to become a schoolteacher. But Calvin had little enthusiasm for this job.

Finally, John Coolidge had enough money to send Calvin to the Black River Academy, a private school twelve miles from home. After graduating from the academy in 1891, Calvin entered Massachusett's Amherst College. He was, at first, a true picture of Yankee singlemindedness. The young man from Vermont joined no clubs and participated in no sports, he just studied. In the beginning he was only an average student, but by his senior year at Amherst things were better for him in every way. Calvin found he could make people laugh and this erased some of his shyness and helped him make friends. Classmates found Coolidge quiet but enjoyed his sly sense of humor. He joined a fraternity in his senior year. Social success gave Calvin confidence in himself and his grades improved. He graduated from Amherst in 1895 with high academic honors.

In the fall of that year Calvin Coolidge decided upon a law career. With his father's blessing, he entered the Northampton, Massachusetts, law offices of John Hammond and Henry Field. Both lawyers were active Republicans and their law student soon found himself involved in political activity. Immediately after entering their offices, Calvin Coolidge began working on the campaigns to elect Field mayor and Hammond district attorney of Northampton. Both men won. Politics had proved interesting, but the determined young man from Vermont kept at his law studies. In 1897 Coolidge passed the Massachusetts bar examination and hung out his shingle in Northampton. Northampton's people found lawyer Coolidge hardworking and hard to know. Some thought of him as an "odd stick." Gradually the shy young man earned the respect and admiration of the town for his honest work. Those who broke through his protective shell of shyness, found him to be a fine, faithful friend. Coolidge's friendships were with the people who made him feel at ease. He was friends with shopkeepers, the barber, and in particular, Jim

Mrs. Coolidge dressed up her white collie Rob Roy in a bonnet for a White House garden party in June 1926.

WONDERFUL INVENTION BUT COSTLY

"CAREFUL CAL."

This political cartoon, by G. K. Berryman of the Washington Evening Star, pokes fun at President Coolidge for his thrifty ways.

Lucey, the Northampton shoemaker, with whom he could freely discuss anything.

It is often said that opposite personalities are attracted to each other. This was not the case with Coolidge's plain-thinking, hard-working friend, Jim Lucey, but it most certainly was true with Miss Grace Goodhue. Coolidge had been a bachelor for many years when he met and fell in love with attractive Miss Goodhue, a teacher at the school for the deaf in Northampton. This high-spirited young lady returned the shy lawyer's love and accepted when he proposed marriage. They were married in October 1905. The match was a fortunate one for both. Grace helped her husband socially by smoothing out his rough edges. At home Calvin calmed down his spirited wife by his firm New England manner. The Coolidges lived in a simple two-family house on a quiet Northampton street. The couple had two sons, John who was born in late 1906, and Calvin, Jr., who was born in 1908.

By 1908, "Coolidge luck" was often talked about in Northampton politics. Calvin had been elected to many offices: first the town council, then city solicitor, then clerk of the county courts, and then to the Massachusetts legislature. By winning election after election, Coolidge was a marvel to his Republican colleagues. He was truly a non-political person with his shy, silent ways. There were no tricks hidden in his political basket. Local political sages threw up their hands in surprise each time he won and suggested Coolidge's success was luck. Luck had nothing to do with it. The Massachusetts voters liked Calvin Coolidge's hard-working, honest approach to politics. He was a man they trusted to represent them against silver-tongued politicians.

Coolidge climbed higher on the political ladder when he was elected Northampton's mayor in 1910. Two years later, the voters sent him to the Massachusetts Senate, and 1915 he was elected lieutenant governor of that state. Calvin Coolidge gained the top job in state politics in 1918 when he was elected governor.

Strangely enough he had not really wanted a career in politics. The life of a lawyer was more appealing to him. Coolidge explained his political activity to Grace and his friends by saying it was a way to please his father, while making valuable contacts for his law practice. Political activity was painful for the shy Coolidge. Discussing this with a friend he said:

"When I was a little fellow . . . I would go into a panic if I heard strange voices in the kitchen . . . and the hardest thing in the world was to have to go through the kitchen door and give them greeting . . . I'm all right with old friends, but every time I meet a stranger, I've got to go through the old kitchen door back home, and it's not easy."

For this shy man political life was uncomfortable. But by the time he was elected governor, he knew that politics was to be his career. Calvin Coolidge knew that honesty and straightforwardness were needed in politics. The simple people needed someone to carry their banner. Highlighting his years in the Massachusetts statehouse were the efforts he made in 1919 to settle the Boston police strike. His settlement of this matter made him a national hero in the eyes of the American voter. They saw Coolidge as a man who would fight against anyone or any organization standing against the public safety and the public welfare.

Then Massachusetts friends and well-wishers began to plant the seeds of presidential aspiration in the mind of the governor. They collected fifty thousand dollars to publish and distribute throughout the nation a book of Coolidge speeches. His clever, simple statements on government and politics were appealing to the Americans who read them. It was fun swapping "Coolidgisms" with friends: "We need more of the office desk and less of the show window in politics . . . Expect to be called a standpatter, but don't be a standpatter . . . Let men in office substitute the midnight oil for the limelight." Delegates to the 1920 Republican National Convention had also read "Coolidgisms," and surprised the nation by nominating Calvin Coolidge as Warren Harding's vice-presidential running mate.

Political sages chuckled at the personality contrast on the Republican ticket. The two men were miles apart. Harding was a handsome, cigar-smoking, backroom, caucus politician and Coolidge was a plain, frontroom, political puritan. The sages said this pairing would never work. But it did. The voters sent the unlikely Republican pair to Washington in the November 1920 election.

The vice president was awakened in the middle of the night on August 2, 1923, at his father's Vermont farmhouse. Every summer the two Coolidge men got together and Calvin discussed

President Coolidge and his family (left to right) John, Mrs. Coolidge, and Calvin, Jr., gaze at their reflections in the White House pool.

the events of American life with his father. That night the bewildered vice president was awakened and told of Warren Harding's death in San Francisco. Inside the farmhouse, which had few comforts and none of the twentieth century conveniences, John Coolidge took charge with twentieth century efficiency. The nation needed a leader. In this lamplit sitting room, he solemnly administered the oath of office which made his son President of the United States.

The next morning, before leaving for Washington, Calvin Coolidge turned aside from the mob of government officials and newsmen who swarmed over the Vermont farm. The new president visited his mother's grave alone. He needed a time to remember her wisdom and kindness, a time to remember her Yankee clear-headedness. These memories would help guide him in the enormous task that lay ahead.

Back in the capital, President Coolidge set about his new job with the firm belief that the country needed peace, prosperity, and calmness. The president wanted strong men in important government jobs to help him. He made wise choices, and then let the men he selected move ahead with firm action while he acted as overseer to his Cabinet. The president did not give his Cabinet members orders, he watched and approved their actions.

"Silent Cal," as his enemies loved to call him, sat back when the messy "Teapot Dome" scandals came to light, and did little to punish the wrongdoers. He decided to let the law do its job without interference. The Republicans and the general public gathered around the president in sympathetic support when Democrats tried to show he had taken part in the illegal activities. In the 1924 election, Coolidge and Dawes were placed in office by a two-and-a-half million vote majority.

After the 1924 victory, "Coolidge prosperity," dominated the land for a time. The president had a good radio personality and was able to make his aims clear to those who listened. The people let Coolidge set about accomplishing his belief that "the business of America is business." Coolidge encouraged private industrial expansion and held back on the federal government's spending. Businessmen and workingmen prospered, but trouble lay ahead. This great prosperity stood upon the shaky legs of an extremely active and unstable stock market. Economic experts warned President Coolidge and Secretary of the Treasury Andrew Mellon of the dangers that could come from this "sky's the limit" stock market. Perhaps President Coolidge believed the experts, but his policy of "watchful waiting" would not allow him to heed these

President Calvin Coolidge.

warnings. He would not interfere with the stock market on Wall Street. This was a New York state problem.

"Watchful waiting" was not so strictly applied to foreign affairs. President Coolidge was an active diplomat. A month after he came into office in 1923, a terrible earthquake and typhoon ripped across Japan. The president quickly sent the U.S. Pacific Fleet to the Japanese port of Yokohama to help the devastated country. Relations between the United States and Japan reached an all-time high because of the quick actions of the American president. Coolidge also worked to improve relations with Latin American countries. He chose efficient, tactful U.S. representatives to work in South American nations.

Behind his calm mask the president showed the nation there was a man with deep feelings and strong emotions. A few days after he became president, Coolidge thought of his good friend and advisor Jim Lucey. He wrote to Lucey, "If it were not for you I should not be here and I want to tell you how much I love you." He found it more difficult to outwardly express love for his wife and two sons, but it was there, strong and deep. One day on vacation, Grace Coolidge was late coming back from a hike. The president had worried so that his relief turned to anger when she returned safely. He had the secret service man who accompanied Mrs. Coolidge transferred, and would not speak to his wife for days for frightening him so.

Calvin Coolidge brought his two sons up in the same hard-working ways he had learned on the farm in New England. This method did not change when the Coolidge's moved into the White House. One summer vacation, Calvin, Jr., was sent to work on a tobacco farm not far from the nation's capital. Another worker teased him by saying, "If my father were president, I wouldn't have to work." Young Calvin smiled and retorted, "If my father were your father you would!" Not long afterward, when playing tennis vigorously, young Calvin developed a large blister on his hand. This seemingly harmless blister led to a severe case of blood poisoning. Soon the fourteen year old boy was dead. Calvin Coolidge's strong belief in the ways of God was again tested. The grief-stricken president wrote: "I do not know why such a price was exacted for occupying the White House."

Yankee Coolidge's lifelong habit of thrift was not changed by living in the White House. He carefully supervised White House guest lists and menus, and rarely let his more free-spending wife in on the planning. Guests to White House receptions were sometimes served only plain ice water in paper cups. "Silent Cal" relaxed by taking occasional fishing trips or riding an electric horse that bucked up and down in the White House gymnasium. Nearly every night he was in bed by ten, and each afternoon he took a two-hour nap. To some, his life style seemed almost stingy. Perhaps Coolidge knew that presidential plain-living was exactly the thing needed to impress a nation tired of the "Roaring Twenties" and the Harding scandals.

Plain-living was Coolidge's rule, but humor was also present. Inside the Executive Mansion he delighted in pressing buttons to call assistants and then hiding to watch the fun as they searched for him. He could take a joke about himself as well as any man. When a comedian in a theater saw the president in the audience, he poked fun at Cal for being up past his bedtime. Coolidge laughed along with the audience. The shy chief executive hated having his picture taken. But he was photographed more than any of his predecessors, and said to a friend that his main source of exercise was "having his picture taken." Friends objected to his almost clownish appearance when he had his picture taken dressed as a cowboy. President Coolidge was a bit embarrassed about this picture, too, but commented that it was good for the American people to laugh, even at their president.

The presidential office, with its duties and decisions and strains, was exhausting to Calvin Coolidge. He also realized that the time was coming when the country would need a different direction than his watchful waiting policies could accomplish. He disappointed the Republicans and the nation by stating firmly in 1928 that he would not run again for president.

He returned to Northampton, to his plain, two-family house in 1929. But the quiet Yankee and his wife often found their privacy invaded by visitors who traveled to the little Massachusetts town just to catch a glimpse of the ex-president they admired. One year of this was enough for Coolidge. He and Grace moved out of town to a secluded twelve-room home, "The Beeches." There they could sit on their front porch undisturbed. He devoted the rest of his life to writing his autobiography and, for a year, wrote a daily newspaper column. Death came to the unassuming man from Vermont, January 5, 1933.

Grace Goodhue Coolidge did not entertain much as First Lady due to the death of her son, Calvin, Jr., in 1924, and the death of her father-in-law, John Coolidge, in 1926.

HERBERT HOOVER

Thirty-First President (1929-1933)

His story was like
a Horatio Alger tale of success.
Starting as a poor Iowa farm
boy, his life went from
rags to riches and fired the
imagination of millions.
In his lifetime, he lived in the "White House"
on England's Thames River, and in the
White House on America's Potomac River.
Living in the "White House" on the Thames, he
reached the peak of success and prosperity
as a world-renowned mining engineer and executive.
As a resident of America's greatest
house, he experienced a low point
in his long and productive life.
A black cloud of despair broke
over the thirty-first president, Herbert Hoover,
and his country in 1929.
The "rugged individualist" did
not have the political prowess to lift
the United States out of
this terrible time of trial.

Herbert Hoover's birthplace in West Branch, Iowa.

A "RUGGED INDIVIDUALIST" IN THE WHITE HOUSE

Herbert Clark Hoover was the second son of Jesse and Hulda Minthorn Hoover. He was born August 10, 1874, in West Branch, Iowa. His father was a blacksmith, his mother a hard-working housewife. Young Herbert never knew either of them well, because by the time he was eight both parents had died. The eight year old orphan went to live in a small town in Oregon, where he grew up in the household of an uncle.

Herbert went south to Palo Alto, California, tall, lean, and bashful at seventeen. With only three hundred dollars in his pocket and the determination he learned from his Quaker upbringing, he enrolled at Leland Stanford University. He selected engineering as his major field of study. To meet his college expenses he worked at many jobs. He was an office boy, delivered newspapers, and worked a laundry route. Each summer vacation he earned money working in the mountains as a member of mining and geological expeditions. The hardworking Hoover was not a brilliant student, but he earned good marks in his engineering courses and had many college friends. Stanford classmate, Will Irwin, discussing Hoover said, "Popularity is not exactly the word for (Hoover's influence) on his fellows, a better word would probably be 'standing!'." He earned more than "standing" with Lou Henry, another Stanford student whom he met in a geologist's laboratory at the university. They fell in love and planned to marry when

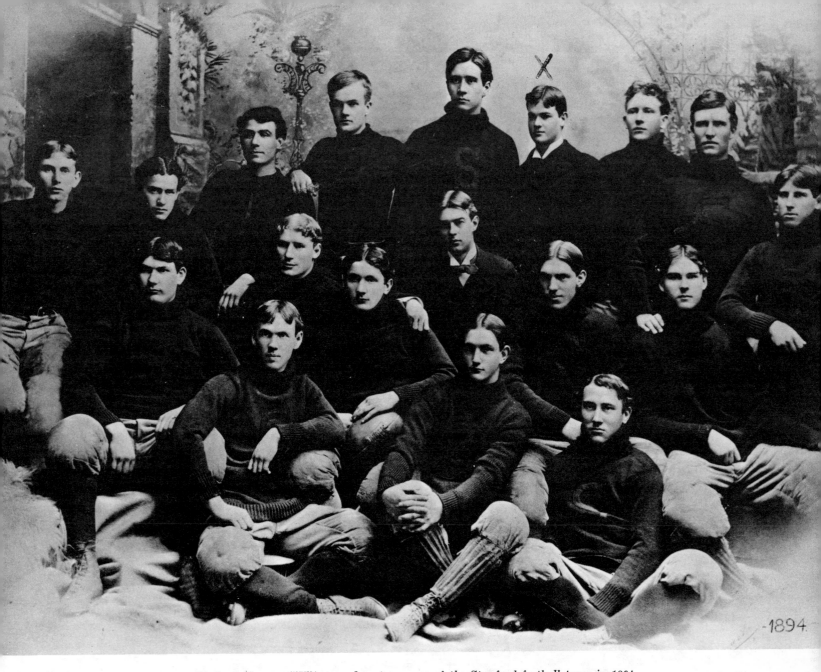

Herbert Hoover ("X") served as treasurer of the Stanford football team in 1894.

Herbert was established in the engineering world after graduation.

Herbert Hoover was a member of the first graduating class at Stanford in 1895. He took with him an engineering degree and a determination to do well. The young engineer went out into a business world where jobs were hard to find because times were hard. With high hopes, Hoover headed for the gold-mining district of Nevada. He found a job for fourteen dollars a week using a pick and shovel. Working as a laborer in the mines, he toiled ten hours a day, seven days a week. In a few months even this job was gone. "Then I learned what the bottom levels of real human despair are paved with," he said later.

Then the energy and refusal to quit that characterized Herbert Hoover's life took hold of him. He traveled to San Francisco to seek em-

ployment. The mining engineer who hired him at a salary of fifty dollars a month soon saw that he had a bargain in Herbert Hoover. The young man was a worker and he really knew mining engineering. When Hoover's new employer was asked by a British company to send an engineer to Australia to install American machinery, young Hoover was chosen. When he arrived, a gold rush was booming. The Australian mines were crowded, inefficient, and the workers were excited. But Hoover set to work and did it well.

Success on this job made him a well-known mining engineer. Twenty-four year old Hoover was sent to another job in China. Proposing marriage to Miss Henry by cablegram, Hoover made a quick trip to California so they could be married. The couple honeymooned on their way to his new job in China.

When his work in China was successfully

Mining engineer Herbert Hoover (center) with his friend D.P. Mitchell (right) in Australia in 1903.

In his job as Chairman of the European Relief Council, Herbert Hoover supervises the loading of food for Europe in 1921 in New York City.

THE BANDWAGON RUSH

Hoover's popularity as a 1928 presidential candidate is shown in this political cartoon.

The great depression that came shortly after President Hoover's inauguration hit people across America from all walks of life. The despair of the times can be seen in the face of this migrant mother.

completed, Hoover was asked to join a London mining firm. Lou and Herbert Hoover moved to London and lived there from 1902 to 1917. Both of their sons were born in the English capital. However, much of their time in those years was spent traveling to distant places on the globe, wherever Hoover's job called him – Ceylon, Burma, Malaya, Russia, Siberia, and Africa. When the Hoover family was at home in London, they lived at the "Red House." The Hoover boys especially enjoyed the times spent at their lovely country home, outside London on the Thames River, which they called the "White House."

Herbert Hoover's humble beginnings taught him to work hard and mining engineering was a life he truly enjoyed. Hoover became a prosperous mining director in London and an owner of mining properties throughout the world because he was a fine executive and could make quick, correct decisions. By 1914, the poor boy from Oregon had become a millionaire with a chain of offices around the globe, in London, Melbourne, Shanghai, San Francisco, and New York.

The outbreak of World War I in Europe brought his mining career to an end, but opened up another to Hoover's administrative genius. Frightened American tourists were caught by the war in Europe. Given the job of gathering together thousands of American vacationers in the most difficult of circumstances, Hoover calmly and efficiently packed them all up and shipped them safely home.

Next he was selected for an even greater task. During the war thousands had been left homeless and hungry in Belgium. Herbert Hoover was asked to head the Commission for Relief to Belgium. He agreed to take on the work of feeding and housing needy Belgians; and he did it with great skill and at top speed.

When the United States entered the war in 1917, he returned home to serve President Wilson and the country as Food Administrator. It was his duty to see that the American Army and the Allies in Europe were well fed. This was no easy job. To accomplish this task, Hoover had to convince the American public to ration itself. He did this by appealing to American patriotism. The word "Hooverize" became the cry across the country. At Hoover's request, Americans gladly accepted "meatless" and "wheatless" days every week to help the war effort.

At the conclusion of World War I, Herbert Hoover returned to Europe to continue his humanitarian work. He helped to stop starvation on the bombed and burned continent. Between 1914 and 1921, commissions headed by Hoover spent over a billion dollars keeping millions of Europeans alive with necessary food supplies. For seven years he worked to overcome the devastation of war and, at his request, he received not one penny in salary.

When the European situation eased, he returned to America in 1921. Watching him depart, a Food Commission colleague of many years raised his hat in deep respect and called Herbert Hoover "The Weary Titan."

When Herbert Hoover emerged from the ashes of World War I, his name was known in every country. To the American public, he had managed the miracle of feeding the American Army, the war's civilian victims, and finally, the starving enemy in Germany. He was a humanitarian hero, and seemed a natural for political life.

President Harding promptly appointed Hoover as Secretary of Commerce. At that time the Department of Commerce was ineffective and inefficient. It had been established for some time but had accomplished very little. What could Hoover do with it? The extent to which Secretary of Commerce Hoover built up this department seemed another of his miracles. Believing in hard work and self-reliance, he encouraged and inspired these values in Commerce Department workers. He saved a great deal of money for the country by ending wasteful Commerce Department practices. In a short time, Herbert Hoover, the businessman administrator, turned the department into a well-organized, well-run part of the federal government.

When Calvin Coolidge decided not to run for the presidency in 1928, Hoover was the logical and popular choice of the Republicans. They knew Herbert Hoover could win the election if he campaigned carefully against Democrat Alfred E. Smith, the popular governor of New York. Candidate Hoover made no mistakes. He cashed in on the appealing theme of continuing "Coolidge prosperity." Telling the voters there was more of the same coming, he promised "a chicken in every pot" and spoke about the great numbers of automobiles, radios, and washing machines in American homes. The voters liked his message and sent Herbert Hoover to the White House on the Potomac with a smashing

444 to 87 electoral college majority over Smith.

Americans sat back and smiled. Now they had a businessman, not a politician, at the helm. At last the government was in good hands and things could only get better. President Hoover continued to work as hard as he had all his life. He took no vacation and played no golf or other games for four years. The president arose at seven each morning and went straight out to the White House lawn in old clothes. Friends were always waiting to exercise with him by throwing a heavy medicine ball back and forth. The exercise period was not long. He was soon behind his desk carrying on the nation's business. President Hoover was often so deep in his work he hardly lifted his eyes from the desk to greet callers.

But it was not long before the people began to look upon him as a humorless man of all work and no play. They wanted to laugh with him and could not. And when it came time to cry with him, they would not. Eight months after his inauguration Hoover's version of "Coolidge prosperity" disappeared overnight. Black Thursday came to Wall Street in New York City in October of 1929 and sent stock prices spiraling downward. Millionaires became instant paupers and some jumped from windows of Manhattan skyscrapers, unable to face bankruptcy. The nation came crashing down after them. Factories shut down, business failed, and banks closed their doors. Unemployment rose to twelve million in 1932. Private organizations began breadlines around the country so that the hungry would not starve. Nearly two million jobless men roamed the country trying to make some sort of living.

The worst economic depression in American history had citizens struggling for their existence. During World War I "Hooverizing" was popular. During the depression the word "Hoover" was applied to anything that meant hardship and despair. Broken down automobiles were called "Hoover wagons." "Hoover blankets" were newspapers wrapped around bodies of the thousands who could not afford coats to keep away the cold. Empty pockets turned inside out to show the penniless condition of their owners became "Hoover flags." These economic conditions had been developing for years before Hoover took office and they raced out of his control. Once again the President of the United States had to answer for the agony of his people.

In spite of the trying times of his presidency, Herbert Hoover had a good sense of humor. He liked this 1932 caricature of himself.

Back in Washington, Hoover heard the people's cries and ached for their troubles. He worked harder than ever, directing meetings, getting laws passed, and creating bureaus he thought would help. The president's actions were meant to encourage industry in hopes that some money would trickle down to the workers. It did not. In the cities, girls worked fifty-five hours a week in "sweat-shops" for less than a dollar a day.

Appeals came to the president from everywhere. The government must do something to ease this despair and suffering. Why not pay directly for hungry Americans' food? Why not create government projects that would give jobs to some of the unemployed thousands. Herbert Hoover did not like these suggestions. He felt

President Hoover strolls on the White House lawn with his wife. Behind them (with the naval officer) is Mrs. Theodore Roosevelt.

the country would be weakened by giving people something for nothing. In turning down a suggested two billion dollar public works program created to employ and feed thousands of hungry Americans, President Hoover said, "It is the most gigantic pork-barrel ever (created) by the American Congress."

The President stood firmly in this position and would not move. He substituted words for the work that troubled people needed for their self-respect and survival. "Rugged individualism" had gotten him where he was in life, and he felt it would carry Americans through their troubles. Hoover did not want direct federal payments to the needy. He called it putting them "on the dole." President Hoover believed that local government and private charities must accept this responsibility. He asked America to

recall its vigorous and active history of victory over enemies and hard times. The "rugged individualist" in each American must once again rise up to defeat the depression.

But things got no better in spite of the president's hopes and efforts. "Hoovervilles" sprang up around the country. These were broken-down, tarpaper and wood huts thrown together on the edge of many American towns. Jobless men and their families, who had been thrown out of their own homes, gathered in these pitiful dwellings. One of the largest "Hoovervilles" appeared just outside Washington, D.C. Thousands of World War I veterans and their families lived there. They came from all corners of the United States to speak directly to the president. These ex-soldiers remembered President Hoover's help to homeless and hungry millions in

Europe after World War I. Now it was his time to help them. They asked for immediate payment of their veterans' benefits. The law said these benefits could not come to them until 1945. They could not wait. It was their hope President Hoover would know why and would do something to help.

But Herbert Hoover turned a deaf ear to the veterans' outcries. He refused to see any of their leaders. The frustrated veterans, calling themselves the Bonus Expeditionary Force, marched on Washington to appeal to the president and Congress. Hoover would not see them. Congress would not act. The veterans then started to occupy government buildings in the daytime and Washington parks at night. They would not be forgotten. An angry President Hoover went into action. Calling in the army, he forcibly removed the marchers from the capital and had their tattered shacks in "Hooverville" burned to the ground. Many people were hurt when the army took this action, among them some wives and children of the veterans.

Four years of energetic activity upon the part of President Hoover did not ease the depression in America. The businessman chief executive never stopped working, never stopped trying to help, and never changed his mind about the way to do it. Newspapers and radios carried his messages again and again. He told the country that rugged individualists could work their way out of the depression. The government would not dole out money or food.

The voters now knew they had been wrong in 1928. This hard-working man in the White House was not the right president for that time. They turned away from Hoover and the Republicans in the presidential election of 1932. The country had to have a chief executive who would listen, compromise, and try new things.

Herbert Hoover left office on March 4, 1933. The country was at the bottom of a dry well and his image was there too. He had been wrongfully accused of causing the depression, and savagely attacked when his efforts to bring the country out of this terrible dilemma had failed. Herbert Hoover was a tired man.

Following Franklin Delano Roosevelt's inauguration, Lou and Herbert Hoover returned to Palo Alto, California, to rest. But Herbert Hoover was never a man to remain idle for long. He lived longer than any other chief executive after retiring from office. His last career

as an ex-president was a fruitful one. At Stanford he organized and administered the Hoover Institute on War, Revolution, and Peace. In 1945, at the end of World War II President Truman asked Hoover to return to Europe and act as the Coordinator of the European Food Program. He was also twice chairman of the Hoover Commission on Administrative Reform in Washington. This commission was set up to increase efficiency in the Executive Branch. For his continued good work Hoover received the thanks of two presidents. He died on October 20, 1964, in New York City.

Herbert Hoover's life proved the American dream, that a man can rise through hard work and creative thought to the heights of fame and success, no matter where his position in society starts. In his long life he had three separate careers, in business, philanthropy, and politics. His presidency was a most troubled one and it may best be summarized this way, his belief in "rugged individualism" perhaps was right, but it appeared at the wrong time.

Lou Henry Hoover lived in Washington while her husband was Secretary of Commerce under Presidents Harding and Coolidge. As a result she had many personal friends in the nation's capitol when she became First Lady. There were many friendly White House social functions for these friends while her husband was president.

For his fine humanitarian work in war-torn Europe after World War II, Ex-president Hoover was greeted enthusiastically by Europeans everywhere he went. Here he is greeted by children in Helsinki, Finland in 1946.

Ex-president Hoover talks with President John F. Kennedy shortly after the young Democrat took office. Hoover was eighty-six.

FRANKLIN D. ROOSEVELT

Thirty-Second President (1933-1945)

Doctors once said
that this six-foot,two-inch
man would have to be
carried about like a baby.
He had been cut down in the middle
of his active life by polio.
But with a determined will that
would not give in to this great personal
tragedy, he remained hopeful.
First he used a wheelchair.
Then knee braces helped him walk.
In this crippled condition,
Franklin D. Roosevelt was elected
the thirty-second president.
The courage and determination he
acquired from his bout with polio were
applied to solving gigantic
problems facing the country.
The great depression and World War II
were met and overcome during his
twelve-year administration.
He faced these problems without fear.
"If you have spent two years in bed trying
to wiggle your big toe," he said,
"everything else seems easy."

The birthplace and home of Franklin D. Roosevelt in Hyde Park, New York.

THE BOLD BATTLER IN KNEE BRACES

January 30, 1882, was the birthdate of Franklin, the only child of James and Sara Delano Roosevelt. The senior Roosevelt was a wealthy gentleman farmer who had made his money with business interests in railroads, shipping, and the coal industry. Franklin was raised in luxury on his father's Hyde Park estate in New York. Young Franklin had all the privileges and benefits money could buy. He had private tutors, a governess, dancing lessons, and riding lessons on his own pony. The Roosevelts were extremely fond of their only son, especially Sara, who devoted much of her time to the boy's best interests. Being the only child on this large estate, Franklin was sometimes lonely and spent a great deal of time reading. He particularly enjoyed

the exciting stories of Mark Twain. The boy grew to love the sport of sailing. He felt refreshed and excited when his boat cut through large swells and cold salt water sprayed into his face.

At fourteen, young Roosevelt was sent to Massachusetts to enroll in the Groton School. This was an academy that polished wealthy young men's manners and prepared them for enrollment in one of the Ivy League colleges. At Groton, Franklin was only an average scholar. He was disappointed because he did not do well in competitive sports. But with his usual good nature, he settled for being the manager of the baseball team.

Franklin went the way of many Groton graduates when he entered Harvard University in the fall of 1900. Nearly six-feet-two, he decided to try out for the football team. Again he was disappointed, because at one hundred forty pounds he was just too light for the rough-and-tumble game of football. Once again he refused to give in to disappointment. He just changed his plans and stayed close to the excitement of football as one of the school's cheerleaders.

If he didn't develop his football powers, he did develop a prowess with people. The young man from Hyde Park had a charm that made college friends and acquaintances flock to him. This charming and personable manner was greatly enhanced by a handsome face and a winning smile.

Franklin also found romance on the Harvard campus. During his junior year he invited his distant cousin, Eleanor Roosevelt, to visit him. Franklin wanted the young lady to help organize an important party in which he was involved. Miss Roosevelt organized the party and also won the heart of Franklin Roosevelt. Eleanor made quite a contrast to her distant cousin. She was extremely shy and thought herself to be awkward and plain-looking. Handsome Mr. Roosevelt did not agree. With the understanding he had developed for people, he saw her inner beauty and great strength of character.

The two Roosevelts were married in March 1905 after Franklin's graduation from Harvard, and shortly after his entrance into the Columbia Law School in New York. Eleanor Roosevelt's father was dead so she asked her cousin, President Theodore Roosevelt, to give her away at the wedding. During the ceremony the two male Roosevelts, who were cousins, met at the altar and grinned at each other. Teddy was delighted to give the bride away because he was keeping Eleanor's name in the family!

Franklin and Eleanor Roosevelt raised four sons and one daughter. Their forty-year marriage proved a remarkable and fruitful one. The husband and wife continually inspired one another. In later years Eleanor's strength helped her husband out of the depths of helplessness and despair during his illness. Franklin's love helped his wife lose her "ugly duckling" complex. He encouraged her in good works throughout their marriage, and she later became known as "First Lady of the World."

Ten year old Franklin practices archery on a trip to Germany in 1892.

Roosevelt (front row center) served as president of his college newspaper, The Harvard Crimson.

Roosevelt, in 1920, aboard his sailboat Vireo with his sons James and Elliot.

On a 1928 trip to Warm Springs, Georgia, FDR exercises his polio-damaged legs in the enclosed pool.

After their marriage Franklin applied himself to his law studies at Columbia and graduated in 1907. That same year he became a practicing New York attorney. For three years he enjoyed life as a wealthy city lawyer. There was time for work in the courtroom, time for pleasant days at Hyde Park, and time for weekends of sailing on the Atlantic.

When politics entered the life of Franklin D. Roosevelt his leisurely existence came to an end. He was shaken when Eleanor, who was working as a settlement worker, showed him the miserable lives led by people who lived in New York City tenements. He had not believed that human beings could live in such conditions and this picture of poverty never left him. In 1910 the wealthy young man from Hyde Park was asked by state Democratic leaders to run for the New York Senate. Roosevelt believed politicians could make laws that would force landowners to end some of the misery of tenement dwellers. He believed a politician could and should make laws to assist the helpless and troubled.

The state senate nomination really wasn't much of a plum. Democratic politicians offered him a chance to run for the senate seat from Poughkeepsie which had been held by a Republican for years. This was the first test which showed that the greater the odds, the harder he would fight. The twenty-eight year old candidate took the campaign seriously, even if the New York Democratic leaders did not. He drove up and down roads in the district to meet the people. The voters came out to see the young politician who ran his campaign from a motorcar. Standing up in the back seat, Roosevelt spoke against political bosses and corruption which kept lawmakers from helping those who needed it. The Roosevelt charm and the truth in his speeches won him this impossible election.

Senator Roosevelt spent two years in Albany learning valuable political lessons. F.D.R. later profited by these lessons. He learned how to run a campaign, how to meet and influence people in important positions, and how to push for legislation. Senate work in Albany gave him a strong desire to serve in the federal government. He believed he could do much more for his fellow citizens on the national level.

In 1913, during President Wilson's administration, Roosevelt was appointed Assistant Secretary of the Navy. In this job the young New York politician cut his political wisdom teeth while learning the workings of the federal government. Largely due to his efforts, the United States Navy was ready when America entered World War I. His political standing increased even more when he represented the Department of the Navy at the Versailles Peace Conference in France at the conclusion of the war. It was at Versailles that Franklin D. Roosevelt took up Woodrow Wilson's beliefs in the League of Nations. Watching Wilson design the structure for a world government which might bring permanent peace, Roosevelt eagerly accepted the president's philosophy.

Franklin D. Roosevelt was becoming well-known politically. He was pleasant, hard-working, and got things done. The Democrats recognized this at their 1920 convention, and nominated the thirty-eight year old New Yorker to run for vice president with James M. Cox. Roosevelt worked very hard for the party and for its League of Nations platform. But the Democratic ticket lost to handsome Warren Harding's smooth front porch campaign. By losing this nomination Roosevelt joined an exclusive club in American political history. Many presidents have been defeated for lesser offices and later were elected to the country's highest office.

The defeated candidate returned to private life and a law practice in New York City. Roosevelt spent the next year traveling between Manhattan and his Hyde Park home. This was perhaps the most pleasant year of his life because he spent many hours with his wife and children. He enjoyed golfing, hunting, sailing, and stamp collecting.

In August 1921, the vigorous, handsome figure of Franklin D. Roosevelt was suddenly crushed by a tragic illness. After an energetic day of sailing and swimming, Roosevelt exhausted himself by helping to beat out a brush fire not far from his summer home. Completely exhausted, he went to bed in his cottage on Campobello Island in the Bay of Fundy. The next morning he felt ill. Three days later the muscles of his legs would not support him. Doctors were called in but could not agree upon the nature of his illness. Finally, Eleanor Roosevelt called in a specialist who cast a cloud of doom across Campobello with his findings. Roosevelt had a severe case of polio.

It seemed probable that F.D.R., the vigorous outdoorsman and active politician, would never

During the depression "breadlines" were a common sight. In the absence of adequate government relief programs during 1932, free food was distributed to the unemployed by private agencies in some cities.

again walk, stand, sit, or rise from a chair without help. Doctors said if he ever moved under his own power, he would have to drag himself from room to room. It seemed that the man his son James called "the handsomest, strongest, most glamorous, vigorous, physical father in the world," would spend the rest of his life as a cripple, dependent on others for his every need.

Eleanor Roosevelt refused to pity her husband, and the crippled man would not accept the sorrow he saw in his friends' eyes. "I'll beat this thing," he said. Then the painful, agonizing road back from helplessness began. The struggle also brought about a strengthened character. For two years he struggled to gain control of his body, and to conquer fear and pain. Franklin D. Roosevelt gained a new kind of strength and developed a greater understanding of his fellow man.

His first major achievement was sitting up. F.D.R. accomplished this by the end of the first year. The following spring he put on heavy leg braces which were strapped around his waist, attached under the heels of his shoes, and clamped at his knees. These braces were painful, but he could stand and move about in public

with assistance. At home he moved around in a wheelchair. Daily sessions of painful exercises strengthened his upper body. Looking at his thin, helpless legs he would joke, "My legs aren't so good, but look at those shoulders. Jack Dempsey would be green with envy."

Friends soon found Roosevelt wrestling on the floor at home with his children, driving around in a hand-operated automobile, even riding horseback through the countryside. In 1924 he discovered the soothing waters of Warm Springs, Georgia. As he swam in the 88 degree waters, Roosevelt promised Eleanor and his family he would swim strength back into his legs.

That same year he also returned to political action. Franklin D. Roosevelt was asked to nominate New York's governor, Alfred E. Smith, for the presidency at the Democratic National Convention in June. Roosevelt leaped at the chance. Now he could show party members how far he had come along the road to recovery. The crippled man set to work. He was determined to walk without help across the speaker's platform. Weeks of daily practice followed. Walking a few steps alone was a difficult and agonizing task, but he kept at it.

This political cartoon pokes fun at President Roosevelt and his "Alphabet Soup." The caption read, "Ring around a Roosevelt, pockets full of dough."

On June 26, 1924, Roosevelt walked to the speaker's rostrum at Madison Square Garden. That event is now recorded as one of the most dramatic moments in American political history. His name was announced and a hush fell over the audience. His face clouded with uncertainty over the task that lay ahead. The ten steps to the rostrum seemed like ten miles. The audience was completely silent as he slowly took one step at a time. Concentration twisted his face. Finally his hands gripped the speaker's stand. He had made it. In a gesture that was to become characteristic during his presidential years, Franklin D. Roosevelt tossed his head

back and broke into a wide grin. The audience went wild at this show of courage and gave him a long standing ovation.

Roosevelt's demonstration of courage and strength got him what he wanted. In 1928, the Democrats nominated him for the governorship of New York. Mocking the Republican challenges that he was too crippled to handle the job, he stumped the state. Sometimes covering up to two hundred miles in a day, he proved to voters that he was most certainly fit. The people saw him for themselves and sent him to the governor's mansion in Albany.

The courage that led Roosevelt from a sickbed now helped him as New York's governor. His four years in Albany are remembered for his spirit, his vigorous energy, and his willingness to try new things. Governor Roosevelt was determined to lead his state out of the depression. He pushed for legislation that would assist the poor and hungry. His greatest achievement was the establishment of the Temporary Emergency Relief Administration. This agency, with a grant of thirty million dollars, made New York the first state to give desperately needed unemployment relief and welfare to the needy.

During his second term in Albany the energetic governor said, "The country needs and ... the country demands bold, persistent experimentation ... Above all, try something." With these words as his theme, he decided to try for the 1932 Democratic presidential nomination. On the fourth ballot at the party's national convention in Chicago, Roosevelt's wishes came true. The Democrats decided to give him a chance

Eleanor Roosevelt was an extremely active First Lady during the twelve years her husband was in office. Here she prepares to descend into an Ohio coal mine, in May 1935, to investigate working conditions there.

to prove his bold statement. In his acceptance speech he promised a "New Deal" for the country. He campaigned against Herbert Hoover with endless energy. He visited forty-one states to spread his New Deal message. The despairing country listened and liked what it heard. In November, Roosevelt was swept into office by a seven million majority over Hoover.

On Inauguration Day, March 4, 1933, President Franklin D. Roosevelt addressed the troubled nation saying, "The only thing we have to fear is fear itself." Leaving the inauguration ceremonies the new president went into action. For the first time a president's Cabinet was nominated, accepted, sworn in, and called into session on Inauguration Day. In this group was Secretary of Labor, Frances Perkins, the first woman to serve on the Cabinet in U.S. history. The president called Congress into a special session on March 9. During that "hundred days" session many daring New Deal measures were pushed through to cure America of her economic sickness.

Roosevelt's first administration was called "Alphabet Soup" by political enemies who criticized his use of letter abbreviations. But to F.D.R. abbreviations were quick and to the point. So were the organizations for which they stood. Among the most famous and successful programs established during the "hundred days" were the "C.C.C.," the "A.A.A." and the "T.V.A." The C.C.C. (Civilian Conservation Corps) was created on March 31, 1933, to employ jobless young men on government work projects like dam building, planting new forests, and constructing new federal and state parks. On May 12, 1933, the A.A.A. (Agricultural Adjustment Administration) was established to help farmers control crop growth and thus avoid price-lowering because of overproduction.

President Roosevelt's most famous ingredient in the "Alphabet Soup" was the T.V.A., the Tennessee Valley Authority, established May 18, 1933. This program covered the entire Tennessee River Valley basin with government projects such as cheap production of electric power, soil conservation programs, flood control, and industrial development.

Another great New Deal achievement was the passage of the Social Security Act. To this day this law is still the source of help for the needy, and gives pensions to retired persons. It also provides money for the blind, dependent mothers, and uncared for children. It is financed through payroll taxes on employers and employees.

During his first years in office President Roosevelt tried many daring programs. Many were successful and many were not. He was willing to try anything to help a weakened America. When something didn't work, it was dropped in favor of something else. Problems as enormous as those of the great depression could not be solved overnight. But F.D.R.'s programs began to catch on, and the country gradually began to heal its economic wounds. The people took heart. They grew to love the smiling "Squire from Hyde Park" and returned him to the presidency in 1936. Roosevelt won the electoral votes in all but two states when he defeated his Republican opponent, Alfred Landon, by a majority vote of eight million.

At the beginning of his presidential administration, F.D.R. realized the importance of communication with the people. He held press conferences once a week, and had his plans and ideas regularly placed in newspapers across the nation. More important was his use of the radio. At the end of his first week in office, he began his weekly "fireside chats" which soon became world famous. Each week he talked of the problems of the nation to twenty million listeners. His pleasant radio voice and personality made it seem as if the president was sitting down to have a heart-to-heart talk with each family that listened. Roosevelt's use of newspapers and the radio made Americans feel they knew him. They were aware of his hopes and trials on their behalf. Mail to the White House shot up to thirty-eight hundred letters a day. On his first birthday as president F.D.R. received over 300,000 greetings.

President Roosevelt wasn't the only "New Dealer" living in the White House. Breaking out of the quiet hostess tradition of former First Ladies, Eleanor Roosevelt's philanthrophic spirit went into action. Her personal mail was more than some previous presidents received, twenty-five hundred letters a week. Most of it praised her vigorous actions. She crawled down into coal mines and climbed to the top of dams to broadcast her message of assistance for the thousands of Americans whose living conditions were so bad they were almost without hope.

President Roosevelt worked long, hard hours in the best interests of his country. During the day, he rarely left his office in the White House and usually had his lunch sent in on a tray. Now there were fewer times for the strength-giving trips to the waters of Warm Springs. Friends worried about this and decided to bring the warm waters to the president. They collected money and constructed a heated swimming pool at the White House. When the pool was ready, F.D.R. strengthened his body daily by swimming in the warm water.

In 1939, the New Deal was overshadowed by troublesome international problems. The European countries of Germany and Italy and the Asian country of Japan were acting against world peace. These three countries hoped to increase their industrial and economic strength by taking over or occupying weaker countries. Austria, Czechoslovakia, and Albania fell to Germany and Italy. When the Germans invaded Poland in September 1939, England and France declared war upon these Axis powers. World War II had begun and the League of Nations was shattered.

With the Atlantic Ocean between them and the war in Europe, the American people were largely in favor of a neutral position. F.D.R. listened to them and agreed for a time. But he knew this war was being fought to preserve universal human rights. America would soon have to become involved. Efficiently and without much publicity he went about preparing the country for an emergency. In the spring of 1940 he increased airplane production, and in September managed to establish the country's first peacetime draft.

Meanwhile, 1940 brought another obstacle before Franklin D. Roosevelt. It was a presidential election year. No president had ever tried for three successive terms. Election to a third term seemed almost as great a challenge as the war in Europe, but F.D.R. was never one to run away. He ran against Republican Wendell Willkie and the third term issue was the greatest of the campaign. Willkie supporters

FDR during one of his weekly "fireside chats."

around the country wore buttons which said: "Washington Wouldn't, Grant Couldn't, Roosevelt Shouldn't," or "No Man is Good Three Times," or "Two Times is Enough for Any Man."

But two times was not enough for the fighting F.D.R. because his job was not done. He easily defeated Willkie by five million votes. (He was to go on to gain a fourth victory over Thomas E. Dewey in 1944). America continued to stay out of the war, but the president went on with his preparations. He established a defense board. He modernized the War and the Navy Department, and built up the Pacific and Atlantic Fleets of the navy. Americans could now sit back and wish the diplomats well. The public was secure in the thought that they were prepared for anything. But on Sunday morning, December 7, 1941, they found there was something for which they weren't prepared. On that day, Japan attacked and almost completely destroyed the U.S. Pacific Fleet at Pearl Harbor, Hawaii.

A nation whose defenses were terribly hurt listened somberly the next day as President Roosevelt asked for a declaration of war against Japan. Very soon afterwards, war was also declared upon Germany and Italy. The president made fine appointments of civilian and military men to head the war effort overseas and the industrial expansion at home. General Dwight D. Eisenhower was named to command the Allies in Europe, and General Douglas MacArthur was selected to direct the war effort in the Pacific. Civilians Donald Nelson and William S. Knudsen were chosen to lead the war effort inside the United States. This cooperative effort between the American public and their leaders broke all records for efficiency and high production.

F.D.R.'s fireside chats told Americans to "remember Pearl Harbor." They did. Young men went to war, older men went to work in factories and war plants, and women put on dungarees and learned how to build the airplanes and ships that were so badly needed by the fighting men. Volunteer workers rolled bandages, packed kits

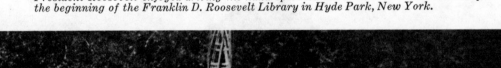

President Roosevelt enjoyed driving his hand-operated Ford. In 1939 he drove to inspect the beginning of the Franklin D. Roosevelt Library in Hyde Park, New York.

The Roosevelt Family celebrating Christmas 1939 in the White House.

In this 1940 election billboard opponents of a third presidential term for FDR have Uncle Sam against the president. Roosevelt won by five million votes.

The United States Pacific Fleet at Pearl Harbor, Hawaii, after the Japanese attack December 7, 1941.
This signaled America's entry into World War II.

Albert Einstein (1879–1955), a German-born scientist who became an American citizen. For his theory of relativity and other far-reaching scientific contributions he won the Nobel Prize in Science in 1921. He accepted a position at Princeton University in 1933 and remained there until his death. In August 1939 this world-famous scientist became alarmed at German scientists' progress in atomic research and wrote to President Roosevelt. Einstein urged American development of atomic weapons. His plea led to U.S. development of the atomic bomb in 1945.

The president and his First Lady in a rare moment of relaxation together in 1941.

During her August-September 1943 journey to the South Pacific to hearten American troops, Eleanor Roosevelt speaks to the Second Marine Raiders.

for servicemen, and established USO centers for lonely soldiers and sailors away from home and friends. Older men acted as air raid wardens, housewives had ration stamps to use for many foods, and gasoline was rationed. Books were printed on cheap paper, children's supplies of bubble gum were limited, and people going to movies read "The End—Buy War Bonds" at the conclusion of each motion picture. The war effort touched everyone from grandfathers down to tots. America was prepared to sacrifice whatever was needed to defeat the three Axis enemies.

Franklin D. Roosevelt's contributions at this time were magnificent. His personal magnetism and confidence in the task before the country inspired the civilians at home and encouraged fighting men overseas. He made three trips to Europe to coordinate Allied war efforts and prepare a plan for peace after the war had ended. The League of Nations had failed, but lessons are learned by mistakes. F.D.R. still believed that an international organization for world peace was possible. He labored for a new dream, the United Nations. On January 1, 1942, twenty-six nations signed a declaration for membership in the United Nations. As battle after battle was won by the Allies in the Atlantic and Pacific, peace came closer. The establishment of the United Nations came closer to reality, too, largely due to the efforts of the American president. In November 1943, forty-four nations signed for membership in the United Nations Relief and Rehabilitation Administration for peacetime rebuilding. The final steps to establish the great world organization were taken in August 1944. The Allies met at Dumbarton Oaks to design the preliminary structure for the United Nations.

F.D.R. was worn out from his great efforts during the presidential campaign of 1944, from his position as Commander-in-Chief of the American Armed Forces, and from working as a diplomat to establish the United Nations. For months the Roosevelt family had been concerned about F.D.R.'s health. When he collapsed after his fourth inauguration, January 20, 1945, into his

The Allies began their final push toward victory in Europe after D-day in June of 1944. Here members of an American landing party help their wounded buddies ashore in Northern France.

son James' arms, they feared for his life. Family and friends worried about his haggard appearance when he left in February 1945 for Yalta on the Crimean Peninsula in the U.S.S.R. He journeyed there to confer with Allied leaders, Winston Churchill of England and Joseph Stalin of Russia. At Yalta, they agreed that a conference on the United Nations would be called in San Francisco on April 25, 1945.

Roosevelt left Yalta exhausted from his twelve years in office, but happy. He was content with the world situation. World War II was rapidly coming to a close with an Allied victory assured, and his beloved United Nations organization would soon be a reality. "The President," as he was affectionately called by many people around the world, was never to see his efforts bear fruit. After the Yalta Conference, doctors ordered him to take a complete rest. This time he listened. He returned to his favorite spot, peaceful Warm Springs. There he felt he would be refreshed by the soothing waters and bounce back as he always had before. But Roosevelt was an older man of sixty-two now, and his body did not strengthen.

He was sitting for a portrait in his Warm Springs cottage on April 12, 1945, when he complained of a terrible headache and slumped over unconscious. Two-and-a-half hours later the man who had moved nations with his powerful force of ideas was dead of a cerebral hemorrhage.

As news of his death was carried across the sea, soldiers wept. In Russia, for the first time in years, foreign news appeared on the front page to pay tribute to the American president and his great work. Two weeks later, the United Nations Conference sadly went into session without the opening address that was to have been given by Roosevelt.

The world was deeply saddened, but not disheartened by the death of Franklin Delano Roosevelt. His spirit was still alive. In a few months World War II ended. April 1945 saw the birth of the United Nations. Today the magnificent United Nations Building stands in Roosevelt's home state casting a proud shadow on New York's East River. This organization like Franklin Roosevelt, its prime founder, has had successes and failures, but it still works for world peace and for better things for all men.

FDR, February 9, 1945, with Winston Churchill of England (left) and Joseph Stalin of Russia (right) at Yalta.

HARRY S. TRUMAN

Thirty-Third President (1945-1953)

He entered politics by the
side door, after his business
in Kansas City failed.
Out of work, the thirty-third president
turned to public service as a career.
Before entering public life,
this man from Indpendence was
average in many ways.
He had followed the up-and-down
road that life deals out to most people.
He was not wealthy, not poor, had an
education that ended with high school, and
knew success as an army officer
during World War I.
He failed in a private
business venture after the war.
His life matched tens of thousands
of average American men.
But there was one way in which
he could never be considered average.
His complete honesty made
him a man to be noticed.
Harry S. Truman followed a political giant
into the president's chair.
But he refused to be written off as a
man too small for the presidency.
He courageously stood up and fought for
the country, leading it well
through years of
great turmoil.

Harry S. Truman, age thirteen.

THE UNDERDOG FROM INDEPENDENCE

The oldest of three children in the family of John and Martha Young Truman, Harry was born May 8, 1884, in Lamar, Missouri. A problem arose around naming this first Truman offspring. Not wanting to show favoritism to either grandfather, Anderson Shippe Truman or Solomon Young, Harry's parents gave him only a middle initial. The "S." did not stand for anything, but each grandfather secretly thought Harry S. was named for him.

When Harry was six the family moved to Independence, Missouri. In this small town, where so many wagon trains started west in the last half of the nineteenth century, the Trumans settled down to hard-working farm life. John Truman ran the family farm and worked as a livestock dealer.

The Truman family was never poor, but there was little money to spare. Young Harry worked at many part-time jobs after school to help the family. He began his first job at nine, working at the Clinton Drug Store in Independence for three dollars a week. About that time his parents discovered his poor eyesight and purchased strong eyeglasses which he wore for the rest of his life. These round, gold-rimmed glasses perched on the bridge of his nose, were as much a part of Harry Truman as the wide grin that would one day become world famous.

At first young Harry found it hard to grin about his glasses; they interferred with many of his activities. Fearful of breaking the expensive glasses and terribly nearsighted without them, he could not take part in most sports. Being a spectator was no fun for the active young man. He found a middle road. In baseball games Harry became the umpire because he could not see well enough to bat. Poor eyesight hurt him in other ways, too. After graduating from high school, he had hoped for a West Point appointment but his weak eyes kept him out.

Throughout his school years in Independence, Harry was a bright and personable student. His likeable, outgoing personality brought him many friends and made him a favorite with many of his teachers. Harry later admitted that he played a game with himself to see how long it would take to discover what pleased his teachers. His school marks were good, not because he was a teacher's pet, but because he knew how to study. His poor eyesight had cut him off from sports, but they did not keep him from reading. By the time he was in his mid-teens, Harry had read all the books in the Independence Public Library. His favorite subject was history, which he continued to study with great interest throughout his life.

Turned down by West Point and unable to attend college because of lack of money, Harry Truman traveled to Kansas City to begin a career in the business world. He worked at a variety of office jobs, including service in the mail room of a Kansas City newspaper and clerking at two banks. In 1906 he returned home to go into partnership with his father on the Truman farm. After the bustle of Kansas City, Harry enjoyed small-town life. He especially liked to work close to the soil. His mother was proud of Harry's farming and boasted that he could plow the straightest row of corn in Jackson County.

World War I took Harry S. Truman away from farming. In 1906 he had joined the Missouri National Guard, and when war broke out the guard members were called to action. Truman had always been interested in military life and he served gladly. His heroes had been the Civil War Confederate generals. For years he had studied their campaign tactics through books. Now he would have the chance to try a few battle tactics of his own against the enemy.

He was commissioned into the army as a first lieutenant in the field artillery. After training in the United States, Harry's unit was sent to the front in France. There the young officer from Missouri stood the tests of friendship, courage, and good judgment very well. He became an artillery expert and won the admiration and respect of other officers as well as his men. When the war ended he left the army as a major.

Friendships with army friends played a major role in his life when he returned home to

Missouri. Truman went into the men's clothing business in Kansas City with an army friend, Eddie Jacobson. Thirty-five year old Truman now felt he had money enough to propose marriage to his childhood sweetheart, Elizabeth Wallace. The two had met twenty-five years earlier in the fifth grade, and Bess had been the only girl Harry had ever gone with. For years there had been an "understanding" and now there was money enough for a start. They were married in June 1919. Their only daughter, Margaret, was born five years later.

At first the Jacobson and Truman men's clothing store did well. Then, in 1921, a national financial recession badly hurt the business. Their shop closed in 1922 with Harry Truman refusing to declare bankruptcy. Bankruptcy would have relieved him of many of his debts, but this was not Truman's way. His tough Missouri honesty made Harry Truman determined to pay back every cent he owed. After many years, he managed to pay back every penny to his creditors.

Fortunately, another army friend reentered Truman's life just as his business was failing. Mike Pendergast introduced Harry to his brother Tom. "Big Tom" Pendergast was a powerful Kansas City political boss and at once saw possibilities for Truman in politics. Truman liked the idea of a political career and joined the Pendergast machine. He was elected as a Jackson County Court judge in 1922. (This was an administrative position and not a judicial one.) While in this office, Harry Truman became interested in law and studied nights at Kansas City Law School for two years. In 1926 he entered the judicial world by being elected a presiding judge in Jackson County.

Through the years Harry Truman proved to "Big Tom" Pendergast that he was a man of absolute honesty, a man who could not be managed. Therefore, in 1934, when Pendergast began looking for someone to run for the United States Senate, he did not want to select Harry S. Truman. But Truman was the candidate he had to accept when several other men refused to run. Pendergast again put his political machine behind the man from Independence and Harry Truman won the election.

During his first term in Washington the new senator from Missouri had a difficult time establishing himself. His reputation was unfairly tied to the shady Kansas City boss. When Tom Pendergast was jailed for failure to pay his in-

Truman (second row, third from right) posed with the 129th Field Artillery at Chateau le Chenay, France, in April 1919.

Harry Truman (far left) stands proudly inside his new men's clothing store at 104 West 12th Street in Kansas City, Missouri.

come tax, Senator Truman's job became even harder. No one wished to be associated with a man whose friend was a jailbird.

Harry Truman continued to work hard at his Senate job and made a few gains. He decided to run for reelection in 1940. By this time the Pendergast machine had completely broken down and Truman had to campaign on his own. There was no money for radio broadcasts, for political rallies, or for buttons and banners. With no Pendergast bank account to back him, the task seemed hopeless. Harry Truman rose to meet his first great political challenge. Definitely the underdog, Harry drove around the state in his own car, often with his wife at his side, and met the voters where they lived and worked. A majority of the "show-me" Missouri voters liked the honesty and spunk of Senator Truman and sent him back to Washington for a second term.

This time Harry S. Truman was highly successful. The Missouri senator had been concerned about the waste and laxity he saw in the defense plants and army bases he had visited during his campaign. He spoke out in the Senate against this and was made chairman of a Special Committee to Investigate the National Defense Program. This committee did good work. Truman made the headlines uncovering dishonest companies that were getting rich on the war contracts. The threat of Truman's committee action kept many manufacturers from using short-cuts to turn out imperfect war goods. It was estimated that by 1944, Senator Truman's committee had saved the taxpayers nearly fifteen billion dollars. By these efforts to improve the defense industry, Harry S. Truman became known to the public and to the president.

The year 1944 was another presidential election year and F.D.R. needed a new vice presidential running mate. Roosevelt wanted the fiery senator from Missouri. Truman, now well-established and highly-respected in the Senate, was reluctant to run. A personal phone call from Roosevelt during the Democratic National Convention changed his mind. Shortly after the phone call, Truman told Bess of his acceptance. His wife asked a question that stopped him cold. "But, Harry, what if the president should die?"

Three months after his January 20, 1945, inauguration, Vice President Truman was called to the White House. When he arrived he was given the unreleased news that F.D.R. was dead.

The stunned man did not forget his kindness when he asked Mrs. Roosevelt if he could help. Characteristically she replied, "Is there anyway we can help you, Harry?" The next day Harry Truman was president. In sincere humility he spoke to a group of reporters who had gathered about him: "Last night the whole weight of the moon and the stars fell on me. I've got the most awful responsibility a man ever had. If you fellows ever pray, pray for me."

The "awful responsibility" fell upon President Truman's shoulders only minutes after he was sworn in as chief executive. He called an emergency Cabinet meeting and asked for and received the promise of the members to stay on at their jobs. As the meeting broke up, Secretary of War Henry L. Stimson remained and passed a terrible burden of power onto Harry S. Truman. When they were alone, Stimson told the new president of an awesome new weapon that would soon be ready to use against the enemy, the atomic bomb. When this fearful weapon was ready, it would be the president alone who must make the final decision for its use.

The bomb was ready in July 1945. The war against Japan was going well, but Truman was warned that it could continue for another year. Japanese kamikaze pilots were delaying the victory. These human bombs, their planes loaded with explosives, flew right into American ships, killing themselves and hundreds of Americans with each strike.

The troubled president agonized over his decision. On either side there was death and destruction. Then he acted. The United States dropped the first atomic bomb on Hiroshima on August 6, 1945. On August 9, a second atomic bomb was dropped on Nagasaki. The results were devastating. Five days later Japan surrendered. Historians will argue for years about President Truman's decision to use this terrible weapon. The two atomic explosions killed over one hundred thousand people and injured countless more. But Truman's decision also stopped a bitter war which might have dragged on for many months.

In August 1946, President Truman authorized the creation of the Atomic Energy Commission to develop peaceful uses of the powerful atom. Several nations have now tested atomic bombs and the more powerful hydrogen bombs.

FDR and his vice presidential running mate, Harry S. Truman, discuss campaign strategy in August of 1944.

Vice President Truman and actress Lauren Bacall entertained servicemen at the National Press Club Canteen on February 10, 1945.

But these terrible agents of destruction have not been used against human beings since World War II.

The main interest of Harry S. Truman's administration was foreign policy. The man whom people thought would be only a hapless stand-in for Roosevelt, began firm international action at the end of World War II. The war-torn countries of the world had to be rebuilt and made safe against the expansion of Communism. These responsibilities lay, in President Truman's opinion, with the United States.

In May of 1947, Congress approved the "Truman Doctrine" which gave aid to Turkey and Greece to help these countries remain strong against the expansion of Russian Communism. Early in 1948 with Truman's approval, Secretary of State George Marshall's brilliant plan to give economic and industrial aid to Europe went into operation. It was called the Marshall Plan and it poured billions of U.S. dollars into western Europe. This money helped rebuild many war-damaged European countries. Equally important, the Marshall Plan greatly strengthened western Europe's political ties with America.

Harry Truman faced an election in 1948. His enemies shouted "to err is Truman." Because Truman had many troubles inside America, Republicans believed he could easily be beaten. Many Democrats were also disappointed in Truman. Liberal Democrats formed the Progressive Party and conservative Democrats formed the Dixiecrat Party. The people who remained in the Democratic Party gave Harry S. Truman the 1948 Democratic presidential nomination. Campaign contributions were scarce. Most Democrats felt it would be like throwing money down a bottomless well. Everyone knew that Republican Thomas E. Dewey, the popular governor of New York, would easily win. He was a well-known politician and had all the money he needed to run his campaign.

During his acceptance speech in July, Truman told the delegates at the Democratic National Convention that he would win. These words brought secret smiles throughout the huge arena. Very few believed this possible. With fiery spirit and the will to win, Harry S. Truman traveled the campaign road. While Tom Dewey delivered smooth radio speeches to the country from the east coast, the "Man from Missouri" traveled around the country by train to meet the people in person. Truman spoke to farmers in the Midwest, field workers in California, and slum dwellers in eastern cities, telling them exactly what he would do to help. "You tell 'em Harry!" the enthusiastic crowds would reply.

And he continued to deliver his powerful, earthy speeches at "whistle-stops" throughout the land. When the campaign came to an end the day before the national election in November, Harry S. Truman went back to Independence to await the outcome. Some members of Truman's Cabinet were so discouraged by reports of his campaign progress they had already packed up their personal belongings and sent them home. They knew Dewey would win. All the experts and all the public opinion polls still had Dewey ahead, but Truman knew he had successfully delivered his message to the people. He would win.

On election night the results began to come in showing Truman ahead. Experts said the trend would change. Later results came in with Truman's lead growing. Experts reported that the Dewey strength would come through soon. The next morning, newspaper front pages around the country announced the winner— Harry S. Truman. Flashing his wide grin, the president was photographed holding a newspaper headline above his head which read "Dewey Defeats Truman."

President Truman's second administration began with his family's exit from the White House. Worried about the creaks he heard, and the weakened beams he saw, the president convinced Congress that the Executive Mansion had to be rebuilt. Harry, Bess, and Margaret moved across the street to Blair House for a three-year stay while the rebuilding took place. The president amazed his younger aides as he stepped out of Blair House each morning for a morning stroll. Chatting with reporters and citizens, Harry Truman walked at a pace that tired younger men.

Bess Truman was a quiet First Lady. There were small groups of friends she enjoyed entertaining, but she much preferred to keep out of the public eye. This was not true of daughter Margaret. Miss Truman had studied voice and wanted to become a concert singer. During her father's presidency, she made many singing appearances on television and gave private performances in Blair House for friends. Her father liked to accompany her on the piano at these private concerts. After one of Margaret's public performances, President Truman received bad

President Truman (second from left) looks on proudly as Secretary of State Edward R. Stettinius signs the United Nations Charter, June 26, 1945, in San Francisco, California.

President Truman and secret service men on a brisk walk through the Washington Monument grounds in 1946.

The subject of this political cartoon was the presidential campaign of 1948. It shows President Truman anxiously looking over his shoulder at the Republican truth squad that followed him around the country during his whistle-stop campaign.

The smiling winner holds up the November 4, 1948, issue of the Chicago Tribune. *Truman was delighted with this erroneous headline and held it up for the world to see.*

publicity for writing a harsh letter to a critic who had reviewed his daughter's concert unfavorably.

This action was just a case of fatherly love getting the better of his judgment. He could become angry quickly and his sharp, angry comments sometimes got him into hot water. Most of the time he was much too busy to remain angry at anyone for long.

The second Truman term was one of the most explosive in American history. It was the time of the "Red Scare" and the Korean War. In 1948 Congress established an Un-American Activities Committee. Joseph McCarthy, a senator from Wisconsin, wanted a campaign issue to reelect him. McCarthy and the Un-American Activities Committee said the country was being weakened from within by undercover Communists. Thousands of government officials were dismissed and ruined by the charges made by Senator McCarthy and the Congressional committee. Dismissed government employees were not allowed to defend themselves against these charges. President Truman was not involved in these activities and openly criticized the anti-Communist rampage. He charged that McCarthy's actions were unfair, unfounded, and unconstitutional. But Truman's words were not heeded. The "Red Scare" had to run its course.

A very real Communist threat to the free world arose in June 1950 to occupy the president's attention. North Korean Communist troops crossed the 38th parallel and invaded the South Korean republic. The United Nations declared this action illegal and sent in troops from many countries to assist the South Koreans. Ninety per cent of the United Nations troops were American, and President Truman made General Douglas MacArthur the commander of the United Nations forces. General MacArthur led his armies from defeat to victory against the North Korean Army and carried the war into North Korea.

Free world leaders were worried about Communist China, a neighbor of North Korea. General MacArthur reported to President Truman that things were going well and told him the Communist Chinese would never enter the action. However, in November of 1950, they did. Fearing the start of World War III, the United Nations and President Truman ordered MacArthur to keep all fighting inside the boundaries of Korea. MacArthur became frustrated with these orders. He wanted to carry the war into China. Communist planes were bombing his troops and supply lines and returning unchallenged to the protection of their bases in China. The general began publicly criticizing the United Nations and President Truman. He was ordered to stop giving his opinions to the press and the public. He did not obey these orders. Finally, in one of the most courageous steps of his life, President Truman ordered the popular general to give up his command and return home.

Harry S. Truman knew the personal criticism this act would bring him. But the prevention of World War III and the second use of atomic weapons were more important considerations than personal popularity. He believed MacArthur's statements were bringing the free world dangerously close to a world war. Douglas MacArthur returned home a hero in the eyes of many Americans. Over seven million people greeted him at a ticker-tape parade in New York City in April 1951.

That same day in the nation's capital, President Harry Truman stood up to throw out the first ball to open the baseball season. As he was announced, boos started around Griffith Stadium.

After he threw the baseball the boos and catcalls reached a thundering peak. The unpleasant din accompanied the president on his long walk out of the stadium. He left with his head bowed against the roar.

Later in an emotional speech to Congress, General Douglas MacArthur bid farewell to the army with the statement, "Old soldiers never die, they just fade away." It might also be said that courageous presidents like Harry S. Truman who will stand up for what they believe is right, will never die, and the memory of them will never fade away.

Harry S. Truman retired from office January 20, 1953, and returned home to a quiet life with Bess in Independence. Much of his time was spent occupied with the organization of his presidential papers at the Truman Library. This building stands in Truman's hometown today, a fine tribute to the underdog from Independence. Harry S. Truman died of natural causes on December 26, 1972, in Kansas City, Missouri, at age 88.

White House renovation, June 16, 1950. Members of the architects' office are examining excavations for concrete footings of permanent steel columns.

President Truman and General MacArthur confer over problems in Korea on Wake Island , October 15, 1950.

The Truman family enjoyed taking trips together.

DWIGHT D. EISENHOWER

Thirty-Fourth President (1953-1961)

"I like Ike!"
This famous political
slogan sprang from
a Broadway musical show
and caught the fancy of the country
many months before the man for
whom it was written agreed to accept
the 1952 Republican presidential nomination.
All through his life, people found it
easy to like the thirty-fourth president.
His all-American image was one
people naturally took to.
He was a small-town Midwest boy, a
high school football hero, a popular West Point
cadet, a distinguished army officer, and
a hero of World War II.
After the war, General Ike's broad
grin and amiable personality were admired
by Americans from the Atlantic to the Pacific.
As "I like Ike" echoed across the land,
he listened to the call and accepted
the appeal for leadership.
During his eight-year administration,
President Dwight D. Eisenhower remained
"Ike" to the people.
He was the man in the White House
they could feel close to,
a man they could trust, and above all,
a man they liked.

Cadet Eisenhower during football practice at West Point in 1912.

Ike (seated, second from left) on a camping trip with his Abilene friends.

Ike (with hands raised) and his high school friends play "Cops and Robber...

ABILENE'S ALL-AMERICAN BOY

David Dwight Eisenhower (he later reversed his given names) was born October 14, 1890, in Denison, Texas. He was the third in a family of seven sons born to David and Ida Stover Eisenhower. While Dwight was still a tot, the family moved to Abilene, Kansas, where his father worked as a mechanic in a creamery. The Eisenhowers were poor but this did not bother them. Mr. Eisenhower held weekly Bible reading sessions at home, and taught his sons faith in God and belief in honesty and justice. All the boys pitched in to help with the family finances. They learned the value of hard work and acceptance of responsibility early in life.

Abilene, Kansas, at the turn of the century, was changing from a wild frontier town to a modern city with sewers, paved streets, streetcars, and telephones. But it was a hard place for people with little money. Railroad tracks ran through the town and separated it into the north side and the south side. People with money lived on the north side. The south side, where Dwight and his family lived, was considered the wrong side of the tracks.

There were bad feelings between boys of the north and south side. The Eisenhower brothers often stuck together for protection when walking through Abilene's north side. Each year it became the custom to select the best fighter to defend his own section of town. The winner was honored by his side of town and won the respect of his friends. When he was fifteen, Dwight was selected to meet Wes Merrifield in the annual fist-fighting contest. Merrifield was bigger and stronger and it seemed an uneven match. Surely Eisenhower would be knocked out quickly. But after two hours of fierce fighting, the two battlers were both standing. Merrifield announced he could not beat Eisenhower. Although it was a draw, the smaller southside boy had won a great moral victory for his side.

"Ike" had many adventures with his friends

while growing up in Abilene. He had been nick-named "Ike" because of his difficult last name. Ei-sen-how-er was a mouthful of syllables and took too long to say. The most spectacular of his boyhood adventures occurred when he was thirteen. It brought him admiration from his friends, but punishment from his worried parents. In the spring of 1903 Abilene was partly flooded. Ike and his friends decided to play sailor. They made some sidewalk planking into a raft and floated down Buckeye Street yelling and brag-ging to all their friends. The young "Huck Finns" had smooth sailing on the calm waters in town, but they became alarmed when they could not keep their raft from entering more dangerous waters. It took a rescue party to save them from the dangerously swirling waters of the Smoky Hill River.

His good-looks, easy-going ways, and happy smile helped Dwight to become a popular mem-ber of his Abilene High School class. Ike was not an outstanding student. He struggled to do well in algebra and to improve his handwriting. However, he did enjoy spelling, arithmetic, and sports. By the time he reached his senior year, he was a campus celebrity as the star of the baseball and football teams. He particularly liked football and hoped to continue playing in college.

While in high school he had an accident that might have ended his athletic activities forever. Ike fell and skinned his knee. The scrape was a bad one; blood poisoning developed and spread through his entire leg. Doctors, fearing for his life, told the Eisenhowers their son's leg would have to be amputated. Sobbing, Ike begged his older brother, Edgar, to stand over his bed and keep the doctors away, by force if necessary. "I won't be a cripple. I'd rather die," he cried. For two days and nights Edgar remained by his dangerously ill younger brother's bed. Gradu-ally the infection lessened and Ike began to re-cover. He was alive, and thanks to Edgar's perseverance and love, he still had his leg. Throughout his life, when making important de-cisions, Ike recalled Edgar's strength at that time.

In 1909 he graduated from Abilene High School. College had to wait because money was scarce in the Eisenhower household. Ike went to work for a year on the 6:00 p.m. to 6:00 a.m. shift in an Abilene creamery, and sent part of his earnings to help pay Edgar's law school tui-

tion. A friend suggested he apply to the Naval Academy at Annapolis. An appointment there would solve Ike's money problems since his edu-cation would be paid for by the government. Eisenhower liked the idea, and he applied to both Annapolis and West Point. He was ac-cepted by the United States Military Academy and began his studies there in 1911.

The Eisenhower popularity continued on the Hudson River campus. He joined the Cadets football team, first playing lineman and later switching to halfback. He played for Army in a game against Carlisle. During the game, when he tackled All-American Jim Thorpe, the great Indian player, Ike wrenched his knee. In the next game the weakened knee was broken. Foot-ball was over for Ike. This proved to be Cadet Eisenhower's greatest disappointment during his four years at the Academy. But it did not dampen his spirit to succeed. He graduated from West Point in 1915 in the top third of his class.

The young second lieutenant began his army career at Fort Sam Houston in Texas. After two weeks in San Antonio, Lt. Eisenhower met and fell in love with Mamie Doud, a pretty brunette from Denver. Miss Doud was very popular with young men and Ike found it difficult to see her. He once had to book a date one month in advance. But the Eisenhower perseverance was there and he continued to pursue her until she accepted his marriage proposal on Valentine's Day 1916. They were married in July of that year in Denver.

Mamie Eisenhower was a fine army wife. As her husband was transferred from post to post, beginning his advancement through the army ranks, she went with him and set up a comfortable home, sometimes in the most barren of army quarters. She grew accustomed to meet-ing high-ranking officers and important people and was always a good hostess. Their first son was born a year after the wedding. Three years later the couple suffered the greatest blow of their marriage when the boy died of scarlet fever. This loss was made easier when a second son, John, was born a year later.

Eisenhower continued to impress his superior officers. He had the unusual ability of getting along with other officers and getting the job done. There was no question that Eisenhower was an officer on his way up. His first big army job was as an executive officer for two years in the Panama Canal Zone. Then in 1926, he grad-

General Eisenhower chats
with PFC Marvin Thompson
during a review
of American troops
at Chesham, England,
in May 1944.

uated first in his class at the Command and General Staff School at Fort Leavenworth, Kansas. Eisenhower was now ready to serve in important army staff positions in Washington. For a time he was army executive assistant to the Assistant Secretary of War. From 1935 to 1939, he was on duty in the Philippines. While stationed at army bases in these Pacific islands, he learned to pilot an airplane. By 1941, with a fine record behind him, he had reached the rank of brigadier general.

At the outbreak of World War II General Eisenhower was on duty in Washington. His fine administrative skills were known to President Roosevelt who appointed him commanding general of the European Theater of Operation (ETO). General Eisenhower's command of the Allies in Europe was masterful. He commanded the invasions in North Africa, Sicily, the Italian mainland, D-Day in France, and the defeat of the German armies beyond the Rhine River. He was never a colorful general or a brilliant military tactician. But he was a general who got the job done.

When he took over, ETO was a confusion of Allied commanders, a vast organization of inefficient ideas. Recalling the spirit of teamwork and cooperation he had learned playing football, Ike went to work. Firmly, but in a friendly manner, he wove the elements of the Allied armies into a close-working fighting force. He was an ideal commander, soldier, administrator, and politician. By the time the war was over, General Ike was a hero, loved by Europeans and Americans for his deeds and his character. He returned to the United States to fame and a hero's welcome in November 1945. His new assignment was as Chief of Staff of the United States Army at the Pentagon in Washington.

Three years later, Eisenhower retired from active service in the army. His career had been a long and distinguished one, and his experiences had taught him much more than military excellence. Ike's years in Washington and his important army command positions gave him valuable administrative experiences. He had learned a great deal about politics while working for the federal government. Impressed with his leadership qualities, Columbia University in New York offered him its presidency. He accepted and served as president for two years. Then military services called him again in 1950.

President Truman needed Ike to again work his personal magic in Europe. Ike was given the difficult task of establishing the military forces for the North Atlantic Treaty Organization (NATO). He did the job quickly and efficiently, strengthening the NATO forces and his popularity at home. Ike was now internationally known for his leadership and integrity.

For many years politicians had considered "General Ike" as a presidential candidate. He was a proven leader, a hero, and a vastly popular man. His book, *Crusade in Europe*, showed he was a fine student of history and world affairs. These were tasty ingredients for a winning political recipe. The all-American boy from Abilene was now a sure-fire presidential candidate. Politicians clamored; Ike was not sure. He believed his military life had not prepared him for the tremendous responsibilities of "the most important job in the world." But the politicians kept asking and Ike became impatient with them. During an Eisenhower-for-President movement in 1948, he wrote to a New Hampshire newspaper publisher saying, "I am not available for and could not accept nomination for that high office."

Time changes opinions and the American people continued to ask for Eisenhower. He was the leader who made them recall the World War II spirit of cooperation at home and victory across the sea. Ike was the perfect picture of the average American who had worked his way into high places and succeeded, a man whose great deeds did not change his simple, common humanity. The people's call rose above the politicians' clamor, and Ike finally agreed to accept the Republican presidential nomination in 1952. He was nominated on the first ballot.

Eisenhower ran for office with vice presidential candidate, Richard Nixon. He now found himself in a new role, that of a political campaigner. But his style did not change. Ike saw that he agreed with the public about the troublesome Korean War, and promised to go to Korea and end the war if elected. The genial Eisenhower grin, plus his statement about Korea, was enough for the public. Ike won over Democratic candidate Adlai E. Stevenson by six million votes. His 33,936,234 popular vote was the greatest yet attained by any presidential candidate. Running again with Nixon four years later he again beat Stevenson easily, this time by ten million votes.

The eight-year Eisenhower administration

General Ike is greeted by his mother, Ida Stoever Eisenhower, as he prepares to receive a hero's welcome in Kansas City upon his return from Europe in 1945.

was greatly concerned with foreign policy. Working with his Secretary of State, John Foster Dulles, President Eisenhower led America through eight years of comparative calm in turbulent international affairs. The North Koreans and the Chinese Communists were tired of war and agreed to end the fighting in Korea six months after Eisenhower took office. An armistice line was established at the 38th parallel of that small Asian country.

President Eisenhower's foreign policy showed a determination to stop the spread of international Communism. According to Secretary of State Dulles, "brinksmanship" meant the coun-

try was willing to go to the edge of war to stop Communist takeovers of independent countries.

"Brinksmanship" was severely tested in the Middle East in 1956. Egypt seized control of the Suez Canal and England, France, and Israel, who had strong interests in the canal, opposed the action. The United States, at President Eisenhower's direction, took no part in this action. Egypt kept control of this important canal. Critics said Eisenhower should have gone "closer to the brink" and taken a firmer hand. Supporters said this action might have involved the Communists directly, and suggested the president had helped to prevent a serious war in the

This political cartoon had the caption, "No fury like a politician scorned!" It shows the Democratic bosses turnabout when Ike decided to run on the Republican ticket.

The Eisenhower family celebrating Christmas at the White House in 1957.

Middle Eastern area of the world.

In March of 1957 President Eisenhower got a little tougher. The "Eisenhower Doctrine" was passed by Congress. The doctrine stated that U.S. troops would assist any Middle Eastern country that asked for aid when threatened by Communist nations. Communist-backed Egypt began to move into Lebanon and the Lebanese government called for American assistance. President Eisenhower took action immediately. From July to October 1958, fourteen thousand U.S. troops landed in Lebanon and the American Sixth Fleet cruised off shore. The Communist threat was stopped and Lebanon remained free. This time President Eisenhower was criticized for acting too quickly and too harshly. Some critics thought the Eisenhower Doctrine, as applied in Lebanon, had brought us close to war. One fact remained unchallenged. At Suez and in Lebanon, Eisenhower's actions had kept America from involvement in serious international warfare in the Middle East.

Another great test of "brinksmanship" happened during the bloody Hungarian Revolt in November 1956. The Iron Curtain country of Hungary declared its independence from Russia. The Soviet Union would not allow this. On the morning of November 4, 1956, in a display of awesome power meant to quiet the Hungarians, two hundred thousand Russian troops were sent to occupy the capital city, Budapest. A bloodbath followed. Before the fighting ended, thirty-two thousand people had been killed and nearly two hundred thousand Hungarians went into exile. Promptly responding to the homeless Hungarian refugees' plight, President Eisenhower offered to admit them to the United States. Critics now shouted that Eisenhower should have sent troops to help the Hungarians. But this would have meant a direct confrontation with the Soviet Union and the possibility of World War III.

Throughout his administration, Dwight D. Eisenhower worked for some kind of international control over atomic weapons. A man with his military background knew what their use could mean to the world. In 1953, he proposed to the United Nations that an international stockpile of atomic materials be established for peaceful purposes. The plan failed because the Communist countries voted in a bloc against it. President Eisenhower later admitted that when this proposal for peace was turned down it was his greatest disappointment as president. He kept working towards controls in the use of atomic energy and was rewarded in 1957. That year an international Atomic Energy Agency was established to pool atomic resources for peaceful purposes.

The cold war between the United States and Russia took a new turn in October of 1957 when the U.S.S.R. launched Sputnik I, the first space satellite. Sputnik I put Russia ahead in space travel and put fear into some American hearts. We weren't used to being second. Russia's "first" in space seemed to point out a weakness in our educational program, particularly in the sciences. With President Eisenhower's hearty endorsement, new programs pushing the sciences were started in schools across the country. On January 31, 1958, the United States sent Explorer I into space. With President Eisenhower's approval, the National Aeronautics and Space Administration was established to increase our efforts in the new world of space. Soon the United States space program was flourishing.

Eisenhower worked endlessly to improve relations between the United States and Russia. He reasoned if the two most powerful countries on earth could develop a spirit of mutual trust and cooperation, the world would be a safer place in which to live. A conference to discuss these hopes was set for May 16, 1960. Eisenhower and Russia's Premier Khrushchev were scheduled to attend. Hopes for this conference were ended when the Soviets discovered Francis Gary Powers, an American pilot, and his high-altitude U-2 spy plane flying over Russia. The U-2 went down inside Russian borders and Powers admitted the purpose of his flight was to take photographs. When President Eisenhower admitted this was true, Russian leaders became extremely angry and cancelled the conference.

No president's illnesses were ever reported more widely than Eisenhower's. Three times during his presidency he was struck down with a disabling illness, and three times he fought back and successfully regained his health. During each recovery period the American people worried about their president and sighed with relief as the famous Eisenhower grin once again appeared on the front pages across the country. But his illnesses raised serious questions. How should the business of the nation be handled if the president was not able to perform his duties?

Dwight Eisenhower was hampered during most of his eight year administration by a Democratic majority in Congress. Realizing this handicap, the pull-together spirit that led him to victory in World War II was used again in Washington. The president did not like to play partisan politics. He wanted to create harmony between the White House and the Capitol Building. To get desired legislation passed early in his first term, Ike invited every one of the 531 members of Congress to luncheon or dinner in small groups at the White House. He wanted to know the men with whom he would be dealing and he hoped to win their confidence.

This man in the White House was willing to entertain his congressmen or shoot a round of golf with them. But he continually refused to use the power of his office to place undue pressure on congressmen to swing legislation his way. He used all the fair means at his disposal, and then let congressmen make up their own minds.

There was some criticism of Eisenhower's domestic programs during his eight years in office. He was criticized for not cracking the presidential whip hard enough when an important bill was up for passage. Looking over the returns, his batting average on domestic issues was good. Alaska and Hawaii became our forty-ninth and fiftieth states. The Department of Health, Education and Welfare was created. The Air Force Academy was established at Boulder, Colorado. In cooperation with Canada, the gigantic St. Lawrence Seaway project was started and completed. Social Security benefits were expanded to reach ten million more Americans, and minimum wages were raised to one dollar an hour.

Civil rights was the greatest domestic problem. For the first time in decades, the civil rights issue was dealt with in America. On May

Mamie Doud Eisenhower was a reserved First Lady who avoided all unnecessary publicity.

President Eisenhower's portrait hangs over the fireplace in the Cabinet Room of the White House.

17, 1954, the Supreme Court, led by Eisenhower-appointed Chief Justice Earl Warren, ruled that segregation in the public schools of America was unconstitutional. There was a great national uproar. Southern newspapers screamed their anger in headlines. Southern senators and congressmen pledged their total efforts to overturn a decision they believed was wrong. In spite of the outcries and criticism, the Supreme Court's decision was firm. Again Eisenhower critics said the president wasn't acting fast enough or firmly enough. Although progress was slow, the wheels of human rights were turning in Washington. Congress established a Civil Rights Commission to speed action around the country.

Two weeks after the creation of the Civil Rights Commission, President Eisenhower was faced with a civil rights confrontation that stirred the entire nation. The Supreme Court's desegregation ruling was being openly challenged in Arkansas. Governor Orval Faubus ordered state national guard troops to keep black students from entering Central High School in Little Rock. Rioting broke out. Eisenhower sent one thousand paratroopers to Little Rock and called ten thousand Arkansas national guardsmen into service. Order was restored and the black students entered Central High School.

Dwight D. Eisenhower retired from office January 20, 1961, more popular than when he was first elected. He was the first president to reach his seventieth birthday while in office, and, after forty-six years service to his country, he was ready for a rest. There was time now for writing and relaxation on his farm in Gettysburg, Pennsylvania. There was leisure time for playing golf in the warm winter sun of Palm Springs, California. There was also time for conferences with the presidents who followed him. They, too, liked the amiable man from Abilene, and respected the wisdom eight years in office had given him.

Shortly before his death, he received a great tribute. In 1968 there was a national public opinion poll and one of the questions asked was, "What man do you most admire and respect?" The winner in a runaway was Dwight D. Eisenhower. Although he had been absent from the presidential chair for eight years, America had not forgotten the thirty-fourth president. They still said with affection and firm resolve, "I like Ike!"

Ike relaxes on the golf course in August 1958.

The new fifty-star flag was unfurled in the White House after President Eisenhower signed the proclamation admitting Hawaii into the Union. Next to the president is Representative Daniel R. Inouye of Hawaii and Speaker of the House Sam Rayburn of Texas.

JOHN F. KENNEDY

Thirty-Fifth President (1961-1963)

John F. Kennedy traveled
a great deal during his years
as president to discuss serious
problems with world
leaders and to promote international
understanding and good will.
One trip was mainly for personal pleasure.
In 1963 he made a sentimental journey to
Ireland, the homeland of his ancestors.
This land of shamrocks and leprechauns
welcomed Jack Kennedy
with open arms.
The charm and earthy
enthusiasm of the Irish people
delighted the young man from Massachusetts.
Telling the Irish people of his affection
for them, he spoke the words of an old
Irish song: "Come back around to
the land of thy birth.
Come with the shamrocks in the
springtime."
In speaking of his love
for the happy people and green
hills of Ireland, the young
American president talked hopefully
of returning one day soon
"back in the springtime."
It was never to be.

Jack Kennedy loved sailing on the Atlantic near his Hyannis Port home.

THE YOUNG MAN FROM BOSTON

John F. Kennedy's Irish ancestry was unquestioned from the instant of his birth. He was born May 29, 1917, the second child in Joseph and Rose Fitzgerald Kennedy's family of nine. The Boston Irish are a fiercely proud, hard-working, hard-fighting American group. Because of their years of involvement in local politics, the Kennedys stood at the top of this group. Rose Kennedy's father had been a popular mayor of Boston, and Joseph Kennedy's father was one of the city's most powerful Democratic ward bosses.

Shortly after his marriage, Joseph Kennedy gave up active participation in politics. He be-

lieved that wealth opened the doors that lead into the halls of power. He became the nation's youngest bank president at twenty-five. By the end of the 1920's, this clever and ambitious man had left his mark on the world of finance in eastern America. Joseph Kennedy had become a millionaire with power and influence. In 1925, he began the first of the trust funds that made each of his children millionaires at twenty-one.

The Kennedy children spent summers at their Hyannis Port, Massachusetts, home and winters at their Palm Beach, Florida, home. Luxury and servants were part of their everyday life. But Rose and Joseph Kennedy did not spoil their children. Each child was told he had to earn his way through school and through life. Rose saw to it that her brood had a thorough religious education. She set an example by attending Mass every day. Joseph Kennedy did not permit his children to sit back and wait to inherit fortunes. Fearing his children would become soft, Joseph drove them saying, "Second best is a loser." He hoped each of his four sons would rise to political heights greater than those reached by their grandfathers.

The young Kennedys were taught to think of everything as a contest which must be won, from school grades to games after school. Their competitive spirit was sharpened by family football games on the sprawling lawn of their Hyannis Port home. These games were always fun but everyone played to win. The same was true of swimming and sailboat racing.

Joseph Kennedy's highest hopes were for his eldest son, Joseph Junior. Joe was a tall, strong, handsome young man with superior athletic and scholastic abilities. It was difficult for second son, John, to follow in his older brother's footsteps. Strong competition between the two did not destroy brotherly affection, but it strained their relations at times. At home John was often beaten in fistfights by his older, stronger brother. But John was a Kennedy. He kept at it and won a few of his own. He disliked having to compete with Joe's record in New England private schools. Sometimes he did not try. The result was only an average scholastic record and little success in sports.

Partly to avoid further competition with his older brother, Jack Kennedy decided not to follow him into Harvard, and enrolled instead at Princeton University. Illness forced Jack to drop out of Princeton during his first year. In the fall of 1936, he enrolled at Harvard and again found himself several steps behind on Joe's path. During his first two years, Jack followed the usual pattern of making only average grades.

Joseph Kennedy Senior's appointment as United States Ambassador to England ended Jack's "second-fiddle" playing forever. In 1938 Jack sailed to England to act as his father's secretary. This job gave him a chance to travel throughout war-clouded Europe. His father's diplomatic position allowed him to meet many of England's and Europe's greatest and most powerful men.

These European experiences polished his manners, sharpened his mind, and strengthened his self-confidence. When Jack Kennedy returned to Harvard he was more than able to compete with Joe's record. His Irish zest for action revealed itself. He studied hard and his grades soared. When he graduated in June of 1940, Jack Kennedy was an honor student. His undergraduate thesis in political science, based upon his observations of the European area, was later published in book form. *Why England Slept* made him a best-selling author at twenty-three.

After the Japanese attack on Pearl Harbor in December 1941, the two oldest Kennedy boys went into uniform. Joe became a pilot in the Army Air Corps and Jack joined the navy. They separated for the last time when Joe was sent to Europe and Jack was ordered to the Pacific.

By April 1943, Lieutenant John F. Kennedy had taken command of PT-109, an eighty foot torpedo boat with a crew of seventeen. These quick little fighting ships attacked and sank much larger ships with torpedos and sometimes with gunfire. The PT's were fast and difficult to sink. But service on a PT boat was always dangerous duty because Japanese gunners had a special grudge against the troublesome little boats.

Shortly after the sun went down on the cloud-darkened evening of August 1, 1943, Lieutenant Kennedy's PT-109 moved out of Rendova Harbor in the Solomon Islands. With several other PT boats, Kennedy and his crew were being sent on a most important mission. They were sent to patrol Blackett Strait and ordered to stop a large force of Japanese ships.

The hours of the patrol passed slowly on that black night. No one knew how many enemy ships they might meet. To fighting men it is often the waiting that is the most terrifying aspect of war. PT-109's twenty-six year old skipper knew this, and moved quietly among his men reassuring them and keeping them alert at their posts. One nervous seaman asked Kennedy to tell him about Winston Churchill. The seaman admired the English leader and Kennedy gladly told him stories about Churchill, whom he had met many times when his father was the American Ambassador in London.

At midnight the inky blackness seemed to deepen. It was impossible to see anything.

President Kennedy reviewing Midshipmen at the United States Naval Academy at Annapolis, Maryland, in June 1961.

Blackett Strait was well named. A few moments later a crewman shouted, "Ship at two o'clock." One minute later the Japanese destroyer *Amagiri* rammed PT-109. Kennedy was knocked down by the collision. Two of the crew were drowned when the stern of the boat sank. Gasoline tanks exploded, and the survivors tried to swim away from the flames which surrounded the wreckage. The other PT boats attacked the *Amagiri* unsuccessfully.

When things calmed down in the black, cold waters, Lieutenant Kennedy took charge, checking the men clinging to the wreckage. Eight men were not seriously injured. His friend Ensign George Ross was all right. But Patrick McMahon was not. McMahon, at thirty-seven the oldest member of the crew, had been seriously burned and could not swim. Kennedy ordered the other men to swim to a nearby island, directing them to hold onto a plank so they would not become separated. Then he took McMahon's life preserver strap, clamped it between his teeth, and began to swim pulling the injured seaman behind him. Kennedy's back, which had been hurt in a college football game, had been reinjured in the crash. Each stroke of his four-hour swim to land was agony.

After their arrival on the small strip of land, his spunk kept the crew from giving up hope of rescue. Because the tiny piece of land was barren, the group swam to a larger island. Kennedy again towed McMahon. They hoped to find food but did not. By this time the men were desperate for food so Kennedy and Ensign Ross swam to a third island. There they discovered a case of hard candy on a wrecked Japanese ship. Swimming back with this treasure, they were surprised to find the crew with visitors —natives working for the Allies. The friendly natives took the message of the crew's survival back to the American forces and soon Kennedy and his men were rescued. For saving McMahon's life, John Kennedy was given the Navy and Marine Corps Medal.

Four months after the rescue in the Solomon Islands, Kennedy was sent to Chelsea Naval Hospital near Boston. He had malaria and his back injury had proved serious. A back operation was performed at the naval hospital. While he was recovering, Jack Kennedy learned his brother Joe had been killed in action while flying an air mission over Europe. Jack was now the oldest Kennedy brother. He recovered from

President and Mrs. Kennedy congratulate cellist, Pablo Casals, after his White House concert, November 13, 1961. The president's mother, Mrs. Rose Kennedy, applauds at the far right.

surgery when the war was nearly over and left the navy early in 1945.

One year later, much to the delight of his father, he took up the Kennedy political banner. Jack announced his candidacy for the Eleventh Congressional District of East Boston. With whirlwind vigor all the Kennedys went to work for Jack. A campaign technique that came to be known as the "Kennedy blitz" was born. Appealing Kennedys seemed to be everywhere in East Boston. The Kennedy ladies held tea parties, they handed out campaign literature, and they talked to everyone about Jack. Grandfather Fitzgerald, the former mayor, still spry in his eighties, jumped into the political activity with gusto. Jack's old college friends and navy friends from all parts of the country came to help. Twenty year old Robert Kennedy, with father Joseph's checkbook to help, had thousands of *Reader's Digest* articles about PT-109 circulated to the voters. He rocked East Boston into an awareness of his naval-hero brother.

Shining above this high-speed race was the handsome candidate himself. With the help of his small army of smiling supporters, John F. Kennedy, with his easy wit and smooth speeches, bowled over all opponents. In November

ber 1946, another Boston Irishman was on his way to the nation's capital. In January 1947, when he first took his seat in the House of Representatives, he looked much younger than his twenty-nine years, and was sometimes mistaken for a Capitol Building elevator operator!

In 1952, the Kennedy clan felt Jack was ready for a bigger political prize. In April he announced his candidacy for the U.S. Senate seat held by Henry Cabot Lodge II. The campaign this time would be difficult. Lodge was a well-known member of a politically powerful Massachusetts Republican family. To make it even harder, Dwight Eisenhower was running for the presidency and seemed a sure winner, almost certain to carry the state for Lodge.

The Kennedy blitz was on again, this time across all of Massachusetts. The state was filled with billboards, PT-109 reprints, tea parties, and political rallies. Although Dwight Eisenhower won in Massachusetts in November 1952, John Kennedy defeated Lodge by more than 70,000 votes.

Back in Washington, the young senator from Massachusetts did not take long to become a political force. But the two accomplishments which brought him the most attention during his

A pleasant presidential duty is greeting visiting heads of state. Here President and Mrs. Kennedy entertain Ayub Khan of Pakistan at a reception at Mount Vernon.

eight years in the Senate did not happen in the Capitol Building. In September 1953, John Kennedy, Washington's most eligible bachelor, married beautiful Miss Jacqueline Bouvier in a society wedding at Newport, Rhode Island. The handsome pair had known each other two years. The new Mrs. Kennedy was as attractive and talented as her husband.

John F. Kennedy received national attention in 1957 by winning the Pulitzer Prize in biography for writing *Profiles in Courage*. The book was on the best seller list for weeks. Steadily hampered by back problems since 1945, Kennedy found he could get around only with the aid of crutches. The vigorous touch-football player from Hyannis Port said, "I'd rather die than spend the rest of my life on these things." It took two painful operations, in October 1954

and February 1955, to correct the problem. During the early months of his recovery, he was sent to rest at his father's Palm Beach home. The energetic Irishman found the time he had to spend lying in bed unbearable. He dove into the only action he was allowed. Kennedy studied the lives of Americans whom he admired for their bravery. The result was *Profiles in Courage*.

Both back operations had been extremely dangerous. After the first operation, Jack Kennedy lay close to death on two different occasions. His back condition was never completely cured. In 1961, when he took part in a tree-planting ceremony in Canada, he injured it again. He never had a day without pain from that time on. An old rocking chair was put in his White House office. This type of chair eased the pain in his spine. Aides, visitors, and Cabinet members often found him sitting in it during conferences.

The one great disappointment of his Senate years occurred in 1956. He had recovered from surgery and had returned to political life. That year John Kennedy sought a higher political office. He tried for the Democratic vice presidential nomination, and was defeated at the Democratic National Convention by Senator Estes Kefauver of Tennessee. But Kennedy's vigorous campaigning for the Democratic ticket won the admiration of many important Democratic politicians. After his Senate reelection in 1958, Kennedy became the favorite among Democrats for the 1960 vice presidential nomination. When the Democratic leaders suggested this to Jack Kennedy he replied, "I'm now running for president."

This ambition seemed impossible. His critics said he was too brash and too young for the job. Political sages believed his great wealth and his Roman Catholic religion (a Catholic had never been elected president) would cause many Americans to vote against him. John Kennedy answered everyone with straightforward talk. He told audiences that at forty-three he was not too young. Thomas Jefferson, when he wrote the Declaration of Independence, and George Washington, when he was Commander-in-Chief of the American Army, had both been younger. He had experienced fourteen years under the Capitol dome and this made him better prepared than many former presidential candidates. When Kennedy told a large Protestant audience that he believed in the separation of church and state, the issue of his Roman Catholicism was quieted.

Words were cheap. He had to prove to Democratic leaders that he was a winner. John Kennedy and an army of family and friends took his candidacy directly to the voters in several 1960 primary elections. Kennedy proved to the Democrats he could win by defeating Senator Hubert Humphrey in Wisconsin. This state had always been a political stronghold for Humphrey. Something new was added to the Kennedy blitz during these primary campaigns, a family airplane called the *Caroline*, named for John Kennedy's three year old daughter.

The greatest primary election test was in Protestant West Virginia, one of the poorest states in the country. The Democratic leaders felt if wealthy, Catholic Kennedy could win

there, he could win anywhere. John F. Kennedy did win, and the Democrats nominated him on the first ballot at their July 1960 convention in Los Angeles.

Together with vice presidential candidate Lyndon B. Johnson of Texas, Kennedy began his political campaign. He knew he would be in a nose-to-nose horserace. Republican candidate Richard Nixon had eight years of publicity and experience in the Executive Branch as Dwight Eisenhower's vice president. Nixon would be hard to beat.

Many think the turning point of the campaign came when the two presidential candidates agreed to a series of live television debates in September and October of 1960. Seventy million people watched as handsome, eloquent John Kennedy came out ahead in these debates. John Kennedy also won the presidential election by the narrow margin of 113,057 votes.

Although this was not an overwhelming victory, the youngest man ever elected to the presidency accepted the office as a smiling, confident leader. His inaugural speech was inspiring. President Kennedy spoke to the millions of Americans listening and watching. He spoke of an America coming into a new age. The 1960's would show a "New Frontier" of activity where the public good would replace individual interests. "Ask not what your country can do for you—ask what you can do for your country." This memorable line from his speech echoed across the land.

The thirty-fifth president's message was an appeal for action to the young men and women of America. To them Kennedy was the perfect picture of youth, strength, and justice. Young Americans listened to John F. Kennedy, loved him, and went to work for him. Six weeks after his inauguration, President Kennedy started the Peace Corps. American youths by the thousands joined to serve in the impoverished and underprivileged countries of the world. Imitating their vigorous young president, they spread American good will and American knowhow around the globe—in Asia, in Africa, in Central and South America.

President Kennedy realized that civil rights was his greatest domestic problem. This was not something to be corrected overnight. In partnership with brother Robert, the Attorney General, he tried to solve it. The Kennedy brothers decided to build up black voter registration everywhere. Although the Fourteenth

The busy young president relaxes in his office at the White House with his children Caroline and John.

The Kennedys at Hyannis Port in 1962.

Amendment to the Constitution, allowing blacks to vote, had been in effect for almost a hundred years, few black men voted in the south. President Kennedy felt that if black men could vote, they could help themselves out of poverty and despair. Inspired young Americans again went south to register black voters, backed by law enforcement from Robert Kennedy's Justice Department. The plan began to work. Black men began electing black officials to serve them.

Just as President Eisenhower had been called upon to support the Supreme Court's ruling on desegregation of public schools, so was John Kennedy. Twice he had to call out national guard troops to support the entrance of blacks into the University of Mississippi and the University of Alabama. Both times he was successful.

President Kennedy won many admirers and supporters with his television press conferences. His Irish wit and well-informed mind impressed the public. Many considered him to be our best informed president. The president often surprised officials in government departments with telephone calls asking for the details of some important project. Close associates and government colleagues never ceased to be amazed by the span of President Kennedy's knowledge of government affairs and his ability to cut through unimportant details to get to the point.

John Kennedy's thousand day administration brought great advances in space exploration. On May 5, 1961, the New Frontier seemed to stretch out endlessly as Astronaut Alan Shepherd became the first U.S. spaceman. The flight was one hundred fifteen miles in space above Florida's Cape Canaveral. Nine months later Astronaut John Glenn, Jr., thrilled America as he became the first American spaceman to orbit the earth. More orbital flights were made by Astronauts Scott Carpenter, Walter Shirra, and Gordon Cooper. These men proved man could survive flights in weightless conditions. President Kennedy increased the space program and promised excited Americans that we would land the first man on the moon by 1970.

The road of foreign policy wasn't entirely free of obstacles for the young president. His greatest setback occurred three months after his inauguration when the "Bay of Pigs" invasion took place in Communist Cuba. Months before John Kennedy became president, the Central Intelligence Agency (CIA) had secretly organized and trained a small army of anti-Communist Cubans to invade and free their homeland. After becoming president, John Kennedy learned of these plans and let military men talk him into the invasion. Cuban Premier Fidel Castro's troops were waiting when the CIA-trained force waded ashore. They were badly beaten. Many were killed and hundreds were taken prisoner. When President Kennedy bravely admitted his error in public, even greater damage was done. American standing around the world spiraled downward. Some Americans began to doubt the judgment of the president. Things became worse when East Germany built a brick wall to separate East and West Berlin. The Berlin wall was built to keep Germans from escaping to West Berlin. Although its existence greatly hurt American prestige, Kennedy was forced to quietly sit by rather than risk an armed confrontation with Russian troops.

These had been hard lessons for John Kennedy. However, he learned from these experiences. In his inauguration speech he told an America weary of the cold war: "Let us never negotiate out of fear. But let us never fear to negotiate." These words became real in October

1962. The scene was again Cuba. CIA agents told the president that photographs showed the Russians were installing offensive missile bases there. The situation was a terrible one for Kennedy. He was faced with two impossible responses. Should he allow these bases, with missiles that could destroy the United States in a matter of minutes, to remain? Or should he face armed confrontation with Russia and risk starting World War III? John Kennedy thought long and hard and then acted with courage and firmness.

Americans were greeted by an unfamiliar sight, as a somber-faced Kennedy spoke to them from their television screens announcing his plan. The United States would put Cuba in "quarantine." The Russian supply ships on their way to the Caribbean country would be stopped. The world held its breath as Russian ships steamed toward the American fleet blockading Cuba. The Russian ships turned back. They knew President John Kennedy was not bluffing. Six days later Russia's Premier Khrushchev agreed to tear down the Cuban missile bases and remove the rockets under United Nations supervision.

The Kennedy years inside the White House were full of beauty and charm. The handsome chief executive, his beautiful First Lady, and their two children, Caroline and John, were al-

On the steps of the White House, President Kennedy shows three year old John how to use his toy horse.

JFK speaking in Italy in June 1963.

The children of Ireland in June 1963, wave American flags to show their love for the young American president.

The hearts of Dublin (Ireland's capital city) went out to the young Irish-American president when he visited there in June 1963.

Ten days before his death, President Kennedy and his family view the famed Black Watch, the Royal Highland Regiment from Scotland. A member of the Black Watch sits next to the president on a White House balcony.

The popularity of his First Lady often brought out the Irish wit of her president-husband. When she accompanied him on an official visit to Paris, President Kennedy introduced himself as the man who came to France with Jacqueline Kennedy.

ways in the news. John Kennedy was compared with Thomas Jefferson as a patron of the arts. World famous authors and poets (among them Ernest Hemingway, John Steinbeck, and Robert Frost) visited the Executive Mansion. Kennedy guests were often treated to concerts by world-famous artists like cellist Pablo Casals. White House parties were sophisticated affairs. The chandeliers glittered and the rooms were filled with beautiful music, gay talk, and the clink of champagne glasses. The press reported the White House was livelier than it had been for years.

Beautiful Jacqueline Kennedy was an active First Lady. She traveled with her husband on foreign goodwill tours and met important world leaders. Charles DeGaulle of France was particularly impressed with Mrs. Kennedy's charm and linguistic abilities. An elephant ride she took on a tour of India made headlines around the world.

At home "Jackie" set the styles for thousands of American women in clothing and hairdos. Imitation Jackie-hair styles and copied Jackie-dresses were everywhere. Wishing to turn attention away from her wardrobe, the First Lady studied old books and pictures to find out about the White House of other presiden-

tial eras. By digging into dusty storerooms and personally directing the activities of interior decorators, she supervised a complete redecoration of White House rooms. When the job was done, a sparkling Executive Mansion was shown on national television. An equally sparkling First Lady acted as hostess on the tour.

The Kennedy years moved along at a glittering gallop. Late in 1963, reelection the following year seemed like a strong possibility. Kennedy decided to make a trip through Texas in November to strengthen the Democratic Party there. This was a state he would definitely need in 1964 if he was to win. Advisors and friends warned of possible danger because there were areas of great Kennedy unpopularity in the state. Only a month earlier, Adlai Stevenson, our Ambassador to the United Nations, had been hit with a sign by demonstrators in Dallas. Stevenson warned the president that he might not be safe in that city because some groups openly expresed a hatred for Kennedy.

John Kennedy would not listen. There were some badly damaged political fences that he personally had to fix. On November 21, he and his wife landed in Texas in his presidential jet, *Air Force One.* He received warm welcomes in San Antonio, Houston, and Fort Worth. Texas Democrats heaved a sigh of relief—all was going well. At noon on November 22, *Air Force*

President John F. Kennedy

One, landed at Dallas' Love Field. The President and First Lady rode in a convertible and enjoyed the warm Texas sun as they waved to the thousands who lined the roadway to greet them. President Kennedy grinned when Texas Governor John Connally's wife said, "You certainly can't say the people of Dallas haven't given you a nice welcome."

Moments later, at approximately 12:30 p.m., their open car passed the Texas School Book Depository. Shots from a high-powered rifle rang out. The first bullet pierced John Kennedy's neck, the second shattered his brain. "My God, I've been hit," were the young husband's last words as he died with his head resting on his wife's bloodstained lap. He was pronounced dead a half-hour later at Parkland Hospital.

Shocked Americans watched on national television as a series of tragic events took place the next two days in Dallas. The sniper-assassin was caught. He had been a misfit all his life and had apparently turned all his hatred and frustration toward the president. As the assassin was led from Dallas Police Headquarters, handcuffed and surrounded by policemen, another chapter in this meaningless tragedy opened. A Dallas nightclub owner, crazed over his grief for Jack Kennedy, calmly walked up and fired into the chest of the assassin. He

died instantly. The nightclub owner was immediately taken into custody.

Hundreds of miles away in Washington, the nation grieved with the First Lady and her fatherless children. Her courage carried the country through the stabbing sadness of the presidential funeral. John Kennedy's body lay in state under the Capitol Rotunda. Thousands paid their last respects in person. Millions sobbed in front of their television screens. Leaders from throughout the world came to mourn.

For the fourth time in American history, the madness of an assassin had cut down an American president. For the fourth time the victim had been one who was loved and admired. For a time, bullets shattered the budding New Frontier as effectively as they had its leader's body. The youth of America, in particular, seemed lost. For them hope seemed to die with John F. Kennedy.

Closing the presidential burial ceremony at Arlington National Cemetery, Kennedy's widow leaned over to light a flame that burns near his grave. Months passed and the nation began to take heart. Young people once again rose to action, their hope rebuilt by thoughts of the everlasting flame at Arlington. As the years pass the memory of John F. Kennedy continues to give springtime strength and hope to America.

LYNDON B. JOHNSON

Thirty-Sixth President (1963-1969)

Sometimes there
are fascinating parallels
in politics.
One of the strangest
comparisons in our history
is between the seventeenth and the
thirty-sixth president.
The parallel development of their lives,
separated by almost a century,
is striking.
Although not related,
both were southerners
who had the same last name.
Both men served in the Senate before
becoming vice president.
The tragedy of well-placed assassins' bullets
shot into the brains of Abraham Lincoln
and John Kennedy elevated these
vice-presidents to the presidency.
Both vice presidents were strong, patriotic Americans
who battled unfair comparisons made between
themselves and the slain president.
Andrew Johnson of Tennessee and
Lyndon B. Johnson of Texas toiled valiantly
for their country against turbulent and
troubled times that sometimes raced out of control.

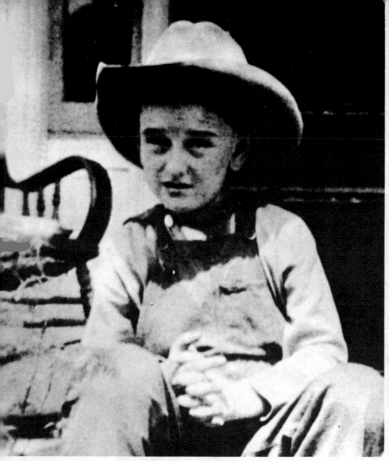

Lyndon Johnson at the family home near Johnson City, Texas.

As a college student, Lyndon Johnson (right) organized his busy schedule to allow much time for his studies.

HE PLANNED "THE GREAT SOCIETY"

Politics had been in the Johnson family bloodstream long before Lyndon Baines was born on August 27, 1908, to Sam, Jr., and Rebekah Baines Johnson. One of Lyndon's ancestors was a governor of Kentucky. One grandfather had been a member of the Texas legislature and Texas Secretary of State. His father divided his time between farming, schoolteaching, and service in the Texas legislature. His other grandfather, Sam Johnson, Sr., for whom their hometown Johnson City was named, had long taken a great interest in local and state politics. When baby Lyndon arrived, Grandfather Sam proudly boasted to his friends, "A United States senator was born this morning!" Little did he dream his grandson would go far beyond this high goal which had been set for him.

Lyndon and his four younger brothers and sisters grew up on their father's farm in the southwest hill country of Texas. The Johnson family was never poor, but when the sun scorched the land and burned out their crops, they knew what hard times were. By the time he was fourteen, Lyndon had decided the unpre-dictable life of a farmer was not for him. Throughout his life he kept a great respect for these men who battled against the weather and low-priced markets to bring forth food from the land.

As his desire not to be a farmer grew, so did his stature. At fifteen, Sam,Sr.'s,grandson was already six feet tall and "thin as a willow fishing pole." After school, Lyndon loved to spend time with his friends talking over the possibilities for the future. Not certain of his goals, he found it fun to talk of the future with other Johnson City boys. There was not much time for daydreaming because he had to earn his own spending money by working at part time jobs shining shoes at the Johnson City barber shop or picking cotton.

When he graduated from high school in 1924, sixteen year old Lyndon was still uncertain about the future. His parents wisely let their oldest son leave home to try out his wings. Lyndon decided to head west. He traveled up and down the Pacific Coast for several months stopping wherever he could find work. He washed dishes, waited on tables in diners, and worked as a farmhand until homesickness got

Newly-elected Congressman Johnson of Texas proudly poses in 1937 on the steps of the Capitol Building in Washington.

Lieutenant Commander Lyndon B. Johnson was the first member of Congress to go into uniform. He was sent to the South Pacific as President Roosevelt's special representative in 1942.

the best of him. Thinner than ever, the tall young Texan returned home to Johnson City. But Lyndon was still undecided about a career. He worked for many months at several jobs around Johnson City while he tried to decide what to do.

Rebekah Johnson was a wise and patient mother. Lyndon was almost two years out of high school with no definite plans and she felt she had been silent long enough. Realizing her son could get more out of life, she had some serious heart-to-heart talks with him. He agreed with a plan suggested by his mother and in 1927 entered Southwest Texas State Teachers College. Older than most of his classmates, Lyndon decided to take extra classes to graduate in three years. This heavy load of classes and studies was burdened by having to support himself. He arranged his work, as a secretary in the college president's office and as a school custodian, around his class and study schedule. This formula worked and he graduated in 1930.

Another of his student jobs was teaching in an elementary school near the college campus. Lyndon Johnson enjoyed this work and decided

teaching would be a good profession to pursue. He took a job in Houston, Texas, at Sam Houston High School. For three semesters the young public speaking teacher did well working with his students. In 1931, Johnson transferred his public speaking talents outside the classroom when he campaigned for congressional candidate Richard Kleberg. Kleberg won the election and asked the personable young teacher to come with him to Washington as his secretary.

Accompanying the congressman to Washington in 1932, Lyndon Johnson's abilities in politics bloomed. As the Roosevelt New Deal era burst forth, the political and organizational genius which typified Johnson's long career in politics began. Helped by Sam Rayburn, the powerful Texas congressman, Lyndon Johnson grew in reputation and political polish. Rayburn and other high-ranking Texas politicians believed he was ready for bigger things in the spring of 1935.

With their help, Lyndon Johnson returned to Texas and began eighteen months service as state director of President Roosevelt's National Youth Administration (NYA). The NYA was

Senator Johnson of Texas, shown here leading a Senate committee, was one of the most dynamic Senate Majority leaders in U.S. history.

particularly close to Johnson's heart because one of its main duties was to find part-time work for needy college students. Thinking back to his struggle eight years earlier, he worked long hours to help college students. Under his direction the NYA in Texas helped over seventy-five thousand students stay in college. This position also helped Lyndon Johnson increase his powerful connections across the state, and built up his name with the public. Early in 1937, he decided to run for Congress.

By this time, Johnson had married Claudia Taylor in San Antonio, Texas. Mrs. Johnson had been called "Lady Bird" since early childhood because the family cook announced she was "pretty as a lady bird." She was the daughter of a wealthy East Texas landowner. This did not keep the bridegroom from putting a two-dollar ring on her finger during the wedding ceremony. It was all he could afford. Lady Bird was a pleasant hostess to Lyndon Johnson's political friends. There were two small Johnson daughters, Lynda and Lucy (Luci), but she still had time to take an active interest in her husband's work.

Lady Bird helped her twenty-eight year old husband in his first campaign for Congress. Can-didate Johnson ran his campaign in firm support of the New Deal. He told audiences that a vote for him was a vote for President Roosevelt. The strategy worked and he was elected to Congress on April 10, 1937. The next day in Galveston, Texas, the new congressman had a fortunate meeting with Franklin Roosevelt, and accepted the president's invitation to accompany him on a trip across Texas. During this trip the two men became friends. Roosevelt found the young Texan to be a man with good political instincts. Back in Washington, Congressman Johnson, with F.D.R.'s interested eye upon him, soon became a politician to watch.

The Johnson political express was temporarily derailed in 1941. That year he lost his first try for a United States Senate seat from Texas. But this setback just turned Congressman Johnson toward service to his country in another way. He joined the navy.

In May 1942, Lieutenant Commander Johnson flew to the South Pacific to report for duty. Riding as an observer in a B-26 on a bombing mission, Commander Johnson and the airplane's crew had a close call. One of the plane's engines failed, forcing it to drop out of formation. The crippled bomber was now an easy target for

The winning team of the 1964 presidential election, Democrats Lyndon Johnson and Hubert Humphrey, relax on a horseback ride on the LBJ Ranch.

Chief Justice of the Supreme Court Earl Warren (right), administers the oath of office to President Lyndon B. Johnson during the inauguration ceremonies January 20, 1965. Mrs. Johnson proudly looks on.

Japanese fighter planes. Although it was hit many times, the B-26 managed to limp back to its home base. For his coolness under fire Lyndon Johnson was given the Silver Star. His military career ended when President Roosevelt ordered all congressmen in the armed forces to return to Washington.

Congressman Johnson continued his organized, efficient ways in the House, serving on the important Joint Committee on Atomic Energy and the Naval Affairs Committee. All the while his knowledge of the workings of the federal government and his influence with the men who ran it was growing. When he decided to run again for the Senate in 1948, his powerful friends backed him. Lyndon Johnson won this election by easily beating his Republican opponent in the November election.

The Senate was happy to receive the popular six-foot, three-inch Texan. Men with his politi-

cal knowhow were needed in those days of cold war troubles. During his early years in the Senate, Johnson's main work was for America's military preparedness against Communism. He worked particularly hard to strengthen the Air Force. Senator Johnson's influence rose steadily in the halls of the Capitol Building. Democrat Johnson impressed the country with his spirit of fairplay after Republican Dwight Eisenhower's election in 1952. He told the press he would cooperate with the Republican president because: "Any jackass can hack a barn down. It takes a good carpenter to build a barn. We aim to build." Democratic colleagues in the Senate were also impressed with Lyndon Johnson's cooperative spirit. Early in 1953, they elected him Minority Leader of the Senate.

Lyndon Johnson, the creative builder in government, was easily elected in 1954 to serve a second Senate term. In that same national election, the Democrats gained control of the Senate. Johnson then became Senate Majority Leader, a position often called the second most important in Washington. He always put the best interests of the country ahead of his political party. Majority Leader Johnson helped President Eisenhower pass the major legislation of his administration. He was particularly proud of his part in pushing through the first civil rights legislation to be passed in eighty-two years.

The tall Texan was now a familiar sight to the most powerful politicians in Washington. Lyndon Johnson was a member of the political aristocracy. In 1960 he was a leading Democratic candidate for the presidential nomination. Refusing to hit the primary campaign trail against his main opponent, John Kennedy, the Majority Leader said he had to stay home and "tend the store" in Washington. In doing so, Johnson sacrificed his presidential chances. At the July convention in Los Angeles, the Democrats nominated John F. Kennedy on the first ballot. Then, in a piece of political strategy that surprised everyone, Kennedy asked Lyndon Johnson to become his vice president. Johnson accepted. They won the election in a very close race against Richard Nixon and Henry Cabot Lodge.

Lyndon B. Johnson's three years as vice president were frustrating ones. He was given many jobs by President Kennedy, but they were not enough to burn up his tremendous energy or fire his tremendous ambition. Even the familiar Senate chambers were off limits. As the presiding officer of the Senate, Johnson was no longer a member of the club. He had risen above it into the Executive Branch. Vice President Johnson did not complain, but his friends and family knew of his inner turmoil.

Turmoil changed to tragedy and then awesome reality when John Kennedy was murdered by an assassin in Dallas. Two hours later with Lady Bird and Jacqueline Kennedy, still in her blood-stained suit, by his side, a saddened Lyndon Baines Johnson took the oath of office from a federal judge aboard *Air Force One*. As the jet sped toward Washington, the thirty-sixth president thought about the office he now held, the office he had wanted but had given up hope of achieving. He thought of the dead Kennedy in a coffin at the back of the jet and the grieving young widow a few seats away. Thinking of the complete waste of it all, Lyndon Johnson became angry. This anger fired his determination to show the country and all assassins that the nation could not be stopped with bullets.

Five days after Kennedy's assassination, the new president addressed a joint session of Congress. He reminded them that President Kennedy had said, "Let us begin," and Johnson added, "I would say to all my fellow Americans, let us continue." Then President Johnson declared that the greatest tribute Congress could give to Kennedy was to pass the Civil Rights Bill. In a cooperative nonpartisan spirit rarely seen under the Capitol dome, the Civil Rights Bill was passed in July 1964. This far-reaching bill gave new hope to millions of blacks across the land. The law provided fair employment for any person and the right to all public accommodation for everyone. Before he was finished Lyndon B. Johnson, a southerner, directed the passage of the greatest group of Civil Rights laws in United States history.

The first months in the presidency were difficult ones for Lyndon Johnson. L.B.J. had three famous initials like J.F.K., but otherwise they were very different. The saddened country and close Kennedy associates in Washington looked at President Johnson with grief-clouded vision. The plain-living Texan suffered from comparison made between Jack Kennedy and himself. Somehow, and not very sensibly, the bitter fact that Kennedy had been murdered in Johnson's home state was not forgotten or forgiven by some.

The elegant "Kennedy style" was replaced by the leisurely, folksiness of the southwest when the Johnsons moved into the White House. President Johnson was an outdoors man and not a patron of the arts. The Johnsons enjoyed going back to their LBJ Ranch in Texas to ride horseback, and plan outdoor barbecues for government guests and personal friends. The Johnson ranch get-togethers featured roasting beef in an open pit on the banks of the Pedernales River, cowboy music, and western clothing. This was very different from the musical evenings of the Kennedy White House.

Not since the days of the Wilson girls had the Executive Mansion seen such a flurry of feminine activity. The two attractive Johnson daughters seemed to be everywhere. Lynda, a student at the University of Texas, found time for trips to Mexico and for dates with a movie

Lady Bird Johnson was never afraid to "get in and dig" for national beautification. As Secretary of the Interior Stewart Udall (left) looks on, Mrs. Johnson in a March 1965 ceremony, plants flowers in a public park.

say it hardened the Texan a little. He simply was not like John Kennedy and would not try to be.

But it was agreed by all that Presidents Kennedy and Johnson shared one common belief. Kennedy's "New Frontier" and Johnson's "Great Society" both tried to do the best for poor Americans. Both men disliked the suffering and poverty of millions of Americans in Appalachia, on poor southern farms, and in rat-infested city ghettos. Both were determined to change these terrible situations.

The comparisons eased off when Lyndon Johnson won the presidential election of 1964 over Republican Barry Goldwater by a landslide of 16,000,000 votes, the largest popular majority in history. This smashing victory gave President Johnson the encouragement he needed

star. Luci stayed closer to home, attending nursing school and taking part in charity projects. During their father's five years in office, both girls fell in love and were married in large Washington weddings which received much national publicity.

Lady Bird Johnson was one of the hardest working First Ladies in history. With her winning smile and soft Texas voice, she won friends all over the country as she worked for a more beautiful America. Mrs. Johnson believed that the United States was hurt seriously by carelessness and waste. She worked endlessly to change this destructive trend. Largely because of her well-known efforts on behalf of the ecology movement, the Congress of the United States passed a National Highways Beautification Bill.

At home in the White House, the Johnsons enjoyed relaxed gatherings with their friends. The president was nicknamed "Lightbulb Johnson" by the newspapers who reported his habit of switching off lights in empty White House rooms. His early days in Johnson City had taught him that much money could be saved on the electric bill by doing this. And even as President of the United States, this was a thrifty habit Lyndon Johnson did not wish to break.

Comparison of presidents is always done, but it was particularly hard for Lyndon Johnson to accept. The comparison between Kennedy and Johnson continued month after month and some

to put his programs into operation. The first hundred days after the inauguration of Lyndon Johnson are sometimes compared with the first hundred days of the F.D.R. New Deal in 1933. Johnson used a forceful, direct approach to get his legislation passed. President Johnson often picked up the telephone and spoke personally to congressmen or senators who were uncertain about his legislative programs. Some critics thought the president was putting too much pressure on members of Congress. L.B.J. just wanted to get things moving.

Lyndon B. Johnson's "hundred days" brought many changes. Within three months, a Job Corps to train young people while they worked on public projects went into operation. The Medicare Bill was passed. This bill allowed free medical care and hospitalization for people over sixty-five. Johnson's "hundred days" also gave federal aid to the poor areas of the Appalachian Mountains.

The legislative landslide continued late in 1965 with the passage of the Voting Rights Bill. The Department of Housing and Urban Development was created and its director, Robert C. Weaver, was the first black man to serve on a president's Cabinet. Later President Johnson appointed Thurgood Marshall, a black man, as an Associate Justice of the Supreme Court.

In the last part of Lyndon Johnson's presidential administration the Department of Transportation was created. The poor of America were further helped by a Social Security bill which increased, by thirteen percent, the payments to 24,000,000 people. For non-farmwork-

A bill became a law on July 23, 1965, when President Johnson signed an Act of Congress which changed the coinage of silver. After he signed bills into law, President Johnson often gave away the pens he used as souvenirs to onlookers.

ers, the minimum wage was increased to $1.50 an hour.

The space program moved ahead under President Johnson's leadership. L.B.J.'s interest in the National Aeronautics and Space Administration continued from his Senate days when he was chairman of the Committee on Aeronautical and Space Science. Often traveling down to Cape Kennedy to view the launching of the Gemini and Apollo space crafts, the president was filled with pride after the successful conclusion of each flight. In June 1965, Astronaut Edward White took the first American spacewalk outside his *Gemini 4* capsule. That year the first U.S. commercial communications satellite was launched. In January 1967, *Surveyor 7* made a successful soft landing on the moon and broadcast pictures back to Earth.

Progress in domestic affairs under President Johnson was tremendous. An aide suggested that President Johnson, like a symphony conductor, was able to inspire his Congressional orchestra. But when this wave of harmony be-

"WATCH IT!"

TO PRESIDENT
LYNDON B. JOHNSON
with Best Wishes
Joaquin de Alba

DE ALBA.

President Johnson enjoyed this political cartoon drawn to poke fun at his civil rights problems.

gan to crack on the field of foreign affairs, the L.B.J. music began to sour.

In the Caribbean, President Johnson had a draw. Early in 1964 Communist Premier Castro of Cuba, perhaps to test the new president, shut off the water supply into Guantanamo Naval Base. Castro demanded the base be returned to Cuba. President Johnson directed the base to make its own emergency water supply and seized Cuban fishing boats that strayed into United States waters. Castro fumed and then turned the water back on.

L.B.J. didn't do as well the following year when a revolt broke out in the Dominican Republic. Fearing a Communist takeover, President Johnson sent in American troops to stop the fighting and the revolt ended. When a Communist plot could not be proved, the United States was criticized for meddling in another country's affairs.

Vietnam caused L.B.J. even greater difficulty. Problems in Southeast Asia were not new, they had troubled Truman, Eisenhower, and Kennedy. Historian Theodore White said the Asian continent was the home of the "roots of madness." Three American presidents had talked much about sending American military aid and American advisors to South Vietnam. In fact, the war between North Vietnam and South Vietnam had been going on for years without much notice by Americans.

Then came August 1964 and Congress' Gulf of Tonkin resolution. U.S. destroyers cruising in international waters eleven miles off shore were fired upon by North Vietnamese torpedo boats. The next day President Johnson requested that Congress approve a resolution allowing him to retaliate with all means necessary when United States forces were threatened in Vietnam.

Then American involvement in the war grew. President Johnson listened to military advisors, who feared the spread of international Communism in Asia, and increased American participation in the war. American ground troops were sent in greater numbers. Naval and Marine pilots were sent into the action, and part of the Pacific Fleet was sent to support them. To supply the necessary troops, American young men were drafted each month by the thousands. The president next authorized the bombing of North Vietnam. Slowly the terrible truth of the Vietnam War became clear to

*President Johnson giving his State of the Union message before
a joint session of Congress, January 10, 1967.*

Animal-lover Johnson romps with his pet beagles on the lawn of the White House.

On August 16, 1967, the sightseers' line, waiting for the White House tour, got an unexpected treat as President Johnson greeted them personally.

President Johnson presides over a February 1968 Cabinet meeting.

Americans. We weren't gaining and we weren't losing. Experts told the public this was a war we couldn't win. A terrible price was being paid for this draw. By mid-1967, billions of dollars had been poured into the Vietnamese War, and American casualties rose to 11,323 killed and 68,341 wounded.

"Hawks" and "doves" began making appearances on television and in newspapers around the country. Their opinions polarized the nation. Hawks in the government and in civilian life called for greater American participation and a win-at-all costs effort. Doves said the Vietnam War was the greatest tragedy in our history. They called it a bloodbath that was killing hundreds of American men each week. Lyndon B. Johnson got caught in the middle. He wasn't doing enough to please either side.

With his civilian and military advisors, the president directed the Vietnam military effort from the White House, but said little to the American public about his actions. With servicemen dying daily, the American public needed a comforting word from the president. These words did not come. A new political term appeared on the national scene, "credibility gap."

Newspapers and private citizens used it to suggest that perhaps, where the war was concerned, L.B.J. was not to be believed.

To make matters worse, there was trouble at home. Violence exploded across the land. Tired of injustice and impatient with the slow-working machinery of the law, some blacks rioted in big city ghettos from coast to coast. Fires were started, rocks were thrown, stores were robbed, snipers went into action, and many lives were lost.

On some college campuses students used the same tactics to protest against the draft, social injustice, and college administrators. Fire bombs and rocks were thrown. Clubs, sticks and, sometimes, guns were used by radical students. In the ghettos and on the college campuses, the police and the national guard were called in to bring back order.

One cause of this terror was the Vietnam War. Young men went to jail rather than be forced into military service that might send them to death across the Pacific. Why should they go when they did not believe there were good reasons for the fighting? Many Americans wanted the billions of dollars being spent on the war to be used at home in the United States. They said the money was needed to repair the scars of burned-out ghettos, to fill the stomachs of the hungry, and to build hope for the poor. Many people grieved over the thousands of men killed or injured in a war they felt was useless.

Then Senate doves, Eugene McCarthy of Minnesota and Robert Kennedy of New York, announced they would try to take the 1968 Democratic presidential nomination from Lyndon Johnson. The tired and troubled president decided not to run. He had not been in the best of health since his severe 1955 heart attack, and angry criticisms that seemed to come from everywhere did not help. Lyndon Johnson's face showed the strain of five turbulent years in office, when he spoke by television to America on March 31, 1968. He said he would not run again, but instead would spend his remaining months in office in efforts to bring about a peaceful settlement in Vietnam.

He retired from the presidency January 20, 1969, to raise Hereford stock on the LBJ Ranch and to prepare his presidential papers for the Johnson Memorial Library on the campus of the University of Texas. As he prepared to leave office it was impossible for even his greatest critics to find fault with the parting words of his final speech to Congress: "At least it will be said (I) tried." Lyndon B. Johnson died on January 22, 1973, in San Antonio, Texas at age 64. He was tireless in working for his country. And his "Great Society" made positive and lasting changes in America.

The line forms to the rear! President and Mrs. Johnson serve a Texas-style barbecue to guests.

The proud grandparents relax in a White House dining room with their first grandchild, Patrick Lyndon Nugent. The telephone under the table is for emergency calls to the president.

President and Mrs. Johnson happily look on as their daughter Lynda Johnson Robb cuts the cake at her December 9, 1967, White House wedding reception. The groom, Captain Charles Robb, U.S.M.C., assists.

RICHARD M. NIXON

Thirty-Seventh President (1969-1974)

*During his college career our
thirty-seventh president longed to be a member of
the football team's first string. Throughout
his long career in politics he never lost his
appreciation for sports stars. Richard Nixon
loved a winner and felt empathy for a loser. He
had been both in his three campaigns for the
presidency. As a premier man in American public
life, he shared the sports superstar's love-hate
relationship with the press. Gradually, as aides
and advisors isolated him in the Oval Office, he
lost his perspective, and newsmen became anathema
to him. The press began to question his actions
after a burglary at the Watergate Office Building
was uncovered. As time passed, the press
questions grew louder. The President brooded and
remained silent. The questions turned into
probes. Finally, the Watergate dam spilled over
and drowned Richard Nixon's hopes for a high
place in American history.*

HE MADE THE POLITICAL "FIRST STRING"

Richard Nixon was born January 9, 1913, in Yorba Linda, California, the second of five sons in the family of Francis and Hannah Milhous Nixon. Richard spent the first nine years of his life in the small town of Yorba Linda where his father ranched and worked as a carpenter. Then the family moved to Whittier, California, where the Nixons opened a grocery store. The Nixon boys divided their time between school and helping out around the store. In this hard-working family there wasn't much time for play.

After he entered the East Whittier Elementary School, his teachers soon discovered that Richard was a student who worked hard. Usually the first to raise his hand to answer questions, his teachers had to gently remind the enthusiastic Richard that he must give his classmates a chance. The boy worked to break himself of this habit. Richard showed an interest in politics during his elementary school years. At age eleven, he heard his parents discussing the Teapot Dome scandal. He listened with deep interest and then announced, "When I get big, I'll be a lawyer who can't be bribed."

When Richard Nixon set his mind to something it was carefully thought out and planned. If he was to become a lawyer and a politician, he must learn to speak well. Young Richard began work on this plan as a seventh grader by taking part in a debate. He was given a difficult issue to discuss: "Resolved: It is better to rent than to own a home." Richard's parents owned their home and often spoke to their children of the satisfaction of ownership. But he studied the other side of the question and argued so well he won the debate.

Graduating from elementary school in 1926, he attended Fullerton High School for two years, and then transferred to Whittier High School as a junior. Richard's grades were always high. He was an honors student throughout his school career. Although he was serious-minded, Richard Nixon was a person who earned the respect and friendship of his classmates. They admired his honesty, his abilities, and his easy sense of humor.

A few months after entering Whittier High, Nixon was nominated for the office of student body president. He ran against his friend Roy Newsom and Robert Logue. Nixon and Newson conducted a friendly, easy campaign and were amazed by their opponent's energy. Logue ran a vigorous campaign during recess and lunch periods, speaking directly to students in hopes of gaining their votes. The result was a well-earned victory for Robert Logue and a lasting lesson in politics for Richard Nixon. He vowed in any future campaign he would not be caught sitting back or napping.

Nixon's extra-curricular activities took a turn for the better after that defeat. He was the general manager of the associated student body and organized many student projects. In his senior year, he was supervisor of the athletic team managers who handled team equipment and arranged transportation to the games. Sports fan Nixon, not skilled enough to make the team, took part in the Whittier High athletic program in another way.

His abilities in debate were well-known at school and in the community. Winning debating contests became a habit with him. As Whittier High School's best speaker, he won a debating championship with a speech entitled. "Our Privileges Under the Constitution." After that, customers in the Nixon grocery store congratulated his parents by speaking of the day when Richard would be President of the United States. The parents smiled but thought this was a bit of an exaggeration.

Richard Nixon was a serious student and politician, but he also found time to enjoy himself. Dick enjoyed some sports, especially ice-skating. He was close to his brother, Donald, who was only a year younger. The brothers had the usual arguments and most of them were won by Dick if they involved discussion. When the action was more vigorous, Don held his own.

Richard graduated from high school with honors and enrolled in Whittier College in September of 1930. His major was constitutional history. One day Dick found his high school and college friend, Roy Newsom, greatly depressed. Roy was disappointed over an examination grade he had just received. He believed it should have been higher. Dick read the test and agreed. He managed to get Roy to go and

Richard (right) was three-and-a-half when this Nixon family photograph was taken. Nixon's brother Donald sits on his mother's lap while his brother Harold stands at the left.

Richard Nixon was always an enthusiastic member of the Whittier College football team.

Richard Nixon served six years under this Capitol dome as a congressman (1946-1950) and a senator (1950-1953) from California.

Lieutenant Commander Richard M. Nixon served with distinction in the United States Navy for five years during World War II.

Congressman Nixon (second from left) arrives in Athens, Greece, in 1947 as a member of the Herter Commission. After this trip Nixon returned to Washington to fight for the passage of the Marshall Plan in Congress.

argue his point with the professor by going along to supply moral support. Newsom later said of his friend: "I recognize this same kind of characteristic in Richard Nixon's campaigns. When he sees something that he thinks ought to be different, he'll go right to bat."

Football had always been of great interest to Richard Nixon. At Whittier College he decided to try out for the team. His position was tackle and he played well. But his coach, Wallace P. Newman, said that at one hundred fifty pounds he was just too light. Coach Newman remembered the hard-working young man this way:

"Weeks would go by and he wouldn't ever play a minute, but he'd hardly miss a practice, and he worked hard. He was wonderful for morale, because he'd sit there and cheer the rest of the boys, and tell them how well they played . . . Kids like that have more guts than the first string heroes."

Whittier footballers agreed with their coach, Nixon was a good man to have on their team. In later years, many Republican politicians felt exactly the same way.

Thirty-four years later, Coach Newman and Dick Nixon's football teammates honored his sportsmanship by awarding him a Whittier College football letter. Richard Nixon who was then president-elect, admitted that of the hundreds of awards he had received during his long career in public life, this honorary football letter was one he prized most. When accepting the award, he told his coach and teammates that football had prepared him for the hard knocks in American political life.

Football wasn't a strong point, but Dick Nixon excelled in other ways at Whittier College. He was a popular student. His good grades continued. His skill in debating was strong. And in his senior year, he was elected student body president.

After graduating with honors in 1934, Nixon went east to attend Duke University Law School. Three years later he graduated and returned home to study for the difficult California bar examination. He set up a place to study in his Aunt Olive Marshburn's home, and then dropped out of sight for long periods of time to pore over his law books. When the bar examination date came, Richard Nixon was well-prepared and passed with high marks. One of the first goals eleven year old Richard had set was now a reality. He was a lawyer.

For five years Nixon practiced law in the Whittier community. He found time away from his clients to take part in civic and community activities. Nixon's family was proud of him, but his matchmaker uncle, Oscar Marshburn, did not want his nephew to remain a bachelor. To Uncle Oscar, Richard made an incomplete picture as a single man. Mr. Marshburn, who hired teachers for the Whittier School district, began telling his nephew about Patricia Ryan, a pretty young business teacher. The young attorney took the bait and met Miss Ryan at the Whittier Community Theater, where both had parts in the amateur production of "The Dark Tower." During the rehearsals and the play, Pat Ryan and Richard Nixon fell in love. Two years later, when Nixon became a full partner in his law firm, the couple was married.

World War II interrupted Richard Nixon's law career. In 1942, he was commissioned a Lieutenant in the navy and served in the Pacific. In 1945, he was sent to Washington to represent the navy in administrative affairs. Spending time in Washington, watching the ebb and flow of the gigantic machine that is our federal government, increased Nixon's political aspirations. He wanted to be a part of the government and to work for his country. Nixon left the navy in 1946 as a Lieutenant Commander, and returned to Whittier to run for Congress. He won the election by fifteen thousand votes and moved back to Washington with his wife.

Nixon now applied his efficient powers of analysis to his work in Congress. Long before the "Red Scare" of the late 1940's, Richard Nixon had talked with his father about Communism creeping into American life. To the young California congressman, Communism was a threat to the country and its government. Therefore, Nixon was very active as a member of the House Committee on Un-American Activities. He was prominent in the investigation of Alger Hiss, a former State Department aide accused of Communist affiliations. Hiss denied all charges, but Congressman Nixon's vigorous prosecution of the case led to his conviction.

The Hiss conviction was the first conviction coming from the investigations of the Un-American Activities Committee. Richard Nixon

Richard Nixon was selected as Dwight D. Eisenhower's vice presidential running mate with no opposition at the July 1952 Republican National Convention in Chicago. As Mrs. Nixon (left) and Mrs. Eisenhower (right) look on, their smiling husbands greet the convention.

was severely criticized by people who believed the committee actions were illegal and unconstitutional. But he believed Alger Hiss was guilty and spent much time defending the committee which he said had acted honestly and fairly.

California voters believed in the young congressman and elected him to the United States Senate in 1950 by a large majority over his Democratic opponent, Helen Gahagan Douglas. While a member of the Senate, Nixon was active in the passage of many bills. He sponsored bills that made Alaska and Hawaii the forty-ninth and fiftieth states.

In 1952 he became a member of the political first string. At the Republican National Convention, he was selected by Dwight D. Eisenhower as his vice presidential candidate. The thirty-nine year old Nixon conducted a vigor-

ous campaign and used his debating skills to speak out strongly on the issues. He was eloquent in his attacks on Communism. The Republicans were happy as they watched the energetic Californian plunge into the campaign.

Money had never been in abundance during Richard Nixon's life and a national campaign cannot be run on a congressman's salary. People who supported Nixon knew he needed money and contributed to his campaign fund. The Democratic opposition, in a shop-worn campaign tactic, accused Nixon of improperly using the funds donated to his campaign. Richard Nixon denied wrong doing, but the charges were made and had to be answered. In a nationally televised speech, known as "Checkers speech" because his dog Checkers sat beside him and his family, Nixon made a strong and emotional defense against these charges. The public support for the Californian silenced the charges and Eisenhower and Nixon won easily.

Richard Nixon was the second youngest man to be elected vice president, and he brought new prestige and power to the office during his eight years of service. President Eisenhower placed great trust and confidence in Nixon. The president allowed him to take a greater part in activities of the administration than any previous vice president had taken. Worried about his health, Eisenhower worked out an agreement by which Nixon would serve as acting-president should illness keep him away from his job.

Nixon often represented the United States on official business in foreign countries. He visited fifty-six countries during his eight years as vice president. On one of these tours he made headlines around the world. As the United States representative at the American National Exhibition in Moscow, he met Russian Premier Khrushchev. The famous "kitchen debate" followed. Nixon spoke out strongly for the free enterprise system in America and urged a free exchange of ideas between the United States and the Soviet Union. The Russian premier was so impressed with the American vice president that he allowed him to make an unprecedented television speech to the Soviet people.

Although his political ambitions were great and his vice presidential duties many, Richard Nixon still found time for relaxation. He enjoyed playing golf. Sometimes his partner on the course was President Eisenhower, but they never discussed business. At home he played the piano and listened to music with his family. He was a great fan of football and baseball, and watched many games to take his mind from the problems of the world.

When Dwight Eisenhower retired, it was certain that Richard Nixon would be the choice of the Republicans in 1960. He was young, vigorous, well-known, experienced and a fine speaker. The Republicans thought Nixon was a sure winner. They had a surprise in October 1960 when the debating skills of Richard Nixon took second place to John F. Kennedy. In contrast to the self-assured Kennedy, Richard Nixon appeared over-worked and even unsure of himself at times. In one of the country's closest elections, Ken-

nedy defeated the California Republican by a narrow majority. Deeply disappointed Richard Nixon learned a valuable lesson from his campaign. He now had an enormous respect for television as a tool of persuasion.

Republican supporters knew their man did not give up easily. Back in his home state in 1962, they urged Richard Nixon to run for the governorship of California. Public service was in Nixon's blood and he agreed. In a long and tiring campaign he was defeated by Democrat Pat Brown. When his defeat was a certainty, the overtired and greatly disappointed Nixon let his emotions go on television. Speaking directly to the press, he bitterly told the people of California and the nation that they "wouldn't have Dick Nixon to kick around any longer."

Democrats rejoiced at this televised announcement of Nixon's return to private life. They believed his speech made him a political dead duck. The Democrats should have known better. Richard Nixon's fighting spirit was not dead! Determined to be a first stringer again, he slowly began his climb out of the political graveyard by speaking publicly in support of local and national Republican candidates. In a back-breaking national speaking tour during the 1966 Senate and Congressional elections, Nixon, more than any other Republican, helped his party win back forty-seven House and three Senate seats.

After the 1966 election, the Republicans owed Richard Nixon a great debt. They decided at their 1968 National Convention to give him a second try at the White House. With vice presidential candidate, Spiro Agnew, Nixon ran at a gallop. This time his television image was polished and cool, his speeches wise and confident. A close campaign, much like 1960, took place. But on November 5, 1968, Richard Nixon defeated his Democratic opponent Hubert Humphrey.

Nixon's old friend Dwight Eisenhower, who watched the campaign from his hospital bed, felt deep satisfaction at the victory. Eisenhower was also happy when his grandson, David Eisenhower, married Richard Nixon's daughter, Julie. With the Eisenhower-Nixon team reunited in a younger generation and his former vice president installed in the White House, Dwight Eisenhower was a contented man when he died in March 1969.

Richard Nixon's first term began on a spectacular note for him and for American citizens. Nixon was the man at the helm when the United States space program culminated, over a decade of preparation and experimentation, by landing the first man on the moon. Sputnik I, launched in the late 1950s, had given the Russians a jump in the international public relations race that accompanied all successful experiments in space. This comparative advantage was turned around dramatically when astronaut Neil Armstrong stepped onto the surface of the moon and proclaimed for a worldwide television and radio audience that he was taking "a giant step for mankind."

The new President, a man well-schooled in the advantages of international publicity coups, helped keep America's image on front pages around the globe when he personally greeted astronauts Armstrong, Edwin Aldrin, and Michael Collins aboard the aircraft carrier *U.S.S. Hornet* only minutes after their splashdown in July 1969.

However, America's successful space exploits did little to ease the tension within her borders over the Vietnam War. Ending this disastrous war was Nixon's primary goal. How to end it was the greatest problem he faced. The President wanted to disentangle American troops and bring all other United States involvement to a conclusion. At the same time he felt it to be in America's best interest to leave South Vietnamese forces strong and able to assume their own defense. To accomplish this, Nixon called for an orderly (but for many dissident Americans too painfully slow) United States troop withdrawal. Nixon had inherited a troop level of 543,400 in April 1969. By July 1972 he had reduced American troop strength to 49,000.

Still, neither formal peace negotiations with the North Vietnamese in Paris nor President Nixon's secret peace offers to Hanoi, which he made public in 1972, could secure the peace the war-weary American public desired. Although the demonstrations against the war on college campuses abated, the feelings against this war, so costly in American lives and to the American pocketbook, did not.

President Nixon decided to work to reduce tensions with international Communism on another level. His administration began negotiations in Vienna with Russia in April 1970 to limit strategic-arms development. To begin these talks on the right note, the President announced the United States would unilaterally destroy its stockpile of germ-warfare weapons.

In May of 1972 Nixon traveled to Moscow for a summit meeting with Soviet leaders. The most important achievement of the meeting was a treaty between the two nations to limit strategic nuclear weapons.

Nixon continued American progress in international relations when, in February 1972, he broke through twenty years of diplomatic barriers to seek a working relationship between the United States and mainland China. He visited Peking to hold talks with Chinese leaders Premier Chou En-lai and Chairman Mao Tsetung. These meetings did not bring about formal diplomatic relations, but they did open the doors to a new dialogue and new possibilities for peaceful solutions to many of the problems existing between the two nations. In 1973 this bold international move by Nixon culminated in the establishment of Chinese and American liaison offices in Washington and Peking.

In November 1972 Nixon and Vice Presidential running mate Spiro Agnew defeated their Democratic opponents George McGovern and Sargent Shriver in one of the greatest landslides in American political history. The Republicans won electoral votes in forty-nine states. Three days after Nixon's second inauguration on January 23, 1973, he announced the formal end to the Vietnam War with the signing of a peace treaty with North Vietnam.

The Nixon presidency had succeeded in achieving many of its international goals but, hampered with a Democratic Congress, was not as successful in achieving its domestic goals. Nixon felt one of his major successes at home was in turning a liberal Supreme Court into a more conservative body. Nixon succeeded in appointing four justices, headed by Chief Justice Warren E. Burger, who were well-known for their law-and-order conservative stance. However, this was not an easy victory for Nixon. He had battled with Congress and ultimately lost in his efforts to have Judges Clement Haynsworth and Harrold Carswell appointed to the Supreme Court bench.

Nixon's problems with Congress escalated during 1973 and 1974 into one of the most agonizing political crises in American history. On June 17, 1972, in the midst of the national presidential election, a guard at the Watergate apartment-office building in Washington, D.C., discovered burglars had entered Democratic National Headquarters. A few minutes later police arrested five burglars in the Democrat's sixth-floor offices. However, this was no ordinary burglary. The burglars carried cameras and wiretap equipment, and one of them was the security chief of the Committee for the Reelection of the President.

Nixon committee officials denied any connection with the crime, and his White House aides scoffed at it as a "third-rate burglary." As the election drew to a successful conclusion for Nixon, the Watergate incident seemed to fade away.

However, memories of Watergate would not go away. During the eighteen months of Richard Nixon's second term, a phalanx of investigators from the FBI, the Justice Department, federal grand juries, congressional committees, and the press slowly put together for public view a damning picture of the President and his aides. It was a composite of forged documents, wiretaps, lists of political enemies, political dirty tricks, perjury under oath, and illegal campaign contributions.

The nation watched as several high-ranking members on Nixon's presidential reelection committee and several White House aides were convicted and sent to prison.

Richard Nixon might well have withstood this deluge and subsequent erosion of the public confidence in his presidency had it not been for an almost accidental remark of a former White House aide to a Senate investigating committee in July 1973. The betrayer of Nixon was tape, thousands and thousands of yards of tape of all conversations held in the Oval Office by Nixon and unsuspecting visitors who had no idea that the office was "bugged."

The evidence against Nixon was there. The Senate committee and the Justice Department's special prosecutor asked for tapes of conversations between the President and specific individuals on specific dates. Nixon turned them down, claiming executive privilege. A federal court, an appeals court, and, finally, on July 24, 1974, a unanimous Supreme Court said the President must surrender the tapes. On August 5 a battle-weary Nixon turned over the tapes and released transcripts of the tapes and a statement admitting he had known of the Watergate break-in as early as six days after the burglary. Nixon admitted he had tried to cover up.

Nixon, sensing the angry mood of the nation and knowing that certain impeachment by the Senate lay ahead, resigned from the presidency on August 9, 1974. He had earned a dubious place in history. As America prepared for her Bicentennial celebration, Richard Nixon became the first president who had been forced to resign from office.

GERALD R. FORD

Thirty-Eighth President (1974-1977)

*Our thirty-eighth president entered the
executive office without the reassurance his
predecessors have had. He is the first President
not elected to the vice presidency or the
presidency by American voters. During the
tension-filled days of early August 1974, he had
only seventy-two hours' warning that he would
become President. An Eagle Scout in the
White House? Well, it would be a
refreshing change. The new President had
survived the probes of Congress and the
scrutiny of the press to become Vice President.
Gerald R. Ford was spotless – a heartening
contrast to the smirched spectacle of the
Nixon White House. But were Ford's midwest
amiability and rock-solid integrity enough?
Americans needed, perhaps more than at any time
in their history, an inspiring leader to
take them out of the Watergate mire.
Was Ford the man? A heartening thought.
Number 48 of the Michigan Wolverines had proved
in high school and college, in combat in
World War II, and in twenty-five years in
Congress, that he was not a man who quits.*

Ford as an infant in his mother's arms. His name then was Leslie Lynch King.

Eagle Scout, Gerald R. Ford, folding the flag in 1929.

MICHIGAN'S MAN ON CAPITOL HILL

Ford was born Leslie Lynch King on July 14, 1913, in Omaha, Nebraska, to Dorothy Gardiner King and Leslie King. Before his second birthday the marriage floundered and his parents were divorced. Mrs. King returned to her parents' home in Grand Rapids, Michigan, in 1915 with her two-year-old son.

Not long after her return Dorothy King met Gerald R. Ford, a Grand Rapids paint salesman, at a church social. After their marriage Ford adopted young Leslie and gave him his name, Gerald Rudolf Ford, Jr. The senior Ford took young Jerry as his own and never distinguished between him and his three half-brothers, Tom, born in 1918; Richard, born in 1924; and James, born in 1927. Jerry was unaware that Ford was not his natural father until he was in high school.

Gerald Ford remembers his stepfather with affection and appreciation: "When Dad told us to do something, we did it . . . All of us really looked up to him . . . He could be your friend as well as your father . . . I guess Dad was the strongest influence upon my life."

The senior Ford, because of his reputation for fair dealing and hard work, prospered in his own business, the Ford Paint and Varnish Company.

His sons grew up in comfort as members of Grand Rapids' upper middle class. Jerry's parents were active in community affairs and in charitable activities centered around their church.

Gerald Ford, Sr., helped organize a summer camp for underprivileged youngsters and found time to assist in running Boy Scout Troop 15 in his neighborhood. Teenage Jerry was a member and attained the highest honor in scouting when he became an Eagle Scout. With his father guiding the troop, everyone was certain he had earned it.

The four Ford brothers were not spoiled. Jerry, as the oldest, led the way in household chores. During the long Michigan winters he was chief snow-shoveler, and he regularly saw to it that the household furnace was clean and full of coal.

The Ford family did things together. Sunday picnics were a ritual. Mr. Ford regularly took his boys on fishing and hiking trips. He taught them to swim and play golf and encouraged them to take part in organized sports.

Jerry excelled in sports at school. At Grand Rapids' South High and the University of Michigan athletics dominated his life. He competed on South High's baseball, basketball, and football teams. As his high school career progressed, football became his prime interest. In 1930, Ford's senior year, the football team won the state championship, and Ford was selected as center on the All City and All State teams.

As the 1929 Depression set in, Mr. Ford's paint business waned. The family was forced to sell their elegant home near South High and move into a more modest one miles from the campus. Jerry had to make a fifty-minute bus ride twice a day to get to school. The evening ride home was particularly tedious as he often had to struggle to keep awake after a bruising football practice.

After his high school graduation in 1931, Jerry enrolled at the University of Michigan. His high school coach arranged for scholarship money to help him through the university. Jerry pledged Delta Kappa Epsilon as a sophomore and worked as a dishwasher at the fraternity house to meet his extra expenses.

Ford's football abilities at Michigan were good enough to earn him a spot on the 1935 Shrine East-West game in San Francisco and in the College All Stars game in Chicago. His performances in these games brought offers to play professional football. But twenty-two year old Jerry Ford had another dream—law school.

Ford later said of his law-school career, "I got by." He more than got by, graduating in 1941 near the top of his class.

After his graduation from Yale, Ford returned to Grand Rapids to set up a law practice with his college friend Philip Buchen. Pearl Harbor soon changed these plans. Ford joined the Navy in April, 1942. Lt. Commander Ford left the Navy in 1946 with ten battle stars on his chest.

Ford resumed his law career as a junior member of Butterfield, Keeney and Amberg. Late in 1947, he met Elizabeth Bloomer Warren, a department store fashion consultant and a former Martha Graham dancer and Powers model. Betty and Jerry were married on October 15, 1948.

Ford in 1934 as Most Valuable Player at the University of Michigan.

The Fords set up housekeeping in Washington with Gerald Ford now holding Michigan's Fifth District Congressional seat. This was prior to the opening of the 81st Congress. Betty had all it took to be a good politician's wife. She took the major responsibility in raising their four children and in making the major family decisions. She also became proficient at waiting for the aspiring Congressman from the Fifth District to come home from his political duties and travels.

By 1956 Gerald Ford's name was well-known throughout Michigan. Nationally, Ford had become a popular campaigner for fellow Republicans. In 1961, his Congressional colleagues tabbed him "The Gentle Tiger".

Seven days after the assassination of John F. Kennedy, Gerald Ford was selected to be one of the seven men to serve on the commission headed by Chief Justice Warren which investigated the murder.

Ford's ascent up the Congressional ladder reached the high rung January 4, 1965 when House Republicans voted him to be Minority Leader. When Richard Nixon took office in January, 1969, Gerald Ford was only 27 Congressmen away from the Speaker's job. However, the Minority Leader had trouble at times gaining entrance to Nixon's office. It was difficult to push presidential bills in the House when Nixon could not be reached for consultation.

During the early 1970's Ford's loyalty to Nixon became an increasing public burden. He was forced to make endorsements for things in which he did not personally believe.

In October 1973 Vice President Spiro Agnew resigned. On October 12 Richard Nixon nominated his loyal ally from Capitol Hill to fill the vacancy. Gerald R. Ford was eminently qualified to become Vice President. There was little opposition to his nomination and he was sworn in on December 6, 1973 as the fortieth Vice President of the United States.

Less than eight months later, on August 9, 1974, Gerald Ford became the thirty-eighth President of the United States. Watergate had enveloped Richard Nixon, who had opted to resign rather than face certain impeachment.

President Ford now had the difficult task of reuniting a disbelieving country. The scars of Watergate were not easy to hide. There was severe criticism of Ford's pardon of Richard Nixon. Other criticism leveled at President Ford was that he was a do-nothing. His foreign policy was considered by some to be inept.

Lieutenant Commander Ford on his return home from service in the U. S. Navy during World War II.

Despite a long and hard political fight for the Presidency, in November of 1976, Gerald Ford was not reelected to office. He served the United States as the first and only President who was not elected by the people.

President Ford had an appealing personality, a good mind, a nearly limitless capacity for hard work and an impeccably honest disposition in his conduct of public and personal affairs. He had an easy personal demeanor with which the average American could identify.

A portrait of the First Family. Seated: Betty and Jerry. Standing left to right: Susan, Steve, Jack, Mike, and Gayle.

JAMES EARL CARTER, JR.

Thirty-Ninth President (1977-   )

He was a farmer,
an engineer, a scientist, and a planner.
He was a business man
and the 76th governor of the state of Georgia.
Jimmy Carter, as he was known to one and all,
faced the world with a big smile
and many definite ideas
on how to improve the economy
of this great country he loved.
He was born in a small town
but has traveled the length and breadth
of the United States
meeting and getting to know
the people whom he will now lead.

Carter, in a boyhood photo, taken at a school play.

Jimmy Carter, while attending the U. S. Naval Academy.

FROM PEANUTS TO PRESIDENT

James Earl Carter, Jr. was born in the small town of Plains, in Sumter County, Georgia, on October 1, 1924. His father, James Earl Carter, Sr., was the manager of a grocery store and owner of the town's icehouse and dry-cleaning establishment. His mother, the former Lillian Gordy, was a nurse and was described by many as a most liberal person.

Young Jimmy grew up on the family farm with his brother and two sisters. This was where the Carter family raised most of their own food. They used mules for cultivation and there was no electricity or indoor plumbing until Jimmy was in his teens. The life of a depression rural farmer was what Jimmy absorbed in his early formative years.

Jimmy Carter attended Plains High School where he played basketball and showed a definite aptitude for further study. He was an avid reader all through his boyhood and set his sights early to go to the United States Naval Academy at Annapolis. After graduating from Plains High School in 1941, he applied to the Naval Academy.

However, Jimmy did not receive his Annapolis appointment until 1942. He studied one year at Georgia Southwestern College in Americus and then spent a year at the Georgia Institute of Technology in Atlanta to further qualify himself for his Naval Academy appointment.

The year 1943 found Jimmy Carter at Annapolis as a plebe in the Naval Academy. Because it was during World War II and the programs for the military were accelerated, Jimmy graduated from the Academy in 1946 with honors and his naval commission. He graduated 59th in a class of 820.

Shortly after his graduation, Jimmy Carter married Rosalynn Smith, a childhood neighbor. Rosalynn and Jimmy were married on July 7, 1946. Rosalynn was destined to be a Navy wife for the seven years that Jimmy served.

Jimmy Carter's first assignment in the Navy was aboard the U.S.S. Wyoming at Norfolk, Va. Here he was the officer in charge of enlisted education and the electronics and photography officer. It was two years later in 1948 that he took six months training in submarine school and was then assigned to the U.S.S. Pomfret, based in Hawaii. The young officer made several cruises into Asian waters.

In 1951, Jimmy Carter, now lieutenant commander, began to work with Admiral Hyman G. Rickover on the nuclear submarine program. He became a senior officer in the pre-commissioning crew of the U.S.S. Seawolf, a nuclear submarine. The Seawolf was one of the first submarines to operate on atomic power.

The Naval career of Jimmy Carter was cut off by the death of the young man's father in 1953. It was at that time that Jimmy felt he must return to his native state in order to run the family business. Jimmy resigned his commission and he and Rosalynn returned to Plains. Jimmy Carter was 29 years old.

Carter Farms, Inc. was the business which Jimmy Carter ran. His first year back on the farm, Jimmy listed a profit of only $200. This was the year of the worst drought in Georgia's history. But Jimmy Carter proved himself an able businessman and farmer. The principle crop he worked was seed peanuts. He, in partnership with his brother Billy, became one of Georgia's largest peanut wholesalers.

Although the business of his farm was Jimmy's prime interest, he was also active in civic affairs. From 1955 to 1962, he was chairman of the Sumter County board of education. He also served as chairman of the county hospital authority. He was vitally interested in the future of Georgia and served as the president of the Georgia Planning Association as well as the Georgia Crop Improvement Association.

It was in 1962 that the hazel-eyed, sandy haired man with a smile decided to run for public office. He became a candidate for the Georgia State Senate. The original election returns seemed to indicate a Carter loss. However, Jimmy suspected foul play at the ballot box and challenged the results in court. The election was reversed in his favor. Jimmy Carter was now in the political ring.

Two years later, Jimmy Carter was elected to a second term. His record in office was moderately liberal and he was thought to be one of the most effective members of the State Senate.

Jimmy Carter was not always in tune with the feelings of his neighbors. This was especially true of his liberal attitudes on racial issues. As a Deacon of the Plains Baptist Church, Jimmy Carter was faced with a vote to exclude negroes from the congregation. This was in the racially explosive year of 1965. Jimmy Carter spoke against this exclusion and voted the same way.

Jimmy Carter and his wife, Rosalynn.

Carter taking a large bass out of a net in preparation for a town fish fry.

His lead was followed by his wife, his mother and his two sons. It was this important issue which marked Jimmy Carter for national publicity. He was ready to enter the race as a democratic candidate for Governor of Georgia.

The 1966 election for Governor of Georgia was not won by Jimmy Carter. But the failure to win did not daunt him. He became even more determined to run again and took to the campaign trail with vigor. The story was not the same in 1970. Jimmy Carter was elected 76th Governor of Georgia. In his inaugural speech, he declared,

"The time for racial discrimination is over." This statement brought him to the attention of the entire country. He went on to say,

"No poor, rural, weak or black person should ever have to bear the additional burden of being deprived of the opportunity of an education, a job or a simple justice."

Jimmy Carter speaking at a fund raising breakfast at a Washington hotel.

Carter and Mondale greeting the crowds.

The Carter administration in Georgia included reforms in education, reorganization of the executive branch as well as coordinated planning for the future. Governor Carter, himself, managed to maintain a fairly good relation with the state legislature.

While still serving as Governor of Georgia, Mr. Carter began planning for his future career in politics. He decided to run as the Democratic candidate for president of the United States in 1976.

In 1973, Governor Carter was asked to become the Democratic Party's National Campaign Chairman for the 1974 elections. This program of assistance to the democratic candidates running for office took Governor Carter and his staff members into hundreds of Senate, House and Gubernatorial races all across the country. Jimmy Carter's name and smile were becoming well known and it is said that his campaign effort was the most effective and extensive of any in the party history. The country was getting to know Jimmy Carter.

It was on December 12, 1974 that Jimmy Carter officially announced himself as a candidate for President of the United States. There were many miles to be traveled and many hands to shake before the election was won. Jimmy Carter and his family made an all-out effort to get to know the people and to have the people get to know him.

Not only Mr. Carter, but his wife Rosalynn, his older children—Jack, Chip and Jeff (little Amy was only 8 years old at the time)—and his mother, Lillian, made the all-out effort needed to put Jimmy Carter in the White House as the thirty-ninth President of the United States.

Jimmy Carter and family on the podium after accepting the Democratic Presidential nomination.

The campaign trail was long and hard. There were television debates between Gerald Ford and Jimmy Carter which kept the entire country watching. There were hands to shake, speeches to make and many millions of people to meet. The Jimmy Carter smile never diminished. His political philosophy was unshaken and his goals for the government of the United States did not change.

When the last ballot was cast on November 2, 1976, the country had made its choice and that choice was James Earl Carter, Jr.—thirty-ninth President of the United States—the man who went from peanuts to President.

STATES OF THE UNION BY PRESIDENTIAL TERM

STATE	STATE NICKNAME	DATE OF ENTRY INTO UNION	PRESIDENTIAL TERM
1. Delaware	"The First State"	December 7, 1787	*
2. Pennsylvania	"The Keystone State"	December 12, 1787	*
3. New Jersey	"The Garden State"	December 18, 1787	*
4. Georgia	"Empire State of the South"	February 2, 1788	*
5. Connecticut	"Home of the Yankee Peddler"	January 9, 1788	*
6. Massachusetts	"The Bay State"	February 6, 1788	*
7. Maryland	"The Old Line State"	April 28, 1788	*
8. South Carolina	"The Palmetto State"	May 23, 1788	*
9. New Hampshire	"The Granite State"	June 21, 1788	*
10. Virginia	"The Old Dominion State"	June 26, 1788	*
11. New York	"The Empire State"	July 26, 1788	*
12. North Carolina	"The Tarheel State"	November 21, 1789	*Washington
13. Rhode Island	"Little Rhody"	May 29, 1790	*Washington
14. Vermont	"The Green Mountain State"	March 4, 1791	Washington
15. Kentucky	"The Bluegrass State"	June 1, 1792	Washington
16. Tennessee	"The Volunteer State"	June 1, 1796	Washington
17. Ohio	"The Buckeye State"	March 1, 1803	Jefferson
18. Louisiana	"The Pelican State"	April 30, 1812	Madison
19. Indiana	"The Hoosier State"	December 11, 1816	Madison
20. Mississippi	"The Magnolia State"	December 10, 1817	Monroe
21. Illinois	"Land of Lincoln"	December 3, 1818	Monroe
22. Alabama	"The Cotton State"	December 14, 1819	Monroe
23. Maine	"The Pine Tree State"	March 15, 1820	Monroe
24. Missouri	"The Show Me State"	August 10, 1821	Monroe
25. Arkansas	"The Wonder State"	July 15, 1836	Jackson

*Original 13 States

STATES OF THE UNION BY PRESIDENTIAL TERM

STATE	STATE NICKNAME	DATE OF ENTRY INTO UNION	PRESIDENTIAL TERM
26. Michigan	"The Wolverine State"	June 26, 1837	Jackson
27. Florida	"The Peninsula State"	March 3, 1845	Tyler
28. Texas	"The Lone Star State"	December 29, 1845	Polk
29. Iowa	"The Hawkeye State"	December 28, 1846	Polk
30. Wisconsin	"The Badger State"	May 29, 1848	Polk
31. California	"The Golden State"	September 9, 1850	Fillmore
32. Minnesota	"The Gopher State"	May 11, 1858	Buchanan
33. Oregon	"The Beaver State"	February 14, 1859	Buchanan
34. Kansas	"The Sunflower State"	January 29, 1861	Buchanan
35. West Virginia	"The Mountain State"	June 20, 1863	Lincoln
36. Nevada	"The Silver State"	October 31, 1864	Lincoln
37. Nebraska	"The Cornhusker State"	March 1, 1867	A. Johnson
38. Colorado	"The Centennial State"	August 1, 1876	Grant
39. North Dakota	"The Flickertail State"	November 2, 1889	B. Harrison
40. South Dakota	"The Sunshine State"	November 2, 1889	B. Harrison
41. Montana	"The Treasure State"	November 8, 1889	B. Harrison
42. Washington	"The Evergreen State"	November 11, 1889	B. Harrison
43. Idaho	"The Gem State"	July 3, 1890	B. Harrison
44. Wyoming	"The Equality State"	July 10, 1890	B. Harrison
45. Utah	"The Beehive State"	January 4, 1896	Cleveland
46. Oklahoma	"The Sooner State"	November 16, 1907	T. Roosevelt
47. New Mexico	"Land of Enchantment"	January 6, 1912	Taft
48. Arizona	"The Grand Canyon State"	February 14, 1912	Taft
49. Alaska	"The Last Frontier"	January 3, 1959	Eisenhower
50. Hawaii	"Paradise in the Pacific"	July 4, 1960	Eisenhower

MEN WHO RAN FOR PRESIDENT AND LOST

PRESIDENTIAL CANDIDATE	POLITICAL PARTY	ELECTION	YEAR
No Opposition		First	1789
No Opposition		Second	1792
Thomas Jefferson	Democratic Republican	Third	1796
Aaron Burr	Democratic Republican	Fourth	1800
Charles C. Pinckney	Federalist	Fifth	1804
Charles C. Pinckney	Federalist	Sixth	1808
DeWitt Clinton	Federalist	Seventh	1812
Rufus King	Federalist	Eighth	1816
John Quincy Adams	Democratic Republican	Ninth	1820
Andrew Jackson	Democratic Republican	Tenth	1824
Henry Clay	Democratic Republican	Tenth	1824
William H. Crawford	Democratic Republican	Tenth	1824
John Quincy Adams	National Republican	Eleventh	1828
Henry Clay	National Republican	Twelfth	1832
William Henry Harrison	Whig	Thirteenth	1836
Martin Van Buren	Democratic	Fourteenth	1840
Henry Clay	Whig	Fifteenth	1844
Lewis Cass	Democratic	Sixteenth	1848
Winfield Scott	Whig	Seventeenth	1852
John C. Fremont	Republican	Eighteenth	1856
Stephen A. Douglas	Democratic	Nineteenth	1860
John C. Breckinridge	Democratic	Nineteenth	1860
John Bell	Constitutional Union	Nineteenth	1860
George McClellan	Democratic	Twentieth	1864
Horatio Seymour	Democratic	Twenty-First	1868
Horace Greeley	Democratic	Twenty-Second	1872
Samuel J. Tilden	Democratic	Twenty-Third	1876
Winfield S. Hancock	Democratic	Twenty-Fourth	1880
James G. Blaine	Republican	Twenty-Fifth	1884
Grover Cleveland	Democratic	Twenty-Sixth	1888
Benjamin Harrison	Republican	Twenty-Seventh	1892
James B. Weaver	People's Party	Twenty-Seventh	1892
William Jennings Bryan	Democratic	Twenty-Eighth	1896
William Jennings Bryan	Democratic	Twenty-Ninth	1900
Alton B. Parker	Democratic	Thirtieth	1904
William Jennings Bryan	Democratic	Thirty-First	1908
Theodore Roosevelt	Bull Moose	Thirty-Second	1912
William Howard Taft	Republican	Thirty-Second	1912
Charles Evans Hughes	Republican	Thirty-Third	1916
James M. Cox	Democratic	Thirty-Fourth	1920
John W. Davis	Democratic	Thirty-Fifth	1924
Robert M. LaFollette	Progressive	Thirty-Fifth	1924
Alfred E. Smith	Democratic	Thirty-Sixth	1928
Herbert Hoover	Republican	Thirty-Seventh	1932
Alfred M. Landon	Republican	Thirty-Eighth	1936
Wendell L. Willkie	Republican	Thirty-Ninth	1940
Thomas E. Dewey	Republican	Fortieth	1944
Thomas E. Dewey	Republican	Forty-First	1948
John S. Thurmond	States' Rights	Forty-First	1948
Henry A. Wallace	Progressive	Forty-First	1948
Adlai E. Stevenson	Democratic	Forty-Second	1952
Adlai E. Stevenson	Democratic	Forty-Third	1956
Richard M. Nixon	Republican	Forty-Fourth	1960
Barry Goldwater	Republican	Forty-Fifth	1964
Hubert H. Humphrey	Democratic	Forty-Sixth	1968
George C. Wallace	American Independent	Forty-Sixth	1968
George S. McGovern	Democratic	Forty-Seventh	1972
Gerald R. Ford	Republican	Forty-Eighth	1976

UNITED STATES POPULATION EXPANSION BY PRESIDENTIAL TERM

PRESIDENT	POPULATION	YEAR
1. George Washington	3,929,214	1790
2. John Adams	4,883,209	1797
3. Thomas Jefferson	5,485,528	1801
4. James Madison	7,030,647	1809
5. James Monroe	8,898,892	1817
6. John Quincy Adams	11,252,237	1825
7. Andrew Jackson	12,565,145	1829
8. Martin Van Buren	15,843,452	1837
9. William Henry Harrison	17,732,715	1841
10. John Tyler	17,732,715	1841
11. James K. Polk	20,181,683	1845
12. Zachary Taylor	22,630,654	1849
13. Millard Fillmore	23,260,638	1850
14. Franklin Pierce	25,736,070	1853
15. James Buchanan	29,036,649	1857
16. Abraham Lincoln	32,350,627	1861
17. Andrew Johnson	35,700,678	1865
18. Ulysses S. Grant	39,050,729	1869
19. Rutherford B. Hayes	47,140,727	1877
20. James A. Garfield	51,541,575	1881
21. Chester A. Arthur	51,541,575	1881
22. Grover Cleveland	56,658,347	1885
23. Benjamin Harrison	61,775,121	1889
24. Grover Cleveland	66,970,496	1893
25. William McKinley	72,189,240	1897
26. Theodore Roosevelt	77,585,000	1901
27. William Howard Taft	90,492,000	1909
28. Woodrow Wilson	97,227,000	1913
29. Warren Harding	105,541,000	1921
30. Calvin Coolidge	111,950,000	1923
31. Herbert Hoover	121,770,000	1929
32. Franklin D. Roosevelt	125,579,000	1933
33. Harry S. Truman	132,481,000	1945
34. Dwight D. Eisenhower	158,434,000	1953
35. John F. Kennedy	183,650,000	1961
36. Lyndon B. Johnson	189,042,000	1963 (est.)
37. Richard M. Nixon	203,810,000	1970
38. Gerald R. Ford	211,390,000	1974

UNITED STATES TERRITORIAL EXPANSION BY PRESIDENTIAL TERM

NAME OF TERRITORY	HOW ACQUIRED	PRESIDENTIAL TERM
Louisiana Territory (1803)	Purchased from France for 15 million dollars	Thomas Jefferson
Florida Territory (1819)	Purchased from Spain for 5 million dollars	James Monroe
Texas (1845)	Annexation	John Tyler
Oregon Territory (1846)	Treaty with England	James K. Polk
Southwest Territory (1848)	Treaty and purchase from Mexico	James K. Polk
Gadsden Purchase (1854)	Treaty and purchase from Mexico	Franklin Pierce
Alaska (1867)	Treaty and purchase from Russia	Andrew Johnson
Hawaii (1898)	Annexation	William McKinley
Puerto Rico (1898)	Treaty and purchase from Spain	William McKinley
Guam (1898)	Treaty and purchase from Spain	William McKinley
Philippines (1898)	Treaty and purchase from Spain	William McKinley

PRESIDENTIAL VITAL STATISTICS

PRESIDENT	TERM	BIRTH	DEATH	BIRTHPLACE
George Washington	1789-1797	February 22, 1732	December 14, 1799	Pope's Creek, Virginia
John Adams	1797-1801	October 30, 1735	July 4, 1826	Braintree, Massachusetts
Thomas Jefferson	1801-1809	April 13, 1743	July 4, 1826	Albemarle County, Virginia
James Madison	1809-1817	March 16, 1751	June 28, 1836	Port Conway, Virginia
James Monroe	1817-1825	April 28, 1758	July 4, 1831	Westmorland County, Virginia
John Quincy Adams	1825-1829	July 11, 1767	February 23, 1848	Braintree, Massachusetts
Andrew Jackson	1829-1837	March 15, 1767	June 8, 1845	Waxhaw, South Carolina
Martin Van Buren	1837-1841	December 5, 1782	July 24, 1862	Kinderhook, New York
William Henry Harrison	1841-1841 (1 month)	February 9, 1773	April 4, 1841	Charles County, Virginia
John Tyler	1841-1845	March 29, 1790	January 18, 1862	Charles County, Virginia
James K. Polk	1845-1849	November 2, 1795	June 15, 1849	Mecklenburg County, North Carolina
Zachary Taylor	1849-1850 (16 months)	November 24, 1784	July 9, 1850	Orange County, Virginia
Millard Fillmore	1850-1853	January 7, 1800	March 8, 1874	Cayuga County, New York
Franklin Pierce	1853-1857	November 23, 1804	October 8, 1869	Hillsboro, New Hampshire
James Buchanan	1857-1861	April 23, 1791	June 1, 1868	Cove Gap, Pennsylvania
Abraham Lincoln	1861-1865	February 12, 1809	April 15, 1865	Hodgenville, Kentucky
Andrew Johnson	1865-1869	December 29, 1808	July 31, 1875	Raleigh, North Carolina
Ulysses S. Grant	1869-1877	April 27, 1822	July 23, 1885	Point Pleasant, Ohio
Rutherford B. Hayes	1877-1881	October 4, 1822	January 17, 1893	Delaware, Ohio
James A. Garfield	1881-1881 (7 months)	November 19, 1831	September 19, 1881	Orange, Ohio
Chester A. Arthur	1881-1885	October 5, 1830	November 18, 1886	Fairfield, Vermont
Grover Cleveland	1885-1889	March 18, 1837	June 24, 1908	Caldwell, New Jersey
Benjamin Harrison	1889-1893	August 20, 1833	March 13, 1901	North Bend, Ohio
Grover Cleveland	1893-1897	March 18, 1837	June 24, 1908	Caldwell, New Jersey
William McKinley	1897-1901	January 29, 1843	September 14, 1901	Niles, Ohio
Theodore Roosevelt	1901-1909	October 27, 1858	January 6, 1919	New York, New York
William Howard Taft	1909-1913	September 15, 1857	March 8, 1930	Cincinnati, Ohio
Woodrow Wilson	1913-1921	December 28, 1856	February 3, 1924	Staunton, Virginia
Warren Harding	1921-1923 (29 months)	November 2, 1865	August 2, 1923	Corsica, Ohio
Calvin Coolidge	1923-1929	July 4, 1872	January 5, 1933	Plymouth, Vermont
Herbert Hoover	1929-1933	August 10, 1874	October 20, 1964	West Branch, Iowa
Franklin D. Roosevelt	1933-1945	January 30, 1882	April 12, 1945	Hyde Park, New York
Harry S. Truman	1945-1953	May 8, 1884	December 26, 1972	Lamar, Missouri
Dwight D. Eisenhower	1953-1961	October 14, 1890	March 28, 1969	Denison, Texas
John F. Kennedy	1961-1963 (34 months)	May 29, 1917	November 22, 1963	Brookline, Massachusetts
Lyndon B. Johnson	1963-1969	August 27, 1908	January 22, 1973	Stonewall, Texas
Richard M. Nixon	1969-1974	January 9, 1913		Yorba Linda, California
Gerald R. Ford	1974-1977	July 14, 1913		Omaha, Nebraska
James Earl Carter, Jr.	1977-	October 1, 1924		Plains, Georgia

THE PRESIDENT'S CABINET

CABINET MEMBER	GOVERNMENT DEPARTMENT HE HEADS
1. Attorney General	Department of Justice
2. Secretary of Agriculture	Department of Agriculture
3. Secretary of Commerce	Department of Commerce
4. Secretary of Defense (formerly Secretary of War)	Department of Defense (formerly Department of War)
5. Secretary of Health, Education, and Welfare	Department of Health, Education, and Welfare
6. Secretary of Housing and Urban Development	Department of Housing and Urban Development
7. Secretary of Labor	Department of Labor
8. Secretary of State	Department of State
9. Secretary of the Interior	Department of the Interior
10. Secretary of the Treasury	Department of the Treasury
11. Secretary of Transportation	Department of Transportation

CHIEF JUSTICES OF THE SUPREME COURT

CHIEF JUSTICE	TERM	APPOINTED BY
1. John Jay	1790-1795	George Washington
2. John Rutledge	1795-1795	George Washington
3. Oliver Ellsworth	1796-1800	George Washington
4. John Marshall	1801-1835	John Adams
5. Roger B. Taney	1836-1864	Andrew Jackson
6. Salmon P. Chase	1864-1873	Abraham Lincoln
7. Morrison R. Waite	1874-1886	Ulysses S. Grant
8. Melville W. Fuller	1888-1910	Grover Cleveland
9. Edward D. White	1910-1921	William Howard Taft
10. William Howard Taft	1921-1930	Warren Harding
11. Charles E. Hughes	1930-1941	Herbert Hoover
12. Harlan F. Stone	1941-1946	Franklin D. Roosevelt
13. Fred M. Vinson	1946-1953	Harry S. Truman
14. Earl Warren	1953-1969	Dwight D. Eisenhower
15. Warren Burger	1969-	Richard Nixon